Euroclash

*The EU, European Identity, and
the Future of Europe*

NEIL FLIGSTEIN

OXFORD
UNIVERSITY PRESS

OXFORD
UNIVERSITY PRESS

Great Clarendon Street, Oxford OX2 6DP

Oxford University Press is a department of the University of Oxford.
It furthers the University's objective of excellence in research, scholarship,
and education by publishing worldwide in

Oxford New York

Auckland Cape Town Dar es Salaam Hong Kong Karachi
Kuala Lumpur Madrid Melbourne Mexico City Nairobi
New Delhi Shanghai Taipei Toronto

With offices in

Argentina Austria Brazil Chile Czech Republic France Greece
Guatemala Hungary Italy Japan Poland Portugal Singapore
South Korea Switzerland Thailand Turkey Ukraine Vietnam

Oxford is a registered trade mark of Oxford University Press
in the UK and in certain other countries

Published in the United States
by Oxford University Press Inc., New York

British Library Cataloguing in Publication Data

Data available

Library of Congress Cataloging in Publication Data

Data available

Typeset by SPI Publisher Services, Pondicherry, India
Printed in Great Britain
on acid-free paper by the
MPG Books Group, Bodmin and King's Lynn

ISBN 978–0–19–954256–7
ISBN 978–0–19–958085–9 (pbk.)

1 3 5 7 9 10 8 6 4 2

EUROCLASH

For my father,
Melvin Fligstein

Preface

I became interested in the European Union (hereafter EU) in the mid-1980s, with awareness of the EU's proposal to complete the Single Market. At the time, I was in the process of completing a study of the history of the largest US corporations during the course of much of the twentieth century. My study had convinced me that no one in their right mind would try to rewrite their market rules except under conditions of extreme duress. This is because large firms who benefit from the current legal and political order would simply oppose producing market rules that might undermine their position. The intriguing attempt to create a single market brought me to Europe for the first time to try and puzzle out what was going on.

I quickly began to realize that the Single Market was only part of a complex scenario the beginnings of which stretched back to at least World War II. After spending time in Europe over many years, I understood that many of the old national stereotypes that people held about one another had persisted. It began to dawn on me that the very factors which had led to the two most destructive wars in human history were still in play. This produced for me a deep mystery: how, if the Europeans were still capable of thinking the worst of each other, was it possible that no further war had occurred since 1945, and the chances of Germany, France, and Great Britain going to war are virtually nil?

After all, Europe was the source of much of what had happened in the world in the past 500 years. Europeans invented capitalism, imperialism, the modern state, fascism, and communism. They invented modern military warfare which allowed people to kill one another in the most horrendous fashion in huge numbers. Their colonial adventures transformed the rest of the world. The twentieth century witnessed two world wars, caused by the Europeans, that killed over 100 million people. Of course, Europeans came out of World War II never wanting to repeat the experience, but the same thing could be said after World War I. Certainly the Cold War, whereby the US and its European allies worked to contain the Soviet Union in Europe, played an important part in keeping European governments from focusing on one another as targets, instead deploying their armed forces under NATO on the eastern frontier.

But it was not just the Cold War that brought Europe peace. Europeans turned their attention to rebuilding their economies. The economic miracle that took place across Western Europe after World War II transformed Europe from a set of societies whose economies had thrived on war and colonies to a set of societies that tried to implement systems of social justice (social democracy) and peaceful trade (see Judt's (2005) history of post-war Europe). The EU reflected a commitment on the part of Europe's people, governments, and economic elites to working together to promote trade and economic competition and to avoid war and political competition. The economic project has succeeded beyond anyone's wildest imagination.

Yet, as time has gone by, the people who produced this peace have left the scene. Memories of World War II have faded as that generation has passed. Europe now has a new set of challenges to deal with. Their populations are aging, their economic growth has been uneven, there are worries about immigration, and unemployment remains a serious problem across Europe. The EU has met its key goal, that of creating a Europe-wide market, and two others it did not foresee, i.e. monetary union and enlargement into Eastern Europe. But these new challenges somehow seem beyond the limit of what the EU can accomplish.

I have two goals in writing this book. As an outsider, I am amazed at the degree to which people with such a history of conflict have produced a world of such interesting interdependence and complexity. I decided to try and document some of the important features of this world in order that people, particularly in Europe, might see how far the integration of their economies, societies, and politics has come. I want them to understand some of the myriad ways in which people from different societies have interacted with each other to create the rudiments of a European society.

My second goal is to try and analyze the current situation. In spite of the creation of both a European economy and a nascent European society and polity, there are some crucial problems that create the possibility of a clash between those citizens of member states who have not been the beneficiaries of the economic project of the EU and those who have. The winners are disproportionately from the middle and upper middle classes. They are educated, young, and highly skilled, holding managerial and professional occupations. They work for corporations—often the largest ones—and they work for governments; many as teachers, school administrators, researchers, and professors, and others as members of the bureaucracies that work to produce Europe. The losers are those who have suffered as market competition has heated up around Europe: the less educated, the elderly, and the less skilled, particularly blue-collar workers. In between are those citizens who are in the center of the education and skill distributions. These people tend to be diffusely positive toward the EU project of opening markets because it has created jobs and opportunities to work, play, and go to school in other countries. But they are wary of making sure that enough social protection stays in place. They count on their national governments to protect them from the negative effects of too much market competition. This divide has the effect of pitting citizens in each country against each other and pushing their national governments in different directions. It is this political clash, the clash between the winners of the EU economic and social project and the losers that is at the heart of contemporary political debates on the future of Europe.

The study of the EU is dominated by political scientists who have been mostly interested in the political processes going on in Brussels. The politics that has produced the various treaties, the making of legislation, and the legal decisions of the European Court of Justice have been the main focus of scholarly attention. As a sociologist, it took me a long time to articulate what I thought was wrong with this. Let me see if I can express it simply. Ernie Haas, the founder of EU studies, thought that if European integration was going to work, it would have to move from the purview of governments in Brussels to being a concern of citizens across Europe. As it turns out, it has not happened quite like Haas hoped. While trade has greatly expanded across Europe, the degree to which people in Europe routinely interact with one another has been circumscribed in ways that I will document. As a sociologist, I wanted to try and see how what happened in Brussels had indeed reorganized the European economies and changed the ways that firms work. I also wanted to see how people's lives have changed.

Who were the people who identified more with Europe than with their nation-state? I remember meeting my first European long ago at a conference in Luxembourg. A group of people were at dinner and I was seated next to a German economist who had worked for a while in Brussels. He was living in Paris where he was advising the French Central bank and occasionally writing for the French business press. He had a home in Luxembourg and our conversation was focused on him trying to figure out how he could stay in Paris. Over the years, I have met many more Europeans. But, as I will show in this book, Europeans are a small part of Europe's population.

I set out in this book to try and document what has happened in the economy and society of Europe in as many ways as I could. If I was a novelist, I would perhaps write a fictionalized account of how this has all worked. If I was a historian, I would interpret the long view of these events and their effects. If I was a skilled journalist, I would tell Europe's story through poignant interviews with people to illustrate the general points I want to make. Alas, I was trained as a quantitatively oriented social scientist. This means I am always searching for the big picture, for data to show how things are all over. As such, I apologize in this study for too much jargon, too many statistics, and, perhaps, a confusing kaleidoscope of data gathered from many sources over a very long period of time. But there are many ways in which to try and capture complex and important phenomena. I hope that my strategy will be of interest to people.

Acknowledgments

I have been studying the EU in one way or another for fifteen years, and working on this book on and off since 1999. I am indebted to a lot of people for support, advice, comments, and insight along the way. In 1999, I spent a sabbatical year at the European University Institute (EUI) in Florence, Italy. I would like to thank Stephano Bartolini, who was chair of the Department of Social Science, for letting me be a visitor in the Department. I also wish to thank Yves Meny for an invitation to be a member of the Institute of Advanced Studies at EUI. EUI provided the place where the basic framework for this book was erected. It was a wonderful intellectual environment where I felt supported and encouraged to think of Europe as not just a political project in Brussels, but one that had effects that were reverberating all across Europe.

The penultimate draft of this book was written while I was a Guggenheim Fellow. I was also fortunate enough to spend a final month fine-tuning this manuscript at the Rockefeller Foundation Center at Bellagio, Italy. I extend my thanks to Basak Kus, Jason McNichol, Iona Mara-Drita, Frederic Merand, and Stephanie Mudge for their excellent research assistance over the years.

On an intellectual front, I have been quite fortunate to interact with a great many scholars interested in these topics. First I thank Wayne Sandholtz and Alec Stone Sweet who invited me to join a seminar they were organizing on the EU. That seminar produced important discussions that informed me about what was going on in Europe and offered a place to develop important ideas that are at the core of this project. That group produced two intellectually diverse edited volumes. I would like to thank members of that group, including Paul Pierson, Alberta Sbragia, David Cameron, Jim Caparoso, Martin Shapiro, Patrick Le Gales, Martin Rhodes, and Adrienne Herretier. In particular, I am grateful to Patrick Le Gales who urged me to read Karl Deutsch. I have also had interesting and important conversations over the years with Chris Ansell, Colin Crouch, Ernie Haas, Andrew Moravcsik, Fritz Scharpf, Phillippe Schmitter, Wolfgang Streeck, Steve Weber, Joseph Weiler and Nick Ziegler.

I have also greatly benefited from the detailed written comments of Chris Ansell, Jeff Checkel, Adrian Favell, Juan Fernandez, Peter Katzenstein, Patrick Legales, Doug McAdam, Gary Marks, Frederic Merand, John Meyer, and Wayne Sandholtz, on an earlier draft of this manuscript. I particularly appreciate the help of Juan Diez Medrano and Adrian Favell who both read the manuscript with great care and helped me focus my attention on the issues needing resolution in the final version. I would also like to acknowledge the role of Alec Stone Sweet with whom I co-authored a paper that appeared in the *American Journal of Sociology* and forms the basis for Ch. 2 in this volume. I have given numerous talks on this material and have received interesting insight in seminars given at the Harvard Law School,

Sciences-Po, the Europe Center at Harvard, Institute for International Studies at Berkeley, and the Stanford Economic History Workshop.

On a personal note, Heather Haveman was there for me as I struggled to put this book together. I had several moments along the way where I considered abandoning the effort, as it just seemed to big and too amorphous an undertaking. She continuously lifted my spirits and made it possible to keep going.

This book is dedicated to my father, Melvin Fligstein, who passed away the year I completed the main draft. My family arrived in America as immigrants around the time of World War I. They left because of the terrible economic times in Europe and the persecution they experienced because of their religion. Those who stayed behind were killed in one of the two world wars. The village my grandfather came from was destroyed during World War II. My father was born in the USA, and, given his modest social background, accomplished a great deal. He put himself through university, worked as an aeronautical engineer, raised three children, and accumulated many good friends. He had a community that honored and respected him. He lived a full and wonderful life.

All of this was possible because my grandparents fled Europe, a place that certainly would have made my father's life impossible. The fact that the Europeans have moved beyond the hatred and chaos of the first forty-five years of the twentieth century is something that I think is fundamentally important to understand. In memory of my father, this is my version of at least part of how the Europeans came to find this peace.

Contents

List of Figures

List of Tables

1

The Dynamics of European Society

INTRODUCTION

An observer from 1945 who returned today to the border between Germany and France would be astounded. Instead of devastation, army outposts, and checkpoints, they would simply observe a lack of borders. Cars and trucks pass freely and frequently. Everywhere are signs of prosperity. Opening a newspaper, our observer from 1945 would even be more perplexed. The main Western European actors in that war, Great Britain, France, Germany, and Italy have given up military competition and instead taken up political and economic cooperation. As a result, the people who live in Western Europe enjoy high levels of income and a good quality of life.

This is a remarkable feat given the history of Western Europe and its role in the world in the past 500 years. Europe has morphed from the main site of war and imperialism in the nineteenth and twentieth centuries to a prosperous, peaceful region that has operated as a political conscience for the world. There are many reasons that this has occurred. Among the most important is the hard work of the people who live in Europe. They have chosen leaders committed to peace, prosperity, and social and economic equality. They rebuilt their economies after the war and voted for politicians who have taken chances to build transnational institutions to promote trade and exchange. The peoples of Europe resisted leaders who would have taken them toward rearmament or more belligerent stances toward their neighbors. European governments responded by avoiding the paths taken during the first half of the twentieth century and instead focused on policies to promote peace and economic stability. They have made equality central in their government policies by building extensive welfare states. They have structured their political economies to attempt to promote growth but maintain social justice.

One of the main purposes of this book is to begin to consider how to analyze these accomplishments by focusing on the horizontal linkages that have been constructed across societies as a result of the policies pursued by citizens and governments. My basic assertion is that the growing cooperation amongst the people in Europe is now underpinned by a large number of Europe-wide fields of action, social fields where organized groups, be they governments, firms, nonprofit organizations, or interested groups of citizens from countries across Europe have come together for common purposes. The deepest part of this integration has been in the economy. Firms have moved from being participants in national markets to being involved in Europe-wide markets. They have come to invest all around Europe and employ citizens of many countries. Interest groups and social movement organizations have been part of constructing European political domains both in Brussels and occasionally emergent across national borders. National nonprofit associations have pushed forward cooperation for professions, trade associations, charities, and hobby and sports groups on a trans-European basis. What these social fields have in common is that national-level organizations have formed larger groupings that have reoriented their attention from nations or single states to their counterparts across borders. These fields of action have brought people together from across the continent and now form one of the main supports for a more integrated Europe. Indeed, these horizontal linkages that cross borders form the basis for what can be described as a European society.

The process of creating a European society entails that people from different countries are getting to know one another directly. New and stable social relations have emerged between people from different societies. These direct experiences have ended up affecting how people think of themselves and others. While people from different societies maintain their cultural and linguistic differences, they come to appreciate others from around Western Europe as being part of something that they are part of as well. The overall effect of these interactions is to change the identity of organizations and individuals. People who travel and work across borders do not have just national identities, but come to see themselves as Europeans. Firms are no longer national firms, but European firms. Nonprofit organizations help organize Europe-wide interests. The increasing density and cross-cutting nature of these interactions has come to stabilize and promote more interactions. There is evidence that supports the assertion that more and more of the political and economic affairs of what were previously separate national fields have become European fields. There is very little of national social, economic, and political life that has not in some way been affected by the creation of these European fields.

I am a scholar who has been traveling to Europe for many years. I have been both a formal and informal observer of European political and economic life. What has struck me most about the creation of a European society is the degree to which people in Europe are unaware of it. Most of my conversations have taken place with officials of the European Union, representatives of governments, business people, and academics. I note that many of these people see themselves as Europeans. But even while they see the details of the European project with which they are associated, few of them see how connected Europeans have become. This is for many reasons. People lack time and information about events far away from their central concerns. But it is also because many of these strands are not easily observable. So, for example, few Europeans are aware of the degree to which they are economically interdependent.

From the standpoint of even well-informed citizens, it is hard to see the connections between the representatives of the member states, the European Commission and the various interest groups represented there, and what is going on in their country. Similarly, firms in particular markets understand the nature of who their rivals are and where their markets exist, but few appreciate the degree to which other European markets are integrated. Finally, groups with a European focus meet on a whole variety of topics. Yet their meetings and deliberations do not take them to see how many others are doing the same. Most citizens continue to focus on their differences, differences reinforced by governments and their local settings.

One of my goals is to provide evidence to demonstrate how far the Europe project has gone across many social spheres. This movement has created a great many new social fields and opportunities for new forms of interaction. It has been this process that has provided the glue to connect the people of Europe together. Large numbers are involved to different degrees in working across national borders and traveling for business, vacations, and school. These interactions have produced a newfound cultural understanding of citizens from other countries, which in turn has helped promote security, economic stability, and peace.

This process of building European society forms a kind of circle. The original driving force for the idea of creating a European common market was the vision that if Europeans cooperated on trade they would be less likely to make war. Politics was used to push forward economic interdependence. As this interdependence expanded, two important kinds of dynamics were set in motion. First, people across Europe began to trade with one another more regularly, which fueled demand for more political cooperation. Consequent political discussions were centered in Brussels and new market-opening projects produced more economic interdependence (Fligstein and Stone Sweet 2002).

The second dynamic is that as people from across national boundaries began to get to know one another through their participation in politics or business, their knowledge of and interest in what each other was doing increased in many ways. Many Europeans have learned second languages, and use them regularly for work and leisure. Professional associations, trade associations, charities, and sport and hobby groups now operate on a Europe-wide basis. Such European groups meet at least yearly to discuss issues of common interest (often in resort locations!). People travel across borders for culture and to find the sun. This familiarization of people across Europe with people from other countries has not occurred just through face-to-face interactions. European media such as movies, television, music, and books can be produced in one place and eventually be consumed in other countries. European newspapers cover European business and politics and European events are a staple of the daily press, both print and television.

The process of both market and social integration is no longer tenuous and is not likely to be easily reversed. There are now a great many interests tied up in economic and political interdependence across Europe. There is also a great deal of routine social interaction. In a phrase, Europe has become a part of people's worlds. It has woven new interests and interdependence together to cause people in governments, those involved in businesses, and ordinary citizens to recognize that they need each other.

But these extensive horizontal linkages are very unevenly distributed between the citizens of Europe. A very small number of people are deeply involved with other Europeans on a daily basis. A somewhat larger group has more infrequent contact. The rest have little or no contact with people in other countries. If many of the people directly involved in the process of creating Europe do not appreciate what has occurred, the large mass of the population understands it even less (see Gabel 1998 for a review of the evidence regarding the knowledge of citizens of the European Union). This lack of connection to Europe can be indexed by looking at the percentage of the population which identifies itself as European. Only about 13 per cent (about 46 million people) of the European population in 2004 view themselves as primarily European. An additional 43 per cent sometimes think of themselves as European. This leaves 44 per cent who never think of themselves as European. Given the right circumstances, 56 per cent of people in Europe think of themselves as European (13% + 43%). But under other social conditions, 87 per cent might think of themselves as mostly having a national identity (43% + 44%).

These stark figures hide another important social fact. People who do think of themselves as Europeans are those who have experienced Europe most directly, through business or travel. Those who are most likely to have interactions with their counterparts in other societies are well educated, often holding jobs as managers or professionals, people who are more wealthy, and young people. Being part of Europe mostly involves the middle and upper middle classes who have the opportunities and resources to travel. Young people are more European because they are likely to travel and spend time living in other countries.

The main source of tension and conflict over what might happen next in Europe is the gap between those who participate and benefit from Europe directly and those who do not. There is an immense amount of political cooperation, a more or less well-integrated market for goods and services, and a nascent European politics. There is a great deal of social communication whereby people travel for business and holidays, speak second languages, and share some media and popular culture. But, for most people, this cooperation is not directly experienced. They do not travel or speak second languages, and they consume popular culture in the national vernacular. Given the fact that the beneficiaries of much interaction have been people who are richer and more educated, 'Europe' makes a big potential target for politicians and much of the population who do not think of themselves as Europeans. These citizens can easily view European integration as either a business plot that benefits those who are already better off or an assault on their national identity, state sovereignty, and welfare state. While this is a caricatured view of some of the arguments of the EU's opponents, it is, at some level, a not unreasonable representation that is in sync with what is happening for those who are not involved with the European economic project.

Much of the conflict and occasional stalling of the European process in the past twenty-five years can be understood this way: if citizens see themselves as Europeans, they are likely to favor Europe-wide political solutions to problems. If not, then they will not support Europe-wide policies. Since the swing voters around any European issue are mostly national in identity, but sometimes think of themselves as Europeans, people who live in Europe can be swayed for or against the European project depending on how the particular issue at stake is presented and how it plays out (see Diez Medrano 2003 for a related argument). Under the right conditions, politicians can appeal to constituents that European cooperation is the appropriate method to solve a particular problem; but these same politicians can fail to find ways to cooperate when larger majorities of the European populations are not convinced that something should be done at the European level.

European publics have generally favored creation of the Single Market, creation of the Euro, taking down of border controls, cooperation on issues such as the environment, and having a common foreign and security policy. But they have consistently opposed allowing national welfare state policies such as unemployment benefits, pensions, and labor market policies to be decided in Brussels (Eichenberg and Dalton 1993; Dalton and Eichenberg 1998; Citrin and Sides 2003). The former make sense to citizens as issues to be European about, while the latter people see not as European, but national. So, for example, citizens might see having a Europe-wide foreign policy in Bosnia as a good thing because it is a European issue to be resolved at the European level, but the same citizens are likely to view welfare state issues as national issues. They simply do not 'trust' the politicians in Brussels who are remote from them to serve what they perceive as the national interest on these questions.

This explains why building majorities of the European citizenry to expand the purview of Europe-wide politics is so difficult given the relatively high degree of economic, political, legal, and social integration that already exists across Europe. If only a small percentage of citizens see Europe as the natural place for cooperation, it is far easier to build opposition to European levels of cooperation than it is to build coalitions supporting the expansion of a European state. It is also easier to build opposition to Europe-wide policies within any given country or even across countries.

Indeed, European political, economic, and social integration may have reached a natural limit. Most of the obvious political and economic forms of cooperation have been undertaken and the policies that remain national are unlikely to be pushed to the European level. Without public perception that Europe is the obvious level for political cooperation on many outstanding issues, it is difficult to see where political pressure to engage in new forms of cooperation will come from. Given that most of the population does not view itself as European, they will be skeptical of politicians who want to move national programs to the European level. This does not mean that it is impossible for European integration to be pushed forward. It means instead that it will only do so if citizens who are situational Europeans (i.e. those who sometimes think of themselves as Europeans) can be convinced that the EU is the place to coordinate their policy concerns.

In the rest of this chapter, I will develop this argument in some detail. First, I provide a backdrop of how the European economy, polities, and nations looked before the EU. I consider the key events of the past fifty years that are indicative of the economic, political, and social integration of Europe. Next, I turn to discussing how I conceive of European society as a set of fields. Then I trace out more specifically the evolution of the key dynamics linking the changes in the EU with changes in the economy and European patterns of social interaction. Finally, I compare my approach to the more dominant views of European integration in the political science literature in order to argue about what that literature captures and what it misses.

THE BACKDROP TO MODERN EUROPEAN SOCIETY

There was a set of relations that existed between governments across Europe before World War II (for a review of the historical and theoretical aspects of these relationships, see Katzenstein 2005; for the long view, see Krasner 1988). These relations had a long history and were guided by a 'realist model' of foreign relations that emphasized a world of anarchic states locked in battle over territory. Both German and Italian unification in the nineteenth century occurred mainly in response to the realization that smaller states were less powerful and were likely to be military targets (Moore 1966). The realist model was transformed by the 'Cold War' where the world became divided, at least in the minds of policymakers, into two camps and all international relations were framed by the two main protagonists in these terms (Waltz 1979).

In Europe, there were relationships between businesses mostly within each society, and between labor and capital in each of the societies (Berger and Dore 1996; Boyer and Drache 1996; Crouch and Streeck 1997; Hall and Soskice 2001; Amable 2003 for recent accounts of these continued differences across Europe). Within each society, business elites had links to government and one another. There were systems of property rights to protect their interests and rules to govern economic exchange and competition. Businesses could, in some instances, form cartels and governments could be counted on to be more or less protectionist. As labor mobilized and attained organizational strength, many of the European societies also constructed labor market and social welfare regimes to mediate firm–worker interactions. Governments directly intervened in capital markets and often directed investment and owned firms.

While there was extensive trade across societies before 1914, World War I, the Depression, and the onset of World War II diminished trade substantially across Europe. International trade in the years after World War II accounted for less than 6 per cent of world GDP, down from 14 per cent at the onset of World War I (Fligstein 2001). Nation-state relations during the 1930s were about war making and protecting the interests of the state and the 'nation' (here defined as the sovereignty of the state apparatus in a given territory). Industry was directed to produce for the state as it became obvious that war was coming to Europe. Workers tried to resist both business and the governments by engaging in political actions. But on the eve of World War II, trade and industrial relations became secondary to war making.

The end of World War II altered the whole of Europe dramatically. Much of the physical and institutional infrastructure in Western Europe was shattered. The main governments of the continent were in the process of being reformed. The German, Italian, and French governments were writing new constitutions. There was the possibility of creating a new politics. At one point, for example, the idea was seriously bandied about as to whether or not a United States of Europe should be formed (Duchene 1994; Parsons 2003). The US occupation of Europe meant that the US played an important part in helping to reconstruct the institutions around Europe after the war. Indeed, the US was the strongest external force to push forward democratic government, capitalist economic relations, and free trade. The Marshall Plan aided European economic recovery. The Cold War and the continued presence of American troops on European soil meant that defense issues stayed in the foreground. While some of the US-led institutional projects were put into place, they were also resisted and their implementation was never complete (Djelic 1998).

For the purposes of this book, there were four significant events that produced huge institutional openings that created the possibility of organizing new and different social fields across Europe. The first was the Treaty of Rome, which initiated the process of building a common market area in six Western European countries. It provided a broad set of agreements to try and produce institutional arrangements to promote economic growth through cooperation on trade across Europe. The decision to produce an open-ended organization continuously to promote agreements meant that as firms took advantage of the possibility of producing new economic fields, there was a natural political field in which to discuss their problems. This field could then be used to produce new agreements to govern the continued international opening of markets.

The second event, which was actually a series, institutionalized the Treaty of Rome (see the papers in Stone Sweet, Sandholtz, and Fligstein 2001). These were quiet happenings: the setting up of the European Council of Ministers, the European Commission, the European Court of Justice, and the European Parliament. The problem of how to translate the Treaty of Rome into a workable set of organizations that could produce policy required a great many starts and stops. So, for example, the people who worked at the European Commission had to figure out how to get the many member states to agree to anything. The European Court of Justice had to decide how EU agreements were to fit into national law and how to interpret the Treaty of Rome. As it became apparent that the EU was going to be a place where agreements on opening trade were going to be hammered out, firms and industries took to forming lobbying groups. They did so in order to make sure that whatever was going to be decided would be likely to help them, but also to make sure that it did not obviously hurt their interests.

The third significant event took place in the early part of the 1980s when the European governments decided to relaunch the European Union. This set of events was an outcome of the successes of the first two phases of creating Europe. The European economies had grown together and trade had expanded rapidly between 1960 and 1980. There was demand on Brussels from market participants

for more directives to produce clearer rules about collective economic governance. The result was to open up the possibility for yet further integration of the
European economy. These events and what generated them are still the subject of
scholarly dispute, but everyone agrees that the Single European Act and the Treaty
on European Union laid the groundwork that provided actors in governments,
political parties, social movements, and the private economy to continue and
intensify their creation of Europe-wide social fields.

Finally, the end of the Cold War and German reunification meant that the
security issues that had dominated Europe for forty years had been transformed.
Almost overnight, Europe went from an area with a potentially belligerent
neighbor to the East, to an area that enjoyed great peace and security. This left
the defenders of the states as the preservation of the nation with less leverage
against increased European cooperation and encouraged politics that emphasized
economic growth and individualism. German unification was feared across
Europe because some thought it would encourage Germany, already an economic
powerhouse, to undertake rearmament. Helmut Kohl, German Chancellor,
wanted to make sure that German unification would not result in the possibility
of rearmament. He therefore forcefully pushed forward the project of the monetary union and sought out still stronger forms of political cooperation across
Europe. These historical events provide the backdrop for thinking about the
process of building European fields. The Treaty of Rome, the creation of the
Brussels-Luxembourg-Strasbourg complex, and the relaunched EU of the 1980s
reflected the processes by which European society was being built. The end of the
Cold War pushed governments away from worrying about security concerns and
caused them to focus on issues of social justice and employment and ways to
grow their economies.

THE DEFINITION OF EUROPEAN FIELDS

I have asserted that a kind of European society had come into existence; I will
clarify what I mean by this. There are a great many different ways in which to
define society, so rather than offer some top-down view of what a society is,
I prefer to use a more empirical concept that focuses on the issue of social
interaction. I begin with the idea of a field (also sometimes called a meso-level
social order, a social field, an organizational field, akin to what in political science
would be called a policy domain or policy field and, more generically, a game in
game theory). A field can be defined as an arena of social interaction where
organized individuals or groups such as interest groups, states, firms, and nongovernmental organizations routinely interact under a set of shared understandings about the nature of the goals of the field, the rules governing social
interaction, who has power and why, and how actors make sense of one another's
actions (DiMaggio and Powell 1983; Meyer and Scott 1983; Bourdieu and
Wacquant 1992; Fligstein 2001). This idea focuses attention on field participants,

their knowledge of one another, and the structure of their interactions on a period to period basis.

The central way in which I use this idea here is that Europe-wide social fields are being built where people and organizations from different countries come routinely to interact. In 1950, it is safe to say that few Europe-wide social fields existed. Instead, most of the economic, political, and social fields were organized within each country. They were governed by national states, and populated with local political, social, and economic groups or organizations. What has happened since then, is that a whole new sets of fields has emerged that connect national level organizations and citizens to their counterparts across Europe. These fields bring together citizens and organizations from around Europe to interact not just on a haphazard or random basis, but routinely.

I use the idea of fields generically. There can be political fields, such as the policy domains that exist in Brussels or the national policy domains. Markets are a kind of field as well (Fligstein 1996, 2001). National markets with mainly national firms and governed by national governments were the main kind of market in Europe in 1950. Many of these have disappeared. They have been replaced by markets organized on an EU level where firms from different countries compete under European rules. European citizens participate in Europe-wide trade associations, professional organizations, and nonprofit organizations that focus on charity, sports, hobbies, or any other subject of common interest to people who live in different countries. These organizations were mostly built from the national organizations that came together to form a European association. It is these Europe-wide fields that have potential to create groups whose interests transcend European national boundaries.

It is only as a result of such building of European political, social, and economic fields that one can begin to talk of the possible creation of a European culture, identity, and common politics. It is the groups who participate in these fields who contribute to and help define Europe. These fields may have begun as an outcome of the political projects of the EU, but now they form the main source of support for continuing such a project. They also provide the impetus to continue to push forward the European economic and political project. Indeed, one could argue that the EU is like an iceberg: what goes on in Brussels is like the 10 per cent above the waterline. But the really interesting story is the 90 per cent that is harder to see, that is below the surface, and reflects how European citizens are interacting with one another in economic, social, and political fields outside Brussels.

Central to this analysis is the observation that participation in these kinds of projects transforms people's meanings and identities in subtle ways. While their interactions make them more aware of their differences from other people, mostly they predispose people to favor more social contact. This subtly shifts people's identities. It causes them to view those from other countries as not so different from themselves. It makes them Europeans. As I show in Chs. 5 and 6, those who think of themselves as Europeans are those who have more contact with some European fields.

I cannot map out all the social fields that have been created because the complexity of the picture makes it impossible to do so. Scholarship has generally not paid much attention to the horizontal ties between people and organizations across Europe, and where it has it has done so by looking at cases that come to the fore because of public or scholarly awareness. I will try only to illustrate some interesting cases that I and others have uncovered. It is hoped these cases will give the reader a sense of the myriad ways in which the building of Europe-wide fields has altered the way that people in Europe think of themselves and their relations to citizens of other societies.

Once one considers this general proposition, one can begin to ask the questions that are more interesting. What do the people and organizations who participate in these fields do? Who participates in them? What is the link between the broader top-down projects of the European Union and these horizontal projects of Europeans, firms, and their nongovernmental organizations? Does the construction of these fields change people's identities? How do these fields feed back into their national politics and the politics of the EU? Do these changes in identity affect national politics and the possibility of a European politics that involves citizens more directly?

THE DYNAMICS OF EUROPEAN ECONOMIC, POLITICAL, AND SOCIAL FIELDS

It is one thing to assert that there has been economic, social, and political fields created across Europe, and quite another to theorize their linkages. I want to walk a line here. On the one hand, I do not want to be too deterministic about what has happened. It is the case that politicians, citizens, and corporations did not have to take the opportunities presented to them to create more interaction across Europe. That they did is part of the marvelous character of what has happened. Indeed, the whole European project could easily have died with the Treaty of Rome, a relatively vague document with relatively vague goals.

On the other hand, just to say that European economic, political, and social fields have grown without any sense of the deeper relationships between them would make this a descriptive endeavor that would not give much leverage on what is driving the process forward and causing the underlying tensions. My first purpose in this book is to be descriptive, i.e. to document the myriad ways in which economic, social, and political fields have evolved. But my second purpose is to consider these deeper relationships in order to discover what kinds of contradictions are produced and what social conflicts lie at the core of the European project.

There are three critical dynamics that have been set in motion in Europe. The first reflects the interplay of the political project in the EU and the way in which governments and firms took advantage of it. It was these initial market openings that began to increase the interactions between citizens in Europe. Because the EU project from the beginning was one centered on business, it created opportunities for a particular kind of European social interaction, one focused on the people involved in business and government, such as managers, professionals, white-collar workers, and the affluent, the educated, and the young more generally. European society has for the most part been created by these citizens and for their interests. The identities of these people have shifted as they came to view themselves, as having not just a national identity but also a European identity. This dynamic is at the core of the creation of Europe.

Even if the average citizen does not have routine interactions with other Europeans, the overall effect of the Single Market has been to increase trade, jobs, and economic growth across Europe. It has made it easier to travel for work, vacation, and school. Most middle-class people have been net beneficiaries of economic integration; they were directly affected by being employed in a job that depended on European trade; they were indirectly affected by the increase in the variety of goods and services and the lowering of prices. This variety included the opportunity to take relatively cheap vacations and to study abroad.

But the creation of the Single Market and the single currency has produced not just winners, but losers as well. This has created the second dynamic. There have been distributional issues of how jobs and income have been divided across societies. There are people for whom the past forty years have seen the closing down of economic opportunities. This is particularly true for less-skilled workers in the private sector who were the least able to find jobs as the economy changed. But anyone who might have worked for a government or was protected by their governments through laws guaranteeing job security might also have been hurt. Millions of people across Europe, for example, worked for their state-owned telephone companies as telephone operators. Today, as a result of the massive changes in telecommunications that have been driven partly by technology but also by the privatization of the telephone companies and their equipment manufacturers, such jobs mostly do not exist. Needless to say, these citizens do not identify with the EU or Europe but to continue to view the nation as their main political reference point.

The third dynamic concerns how the two others are responsible for some of the main conflicts in the existing structure of politics in Europe today. The member-state governments have controlled which policy fields have migrated to Brussels and which have remained under national control. They have done this mostly in response to what citizens have wanted. Citizens across Europe recognize that the EU has been a good thing for their country because it has, in general, created more jobs and economic growth. As a result political parties on the center right and center left have converged to a pro-European position.

But, this has not stopped particular groups of citizens from being concerned that certain EU policies might not be in their interest. These politics mostly play out at a national level because citizens expect their governments to protect them. There have been moments when a more transnational debate over issues has occurred and European governments have been pushed to act collectively in order to respond to their publics. The main conduit for these politics is the media which offers extensive coverage of EU politics and events in member states. But this kind of politics that unites citizens across member states, what could be called a horizontal or more descriptively, European politics, remains the least developed.

I begin with the first dynamic. The Treaty of Rome was organized to produce a free trade area in Western Europe. The attempt to create a single market across Western Europe is both a theoretical and political problem. From a theoretical point of view, one must have some conception of what a single market is. Economists would generally focus on markets as fields where prices were determined for a commodity and anonymous market participants from all countries would not face political barriers to entry. In the world of 1950, European markets were fragmented mainly on national lines. Attaining a single market would require political will to reduce trade barriers and level the playing field for all possible market participants.

I choose a more elaborated view of considering what a single market is (Fligstein 1996, 2001). First, a single market would imply a single set of rules governing all firms. This would include rules that govern exchange (banking, insurance, bill payment, health and safety standards), rules governing competition and cooperation within markets (what is called competition policy), and a single system of property rights. A fully integrated market would theoretically contain all three. It should be noted that fully integrated national markets rarely exist. So, for example, in the US, a place where most people would assume there is a single market, the existence of a federal system has produced a certain amount of market fragmentation. States have different laws regarding property rights, minimum wages, and health and safety standards. It is clear that since the Treaty of Rome, Europe has become more of a single market. Most barriers to trade have been removed and it is increasingly difficult for governments to protect their national firms. Rules of exchange have been harmonized across many market settings. Europe has somewhat different competition policies across nation states, but there is now a single set of policies that apply to firms that trade across state boundaries. This creates a situation akin to the US, where interstate trade is governed by federal rules and antitrust laws. It is only in the area of a single set of property rights that Europe has not created a single market. Here national rules continue to predominate. In this regard it is much like the US, where states have different rules regarding property rights.

It is useful to consider what effect the EU project has had on the economies of Europe. In 1960, intra-European exports were 6.2 per cent of GDP for the EU-15, less than the 8.3 per cent share of GDP for exports outside the EU. By 1986, the year of the announcement of the decision to complete the Single Market, intra-EU trade rose to 13.2 per cent of GDP while trade to the rest of the world dropped to 8.1 per cent of GDP (European Economy, 2004: Annex, tables 38, 39). From 1960 to 1986, the EU project redirected the activities of European businesses to opportunities in other countries. As a result of the completion of the Single Market, intra-European exports rose to 18.4 per cent in 2000 and 20.6 per cent of

GDP in 2006. During the same period, the percentage of exports to countries outside the EU rose slightly to 9.4 per cent in 2000 and 9.7 per cent in 2006. The main effect of the existence of the EU is easy to see: trade dramatically increased in size and as a percentage of all economic activity within the EU over the first fifty years of its existence. While European businesses continued to export to the rest of the world, they intensified their focus on Europe.

In 1993, the Eurostat Agency (which gathers statistical data for the European Union) began to count intra-EU trade as internal trade and trade outside the EU as foreign trade. This symbolic shift was supposed to highlight the fact that the Single Market was now a reality. In Chs. 3 and 4, I show how European corporations have responded to the market opening opportunities by redeploying their assets on a Europe-wide scale. I do this by using case studies that consider how particular European markets were reorganized, supplementing this with other datasets to document these changes.

But the increases in trade were not just a one-off outcome of signing the Treaty of Rome. I show in Ch. 2 that the increases in trade created the possibility for more market opening projects in the EU. As traders took advantage of such openings, they began to lobby with their national governments at home and more directly in Brussels for more. This put pressure on governments to decrease their attempts to protect the markets that remained closed to outsiders and give their attention to opening all markets. The lobbying effort paid off, and governments since the mid-1980s have agreed to open many of their previously sacrosanct markets such telecommunications, defense, electricity, water, and banking. The EU political fields were built on the positive feedback between trade opening projects, traders, and governments. Firms were given the ability to expand and grow. Governments gained great success in terms of aggregate economic growth and employment. As a result, between 2000 and 2005, two-thirds of the growth in the European economy came from trade alone. The politics of market opening projects in Brussels has succeeded beyond anyone's expectations. The governments and European corporations are well aware that all such projects have generally helped employment and economic growth.

The creation of Europe-wide markets had one important but largely unintended consequence. It caused people who worked for government and business from across Europe to interact with one another on a routine basis. Government officials and employees got to know their counterparts who worked in the other national governments. This knowledge increased trust and made cooperation easier (with perhaps the notable exception of the British government). While many of the most direct connections between governments were between officials in finance and trade ministries, ministers from other branches of government began to meet routinely as well. Another important effect of the EU on the creation of a European society has been to connect educational and research establishments across countries. Primary and secondary schoolteachers, principals, school superintendents, university professors, researchers, and university administrators have all been brought together in various venues for many purposes under the auspices of the EU. The main participants in the creation of

European markets were business owners, professionals, managers, consultants, marketing people, advertising agencies, lawyers, and sales people. They worked to set up plants and offices and help firms enter new national markets and integrate their production across Europe. They hired new workers from other societies and bought and sold goods and services across national borders.

Both sets of citizens have been active in forming Europe-wide associations. Their national trade and professional associations have led to the formation of European fields where people and organizations from across different societies who share some interest meet. One of the main goals of forming such fields is simply for people to interact, learn more about each other, and try and solve the common problems that groups might face. There are two sorts of groups: some might, in the end, have a narrower pecuniary or political interest in developing ties (such as lawyers from different countries), while others are really trying to seek out counterparts in order to learn more about what they are doing and to interact with them (such as educators or sports fans).

The formation of scientific, professional, managerial, and trade associations are greatly dependent on the ways in which political and economic integration has opened up interactions and discussion between people across societies. Someone has to pay to bring people together from across Europe. Business and governments are the main source of such funds. As a result, not surprisingly, most of the Europe-wide nonprofit organizations are scientific, professional, and trade associations. The increased political and economic interaction makes people interested in how other people in similar situations function. By meeting others, one can learn a great deal about how other countries respond to the challenges of European integration and indeed, people can frame new and innovative collective responses to novel situations as well.

For example, lawyers in Germany might begin to be questioned by their clients about doing mergers in Italy. Lawyers now must develop expertise in Italian business law. This brings them in touch with lawyers in Italy and produces international meetings of lawyers with expertise in mergers. These interactions stimulate the creation of cross-national organizations. In this way, lawyers get information about their counterparts, become knowledgeable and up to date about events occurring in other societies, and develop opinions about important problems facing them and their clients.

These situations that stimulate direct contact between people who give advice to business can also have an effect on national governments. Continuing my example, the German government might be getting complaints from business-men about how difficult it is to execute mergers in Italy. The lawyers involved in these transnational organizations are now in a position to advise their govern-ments on these matters. Governments, relying on these bodies of national and international experts, produce new policies. They train some of their officials to become experts in these matters and continue to monitor the situation. The existence of transnational economic exchange stimulates the production of cross-national organizations, and eventually these same organizations become partici-pants in nation-state deliberations, thereby transforming the policy domains of national governments. This logic applies equally to actors in governments, social movements, and nongovernmental nonprofit organizations. To the degree that their activities are increasingly being affected by the production of new international markets or decision-making across national borders, organizations will want to interact with their cohorts in other nations. This kind of networking has produced much of the explosion of Europe-wide transnational associations.

This is not to say that every social activity will come to be organized transnationally. Again, the opening of new social fields will tend to follow opportunities. If groups are involved in situations where major issues of interest to them are being decided across national borders, then they will seek out contact with others of similar interest. But as soon as national governments transfer some decision-making on certain issues to Brussels, then it behooves social movement organizations to shift their attention to Brussels. This has occurred, for example, in the realm of environmental policy.

The last kind of social fields being created concern people who share similar lifestyle interests, such as sports enthusiasts, hobbyists, and those who share an interest in a particular charity or cause. The ease of international communication and travel can bring football fans, birdwatchers, or fundraisers for research into childhood diseases together. Modern forms of communication such as the internet also promote the opening of transnational fields. These groups are mostly populated with educated and better-off citizens. It is they who have the time, energy, and resources to make such connections. These groups are less likely to result in political lobbying and direct reorganization of national politics. Yet these kinds of lateral ties strengthen the connections between people who live across the continent.

The new social fields being constructed across societies mirror the new ties being forged between governments and firms. Europe-wide associations sprang up to bring professionals, scholars, researchers, business owners, and managers together to discuss topics of mutual interest. These are the people who have time, interest, financial resources, and expertise to participate and create novel European fields. One would also expect that such people would be the main founders of social groups such as hobby and sports groups, groups concerned with cultural issues, and groups interested in charities.

The growth of European trade and Europe-wide associations has created a large and vocal upper-middle class who have come to see themselves not just as citizens of a single country, but as Europeans. Their interactions have brought them interesting work and interesting lives. They have encouraged their governments to continue to expand their cooperation in Europe. They vote for political parties that favor the EU. They are the bedrock of support for the EU in their countries. But it is easy to see that only a tiny part of the population is directly involved, a minority that consists of the most educated and privileged segments of society. The fact that 'Europe' has not directly involved large segments of the population goes some way to explain why it is that in spite of almost fifty years of political and economic cooperation, the EU as a political organization is seen as remote from the interests of average citizens and its activities misunderstood.

It is useful to explore the literature on how national identities have formed historically in order to get some insight into why a European identity has been slow to emerge, and what it might take for that to happen. National identities are the product of the modern era. Benedict Anderson (1983) has argued that national identities represent imagined communities. This is because even in the smallest state, most people never know or meet one another. In spite of this, Anderson argues that they are still communities because, 'regardless of the actual inequality and exploitation that may prevail in each, the nation is always conceived as a deep, horizontal comradeship. Ultimately it is this fraternity that makes it possible, over the past two centuries, for so many millions of people, not so much to kill, as willingly to die for such limited imaginings' (ibid. 5).

History shows that trade, language, religion, and regional or ethnic identities were the basis for national solidarities. Karl Deutsch (1966) has explored this issue. The central problem of modern society for Deutsch was how it would be that occupational and class groups who controlled society could convince those who had less income, wealth, and status that in spite of these inequalities, everyone could be unified by a common cultural identity. To attain this identity, groups higher up in status had to find organizational means and forms of communication to create a horizontal community united by these goals. Nationality is one kind of community than can be created by communicating common values and creating a sense that people share a common culture. But in order to attain this, there has to be an alliance between the members of disparate social groups. Deutsch places the problem of communication and culture at the center of his theory of the emergence of a national identity. A nation-state will come into existence when a national 'story' exists and once in existence, the state apparatus will be used to reproduce the nation. The social groups communicate through extensive networks involving face-to-face interactions, and via organizations that communicate routinely in political, economic, and social arenas and perhaps by means of the media.

Deutsch's theory helps us make sense of what has and has not happened in Europe in the past fifty years. A European identity is first and foremost going to arise among people who associate with each other across national boundaries. As European economic, social, and political fields develop, they cause the regular interaction of people from different societies. It is the people who are involved in these routine interactions who are most likely to come to see themselves as Europeans and as involved in a European national project. In essence, Europeans are going to be people who have the opportunity and inclination to travel to other countries and frequently interact with people in other societies in the Europe-wide economic, social, and political fields.

If we have established an accurate profile of those who are likely to be at the forefront of the emergent Europe, then it follows that there is another sector of Europeans who lack either the interest or opportunity to be there. Most importantly, blue collar and service workers are less likely than managers, professionals, and other white-collar workers to have work that takes them to other countries. Older people will be less adventurous than younger people, and less likely to know other languages, to hold favorable views of their neighbors (they will remember who was on which side in World War II), or to be curious about or want to associate with people from neighboring countries. People who hold conservative political views that value the 'nation' as the most important political unit will be less attracted to travel, know, and interact with people who are 'not like us.' Finally, less educated and less well-off people might lack both the inclination to be attracted to the cultural diversity of Europe and the financial means to travel.

One of the central problems that Deutsch recognized at the core of founding a nation was the problem of dealing with inequalities of wealth, status, and income. He felt that this problem could be solved in one of two ways. First, higher- and lower-status people could mix in certain kinds of institutional settings (such as schools, churches, and the military), thereby bonding them together. In the case of Europe, there are no such mechanisms in place to bring people together across social classes. Indeed, the class basis of European social arenas closes off opportunities for this to happen. The second mechanism that might produce a shared identity is common culture. Here media of all varieties could play an integrative role. Some evidence about whether or not this is occurring in Europe will be presented in Ch. 7. The main conclusion is that popular culture remains nationally oriented with some elements of shared culture. There is some evidence that national media do cover European affairs and politics in a fashion that might produce more solidarity, but they are as likely to cover a European story from a national perspective rather than one that expresses solidarity with Europe.

The overall increase in European trade has generally created positive aggregate economic outcomes for most citizens. Those at the top of the educational and skill distribution categories have benefited the most, but those in the middle have done so too. However, the process of economic integration has also created a group of citizens who are losers. In the Europe of 1950, governments closely protected product markets in order to safeguard jobs. Their most organized workers were able to have high levels of job security and friendly governments to protect occupational privileges. But the tearing down of trade barriers hit industrial workers the hardest. Blue-collar workers were the most likely to find themselves out of work as firms with the most efficient production were able to take market shares from local champions. Governments tried to continue to protect workers by encouraging the building of national champions (a process still going on in many countries). But the ability to preserve manufacturing jobs and other low-skilled employment has eroded.

The best new jobs were in services such as banking, real estate, and insurance or for people with different skills such as computer programming and data services. This has meant that in all societies there has been a national opposition to the European project. The less educated and the less skilled (who frequently were older) saw the new economy based on services and trade as a threat. To them, the new Europe has entailed 'globalization' and the 'triumph of neoliberalism.' Their national governments, in this case, were the enemy. Instead of protecting citizens, their governments appeared to be willing to sell them out to heartless corporations.

Ironically, the EU market opening project has created three constituencies: one that has greatly benefited from trade and increased social interaction, one somewhere in the middle that has benefited to a degree, and a third that has been harmed. These groups map closely onto conventional measures of social class such that the upper-middle class are the most European, the middle classes are more national, but still partly European, and the working and lower classes are the least European. The EU project has created a European market and Europe-wide organizations to facilitate social interaction amongst educated and skilled citizens. These citizens, in turn, over time have supported more market opening and more involvement in Europe. The losers in this market process have come to understand their plight as being caused to some degree by European market opening projects. They have pressured their governments to preserve the nation and to increase protection against market capitalism.

In sum, what have occurred in Europe are centrifugal forces that are not promoting a European national identity across social class groups. The forces that are pushing toward such an identity are concentrated within a minority of the population and the part that is the most elite in educational, occupational, and wealth terms. There is social communication across Europe that is available to wider groups and there are some forms of social interaction (such as travel for vacations, watching European football) that produce a shared sense of being Europeans, albeit in a more fleeting fashion. But, the economic integration project has also produced less favorable economic outcomes as one moves down the scale of education and skill distributions. The effect of economic integration is not to turn these citizens into Europeans, but instead to reinforce their national identities by making them see Europe as the enemy. This produces the underlying tension in European and national politics.

THE POLITICAL DYNAMICS OF THE NEW EUROPE

The creation of a European economy and society has gone on in the context of a set of political processes structured mostly around national governments. To make sense of what might happen next in Europe, it is important to understand how the underlying class dynamics play into the way that the political fields of Europe are structured. It is here that I want to rejoin the more mainstream political science literature on the EU. The central question in the literature is whether or not the EU is an intergovernmental organization (like the United Nations or the World Trade Organization), where states continue to be entirely sovereign powers, or is instead an entity where states have ceded sovereignty to a supranational political body. The EU has been described as a classic intergovernmental organization (Moravscik 1991, 1998; Keohane and Hoffmann 1991), a postmodern state (Caparaso 1996), a regulatory state (Majone 1996), a partial supranational state (Stone Sweet and Sandholtz 1998), a multilevel polity (Schmitter 1996; Marks, Hooghe, and Blank 1996; Hooghe and Marks 2001), and a 'fusionist' state whereby the member-state governments have fused to form a kind of suprational state (Wessels 1997). What all these characterizations agree upon is that the EU is some kind of multilevel polity with European, national, regional, and local levels of government and some division of policy fields by function and jurisdiction between them.

Here, I want to describe the structure of the division of labor between the states and the EU. My position is that the member-state governments are in control of the EU in the most important ways. They decide which issues are open for EU negotiation; they have ultimate voting power over directives that emerge from the political process in Brussels; they have to agree to changes in the Treaties that either emend the voting rules or expand the issues under discussion. Having said this, European governments have committed themselves in Brussels to finding collective solutions to creating a single market in Europe. The process by which directives are created allows member-state governments to decide what their positions are on particular issues, given the input by European-level interest groups, the European Parliament, and the European Commission. Over time, they have changed the voting rules from unanimous to a qualified majority in most of the important policy fields. This has made it easier to attain agreements and occasionally produce log rolling. They have also expanded their purview in Brussels to include cooperation on issues related to the Single Market, such as a single currency and the environment. At home, the member-state governments are the focus of their national political fields. National citizens, interest groups, and social movement organizations lobby, criticize, and demonstrate to attain national policies.

The functional division between policy fields in the EU and the member-state governments is striking. While all issues of trade are open to discussion and decision in Brussels, the governments have firmly kept all issues to do with welfare states, such as pensions, social security, job training, education, and labor relations under their national control. They have also resisted efforts on the part of some member states to harmonize rates of taxation which would, of course, affect the ability of governments to raise money to pay for their welfare state apparatuses. The main reason that this division of policy fields remains intact is that it has proved popular with citizens (Dalton and Eichenberg 1998). Citizens support their governments pooling sovereignty around trade issues because they perceive gains to themselves and their country, but they do not favor creating a Europe-level welfare state. In countries with highly developed welfare state apparatuses, citizens fear that governments would end up dismantling popular programs if they were decided at the EU level.

This functional division of politics has had profound implications for the development of a European politics. The EU politics in Brussels has been institutionalized around a set of policy fields. These fields are organized by the European Commission which is subdivided into Directorates, each of which is in charge of managing particular issues related to trade (Fligstein and McNichol 1998). Member-state governments are the most influential participants in these discussions, but organized interest groups and the European Parliament also play a role. The main interest groups in Brussels are either multinational corporations or the representatives of business groups. These lobby not only their governments but also the Commission and the Parliament. There has been a vast increase in the number of these groups, particularly since the announcement of the Single Market Program. I demonstrate in Ch. 2 that the emergence of these EU political fields was a function of the early successes at opening trade. As EU trade increased, so did the demand for more market openings. This brought interest groups to Brussels to lobby for more open trading.

There are two complaints about the development of these politics. First, is that these politics are undemocratic because citizens lack a real direct voice in the outcomes negotiated in Brussels. This has been called the 'democratic deficit.' A second related complaint is that EU politics is so dominated by business interests that the outcomes are out of line with what voters in Europe would prefer. Since much of Europe is center left or social democratic, they would prefer less market opening and more trade and job protection (Streeck and Schmitter 1991; Scharpf 1999).

I believe that both of these criticisms are somewhat misplaced. First, politicians in governments who were on the left and right in all the countries of Europe have been instrumental in market opening projects. Most of them have bought into such projects because they understood that they would bring new jobs and economic growth, and indeed, for most of Europe's citizens, the result has been an increase more in jobs and opportunities. One piece of evidence for this, shown in Ch. 7, is that both center-left and center-right parties in Europe experimented with anti-EU positions and all had converged on a pro-EU position by the 1990s. They did so because opposing the EU is not a way to win elections. Therefore, it is not clear that Europe's voters would prefer less of a market-friendly agenda in the EU. Indeed, one can argue that median European voters are pro-EU because they believe that trade increases jobs, opportunities, and economic growth; but they are worried about making sure that people have enough protection against the social dislocation that can be caused by market openings. This is why they want to keep the welfare state under their national control to make sure that the more negative outcomes from freer trade can be compensated for by more aggressive welfare state policies.

There has been some development of a European politics outside the context of Brussels. It is here that one can observe how the division of powers between the EU level and the national level of politics creates some elements of a democratic deficit. While citizens across Europe are generally pro-EU, this does not mean that all of them will approve of every policy undertaken by their government in Brussels. When groups of citizens find something they do not like, they generally protest directly to their national governments. They frequently do not have direct access to policymaking in Brussels, and in order to protest some decision that has already been made they direct their attention to their national political fields. This protest can play out in several ways. First, the modal response is for it to be totally contained within the policy fields of a particular country. Here, an aggrieved interest group or social movement organization will petition its government to oppose directly the EU policy or else ameliorate its national effects by granting the injured groups some form of compensation.

Sometimes national groups across countries coordinate their protests against EU policies. In Ch. 7 I show that the European media report extensively on events in Brussels and issues that potentially affect all people in Europe. The media report the same stories in each country and sometimes act as a conduit for Europe-level discussion about a particular issue. This tends to work one of two ways. First, interest groups in a particular society will view their situation as different from their counterparts in other countries. This will cause them to work to get their governments to oppose the groups elsewhere and support the national group. Second, similarly placed groups in different countries will view each other's solutions to a particular problem and agitate with their national government to adopt the solutions from other countries. Occasionally, interest groups or social movement organizations coordinate protest events across national boundaries. To illustrate some of this, I explore two cases of such events in Ch. 7: the election of Jörg Haider in Austria, and the way in which governments responded to genetically modified foods. The Haider episode shows clearly the emergence of a common Europe-wide political position. The case of genetically modified foods and organisms shows how national interest groups promote their own agendas and work with their counterparts in Europe.

One can conclude that there is a kind of European politics, but it is limited in scope because of the current set-up of political institutions and the fact that much of the protest is by national groups who want their governments to protect them from EU policies. The current division of functions between the EU and the member-state governments restricts the ability of citizens to participate directly in EU politics except in a reactive fashion. Most European citizens are happy with this division of power between their governments and the EU. But what they fail to recognize is that it limits their ability to cooperate with their counterparts in other societies who might oppose particular EU-level policies. This means that their main recourse to respond to EU-level policies is after the fact and as a protest. Frequently these protests do not lend themselves to international co-operation because their focus is on the interests and privileges of national groups which will frequently clash with those of groups in other countries. Both the institutions and the interests at stake make it difficult for European groups across societies to cooperate to put pressure either on their own governments or on Brussels. So, while there is a great deal of information about European issues and even about how they are playing out in other countries, there is very little horizontal coordination of political action across Europe.

I argue that this state of affairs is fed by and reflective of the social class differences governing which citizens are most involved in Europe and who is 'a European'. Most European integration has involved the economy and so the kinds of inter-European organizations that have been created are oriented toward the interests of people who are part of this economic expansion. They have created two sorts of organization: lobbying groups who go to Brussels to defend their interests and Europe-wide associations who go to discuss issues related to their industry or their profession. Neither of these kinds of organization is going to create a European politics.

Because of the functional division of issues between the EU and the member-state governments, most citizen groups can enter EU-level discussions only by means of national political fields. Here, they can try and affect the position of their government or work to better their position by getting their government to intervene on their behalf. But because of the institutional division of labor between the EU and the national governments, they have the most difficult time coordinating with their counterparts in different countries. The social class issues play out in obvious ways. Many of the protests in national politics will be pleas to protect the weak against the encroachment of the market. Here, those who have been the most displaced by the EU will oppose more EU-level coordination and more of a return to a national market with stronger social protection. On the other side will be the upper-middle class who will generally favor solutions that produce more market and more international cooperation.

The most important groups in national politics are of citizens in the middle of the scale of education and skills distribution. These are the people who have found jobs because of the increases in trade or have benefited by having access to more and cheaper goods and services. But, they may be more skeptical of EU-level solutions and more sympathetic to their fellow citizens' complaints. They will sometimes support an EU-level solution to a problem, depending on the issue, but they are equally likely to oppose such a solution in favor of protecting some national group. They may be persuaded that the interests of their counter-parts in other countries are not important and, instead, those of their fellow national citizens should prevail. Which side this swing group supports is the central dynamic that is at the core of the future of the EU.

ORGANIZATION OF THE BOOK

The rest of this book is oriented to weaving together the basic ideas put down in this chapter. Chapter 2 considers how the EU as a political and legal organization has affected the economy of Europe in the past fifty years. I present a discussion that outlines how the EU works as a set of organizations, followed by a narrative that documents the historical periods in the growth of the EU. Data are given that show how the EU has produced more legislation, how more cases have ended up being decided by the European Court of Justice, and how lobbying groups have increased their presence in Brussels. Finally, I show that the effect of the increasing legislative output in Brussels has been to increase trade within Europe and that, over time, trade has produced an increase in rules. There has been feedback built up by the process of European political and economic integration. The EU is now a functioning polity whereby economic activity affects the level of litigation and legislation and the subsequent outpouring of legislation increases trade. This has ratcheted up the importance of trade and of trade rules.

Chapters 3 and 4 turn to understanding how the European economy has become integrated over time. The first chapter on the economy examines how these processes played out more widely across Europe. I use aggregate data to show how, over time, trade increased across Europe, and that, as countries join the EU, trade increases and becomes more focused upon it. This has been true not only in the 1970s and 1980s as the EU went from six to nine to fifteen members, but in the past ten years as the countries in Eastern Europe applied for membership. The ten countries in Eastern Europe accounted for only 2 per cent of world trade before their decision to apply for EU membership. Once it became clear that they would become members their trade rapidly increased. Evidence shows that huge foreign investments were made in their economies, their share of world trade leapt to 6 per cent, and most of that trade is with the rest of the EU.

A dataset is presented that shows how the largest European multinationals have deployed their assets in the past twenty-five years. I demonstrate that European multinationals became less national and more European in their investments. The average European multinational does 80 per cent of its business in the EU. Finally, I examine how merger patterns have created larger and larger European firms. There is a great deal of evidence that French and German firms have bought large British, and to a lesser degree American, firms. The total picture is one where the European economy has become more Europeanized.

Chapter 4 presents three case studies: the European defense industry, the telecommunications industry, and the emergence of European football. I show how, in all three cases, the member states and the EU played a part in the deregulation and opening of these markets. Even before the end of the Cold War, European arms producers realized that they were both too small and too fragmented to compete with US firms in the world market. Governments had tried for most of the post-war era to keep arms producers captive so that if they had to go to war they could produce their own armaments. But they began to realize that their producers were too small to survive. Firms began to consider mergers. With the end of the Cold War, this process accelerated. The member-state governments have been wrestling with several issues here. Governments remain uneasy about letting their largest arms producers be bought out by foreign firms. One tentative solution has been for governments to cooperate in purchasing large weapons systems from other national producers or consortia of such producers. As a backdrop to all this has been the ongoing discussion about the construction of a European common foreign and security policy and a European defense force organized to be used in pursuit of that policy. Over time, three large consortia formed that created joint shareholding across firms and across countries.

In the case of telecommunications, governments led the way to deregulate their firms in the mid-1980s. The result was that large state-owned telecommunications firms became privatized. Here, again, governments were reluctant to have their phone companies bought out by private foreign firms. Alliances and joint ventures have emerged in this industry as well. The explosive growth in cellular phones has produced a slew of new companies, most of which are joint ventures between existing telecommunications firms. Only one new player has emerged, Vodaphone (Verizon in the US). The three largest companies remain France Télécom, Deutsche Telekom, and British Telecom.

European football has become more organized at a European level as well. In 1995, the European Court of Justice agreed to allow football players to sign contracts wherever they chose. This created free agency, which meant that the best players no longer played for national teams, but went to teams that bid the highest. This shift in free agency for players was accompanied by an explosive growth in cable TV broadcasting of games. The largest sixteen teams (in terms of revenue bases) threatened to form a European Football League in accord with some of the cable stations in 1999. While they backed away from that, the European Champions' League now holds annual competitions to crown a European champion and the largest teams play one another during the regular season as well as in the play-offs. Football that is being played in different national leagues is now broadcast all over Europe through pay-TV.

Chapters 5 and 6 consider who the people are who have populated the new European political and economic fields. The first chapter uses survey data to assess 'Who are the Europeans?' I show that people who have a European identity are young people, educated people, managers, professionals, or business owners, richer people, and people with political views more to the left. I explore how this varies across European societies. Great Britain, Denmark, and Sweden have the fewest Europeans. It is in these societies that there has been the greatest skepticism toward the European project. I also present evidence that shows that these same people speak second languages and have traveled to other European countries in the past twelve months.

Chapter 7 examines some more concrete ways in which Europeans have come to interact with one another across national borders. I begin by considering the migration of European citizens to work in other countries. Migration is a direct measure of interaction of people from across national borders. At the present time, only 2–3 per cent of the citizens of Europe are working in another EU country. These citizens are highly educated, usually young, and have strong European identities. There are three other major groups of intra-European migrants. Many people migrate to stay united with their families or accompany their spouses when they move to work. Substantial numbers of Europeans are also migrating for shorter periods either to attend school in another country or to retire there. In general, intra-European migration is amongst those who come from middle- or upper-middle-class backgrounds.

Data is presented on Europe-wide associations, which increased greatly in number following the announcement of the Single Market in 1985. This confirms my earlier argument that economic integration has pushed forward the opportunity for social integration. Of associations, professional and trade account for the largest number, but there are also many nonprofit groups such as charities, sports, and hobby groups. These also emerged in the wake of the Single Market, suggesting that the increase in social interaction propelled people toward more collective action.

One of the core groups involved in creating European society is the education establishment. I argue that this reflects the core agreement in the education establishment that being a European is to be someone who is educated and rational, and thereby takes into account the opinions and perspective of people unlike oneself. In essence, for educators, Europe is about the completion of the Enlightenment, a chance to create educated, enlightened European citizens. There are ongoing discussions at every level of schooling about constituting a European education. For primary and secondary schools, there are two issues: the teaching of second languages and the teaching of national history and literature in the context of Europe. I present evidence that European history in different countries is now being taught in the context of Europe. Such history seeks to place the good things that have occurred in a country's history as attributable to the unfolding of a European set of values. At the university level, I explore the expansion of the Erasmus program and students studying abroad. I show that for the 3–4 per cent of students who travel, the experience makes them more likely to work abroad and more European in general. European education ministers have embarked on a reorganization of their universities (called the 'Bologna process'), oriented toward making their degrees compatible. They want to create what they call a 'European higher education space' that will allow students to travel to universities everywhere and be able to transfer credits easily in order to complete their degrees. I conclude that the education establishments in all member-state countries are amongst the leaders in pushing forward a European identity project.

Finally, I consider how music, television, movies, and novels have or have not converged in content across Europe. I show that there is a large influence of American television and movies in Europe. There is less of a presence in music and books, but here there is a substantial persistence of local writers and musicians working in the national language. There are clear examples of books and music that do cross European borders, and even occasionally German, French, and British movies do so as well. There is little evidence of what could be called the emergence of a European culture. A European business press exists. While there are cases of culture moving across national borders, there is also evidence for a continued fragmentation of culture along national lines.

The last substantive chapter, Ch. 8, takes up the implications of all of this for national politics. I begin by outlining how EU and national politics works as a structure. Then I consider how political parties in Great Britain, France, and Germany have campaigned on EU issues over the past forty years. I show that all center-left and center-right parties have a pro-EU stance currently. But, in all three countries, parties did experiment with an anti-EU message at some time in their history. In Great Britain, the Labour Party initially opposed the EU, shifting its position in the 1980s. The Tory Party was initially favorable, but began to oppose the EU in the late 1980s. This issue eventually drove the Tory Party from power and they have subsequently adopted a more neutral EU stance.

There is good evidence that Europe-level political issues are covered extensively by the main newspapers across Europe. These issues are also debated in editorials. The slant on these issues can sometimes be one of solidarity with other countries, but it is also the case that the slant can be about how the nation is affected and needs to be protected from the EU. Evidence is presented that national interest groups and social movement organizations have increased their level of protest to their national governments on EU issues of concern to them. Many of these protests are focused on safeguarding the national group and having the government offer some form of protection. There has been increased coordination of social movement events across national borders, but these forms of coordination remain rare.

A structural division of politics occurs in Europe. Brussels politics is highly organized and focuses on trade issues. The main method of intervention ordinary citizens have into the politics of the EU is through voting. Political parties have taken positions on the EU and most voters favor EU participation. Some citizens form groups that lobby their governments at home and sometimes in Brussels. The focus of these lobbying efforts is usually to preserve or expand the interest of the group. There is evidence that European political issues do travel across countries through the media. Sometimes these issues produce coordination of policy by national governments, but at other times, they reinforce national differences and put governments into conflict with one another. The class character of the EU plays out in interesting ways in these politics. Governments engage in EU-level policies to increase trade and market opportunities. These help middle- and upper-middle-class voters who benefit by getting jobs and more secure employment; at the same time, these policies harm less-skilled citizens. They are more likely to protest directly to their national governments. The degree to which they get satisfaction depends on the political party in power and the sympathy of swing middle-class voters toward their plight.

CONCLUSION

So far in my presentation of my perspective on European economic, social, and political integration I have steered clear of directly engaging the literature in international relations and comparative politics on the nature of the EU, its underlying logic, and its direction. I have done so in order to clear out some ground for a more sociological view of the process. My main argument is that most of the theories of the EU are incomplete. By not understanding how the changes the EU began have played out amongst the citizens of Europe and how they have subsequently fed back into European processes, most theories are unable to specify how the EU changes have produced feedback into the existing political structure of Europe and what challenges those changes will produce.

Given that both the comparative politics and international relations literatures focus only on political processes, they miss how the changes in the economy and in patterns of social action can shift the political calculus in each country. Perhaps most importantly, the economic changes in Europe have benefited the better educated and skilled the most, those in the middle of the scale somewhat, and have impacted most negatively the people at the bottom. The dynamic of integration has created both its proponents and its opponents. The crucial questions in understanding the future of Europe are which group is larger, and where will it make sense to them to have cooperation across countries on decisions concerning critical issues.

There are two main positions in the debate over the nature of the EU. The intergovernmentalists or regime theorists argue that the EU is a political organization formed by nation-states in recognition of their economic interdependencies (Keohane and Hoffman 1991; Moravscik 1991). The states have decided to cooperate on issues of common concern, but in general will only enter into agreements that benefit them. Agreements will have to encompass issues that, in game-theoretic terms, will find the 'lowest common denominator solution' (Garrett 1995). Intergovernmentalists view the EU as a political structure firmly under control of the member-state governments. They also see the legitimacy of that structure as resting primarily on the fact that national governments are democratically elected (Moravscik 2002).

The other alternative posed in the literature is neofunctionalism. Here, the basic mechanism by which agreements are reached concerns the interactions between the international organization and the various constituencies it creates. Neofunctional arguments suggest that increased interdependence leads to the organization of societal and trans-societal actors who will bring new issues to their states and the international organization. This process, called 'spillover,' will result in increased purposes for the international organization over time (Haas 1958; Lindberg and Scheingold 1970). Here, sovereignty is transferred from the states to the international organization resulting in a supranational entity being formed.

This debate has spawned a great deal of scholarship, but it has remained focused on the relationship between EU-level and national politics. From my perspective, the issue of what was going on in Europe had the most to do with the changing effects of European economic integration on the life chances of people who live in Europe. It is the perception of these life chances that drive European attitudes toward the EU. From this perspective, political scientists were missing these deeper dynamics and were trying to explain only part of the story.

I have a great deal of sympathy for intergovernmentalism. I agree that governments remain the most powerful actors in Brussels. Governments have created a self-conscious division of labor between the member-state governments and the EU around policy fields in order to maintain their control. This division of powers reflects the views of most European citizens who favor the focus on trade and monetary issues in the EU but want to keep all issues concerning the welfare state in the national political fields. Governments reflect national views. So, for example, in general, the British voting public is skeptical of the advantages of EU membership. Both Labour and Conservative governments are cautious about joining up with new European ventures in Brussels as a result. At the opposite extreme, the German public has been more pro-EU. Not surprisingly, German politicians have often floated the most federalist conceptions of political structure and were behind the idea of producing a European constitution that would have created a much stronger political union.

I have three main problems with intergovernmentalism. First, governments have been constrained to act in Brussels in accordance with their previous agreements (Pierson 1996). Because new governments are elected with different political constituencies and programs, they have found themselves committed to courses of action that they might not have preferred. So, for example, social democratic governments might not have favored eliminating state aids to ailing corporations. But once member-state governments agreed to severely restrict such aids, new governments were constrained to obey the rules. Second, the political processes of negotiation that go on in Brussels imply that member-state governments need to figure out what is in their interest on any political issue. The process of introducing legislation by the European Commission, comment on the legislation by the European Parliament, and input from various national and Europe-wide interest groups does affect the final form of legislation. While governments do, in the end have to agree to legislation, the process of negotiation can clarify what paths governments will find acceptable.

Most importantly, intergovernmentalism assumes that the division of functions between the EU and the member states is in equilibrium (Moracsvik 2002). This view is based on the idea that the citizens of every country have fixed preferences with regard to the shape of the EU. These preferences are summed up and reflected in their governments. Thus, the separation of powers that exist have been fixed from the beginning and will remain so. My central argument is that the use of EU power to open opportunities for economic and social interactions across Europe changes the preferences of Europe's citizens. It makes some of them more interested in cooperating at the European level and if enough citizens feel that the EU is beneficial this pushes their governments to engage in 'ever closer union.' It is this dynamic that has pushed European integration forward. But, as I have already indicated, this dynamic can also sharpen the debate in member states as citizens who oppose this increasing commitment to the EU are wary of the continuous expansion of EU projects. Citizens who feel that the EU does not reflect their interests organize more vociferously to promote those interests. National political fields become more open battlegrounds for EU issues.

The perspective I develop here has some affinity for neofunctionalist theory in international relations in political science. This view suggests that international organizations produce cooperation amongst their members. By cooperating, actors would discover unintended consequences of their actions and thereby undertake to expand their arenas of cooperation. My position here differs from neofunctionalism in several respects. First, I am skeptical of its claim that 'spillover' into new political fields naturally follows from cooperation.

Much of the process of politics in Brussels has taken place along the lines laid out by the Treaty of Rome (Fligstein and McNichol 1998). So, for example, there has been very little cross-border cooperation on social welfare issues precisely because including these issues in EU cooperation is politically unpopular. From my perspective, spillover has not occurred because the interest groups to promote it at the national level have not formed. Most of the growth in connections between European societies has followed the lines laid down in the Treaty of Rome. It is not surprising that business has the most extensive ties across state lines, followed by governments, nongovernmental organizations, particularly those that represent the interests of professionals and managers, and, finally, ordinary citizens. The Treaty of Rome set up a permanent organization whose major function was to increase economic cooperation across Europe. Much of the project creating Europe has been about creating a single market and that market, by definition, bounds what kinds of spaces might come into existence.

Second, I am not interested only in international agreements and the policy domains they have created in Brussels. The growth in the economic and social fields of Europe has increased awareness of the EU and brought many people into contact all across Europe. These citizens are the strongest source of support for continued European cooperation. They are also creating a European society in response to economic integration. The main way that they express their opinions to their governments is at home through elections or through the existence of interest groups or social movement organizations in national policy fields. The process of spillover is more like 'spill up.' If citizens in the member states view more European cooperation as a good thing, they will be inclined to encourage political parties and governments to pursue increased cooperation at the EU level. If they think it is a bad thing, they will discourage their governments from doing so. They may also take issue with a particular EU policy and organize directly in their national political fields or try and cooperate with citizens of other member states to do so.

It is useful to conclude this chapter by considering what the particular picture of the existence of a European society I have painted implies about the future of Europe. There is substantial evidence that there now exist thousands of fields that routinely bring people from different societies together. Europe has also produced a lot of social interaction outside the context of political activity in Brussels. There is much more connectedness and interaction amongst educated and highly skilled people who are professionals, managers, and similar white-collar workers than those who are poorer, elderly, blue collar, and have fewer educational credentials. In spite of this integration, I want to make the case that one must be circumspect about how far the process of creating a European society has gone. A very small number of people in Europe are interacting with people from other European countries on a daily basis. For most of the population, such interaction is much less frequent and for a substantial percentage, nonexistent.

Nation states are the policy fields where most Europeans continue to look for initiatives. Most Europeans see themselves primarily as citizens of a single country and most expect their governments to tend to their interests. Governments control social policy and remain the site of popular contention and legitimation. How does the creation of a European society matter for the political battles about unemployment, immigration, and the welfare state that are ongoing?

I would like to outline a continuum of various scenarios. At one end is the most negative, a situation where slow economic growth and unemployment push one or more of the big states to pursue a more nationalist solution and even leave the EU. A second possible situation is what could be called 'muddling through.' Here, governments continue to be ineffective in combating slow growth and inflation, but keep the EU at its current institutional level. This could happen without increased cooperation across Europe. In this version, each welfare state decides to follow its own path toward economic and social reform. There may be some borrowing of ideas across societies, but mostly policy choices will be made in national contexts.

A third scenario is for there to be more cooperation amongst member-state governments on issues of employment and social welfare. These more formal agreements might include the attempt to coordinate fiscal policies, create more government spending to create jobs, and produce more market opening initiatives, such as trying to produce a European high technology sector through some form of industrial policy. The fourth possibility is an expansion of the EU apparatus to include social and welfare issues as part of the policy domains in Brussels.

My central argument is that the first and last scenarios are the least likely at this point precisely because of the way Europe has developed. In the first case, even in Great Britain, where skepticism about Europe is the highest, the institutional connectedness of Britain to Europe makes it unlikely that it will leave the EU. The creation of Europe implies that the combination of the importance of the political and economic fields and the collective commitment to the legal institutions that help define those fields makes it unlikely for these institutions to slip backwards.

Consider how such a scenario might play out. A nationalist government in one of the main societies comes to power in a situation of severe fiscal and economic crisis, and asserts its sovereignty by trying to extricate itself from the EU. It would claim that the EU was binding it both economically and socially. Such a government might try to rearm itself to defend against the enemy. This is most likely to happen from the political right where nationalist parties would emphasize the nation and the state over Europe.

Such a scenario would produce a great deal of backlash within that society and across Europe. Put simply, the citizens and groups involved in European social fields would likely react strongly to such a regime. Businesses, in particular, who depend on European markets, and citizens whose jobs depend on European trade would be aghast at the idea that their country would be shut out. The largest economic corporations most involved in trade would be skeptical of the wisdom of such moves. Labor unions, faced with massive lay-offs because of the closing off of European trade, would be in rebellion. A 'nationalist solution' to go it alone, close off borders, and rearm would have to oppose strongly entrenched forces in government bureaucracies and in the economy.

Such a government would also have to face the leaders of the other member-state governments who would remind the recalcitrant government of the agreements that were made by previous regimes. A strong government might be able to push such a project as an ideology, but to move it forward practically would be quite an undertaking. If one of the main societies within the Euro-zone (i.e. Britain, Italy, France, Germany, or Spain) was the site of this contest, it would likely throw all Europe into an economic crisis. Because of the high level of interconnection between European social, economic, and political fields, it is likely that any democratically elected government that began seriously to threaten its neighbors would soon be very unpopular at home. Even in the face of economic crisis, the integration of the European social, political, and economic fields has probably transformed the policy options of most political parties in such a way as to prevent the dismantling of Europe.

Of the other three scenarios, one would have to argue that the transfer of more competencies to Brussels, particularly welfare state functions, seems less likely as well. It is here that the limits of Europe are the easiest to observe. The question is, which is the political constituency within European societies for whom this option makes sense? I think that it is hard to argue that the mass of European voters will find this option very palatable. Those who are the most European may view such solutions as plausible. But, citizens with mainly a national identity fear what would happen to national welfare systems if they are transferred to Brussels. They would strongly oppose such efforts at coordination. Moreover, it is not clear how people who are already the winners of the economic project obviously benefit by increasing this form of cooperation. It is here where national differences in welfare systems will predominate. The British political parties are both committed to more market-friendly labor-market regimes. They have already made it clear that they do not want a European-level expansion of welfare rights. On the more social democratic side, French and German political parties are afraid that an EU-level welfare regime will end up looking more like the British system. The voting publics of these two societies would be in open protest over such a move.

This leaves the middle two solutions. Governments working more or less alone trying to solve their fiscal problems in a piecemeal fashion is probably one of the strongest scenarios. This is particularly true in dealing with an aging population and continuously strained pension and health care systems. No one will be interested in pursuing a European solution because they will be afraid that their benefits will be cut or that their tax dollars might end up in the pockets of citizens of other countries.

There are already existing Europe-wide constituencies in the business and policy community which have more coordinated forms of industrial policy, particularly around issues of finding finance for small and medium-size businesses, promoting entrepreneurship, research and development, technology transfer from universities to business, and job training. Here, a scenario of more cooperation at the European level is possible. This kind of cooperation would mainly be about coordinating policies such as voluntary agreements between member-state governments over targets for policies or further agreements about a set of directives for a particular market opening project. The Lisbon Agenda agreed to by the member-state governments in 2000 is a good model for both these this forms of coordination. Governments committed themselves to creating the 'most dynamic and competitive knowledge based economy in the world by 2010.'

These are the real choices that lie ahead. But before considering the future, it is useful to document what kind of political, economic, and social Europe has been created. What has happened is quite remarkable. It is important to understand how the EU has created opportunities for people to interact with one another, and how this has affected who they are, and what kinds of worlds they have made.

2

Constructing Markets and Politics:
The Formation of the European Union,
1958–2004

INTRODUCTION

The EU started out as the European Coal and Steel Community (ECSC), an organization that was set up to control the levels of production in the coal and steel industries of Western Europe (Haas 1958). In 1957, Belgium, France, Germany, Italy, Luxembourg, and the Netherlands took a quantum leap forward in integrating their economic policies by agreeing to the Treaty of Rome. The Treaty contained a set of blueprints for ongoing cooperation on issues of trade, labor, capital movements, and monetary policy. It created the European Economic Community (EEC), a permanent organization in Brussels to promote this cooperation. Between 1957 and today, the EU grew in size from six, to twelve, to fifteen, to twenty-five, and now twenty-seven member states. As the EU has expanded, the member-state governments revisited the Treaty of Rome and altered it by producing new agreements that include the Single European Act (1987), the Treaty on European Union (1993), the Treaty of Amsterdam (1999), and the Treaty of Nice (2003). These newer treaties have changed several important features of the EU and its decision-making processes. The voting rules for making laws in Brussels have changed from being unanimous to having a qualified majority. This has made collective decision-making easier as the number of member states increased. The European Parliament began direct elections in the 1970s and has been given increasing powers to weigh in on the EU budget and the legislative process. The Treaty of Amsterdam gave the Parliament a formal vote on matters pertaining to the Single Market. EU cooperation has also expanded and several new policy fields have been added that include justice and home affairs, and common foreign and security policy (Noel 1985). Finally, the EU created a single currency, the Euro, and the European Central Bank to administer it.

One of the most remarkable things is that almost *all* European governments of *all* political persuasions have found the benefits of membership to be positive for their economies. Over time, the governments have agreed to expand their fields of cooperation and the rules by which cooperation is attained. Over time, more and more governments in Europe have clamored to join the EU. Not surprisingly, there is a huge outpouring of EU scholarship that tries to make sense of how this process of European economic and political integration took place.

I want to argue that the process of increased cooperation has occurred mainly because many of the firms and citizens of Western Europe have benefited from European economic and political integration. Firms have gained new markets for their products and been able to finance their growth more effectively. Citizens have benefited from the availability of new jobs as market openings have created employment opportunities. As consumers, they have gained access to products and services that they value. Price competition has meant better goods at lower prices. As trade has increased and the benefits of economic integration have become more apparent, governments have been willing to undertake more and more aggressive steps to create a single market for labor, capital, goods, and services in Europe.

This description makes the process of European integration sound straightforward and without conflict. Nothing could be further from the truth. There was nothing inevitable about what has happened. The process has been fraught with difficulties, ambiguities, and crises. The central dynamic of the EU since its inception has been, on the one hand, pressure from some firms and organized citizenry for more Europe-wide cooperation, and on the other, pressure from other firms and citizens about the costs of engaging in EU political agreements. Governments have to face the fact that market opening projects are likely to produce winners and losers in their societies. The potential losers, both firms and workers, are politically connected and have tried to keep their governments from changing the status quo. So, for example, when EU economic integration began in the 1960s, European governments in some countries owned many of their largest firms. This ownership and promotion of national champions made them more reticent to open markets because in doing so, they would threaten the monopoly of these firms over the national market. There was a great deal of fear that increasing competition would lead to the restructuring of those firms and the loss of jobs. In spite of these pressures, European governments after 1980 have been willing to sell off their stakes in these firms and open up their markets in such industries as telecommunications, utilities, and defense. On the political front, the agreement to transfer decision-making authority over economic matters to the EU means that governments have had to give up a certain amount of sovereignty over their internal affairs. Some of Western Europe's voting publics have frequently been concerned that too much has been given up for too little in return.

Indeed, much of the political history of the EU has been about how member-state governments seem at critical moments to have been deadlocked and unable to resolve their differences. While there were constituencies to push European economic integration forward, there was always the worry by member-state governments and some of their political constituencies that they were going to be losers by agreeing to cooperation. The remarkable thing is that at every crisis the governments have found ways to overcome their differences and push forward their cooperative efforts.

One of the important reasons that this has been the case is that governments are in constant contact through their daily involvement in Brussels. The existence of the EU as an ongoing organization has mattered a great deal in a number of ways. The governments are committed to the treaties underlying the EU which provide a legitimate basis for ongoing cooperation. The people employed in Brussels, particularly those who work for the European Commission, are committed to creating a political process that is continuously trying to find grounds for agreement. Political entrepreneurs such as Schumann, Monnet, and Delors have convinced the member-state governments to expand their fields of cooperation. Finally, governments are being lobbied at home and in Brussels by the representatives of their largest and sometimes most dynamic firms (and sectors of their economy), while they are also being lobbied by groups who might suffer at the prospect of more economic integration, member-state governments have usually been responsive to these firms.

One way in which member-state governments have been able to resist organized political opposition to market integration at home has been through their use of welfare state policies. Governments have tried to compensate people who have lost their jobs because of increased competition by providing job training, generous unemployment and pension benefits, and national health care insurance. They have also used their tax policies to insure that increased trade did not produce more inequality in incomes, pensions, and access to healthcare (Leibfried and Pierson 1995; Garrett 1998; Hicks 1999). These policies have been very popular amongst voters across Europe. To keep control over such systems, governments have resisted all efforts to cooperate on most welfare state issues at the EU level. The purpose of this chapter is to document how the Brussels political complex evolved over time to produce a European politics. By this I mean that people have come to Brussels and formed lobbying groups to promote their causes and try to influence European legislation. They litigate under European law and go to the European Court of Justice. This ongoing political apparatus is highly stable and well developed (Mazey and Richardson 1993). This has occurred because users of the Brussels political and legal system have been successful at convincing their governments to increase cooperation and open up new markets. These openings have increased trade, economic growth, and new jobs.

As trade and economic growth have gone forward hand in hand, more people have been encouraged to go to Brussels. Increasing economic integration has energized the political project in Brussels, which in turn has expanded trade across Europe. This dynamic has escalated to create an extensive trading system across member states and a well-developed European polity to regulate economic affairs. I begin by discussing how Brussels works and demonstrate how the EU has come to construct a polity that includes legislative fields and a court. Then I consider exactly what economic policy fields the EU regulates and how this has been structured over time. Finally I demonstrate how litigation concerning trade rules, legislation to produce new trade rules, and trade have moved forward together. Political activity has been accompanied by increases in European trade, which have subsequently driven forward the integration process as firms and lobbying groups go to Brussels to promote their interests by litigation or influencing legislation (Fligstein and Stone Sweet 2002).

The European Union's main goal has been to create a single market for labor, capital, and goods across Europe. While there has been increased attention given to cooperation on justice and security issues in the past fifteen years, the main successes of the EU have been in creating a common market. There are three different but well-known stories that scholars have told about European integration. The first story focuses attention on the consequences for the development of supranational governance of rising economic transactions across borders. The more goods, services, investment, and labor flow across national boundaries, the more governments and the EU's organizations are pushed to remove national barriers to further exchange, and to regulate, in the form of European legislation, the emerging Common Market (Fligstein and Brantley 1995; Stone Sweet and Sandholtz 1998). Traders used the courts to tear down trade barriers (Stone Sweet and Brunell 1998). They also went to Brussels to lobby for new legislation (Mazey and Richardson 1993).

The second story traces the effects of the constitutionalization of the Treaty of Rome. The European Court of Justice interpreted the Treaty of Rome and all subsequent EU legislation as overriding national law. The constitutionalization of the document essentially created a federal structure that divided the jurisdiction of laws into those that were transnational and those that remained national (Weiler 1991, 1999; Burley and Mattli 1993; Stone Sweet 2000). In the fields governed by EU law, this has profoundly altered how individuals and firms pursue their interests, how national judiciaries operate, and how policy is made (Dehousse 1997; Joerges and Neyer 1997; Slaughter, Stone Sweet, and Weiler 1990, 1994, 1999; Poiares 1998). The operation of the legal system, through the Article 177 procedures (De La Mare 1999; Stone Sweet and Brunell 1998), has pushed the integration project in two ways. It made it clear that national governments were not going to be able to protect national firms by ignoring the Treaty of Rome and European law. It thereby encouraged member-state governments and their firms to increase their cooperative activity in Brussels and create more legislation.

The third integration narrative traces the causes and consequences of the growth of lobbying groups and the creation of policy fields in Brussels. As lobbying groups and Commission officials have interacted in specific directorate-generals and within ongoing policy processes, the Commission has worked to develop procedures for consultation within the Brussels complex. A wide range of policy outcomes—from the form and content of directives to the specifics of administrative rules taken pursuant to secondary legislation—can only be understood by taking account of the work of lobby groups (Andersen and Eliasson 1991, 1993; Greenwood and Aspinwall 1998; Mazey and Richardson 1993). The European Commission is a relatively small organization. It lacks the capacity to generate technical proposals on its own. This means that it relies on the expertise of member-state governments, consultants, and the representatives of lobbying groups.

These three stories can be linked together. The main process by which Europe has emerged has been provoked by nonstate actors, particularly—but not exclusively—those representatives of firms or industries seeking to further their own sectoral interests by exploiting opportunities provided by the Treaty of Rome. These actors groped towards determining which issues could be raised, and developed strategies for effective lobbying of the Commission and their national governments, and for litigating matters of EU law before national and European judges. Of course, European Union organizations took part in, and helped to structure the political process in Brussels. As trade increased, the European Court of Justice ruled for traders and against national barriers to trade. The European Commission learned how to respond by recognizing that litigation presented opportunities for legislation. Once new rules were devised or new case law made, new opportunities were opened up for firms and nongovernmental organizations to press their national governments and the Brussels apparatus to continue to open markets.

When it became clear that Brussels was going to be a place where transnational governance was going to occur, business groups, labor groups, and social movement organizations such as women's and environmental groups set up shop in Brussels. They lobbied the European Commission and the member-state governments to increase cooperation. The final result of legislation was the opening of new markets and the increase in trade. Put simply, the European political fields evolved as representatives of an emerging trans-European society, the member-state governments, and the EU organizations came to a set of agreements about how to use and expand the architecture of the Rome Treaty. This architecture, in turn, expanded trade across Western Europe and has altered the character of the European economy entirely in the past forty-five years. This argument is summarized in Fig. 2.1.

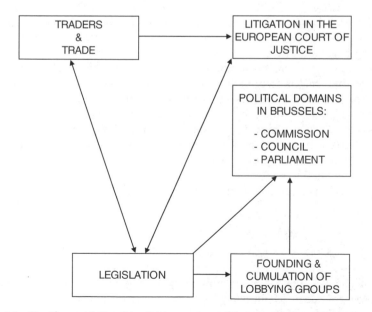

Figure 2.1. Significant relationships in the process of Europeanization, 1958–1996.
Source: Adapted from Fligstein and Stone Sweet 2002.

These events unfolded over time and can be assigned to three periods. From 1957 until 1969 the political and legal fields of the EU were being constructed in Brussels. At the beginning the people who worked in Brussels had to figure out how to implement the Treaty of Rome. The European Commission, the European Court of Justice, and the European Council of Ministers were formed and began to interpret and create European rules. Lobbying groups began to weigh in on policy questions. The most pivotal events centered on the use of the European Court of Justice as a way for traders to promote their rights to market access across Europe. Court rulings opened up market opportunities for firms to sell products and for people to work across borders. By 1970, it was clear that European rules were going to matter for cross-border trade. The second period of EU expansion occurred from 1970 until 1985 with the announcement of the Single Market Program (Ross 1995). The political and legal fields of the EU became the focus of the attention of the representatives of various social and economic interests across Europe. The increase in economic and social transacting brought forth new problems that were most logically solved in Brussels.

The Single European Act (1987) opened up a new era of EU cooperation that witnessed an explosion in laws. It was followed by the Treaty on European Union (1993) the Treaty of Amsterdam (1999), and the Treaty of Nice. The Treaty on European Union pushed forward the decision to create a monetary union and expanded the power of the European Parliament. The Amsterdam Treaty expanded the powers of the Parliament, changed more voting rules to majority agreement, and set in motion the enlargement of the EU from fifteen to twenty-five members. The Treaty of Nice realigned the institutions of the EU in order to make them function better with an enlarged membership. There have been agreements to cooperate on areas such as justice and home affairs and common security policy. However, cooperation here relies on governments unanimously agreeing to a course of action. Such agreements have been difficult to reach.

Within the economic sphere, cooperation has increased in employment, education, environment, the information society, and consumer health and safety. These issues reflect not just the interests of corporations, but also the work being done in Brussels by lobbying groups organized around workers, women's rights, consumer rights, and the environment (Cichowski 2001). Most of the real changes in Brussels have reflected business and trade interests, but representatives of social movement groups that have organized in Brussels now lobby the Commission on a routine basis. The political response of the member states to both sets of pressures has been to expedite the project to create more European cooperation.

THE ORGANIZATION OF THE EUROPEAN UNION

For an outsider, the EU is an administrative nightmare. The proliferation of organizations in Brussels and the complexity of their relationships make the operation of the EU seem impenetrable. One of the big problems is that relationships have evolved over time as the member-state governments have revised the Treaty of Rome to change both the policy fields in which they cooperate and the rules by which they produce legislation. So, for example, the role of the European Parliament has changed dramatically. It began as a relatively powerless advisory organization that was not directly elected by the citizens of Europe. In 1979, direct elections began. These were followed up by an expansion of powers over matters such as the selection of the budget, veto power over the membership of the European Commission, and now, the ability to weigh in on legislative matters (Dinan 1999).

There have also been unintended consequences of the process by which the politics have been done in Brussels. The most important example of this is the proliferation of lobbying groups. The Treaty of Rome did not envisage that groups would come to Brussels to lobby both the Commission and their member-state governments (Groeben 1982), and it has created a layer of European politics that is not formally integrated (although as Mazey and Richardson 2001 argue, the ways in which lobbyists proceed are well organized and understood). Moreover, the EU has developed a set of procedures and an insider's jargon to describe how the EU works. This is supposed to aid the production of agreements (Dogan 1997), but for outsiders it creates high barriers to entry for anyone who has the least interest in trying to understand what is going on.

To cut through this, it is useful to begin the discussion by considering how the EU organizations ostensibly work to produce legislation. The EU is a unique polity. Some observers characterize it as an intergovernmental organization constituted by a voluntary pooling of sovereignty (Keohane and Hoffman 1991; Moravscik 1998). This view highlights that the member-state governments agree to give up some sovereignty in order to attain important joint ends, like market access for their firms. Others see it as a quasi-federal state-like structure not unlike the US under the articles of confederation (Sbragia 1992), and still others as a 'multilevel polity' with a plurality of levels of governance (Marks, Hooghe, and Blank 1996; Hooghe and Marks 2001). Wessels (1997) describes the EU as a 'fusionist' state, whereby the national governments have fused some of their functions together and no longer can be considered separate states. Still others see it as a complex blend of supranational and intergovernmental modes of governance that has varied across time and policy fields (Sandholtz and Stone Sweet 1998). The real differences in these points of view are somewhat esoteric. Everyone agrees that the EU is a political body that continuously produces new legislation and has an effective court in place to interpret that legislation. The disagreements center more on the exact nature of the relationships between the member-state government and these political and legal processes.

For my purposes, the EU is best understood as an evolving system of political governance that makes and enforces mostly market rules. The Treaty of Rome provided a blueprint for a complex set of organizations with jurisdiction over issues of economic exchange defined very broadly. The EU was built from provisions, more-or-less vague, contained in that Treaty. The EU has four major organizations: the European Council of Ministers, the European Commission, the Court (hereafter, ECJ), and the European Parliament (hereafter, EP).

The Council, made up of government ministers from each country, votes on new rules for the whole of Europe (Bulmer and Wessels 1987). The Commission has the power to propose legislation and works to find a consensus across governments and lobbying groups. Before 1986, the Council adopted almost all important legislation by unanimous vote. The unanimity requirement often made attaining agreements very difficult, and left individual Council members with important veto power. With the Single European Act, Treaty on European Union, and the Treaty of Amsterdam, all issues relevant to the creation of a European market are now decided by qualified majority voting. The Treaty of Amsterdam provides the European Parliament with an equal vote to that of the Council.

Once a new piece of legislation has been adopted, each nation-state is obligated to transpose it into its own national law. It has been estimated that half the legislation produced by national parliaments every year is the transposition of EU law (Lodge 1993; Miller 2007). The member states maintain permanent representatives in Brussels, who are in continuous contact with each other and with the Commission. Their representatives are linked to the ministries back home and work to reflect their government's positions on particular issues. So, for example, each government maintains a staff of people concerned with agricultural issues in Brussels. The heads of government meet semi-annually to consider more ambitious initiatives and to discuss the overall direction of the EC.

The member-state governments have occasionally decided to change the Treaty of Rome by engaging in diplomacy outside the context of the EU's day-to-day politics. These so-called 'grand bargains' or 'high politics' (Pierson 1996; Moravcsik 1998) are focused on changing the broader relationships in the EU, such as expanding the fields of cooperation and changing voting rules. The Single Market Act, the Treaty on European Union, and the Treaties of Amsterdam and Nice have altered these rules. The more normal 'low politics' of the EU consists of the day-to-day activity of producing agreements around particular market projects. The relationship between 'high' politics and 'low' politics is complex. The constant political activity in Brussels does bring demands to member-state governments to make it easier to attain more agreements. But, of course, the governments have had to decide whether undertaking these agreements is in the interests of the citizens of their countries. Pierson (1996) argues that new rounds of institutional change in the EU begin with the results of the last round. Experience with cooperation brings demand for more cooperation. This means that Europe is likely at least to remain as organized as it is, and there will always be some pressure for it to proceed forward in some ways. Of course, even with political pressure in Brussels, member-state governments can decide not to engage in more cooperation with one another. Since it takes a unanimous agreement to produce a new treaty, the EU as a political organization is prone to crises that will limit its effectiveness.

The European Commission produces legislative proposals for the Council and the EP to consider, either at its own initiative or at their request. The Commission was created by the Treaty of Rome to help states solve their bargaining problems. It does this by producing policy studies, proposing new measures, negotiating draft legislation with member-state governments and lobbying groups, and ultimately shepherding bills through the Council and the EP. New measures are usually not considered by the Council until extensive negotiations with member-state governments and relevant lobby groups have already taken place. The Commission is divided into directorates, each in charge of some competence delineated by the Treaty of Rome. There are always a great number of proposals, large and small, floating around the Commission, and much political activity among people who work for the directorates and lobbying groups (Mazey and Richardson 1993; for a description of the 'norms' under which these activities are organized, see Richardson and Mazey 2001). People who work for the commission work to broker agreements by trying to understand how to balance off the interests of the representatives of member states with the interests of major lobbying groups (Peters 1992). Every law (called a 'directive' by the EU) the Council of Ministers passes requires the building of a political coalition of interested parties.

The ECJ is the authoritative interpreter of EU law. It enforces the Treaties and secondary legislation pursuant to litigation brought by private organizations, individuals, and states. These decisions are binding on all parties involved, including nation states. In the 1960s, the Court established the principle that EU rules overruled national law in situations in which the two came into conflict. This is called the doctrine of 'supremacy.'[1] The ECJ also decided that, under certain conditions, EU law confers judicially enforceable rights and duties on all who are subject to it, including firms and individuals, rights that national law and courts are obliged to protect. This is called the doctrine of 'direct effect.'[2] Taken together, these decisions transformed the Treaty of Rome and the EU, from an international organization to a vertically integrated, quasi-federal, rule of law polity (Slaughter, Stone Sweet, and Weiler 1998; Weiler 1991).

The EP is directly elected and advises the Commission. With the Single European Act and subsequent treaties, the EP has accrued broader powers (Tsebelis 1994; Lodge 1996). It can ask the Commission to work up new directives. It also has a role in ongoing negotiations about any particular directive. It can comment on directives and seek to alter them. It has final say over the level and composition of EU spending other than the Common Agricultural Policy. It votes to appoint and can dismiss the European Commission. The Treaty of Amsterdam changed the role of the EP from just consulting on directives to actually having to approve them. This gives it an equal role, at least on paper, with the member-state governments in the legislative process. One interpretation of the system is that the EP and the Council of Ministers now look like a bicameral legislature where the states represent the regions of Europe and the Parliament represents the voters more generally (Lodge 2006; Farrell and Scully 2007).

This complex mix of organizational competences, decision rules, and legislative procedures can be confusing to participants and analysts. The member states, through their control of the Council and their ultimate vote on directives would seem to have the upper hand in political processes otherwise managed by the Commission (Pollack 1997, 1998). They ultimately have to approve directives and if they oppose directives strenuously enough, there is little opportunity to pass them. When scholars have asked participants in policymaking in Brussels who is most influential, the answer is typically the member-state governments, followed by lobbying groups, and the European Commission (Wallace and Young 1998; Wallace 2000).

But, the process is complicated. With qualified majority voting and the enhanced role of the EP, governments can find themselves having to accept legislation they may not totally favor. They may also find themselves with an unfriendly Parliament who would oppose their agreement on particular directives. The activist Commission is always pushing the envelope to attain more cooperation. Governments do not control the interpretation or enforcement of EC law, and they have to contend with the possibility that the Commission or a private party may attack them in court for noncompliance with EC rules, which the national courts and the ECJ might view favorably (not an atypical situation, see Stone Sweet and Brunell 1998 and the papers in Stone Sweet, Sandholtz, and Fligstein 2001). Moreover, governments do shift their positions over time on market opening issues and this means that proposals that might appear to be going nowhere at one moment will get a new lease on life as more governments come around to seeing the wisdom in making changes (for an interesting example of this, see Sandholtz's 1998 discussion of telecommunications).

POLICY FIELDS AND THE EU

In order to make more sense of what the EU does and how this has changed over time, it is useful to get closer to the substance of what goes on in EU policy fields. I use the term 'policy field' to refer to a field of political contestation where formal political organizations (in this case, the Council, the Commission, and the EP) and lobbying groups interact in order to influence policies and laws (Laumann and Knoke 1987). Policy fields in the EU are defined by the various Treaties which confer the power to forge such agreements and define the fields in which those agreements can be reached. Fields also require rules by which agreements can be negotiated and organizations to create those agreements. This implies the creation of formal and informal procedures to attain such agreements. I have just described the organizations of the EU and the formal relationships by which EU rules are made which appear in the various Treaties. The Commission has figured out how to organize policy fields informally by consulting with governments, the EP, and lobbying groups to attain agreements (Mazey and Richardson 1993; Richardson and Mazey 2001).

Policy fields imply that special interest groups can legitimately participate in decision-making. One of the most interesting aspects of the politics in Brussels is the role of lobbying groups. In the Treaty of Rome the main legislative dynamic that was envisioned was between the Commission and the Council of Ministers. An organization called the Economic and Social Committee was formed to represent the interests of various constituencies across Europe. It was supposed to funnel the opinions of various groups into the policymaking process. In practice, this organization has played a relatively minor role in the making of European law. This is because the Commission is a relatively small organization. Lobbying groups quickly discovered that if they were interested in a particular issue, they could directly contact members of the Commission or the Council of Ministers, and this has made them more effective.

Table 2.1 describes the policy fields as they are defined by the treaties. Almost all the issue fields have some connection to creating market rules in Europe. Some of the fields are oriented towards increased cooperation in a particular sector, such as agriculture, fisheries, transportation, energy, and information technologies. Others are oriented towards regulation of some market feature, such as the internal market, competition policy, protection of the environment, employment policy, and consumer health and safety.

It is somewhat vague as to what kind of rules are to be made in a particular field. The ostensible purpose of the EU was to create a single market across Europe, but the Treaties never specify what a single market is and what types of rules are necessary to advance such a project. Much of the trial and error in the politics of the past forty years has been about how to remove trade barriers of various kinds while at the same time, leaving in place enough social protection to insure market actors do not produce unsafe or unhealthy products or unduly spoil the environment. Other agreements worry about how to provide compensation to losers. So the biggest program in the EU (measured by Euros spent) has been the agricultural price supports that were put in place under the Common Agricultural Policy to keep farmers solvent. The Agriculture Directorate General (hereafter DG) administers this program. Still others are oriented towards economic development issues. The second biggest program is the regional funds, used to finance infrastructure projects for the less-developed parts of Europe. The EU also supports programs to coordinate scientific work and the integration of transportation systems, both of which are thought to contribute to market integration and development.

The foundations of the EU and its policy fields are laid out in Parts Two, Three, and Five of the Treaty of Rome and these translate into fifteen potential fields for policymaking (European Union 1987). The Single European Act modified the Treaty of Rome by adding three distinct policy fields (law relating to undertakings; common, foreign, and security policy; and environment, consumers, and health protection) and expanding EU organizational and institutional capacity in eight fields that already existed (ibid. 1007–94). The ability to make Europe-wide rules on issues of the environment, consumers, and health protection was a direct result of the realization that market opening projects might lead firms to cut back on worker and consumer health and safety. The creation of Europe-wide standards was justified as a way to prevent governments from using national standards to keep competitors out. European standards also keep governments from lowering standards in order to attract business. The resolve for more cooperation on security issues was a political decision to coordinate foreign policies in the EU, and a clear break with the earlier EU focus on market issues.

TABLE 2.1. *Establishment and expansion of Treaty-based policy domains/analytic categories, 1957–1999*

Treaty of Rome (1957)	Single European Act (1987)
General, financial, and institutional matters	Law relating to undertakings
Customs union and free movement of goods	Common, foreign, and security policy
Agriculture	Environment, consumers, and health protection
Fisheries	(Expanded) Economic and monetary policy and free movement of capital
Freedom of movement of workers and social policy	(Expanded) Science, information, education, and culture
Right of establishment and freedom to provide services	(Expanded) Industrial policy and internal market
Transport policy	(Expanded) Taxation
Competition policy	(Expanded) Energy
External relations	(Expanded) Right of establishment and freedom to provide services
Industrial policy and internal market	(Expanded) Free movement of goods
Economic and monetary policy and free movement of capital	(Expanded) Free movement of capital
Taxation	(Expanded) Regional policy and coordination of structural instrument
Energy	
Regional policy and coordination of structural instruments	
Science, information, education, and culture	

Treaty on European Union (1992)	Amsterdam Treaty (1999)
Cooperation in the fields of justice and home affairs	Enlargement
People's Europe	(Expanded) Justice and home affairs
Monetary union	(Expanded) Common, foreign, and security policy
(Expanded) Freedom of movement of workers and social policy	
(Expanded) Common, foreign, and security policy	(Expanded) Education
(Expanded) Transport	(Expanded) Employment and social affairs
(Expanded) Science, information, education, and culture	(Expanded) Environment
(Expanded) Economic and monetary policy and free movement of capital	(Expanded) Health and consumer protection
(Expanded) Regional policy and coordination of structural instruments	
(Expanded) Energy	
(Expanded) Environment, consumers, and health protection	

Note: See Ch. 2 Appendix for details on coding.

The Treaty on European Union added two new policy fields (cooperation in the fields of justice and home affairs; and 'People's Europe') and substantially added institutional capacity in nine others (European Union 1993; see esp. 12–13). It also prepared the way for monetary union by creating the European Central Bank and the Euro. The Amsterdam Treaty added the area of enlargement in order to accommodate the inclusion of more new member states. It also expanded cooperation in six of the fields. Fifteen of the twenty potential policy fields were specified in the Treaty of Rome. The main modifications to the Treaties changed the voting rules from unanimous to qualified majority voting. They also altered the procedures by which legislation was enacted, giving the EP more of a role in decision-making.

Table 2.1 suggests that there has been a great deal of continuity in how policy fields have been conceived in the EU since 1957. Most of the expansion that has occurred has been changes in voting rules that make attaining agreement easier in issues pertaining to economic matters. The new fields that have been added have mostly reflected concerns related to the Single Market, but there has also been a substantial increase in competencies that are oriented to protecting workers, the environment, and consumers, reflecting the concerns of citizen groups in Brussels. While there has been expansion in cooperation around criminal justice and common foreign and security policy, these fields remain under the control of the member-state governments.

EU policy fields are structured by organizations that directly mirror the concerns of these issues. Both the European Commission and the European Council of Ministers are organized into Directorate Generals that are labeled according to their function based on the Treaties. For example, the DG responsible for agriculture coordinates all policy decisions related to agriculture (an area open to cooperation by the Treaty). In order to see this correspondence, Table 2.2 presents the areas specified by the Treaty of Rome in one column and contains the names of the DG of the European Commission in 1970. There is a direct one-to-one mapping of the fields defined by the Treaty of Rome to the organization of the European Commission.

It is useful to track the organization of the Commission over time in order to see the continuity of the EU policy fields. Table 2.3 presents the structure of the Commission's DGs in 1970, 1980 (before the Single European Act), 1987 (after the Single European Act), 1993 (after the Treaty on European Union), and 2004 (after the Treaty of Amsterdam). Not surprisingly, the basic structure of the DGs has been very constant over time, but one can see the direct effect of the Treaty negotiations on the structure of DGs. There have been some additions and subtractions in the number of DGs. Some issues, such as nuclear safety, have receded; others, such as the environment, health and consumer protection, and education have risen as a result of changes in the Treaties. Several DGs have been consolidated. The DG that controlled the structural funds that were allotted to economically depressed regions has been folded into regional policy, and the energy and transport DGs have been combined. The overall architecture of the

TABLE 2.2. *Policy domains specified by the Treaty of Rome and the organization of the European Commission, 1970*

Treaty of Rome (1957)	DG	DG name/portfolio (1970)
Agriculture	VI	Agriculture
Competition	IV	Competition
Customs union and free movement of goods	III	Industry
Economic and monetary policy and free movement of capital	II	Economic and Financial Affairs
Energy	XVII	Energy
	I	External Relations
	VIII	Development Aid
External relations	IX	Personnel
	X	Information
	XI	External Trade
Fisheries		
Free movement of workers and social policy	V	Social Policy
Industrial policy and internal market	XIV	Internal Market
Regional policy	XVI	Regional Policy
Right of establishment and freedom to provide services	XIII	Enterprise
Science, information, education, and culture	XII	Research and Technology
	XV	Research
Transport	VII	Transport
	XIX	Budgets
	XVIII	Credit and Investments
	XX	Financial Control

Note: See ch. 2 Appendix for data sources and details on coding.

Commission's DGs has remained relatively constant and corresponded closely to the missions outlined in the various Treaties.

I argued above that policy fields require both constitutional and organizational capacity. The organization of the EU's policy fields directly reflects the Treaties and the organized capacity of the Commission. There are several other important features of EU politics that line up with these substantive definitions of policy fields. The EU uses these categories to classify both legislation and court cases (European Union 1995: 13). Policy is made according to these categories and the relevant DG is responsible for trying to generate laws in their particular competence. So, for example, if the Council of Ministers decides it wants to make laws changing agriculture price support payments, it will ask the Agriculture DG to work on the issue. Once laws or rules have been passed in a field, monitoring how they are working will fall to the DG that generated them. Cases brought to the ECJ will reference particular directives. Rulings will rely on the Treaties as a source for their interpretation and will decide whether or not directives are consistent with the provisions of the Treaties.

Finally, policy fields do not contain just the representatives of member states, the Commission, and the ECJ, but also lobbying groups. So, for example, a lobbyist for a banking group who wants rules for interstate banking to change

Table 2.3. *Names of Directorate Generals in 1970, 1980, 1987, 1993, and 2004*

1970	1980	1987	1993	2004
External Affairs	External Affairs	External Affairs	External Affairs	External Relations
Economic and Financial Affairs	Economic and Financial Affairs	Economic and Financial Affairs	Economic and Financial Affairs	Economic and Financial Affairs
Internal Market and Industrial Affairs	Internal Market and Industrial Affairs	Internal Market and Industrial Affairs	Internal Market and Industrial Affairs	Internal Market
Competition	Competition	Competition	Competition	Competition
Employment and Social Affairs	Employment, Industrial Relations and Social Affairs	Employment and Social Affairs	Employment, Industrial Relations and Social Affairs	Employment and Social Affairs
Agriculture	Agriculture	Agriculture	Agriculture	Agriculture
Transportation	Transportation	Transportation	Transportation	Energy and Transport
Development	Development	Development	Development	Development
Personnel and Administration	Personnel and Administration	Personnel and Administration	Personnel and Administration	Personnel and Administration
Information, Communication, and Culture	Information, Communication, and Culture	Information, Communication, and Culture	Information, Communication, and Culture	Education and Culture
Environment, Consumer Protection, and Nuclear Safety	Environment, Nuclear Safety, and Consumer Protection	Environment, Nuclear Safety, and Consumer Protection	Environment, Nuclear Safety, and Consumer Protection	Environment
Science, Research, and Development	Science, Research, and Development	Science, Research, and Development	Science, Research, and Development	Health and Consumer Protection
Telecommunications, Industries and Innovation	Information, Telecommunications and Innovation	Telecommunications Industries and Innovation	Telecommunications Industries and Innovation	Research
Fisheries	Fisheries	Fisheries	Fisheries	Fisheries

(Continued)

TABLE 2.3. (*Continued*)

1970	1980	1987	1993	2004
Financial Institutions and Company Law	Financial Institutions and Company Law	Financial Institutions and Company Law	Financial Institutions and Company Law	[combined with Internal Market]
Regional Policy	Regional Policy	Regional Policy	Regional Policy	Regional Policy
Energy	Energy	Energy	Energy	[combined with Transport]
Credit and Investments	Credit and Investments	Credit and Investments	Credit and Investments	Credit and Investments
Budgets	Budgets	Budgets	Budgets	Budgets
Financial Control	Financial Control	Financial Control	Financial Control	Financial Control
Customs Union and Indirect Taxation	Customs Union and Indirect Taxation	Customs Union and Indirect Taxation	Customs Union and Indirect Taxation	Customs Union and Indirect Taxation
Coordination of Structural Policies	Coordination of Structural Policies	Coordination of Structural Policies	Coordination of Structural Policies	[combined with Regional Policy]
			Enterprise Policy, Distributive Trades, Tourism, and Cooperatives	
				Enlargement
				Enterprise
				Information Society

Source: See Ch. 2 Appendix.

would approach the Internal Market DG, which is in charge of making rules regarding market openings. Philip and Gray (1997) conducted a survey of such groups in order to assess who they lobby in Brussels. It turns out that many groups lobby more than one DG, reflecting the heterogeneity of their interests. Not surprisingly, lobbying groups mainly approach the DG which has the most impact on their issues. So, for example, farm groups all report lobbying the Agriculture DG.

EU policy fields have been set by the various Treaties. The EU has organized itself to produce legislation within the political competences specified by the Treaties. The EU uses these categories to organize and direct legislation. It creates DGs in the Commission where the legislation is negotiated. Lobbying groups attach to the fields in charge of legislation of interest. Brussels policymaking thus follows explicitly the lines laid down by the Treaties. Its main purpose is to produce economic policies within particular industries and also those that might guide action across all industries. Of course, this says little or nothing about the content of those policies, their quantity, their significance, or how they have changed over time. I now turn to considering the dynamics of policymaking in Brussels.

THE DYNAMICS OF EUROPEAN ECONOMIC AND POLITICAL INTEGRATION

The institutionalization of the Rome Treaty has been a process driven by the construction of feedback loops between relatively autonomous economic and political fields in the EU. For my purposes, I identify three such fields: between firms engaged in cross-border trade (seeking to expand markets); between litigants (seeking to vindicate their rights under EU law), national judges (seeking effectively to resolve disputes to which EU law is material), and the European Court; and between lobbying groups (seeking to exercise influence on EU regulation) and EU officials who represent the member states and the Commission in Brussels. Traders who find their activities thwarted by national governments come to the EU for two purposes. First, they will litigate trade grievances in the European Court of Justice. Second, they will try to join with other like-minded traders to lobby the member-state governments and the Commission to make new rules. Other organized interest groups such as labor unions, women's groups, environmentalists, and consumer activists have increasingly come to Brussels to do the same.

One of the most useful ways to understand the EU's main activities is the idea of positive and negative integration (Scharpf 1996). The original Treaty of Rome provided for the dismantling of trade barriers. This has been called a negative integration project because it is oriented towards the dismantling of member-state rules designed intentionally or unintentionally to favor national firms over foreign firms. Governments tried to prevent out-of-country firms from entering their market through the use of tariff and nontariff trade barriers. Some nontariff barriers include such things as excluding foreign firms from certain industries, e.g. telecommunications. Another important nontariff barrier was to make claims about foreign products not being up to national health and safety standards. Changing products proved costly to foreign firms who were forced to modify goods substantially in order to enter the national market. The Treaty of Rome was eventually used to rid national governments of all these tools.

Nonetheless market opening projects sometimes need rules to work, what is called 'positive integration'. For example, in order for banks to operate across borders, governments have a right to demand that foreign banks meet solvency standards. Banks would prefer a single standard across societies, which would produce a demand for a Europe-wide banking rule on the percentage of deposits banks had to hold in reserve (this is in fact something that happened). Generally, firms find that they need some market rules to protect transactions. Governments, workers, and consumers need protection against firms that attempt to undercut each other and do harm to the people who either produce or consume goods and services. This creates the conditions for positive integration, i.e. the construction of market rules that will govern firm interactions in particular markets. One of the main dynamics of EU rules since 1986 has been the concern for protecting workers and consumers from environmental and health and safety risks. The purpose of the politics in Brussels has been mainly to build the market through negative and positive integration processes and to promote those projects by providing for enforcement of those rules by the ECJ.

Using the idea of negative and positive integration, it is useful to think of European integration as being sequenced in three periods. From 1958 to 1969, actors in Brussels were engaged in the process of building the main organizations and figuring out how to make the Treaty of Rome work. The pivotal event during this period was the Court's 'constitutionalization' of the Treaty through the doctrines of supremacy and direct effect by 1969. This established the principles that EU law trumped national law and made it possible for nonstate actors to use the court to litigate. During the second period, 1970–85, the Commission and ECJ worked to dismantle barriers to intra-EC trade and other kinds of transnational exchange (a negative integration project). At the same time, the Commission and the Council sought to replace the disparate regulatory regimes in place at the national level with harmonized EC regulatory frameworks (positive integration).

I will show that the positive integration proceeded more steadily than is often appreciated during this period. However, many important harmonization projects stalled in the Council, often because more ambitious initiatives required the unanimous vote of national ministers. The unanimity rule made it very difficult to forge agreements. At the same time, the cumulative impact of negative integration was to raise the costs of intergovernmental deadlock for an increasing number of social and economic actors who wanted wider and deeper integration. During the early 1980s, it appeared as if the EU was at an impasse (Alter and Meunier-Aitsahalia 1994; Fligstein and Mara-Drita 1996). This impasse ended with the passage of the Single European Act, which altered the voting rules for legislation pertaining to the Single Market Program from unanimity to qualified majority voting in most cases. Subsequent rounds of negotiations have relaxed voting rules even more in other fields and expanded somewhat the competences of the EU (including the implementation of the monetary union). The final period, from 1986 to the present, can be characterized as the most active from the perspective of institutionalizing European market and governance structures through positive integration.

Examining the trends in the data provides some feel for what has occurred in the EC. The institutionalization of the EC took time. The activities of lobbyists, litigators, legislators, and judges started slowly, but began to take off after 1970. In the early 1980s, it seems that institutionalization slowed. The integration project appeared to have reached, or nearly reached, its outward limits, given existing institutional arrangements. After the Single European Act (1986), activity intensified in the EC, and integration was, in fact, 'relaunched.' The subsequent years produced an explosion of litigation and legislation, and, not surprisingly, an enlargement of the EU and three Treaty negotiations.

Figure 2.2 presents the growth in intra-EU exports per capita in constant dollars for the period 1958–94. One observes a low level of exports during the 1960s with a modest increase over the decade. In 1970, as EU rules start to bite, exports rise more steeply. Following 1985, with the announcement of the Single European Act, this rise accelerates. Thus, changes in patterns of intra-European trade coincide with important events within the EU. The rules governing free movement of goods, such as the prohibition of maintaining national quotas and

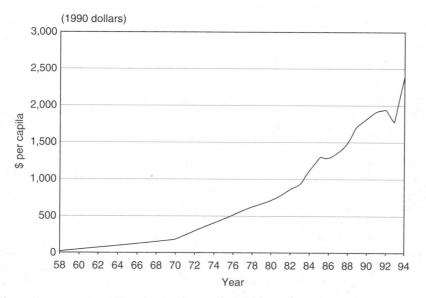

Figure 2.2. Intra-EU exports per capita, 1958–1996.

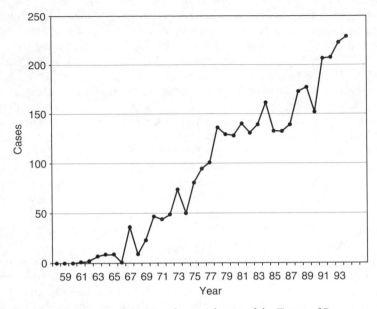

Figure 2.3. Cases referred to the ECJ under Article 177 of the Treaty of Rome.
Source: Fligstein and Stone Sweet 2002.

other measures, entered into force in 1970 and thereby became directly effective for traders. During the recession of the early 1980s, trade growth slowed. But, in 1985, the EC agreed to the completion of the Single Market and to important changes in the voting rules. This encouraged traders to expand their activities across borders.

Changes in trade are mirrored in changes in litigation and legislation. Figure 2.3 tracks increases in the use of Article 177 of the Treaty of Rome. Article 177 allows national judges to send cases involved in disputes over the EU rules to the European Court of Justice. This measure is the best indicator now available of the degree to which litigants have claimed rights issuing from EU law in national courts. National judges around the EU faced the dilemma of deciding cases where national law and EU law conflicted. They sent the most important and tricky cases on to the ECJ. The figure shows that levels of references were very low during the 1960s. As national judges came to accept the doctrines of supremacy and direct effect, they began to refer more cases to the ECJ. References tripled between 1970 and 1980 and then leveled off until 1987. After the Single Act, they shot up once again. Stone Sweet and Brunell (1998) have looked at the link between exports and litigation. They conclude that almost 80 per cent of the variation in court cases is accounted for by growing exports. As exporters took advantage of the expanding market opportunities presented by the Treaty of Rome, they found themselves in conflict with national authorities who were trying to use various kinds of trade barriers to protect national

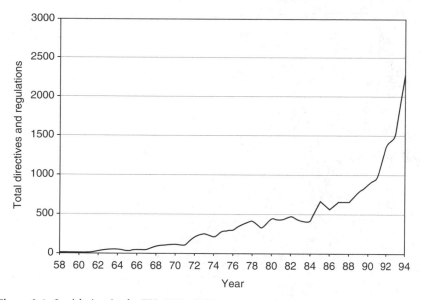

Figure 2.4. Legislation in the EU, 1958–1994.
Source: EU 1995.

producers. These traders turned to national courts and the ECJ to try and have national rules superseded by EU rules. They frequently won.

Figure 2.4 indexes the production of legislation in the EC. Here, the tabulation presents the total number of directives and regulations (the two classes of secondary legislation) adopted each year. The passage of this legislation is a rough indicator of the growth of rules producing positive integration of the market. Most of the legislation was oriented towards producing collective market rules that would apply across member states. As noted, before 1985, most important legislative initiatives required the unanimous vote of the Council to be adopted. But, even here, the pattern that emerges resembles those that appear in the prior two figures. Legislative production during the 1960s was low. During this period, most of the market project was a negative integration project whereby trade barriers were being dismantled by the general Treaty provisions as they were being enforced by the courts. Legislation picks up during the 1970s, and levels off between 1978 and 1985. With the passage of the Single European Act in 1987, the production of legislation takes off.

Fligstein and Stone Sweet (2002) have examined the link between exports, litigation, and legislation over the whole period. They show that exports and litigation cause legislation. They argue that exporters put pressure on their governments and the Brussels bureaucracy to produce more market rules over time. They also argue that litigation begets legislation. Here, the mechanism they identify is that court decisions stimulate political actors to produce new market rules. Their most intriguing finding is that the production of new laws subsequently produces

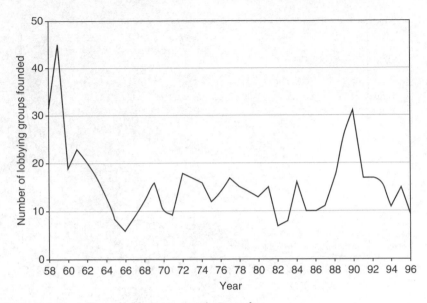

Figure 2.5. Founding of lobbying groups in Brussels.
Source: Philip and Gray 1997.

growth in exports. This implies the process of ratcheting-up that was described earlier. The EU as a political and legal structure was pushed forward by the increase of EU trade, which, once new rules were constructed, in turn had the effect of opening up trade subsequently.

Figure 2.5 presents data on the formation of lobbying groups in Brussels, 1958–96. Data on almost 600 significant lobbying groups were constructed using the survey by Philip and Gray (1997). At the beginning of the EU, a flurry of lobbying groups founded. Numbers of foundings decreased during the mid-1960s, then bounced around during the 1970s and early 1980s. Following the passage of the Single European Act, the establishment of new lobbying groups shot up to their highest levels since the early 1960s. The Act convinced groups from around Europe that being in Brussels mattered. As the laws that would comprise the Single Market were being contemplated, new lobbying groups wanted to be part of the Brussels scene.

Taken together, these figures tell a compelling story. They show that trading, litigating, legislating, and lobbying, which we take to be the key indicators of European integration, grew over time, and that this growth roughly follows similar patterns that broadly conform to our periodization of EC activity. It is useful to break these patterns down by field in order to get a better sense of which fields rose over time and which fell in importance. Table 2.4 presents data on the distribution of legislation across policy fields during each of the three periods. The table shows that during the period of the 1960s, legislative output was relatively tiny, about twenty-five directives and regulations per year. It rose to over 200 during the period 1970–85. In the latest period, 1986–96, the EU averaged almost 600 pieces of legislation a year. Over time, the increase in legislation implies there was work being done to produce market rules that created positive integration.

The most striking result evident in the table is the sheer dominance of agriculture legislation in the EU. This is not surprising: as late as 1992, 70 per cent of the EU budget was being spent on the Common Agricultural Policy (Fligstein and McNichol 1998) a figure that has only decreased to about 50 per cent in 2005. The two next largest categories of legislative activity concerned free movement of goods and single market/industrial policy. Both these fields are integral to building a single market in Europe. This confirms the centrality of the general project of the EU to make trade easier across all kinds of goods and services. The table shows how the rise and fall of certain fields—financial and institutional matters, the right to establish firms and services, transportation, and competition—were more important early on and less so as time passed (even as the absolute number of directives increased in all fields). The fields of free movement of goods/customs union, internal market, external relations, fisheries, and environment/health/education/culture became more important over time. These were all expanded as fields where cooperation could occur during the 1980s and 1990s. The first two

TABLE 2.4. *Number of pieces of legislation by domains and periods, 1958–1969, 1970–1985, 1985–1996* (percentages = % of total legislation, N = 9,396)

Domains	1958–69		1970–85		1986–96	
	legislation	%	legislation	%	legislation	%
Agriculture	118	1.3	1,642	17.5	3,190	34.0
External relations	10	0.1	215	2.2	568	6.0
Customs union and free movement of goods	0	0.0	313	3.3	467	5.0
Industrial policy and internal market	21	0.2	389	4.1	435	4.6
Environment, consumers, and health	4	0.1	136	1.4	339	3.6
Fisheries	2	0.0	67	0.7	245	2.6
Transport policy	13	0.1	66	0.7	166	1.8
Financial and institutional	21	0.2	69	0.7	140	1.4
Right of establishment and free movement of services	34	0.4	64	0.7	119	1.3
Free movement of workers and social policy	6	0.0	72	0.8	92	1.0
Taxation	7	0.1	52	0.6	53	0.6
Competition policy	11	0.1	11	0.1	34	0.4
Science, information, education, and culture	0	0.0	24	0.2	32	0.3
Law relating to undertakings	1	0.0	12	0.1	26	0.3
Regional policy	0	0.0	21	0.2	24	0.2
Energy	8	0.1	30	0.3	16	0.2
Economic and monetary policy	1	0.0	6	0.1	7	0.1

Source: European Communities, *Directory of Community Legislation in Force* (European Union 1995).

TABLE 2.5. *Cases filed under Article 177 by domains and periods, 1958–1969, 1970–1985, 1985–1996* (percentages = % of total cases N = 4,627)

	1958–69		1970–85		1985–96	
Domains	cases	%	cases	%	cases	%
Customs union and free movement of goods	26	0.6	437	9.4	779	16.8
Free movement of workers and social policy	27	0.6	266	5.7	523	11.3
Agriculture	13	0.2	436	9.4	352	7.6
Taxation	14	0.3	78	1.7	320	6.9
Right of establishment and freedom to provide services	10	0.0	45	1.0	217	4.7
Competition	10	0.2	83	1.8	189	4.1
Industrial policy and internal market	1	0.0	55	1.2	178	3.8
Financial and institutional	2	0.0	85	1.8	102	2.3
Environment, consumers, and health	2	0.0	40	0.9	90	1.9
External relations	1	0.0	50	1.2	58	1.3
Transport	0	0.0	25	0.5	52	1.1
Economic and monetary policy	0	0.0	7	0.2	22	0.5
Fisheries	0	0.0	20	0.4	18	0.4
Energy	0	0.0	0	0.0	1	0.0
Regional policy	0	0.0	0	0.0	1	0.0
Science, information, education, and culture	0	0.0	0	0.0	1	0.0
Law relating to undertakings	0	0.0	0	0.0	0	0.0

Source: Stone Sweet and Brunell 1998.

were the main areas where Single Market directives and regulations were negotiated. The external relations policy field includes common foreign and security policy, which expanded following the agreement of the member states to cooperate in these matters. Fisheries became a focus of EU-level rules as recognition of over-fishing in Europe came to the fore. The Single European Act also opened up issues surrounding the environment and consumer protection. Not surprisingly, there was a great deal of legislative activity in this sector.

Table 2.5 shows patterns for Article 177 references that index the types of cases referred from national courts to the ECJ. Litigation during the 1960s was very low, less than ten cases a year. It rose to over 100 during the period 1970–85 and this increased to almost 300 cases a year in 1986–96. The bulk of cases in the data were in the free movement of goods/customs union field, followed by agriculture, and free movement of workers/social policy. There is evidence that some fields declined in importance over time, particularly competition policy, financial/institutional, agriculture, and free movement of workers/social policy (again even as Article 177 references increased). There were also relative increases in cases in establishment/services, internal market/industrial policy, and environment/health/education/culture. The patterns of litigation changed as more directives were written in fields such as internal market/industrial policy and environment. These patterns are consistent with what we know about how negative integration produced positive laws and then these provided the basis for further litigation.

TABLE 2.6. *Founding dates of EC interest groups by policy domain, 1958–1996*

Domain		1958–96	1958–69	1970–85	1985–96
Financial, institutional	%	0.9	0.7	1.1	0.9
	no.	18	6	7	5
Customs union and free movement	%	3.5	3.5	2.7	4.5
of goods	no.	72	31	17	24
Agriculture	%	6.7	9.2	5.5	3.7
	no.	138	83	35	20
Fisheries	%	1.0	0.8	1.2	0.9
	no.	20	7	8	5
Free movement of workers and social	%	8.5	6.6	10.8	8.8
policy	no.	174	59	68	47
Right of establishment and freedom	%	5.9	5.5	6.0	6.4
to provide services	no.	121	49	49	34
Transport	%	4.1	3.9	3.5	4.3
	no.	80	35	22	23
Competition	%	5.1	4.3	2.5	6.0
	no.	94	39	33	32
Taxation	%	3.4	3.6	2.5	3.9
	no.	69	32	16	21
Economic and monetary policy	%	2.7	2.7	3.3	2.1
	no.	56	24	21	11
External relations	%	2.3	2.2	2.4	2.2
	no.	47	20	15	12
Energy	%	2.5	2.1	2.1	3.6
	no.	51	19	13	19
Internal market and industrial policy	%	21.5	26.7	20.2	14.5
	no.	443	238	128	77
Regional policy	%	1.7	1.3	1.9	2.3
	no.	36	12	12	12
Environment, consumers, and health	%	11.5	9.7	12.1	13.6
	no.	237	87	77	73
Science, information, education, and	%	12.0	10.3	11.9	15.1
culture	no.	248	92	92	81
Undertakings	%	7.0	6.5	7.4	7.5
	no.	145	58	47	40
TOTAL	%	100.3	99.6	97.1	100.2
	no.	2,059	891	632	536

Note: Data compiled by the authors from Philip and Gray (1997). Column percentages may not add up to 100 due to rounding up or down.

Table 2.6 breaks the field data down by founding dates of lobbying groups. The patterns are quite consistent with the general story. The first period of the EU witnessed the founding of a large number of organizations. Thus, when the Brussels complex was being formed, interest groups felt it was important to open up interest representation there. This was part of the initial institutionalization of the European Community. The establishing of the Court, the Council of Ministers, and the Commission encouraged interested groups to set up as well. The period 1970–85 witnessed many new organization foundings, but on a per capita basis, the 1986–96 period was higher. What issues were the lobbying groups most interested in? At the beginning, the overwhelming number of groups were business interest groups, as indicated by the high percentage of groups who joined the internal market/industrial policy field and the agricultural fields. Over time, however, business groups became less important in new foundings. The largest increase in group foundings occurred in the regional policy, environment/health/consumer protection, and science/information/education/culture fields. These are clear examples of fields where the problems of positive integration are being tackled. The negative integration project tore down barriers that promoted national differences in legislation in these fields. New lobbying groups in Brussels in the past twenty years have emerged to push agendas forward to deal with the consequences of negative integration as it pertains to citizens and the environment.

These tables show clearly how the EU became a political, legal system as trade grew and was expanded and reinforced by litigation and legislation. In the 1960s, there was a gradual process by which European organizations started to work. Trade was slowly rising and the European Union was organizing itself in Brussels. This period included the construction of the organizations of the community, but it also witnessed the emergence of lobbying groups, primarily those concerned with business issues. Beginning in the 1970s, negative and positive integration began in the EU with some force. Firms used Article 177 to push the negative integration project along and lobbying groups in Brussels began to demand legislation to produce positive integration. The negative and the positive integration projects both fed the growing opportunities for firms to export, and these in turn increased the desire for new rules.

But by the late 1970s, the EC had reached a stage where legislation, lobbying, and litigation were rising, but governments were having more difficulty producing agreements. As integration appeared to have reached its institutional limits, less legislation was produced and, in consequence, fewer lobbying groups formed and the increase in litigation of EC law leveled off. The Single European Act reversed these trends. During the 1980s and 1990s, the Single European Act and the Treaty on European Union encouraged groups to go to Brussels to lobby for issues of concern to citizens. The market building project that was based on tearing down trade barriers was viewed as needing more regulation on the environmental, consumer front. New lobbying groups formed to encourage legislation in these fields. From the tables, it appears that they were successful.

The political cooperation over economic issues that the EC started took ten to fifteen years to develop. It moved forward as opportunistic actors organized as lobbying groups and governments and the Commission learned how to construct and to use new European fields to their advantage. Exporters stimulated litigation and legislation. Groups who went to Brussels to lobby helped to generate legislation, and litigation pushed forward legislation as well. The increase in legislation fed back to produce more opportunities for exporters to grow new markets. This process has produced both markets and a polity in Western Europe.

CONCLUSION

The construction of the European Union has been going on since 1957. The process has been punctuated by discrete and significant political and legal events. But these events have been embedded in a larger flow. Europeanization is about how a large number of actors (firms, interest groups, nonprofit organizations, and governments), operating in both the private economy and in the political fields of Brussels, advanced new forms of economic governance. They have used the existing structures to identify and exploit opportunities for cooperation and, once successful, new structures have produced new opportunities. Strategic actors in firms, lobbying organizations, governments, the European Commission, the legal profession, and the courts have found themselves having to confront one another in market, legal, and political fields. They have managed to attain their interests by building institutions and organizational capacity, thus ratcheting up cooperation. In this way, European markets are integrated, market rules reflect European rules, European law holds sway over national law, and interested parties continue to push for new rules in Brussels. A functioning, stable European political field has been created in Brussels. Lobbying groups lobby, firms, governments, and individuals litigate under EU law, and representatives of the member states legislate.

European economies are now highly integrated, and exports are now critical to economic growth. Almost half the world's trade occurs within the borders of the EC, making it close to a single economy. Firms presumably tell their governments and Brussels officials that European rules and institutions are generally a good thing, because they promote economic growth and work for them. Most European governments realize this. European administrative and legal systems are increasingly integrated as well—legal systems are in some ways the backbone of European integration. National courts enforce EC law, alongside national law, and national bureaucracies implement EC legislation into their procedures and practices. The institutionalization of European fields of governance has occurred through self-reinforcing processes. As one set of European institutions has grown up, it has induced integration elsewhere. Actors across many of the important political, legal, and market structures are now living in worlds where their activities are strongly oriented towards Europe.

This chapter has provided an overview linking the formal politics of Brussels to the market opening project that has increased trade. This discussion opens up broad issues. First and foremost is how this has played out within the European economy. The next two chapters take up this issue. The political science literature mostly focuses on how a particular EU policy came to reorganize markets. It generally fails to examine in any detail how a particular market actually was reorganized. What we lack is a sense of how these rules change the nature of market participants. It also lacks a view as to how generally this has affected the European economy. In particular, the largest European corporations have been the main beneficiaries of increased European trade. It is important to understand how they have responded to this opportunity.

APPENDIX: DATA SOURCES AND CODING

The datasets that I have constructed contain information on EC policy domains from 1958 to 1994. The various Treaties, the Commission, and the Court specify eighteen important arenas or competencies of the EC: financial/institutional; customs/taxation; agriculture; fisheries; employment/social policy; right of establishment; transport policy; competition policy; economic and monetary policy; external relations; energy; internal market and industrial policy; regional policy; environment, consumers, and health; science/information/culture; competition law; justice/home affairs; people's Europe (Fligstein and Mc-Nichol 1998). There are almost no directives, court cases, or lobbying groups for justice/home affairs and the 'people's Europe'. I was able to obtain usable data for the years 1958–94. Thus, for each dataset, I have thirty-six years of information coded into sixteen domains.

The data were compiled from various sources. The data on legislation come from the *Directory of Community Legislation in Force* (European Union 1995). The directory includes all forms of legislation, but I analyzed only the data on regulations and directives here, after coding them into the domain specified by the EC. The observation reflects the total number of pieces of secondary legislation in that domain in a particular year.

I use the *Data Set on Preliminary References in EC Law 1958–98*, compiled by Stone Sweet and Brunell (1998) for data on litigation. Among other information, each reference has a code defining the domain of EC law being raised by the litigant (through the referring question of the national judge). These codes can be mapped directly onto our sixteen policy domains. The measure we use is the total number of directives and regulations passed in a particular domain in a particular year.

The data on lobbying groups were obtained from a volume published by Philip and Gray (1997). They mailed out a survey to almost 1,000 lobbying organizations in Brussels and received answers from about 700. They collected information on each organization's name, size, location, founding date, and purposes, and on the directorate generals with whom they had contact. On the basis of this data, I was able to code 586 organizations. I used the data on founding dates, and the information on whom they lobbied to attach them to a policy domain.

It should be noted that lobbying groups tended to participate in more than one domain. I decided that if organizations claimed to lobby more than one part of the Commission, I counted that organization multiple times. So, for example, if the organization claimed it lobbied in the agriculture domain and the Single Market domain, in the year it was founded we counted it as a founding in both domains. The 586 organizations lobby in an average of 3.5 domains for a total of 2,059. I created two different measures of lobbying presence. For some of the analysis, I use the total number of lobbying groups founded in a particular year by domain. I also create a measure that cumulates the number of lobbying groups in each domain. My theoretical argument suggests that both lobbying group foundation and the number of groups that come to exist in a domain might affect outcomes.

The data on trade are more aggregated. There are two problems. First, exports for particular industries do not neatly correspond to my policy domains. Categories like 'customs/taxation' cut across industries. Second, the EC has expanded from six to twelve and now to fifteen nation-states. Data on exports that only measured trade within the EC zone would show big jumps as soon as the EC zone widened. I decided to use trade data for exports for all of Western Europe that originated in Western Europe and ended up in Western Europe from 1958 to 1994 (United Nations, various volumes).

NOTES

1. First articulated in the *Costa* judgment (ECJ 1963).
2. First announced in the *Van Gend en Loos* judgment (ibid.).

3

The Economic Transformation of Europe

INTRODUCTION

At the core of the European Union has been the creation of a single market across Western Europe. In the second chapter, I showed how trade grew as the EU polity produced more rules and more enforcement. The central theme in this chapter is that European economic integration is near completion in many ways. The EU has provided a common set of rules that make it difficult for governments to raise barriers to entry to foreign firms, and markets—at least formally—are open. Trade accounts for about 40 per cent of GDP across Europe. Over 70 per cent of exports from the countries that make up the EU are to other countries within the EU.

In this chapter I show that as countries have joined the EU, the destination of their exports and the origins of their imports have become more and more focused on the EU. The largest European corporations have made most of their investments in the past twenty years within Europe. These investments have generally been made by engaging in mostly friendly mergers or joint ventures with companies in other European countries, with the result that in many of the largest product markets across Europe, firms with different national identities face off to compete in product markets that instead of being national in orientation are now regional in scope. The interlocking of the economies of Western Europe, as a result, has gone a great distance.

There are a couple of caveats to this. Most of the largest corporations remain national in their ownership. Only a few of the large mergers have produced true cross-European ownership of firms. The largest firms in the European economy remain resolutely British, German, French, Swedish, or Italian in ownership and investment. The main reason for this persistence is that European governments have resisted creating a single market for property rights. It is difficult or impossible to engage in hostile takeovers of continental European firms. So when firms do decide to merge across borders, it is generally a friendly alliance that leaves in place national management. A second caveat is the general British 'exceptionalism' in Europe. Britain has allowed hostile mergers to occur and as such, has been the target for firms from other countries. British firms are also the most aggressive pursuers of mergers with other firms. British firms are also the least European in the sense that they distribute their economic activities more widely around the world, and in particular are big players in the US. Of all European countries, they trade the least with Europe. They are not as extensively invested in Europe. They have also been major players in the US market for corporate control.

The leaders of Europe's largest firms know they are major participants in markets in Europe and to a lesser degree the US. In general, European firms do not have a high Asian profile, which makes their leaders strong supporters of the EU and its continued efforts to open trade. At the same time, a large proportion of shareholders and workers remain in the nation where the firm is headquartered. Shareholders' and workers' experience of Europe and their sense that their firms and jobs depend on Europe is much less pronounced. They remain wedded to a national conception of property rights and labor relations.

In the literatures that compare market arrangements across nation states, there are two images that are juxtaposed. First, there are many scholars who support the view that eventually there will be convergence in the way that markets and firms are organized across societies (for example, see Castells 1996; Strange 1996). The source of this convergence usually emanates from some form of competitive process. The argument is that when firms meet in a market, there is some most efficient way to organize that revolves around the appropriate use of technology, social organization, and investment. Market forces produce convergence towards a single way of doing things.

One way this is typically phrased is to argue that the pressures of economic globalization push firms in every country to converge their corporate governance, organizational strategies and structures, and labor relations to the same forms. There are three common meanings of globalization (Fligstein 2001). First, there is thought to be increasing pressure on developed countries to lower their wage costs because of the lower wage structures of developing countries. Second, the increase in financial integration around the world pushes firms to organize most efficiently in order to attract capital. Finally, the rise of the Asian societies (first Korea, Taiwan, Thailand, Indonesia, and the Philippines and more recently India and China) introduces new competitors into world markets. Those who view these competitive forces as determinative argue that if firms from one society figure out the most efficient way to produce a set of products, then firms from all other societies will have to emulate those firms or fail. A similar argument has been applied to government interventions (Garrett 1995; Boyer and Drache 1996; Crouch and Streeck 1997). Governments that persist in producing trade barriers, protecting workers, and engaging in too much taxation of firms, will eventually lose firms to societies that have friendlier arrangements. This allegedly forces governments to dismantle worker protections, free up capital markets, and deregulate other markets.

The problem with these plausible arguments is that there is little evidence that they are true (for reviews, see Fligstein and Freeland 1995; Wade 1996; Rodrik 1996; 1997; Pauly and Reich 1997; Hall and Soskice 2001; Roe 2004; Fligstein and Choo 2005). As I will show, there is no evidence that developed countries are losing market share in trade to developing countries. There is a great deal of evidence that the world economy contains three large trade zones: the EU, North America, and the Asian area. The trend over time is that these zones have become more and not less economically integrated (for cogent arguments about why these projects have succeeded, see Mattli 1999 and Katzenstein 2005).

Studies typically show that governments continue to sponsor a great number of policy interventions into capital and labor markets. It does not appear that there has been a race to the bottom to undermine the protection of workers in advanced industrial societies. Indeed, what evidence exists suggests exactly the opposite: countries whose economies are more open to trade offer more, not less social protection to workers (Rodrik 1996). Neither does it seem that the so-called global corporation has converged to either a network or 'informational' form (Fligstein 2001). Almost forty years ago, the political economists Raymond Vernon (1971) and Charles Kindleberger (1971) argued that the leaders of multinational firms were people who were quickly building nations unto themselves. They predicted the growth of an international capitalist class that would have no national loyalties. Recently, scholars following in this tradition have argued that globalization is the latest stage of capitalism and that we are now witnessing the birth of a worldwide capitalist class (Sklair 2001; Van Apeldoorn 2003; Robinson 2004). But, today, just as thirty-five years ago, this claim turns out to be hard to sustain, which has brought about attempts by scholars to argue that the national forms of governance must be able to produce some kinds of efficient outcomes and allow managers to be flexible enough to make changes as market conditions change (Hall and Soskice 2001).

Given the contrasting images, one that emphasizes how market forces should produce convergence in firms and government policies, and the other of a world where national capitalisms persist, one is left to wonder about where the truth really lies. One of the purposes of this chapter is to untangle these questions in the context of Europe. What has happened in Europe produces evidence to support both of these arguments. On the one hand, there has been much convergence across Europe in terms of markets emerging with participants from many societies and firms organizing production in similar ways. This convergence is not being pushed by global markets or competition from developing societies. It is instead the outcome of the attempts in Europe to create a single market and the use of a single currency (Rodríguez-Pose 2002). To put it briefly, in Europe, European firms have expanded their European activities. When countries join the EU, EU firms make investments in these new markets and their trade activities both increase and become directed toward other EU countries. In sum, what is going on in Europe is not economic globalization that is being driven by wage competition from the developing world, but the intensification of the creation of the European market.

Yet, in spite of the emergence of Europe-wide markets, there is little evidence that this convergence has produced a capitalist elite that transcends national borders and American-style systems of corporate governance and labor relations. Indeed, large firms remain owned by people in particular societies, by and large, and dependent on their home governments for many things. This produces hybrid markets where firms converge in being organized to serve the European region, but remain wedded to their systems of corporate governance and labor relations. Again, the great fear of European publics that their systems of social protection are under assault by impersonal forces are misplaced. Indeed, the existing systems are robust and have so far responded to challenges presented by the new competition generated by the creation of a European system of markets (Hall and Soskice 2001; Amable 2003).

I begin by defining what an integrated market would look like for a given commodity. I use the theory of fields elaborated in the first chapter and apply it to the case of markets to produce conceptual leverage on this question. An integrated market requires a single system of rules of exchange, property rights, and rules of competition and cooperation (Fligstein 1996, 2001). To produce a particular market (for example, insurance) requires that actors in firms evolve understandings about how to compete and which firms are dominant and which peripheral.

One of the main reasons that national systems have proved to be so robust is because firms depend on their governments and societies for institutional stability. Without governments to provide stable rules, labor market policies, and systems of law, and to promote investments, there would be no markets. Capitalist elites recognize this interdependency. Moreover, most capitalist elites want to try and defend their privileges. This means that they may like free trade if they are 'winning,' but do not like it if they are 'losing.' They also are happy to see their national government protect national ownership of large firms. Governments want to control their national political economies. They generally do not want large parts of their most productive firms owned and controlled from other countries. They fear that outside investors are likely to lay national workers off and increase unemployment.

The purpose of developing this perspective on markets is to apply it to what has occurred in the EU in the past thirty years. My basic argument is that the growing integration of the European economy has meant a great deal of pressure for increasing rules to make trade easier and more transparent, what I call 'rules of exchange.' Indeed, most of the activities of the EU have been of this variety. I will also present evidence that the EU has by and large also come to coordinate rules of competition and cooperation for firms involved in trade across borders. However, there has been little convergence across Europe in property rights. While there is some movement in this direction, national political and economic elites (with the exception of Great Britain) have held fast to rules to protect their control over property rights in the largest and most important firms in society.

I then turn to consider the degree to which markets have become integrated over time. My results provide evidence for the view that the European political project is fundamentally about the degree to which European markets are integrated. Over time, the share of European production that ends up in Europe has increased. As countries have joined the EU, their production becomes more oriented towards the European market. This was true for the countries that joined in the 1980s (Austria, Finland, and Sweden) and it is currently true for the new member states in Eastern Europe. This demonstrates that the continuous shift in European market rules has reoriented national producers toward the European market.

I examine the activities of the largest European corporations over the past fifteen to twenty years. Many of them have become less national in their concentration of production and employment and spread their activities out across Europe, and to a lesser degree America. Data on cross-border mergers suggest that European firms engaged in large numbers of mergers in the wake of the Single Market Act in the 1980s and continued to merge across borders during the 1990s. There is some evidence that large British and Dutch firms, and to a lesser degree, French and German firms, invested in the United States during the merger wave of the late 1990s. But in the past few years, a new merger movement has shifted the world's attention to Europe. There has been a large consolidation of European firms across Europe. All forms of investment in Europe from other European countries have increased. I also present evidence that foreign investment in Europe has predominantly come from other European countries.

WHAT IS AN INTEGRATED MARKET ECONOMY?

Markets are social fields that exist for the production and sale of some good or service, and are characterized by repeated exchanges between buyers and sellers that rely on rules and social structures to guide and organize that exchange. A given market becomes a stable field when the producers are able to produce a status hierarchy of firms whereby some of the largest dominate the market and smaller firms find niches (Fligstein 2001). Once such a structure has emerged, markets can be described as 'self-reproducing role structures' where incumbent and challenger firms reproduce their positions on a period-to-period basis (White 1981).

There are four types of rules relevant to producing social structures in markets: property rights, governance structures, rules of exchange, and conceptions of control (Fligstein 1996; 2001). Property rights define who has claims on the profits of firms (akin to what agency theorists call 'residual claims' on the free cash flow of firms ((Jensen and Meckling 1974)). This leaves open the issues of the different legal forms that exist; the relationship between shareholders and employees, local communities, suppliers, and customers; and the role of the state in directing investment, owning firms, and protecting workers. The constitution of property rights is a continuous and contestable political process, not the outcome of an efficient process (for a similar argument, see Roe 2004 and for a review of the empirical literature see Fligstein and Choo 2005). Organized groups from business, labor, government agencies, and political parties will try to affect the constitution of property rights. The division of property rights is at the core of market society. Property rights define who is in control of the capitalist enterprise and who has rights to claim the surplus.

Governance structures refer to the general rules in a society that define relations of competition, cooperation, and definitions of how firms should be organized. These rules define the legal and illegal forms of how firms can control competition. They take two forms: laws and informal institutional practices. Laws called antitrust, competition, or anti-cartel laws exist in most advanced industrial societies. The passage, enforcement, and judicial interpretation of these laws is contested (Fligstein 2001), and the content of such laws varies widely across societies. Some societies allow extensive cooperation between competitors particularly when foreign trade is involved, while others tend to try to reduce the effects of barriers to entry and promote competition. Competition is not just regulated within societies, but across societies. Countries have tariffs and trade barriers to help national industry to compete with foreign rivals. These laws often benefit particular sectors of the economy.

Rules of exchange define who can transact with whom and the conditions under which transactions are carried out. Rules must be established regarding shipping, billing, insurance, the exchange of money (i.e. banks), and the enforcement of contracts. Rules of exchange also regulate health and safety standards of products and the standardization of products more generally. For example, many pharmaceutical products undergo extensive testing procedures. Health and safety standards help both buyers and sellers and facilitate exchange between parties who may have only fleeting interactions. Products from one country often have to meet the safety standards of those same products from another country. Product standardization has become increasingly important in the context of rules of exchange, particularly in the telecommunications and computer industries. There exist extensive national and international bodies that meet to agree on standards for products across many industries. Standard setting produces shared rules that guarantee that products will be compatible. This facilitates exchange by making it more certain that produce bought and sold will work the way it is intended.

The purpose of action in a given market is to create and maintain stable worlds within and across firms that allow dominant firms to survive. Conceptions of control refer to both the understandings that structure perceptions of how a particular market works and the real relations of domination in the market. A conception of control is simultaneously a worldview that allows actors to interpret the actions of others and a reflection of how the market is structured. Conceptions of control reflect market-specific agreements between actors in firms on principles of internal organization (i.e. forms of hierarchy), tactics for competition or cooperation (i.e. strategies), and the hierarchy or status ordering of firms in a given market. A conception of control is a form of 'local knowledge' (Geertz 1983). Conceptions of control are historical and cultural products. They are historically specific to a certain industry in a certain society. They are cultural in that they form a set of understandings and practices about how things work in a particular market setting.

States are implicated in the building of market institutions by virtue of their claim to sovereignty in a given territory. In practice, state sovereignty is a variable because some states have the capacity to intervene in their societies and economies more effectively than others (Krasner 1988). States have a great deal of interest in maintaining their regulatory capacity. The ability to take action and use legal sanctions is at the core of what sovereignty means, and states are loath to relinquish this form of control. Bureaucracies, courts, police forces, and armies are the organizations that represent the ability of a particular state to act. If these organizations are diminished in their control, the state is weakened. States also differ in the ways in which they intervene in their societies and economies. So, for example, some states such as France, Great Britain, and Germany have owned firms, while others, such as the US federal government, have generally not done so.

In the context of the types of rules necessary to make markets work in modern societies, regulating property rights and competition is more central to states' claims on sovereignty than rules of exchange. These relationships define the relation between states and important economic elites. The elites who own and manage firms have created stable worlds in their markets, worlds dependent on current property rights and conceptions of control. Disrupting these arrangements means that states face the opposition of their best politically organized firms. States will resist another state's standards or rules, particularly in the sensitive areas of property rights and governance structures. Rules of exchange are less symbolically charged because while they facilitate trade with others, they do not by themselves undermine the claims to make rules governing the organization of property.

It is useful to consider how this view of markets, market rules, and the linkages to states and courts defines an integrated market. An integrated market economy will contain firms who can freely trade and invest with each other under a single system of rules that define property rights, sanction legal and illegal forms of competition and cooperation between firms and workers, and produce rules to govern economic transactions between buyers and sellers. Some scholars might add that an integrated market economy requires a single currency and a single regulatory structure. It is obvious that most of the historical cases of integrated market economies have been defined geographically and in reference to a single state.

THE PROBLEM OF THE INTEGRATION OF EUROPEAN MARKETS

There are two sorts of market integration projects that this analysis suggests. First is the political-legal project that would produce a single set of rules to govern market activities. To say that there existed a single market in a geographic area would imply that there exists a single set of rules to govern exchange, to regulate competition and cooperation between firms, and to define property rights. In the real world, there are no single integrated market economies in this way. It may come as a surprise to readers, but the US, which is often held up as a single market, does not have a single set of rules defining property rights and there are some differences in rules of exchange across states. These are caused by the fact that the US is a federal system and in the evolution of the national economy, state governments have kept some jurisdiction over economic activities within their borders. The second way in which markets are integrated concerns exactly who the main market participants are. So, a particular market may be fragmented geographically or not. It is possible that markets are integrated in terms of laws and practices, but that because of which firms are in the markets, they may in reality be fragmented. In the EU observers think that banking services of all kinds are fragmented in exactly this way (EU 2003). There are extensive rules in place for banks to do business in other countries, but in practice, this has not occurred.

If one thinks about this definition in the context of the EU, one can see that the problem of creating a single market across societies is formidable. In 1957 before the signing of the Treaty of Rome, each state in the EU had its own market rules (ie. property rights, governance structures, and rules of exchange). They also had their own currencies and regulatory structures in place. They had longstanding relationships with their organized economic elites who owned, or in the case of state-owned enterprises, managed the national firms. In the European social democracies, this commitment extended to workers as well. This predisposed governments not to undertake any actions that undermined either jobs or the privileges of national firms. Governments also worked hard to keep regulatory capacity under their control in order to maintain their legitimacy (not to mention the jobs of people who worked for them).

Given these constraints, it is quite amazing that the EU governments peacefully agreed to create and complete a single market across Europe and one that eventually also created a single currency. To accomplish the creation of the Single Market, the interests of governments, firms, workers, and consumers had to be balanced. If it looked as though too many people were potentially going to be hurt by the creation of market rules that would open markets to competitors from other countries, then those rules would never gain approval by the representatives of the member states in the Council of Ministers. While it was often possible for governments to make trade-offs, they still had to come out of whatever negotiation they entered believing that they were better off with the rules created than they were before.

The Treaty of Rome presented a set of agreements oriented towards getting European governments to begin to open up their national markets to trade. The Treaty (as I argued in Ch. 2) produced two major accomplishments. First, it set in place organizations in Brussels that produced market rules and a court that claimed the right to enforce them. Second, it created a negative integration project (i.e. it made it difficult for governments to keep tariff and nontariff trade barriers in place) and a positive integration project (i.e. it provided the impetus to put rules in place to promote a single market). In the early 1980s, the European Commission and groups such as the European Business Roundtable began to lobby for rules that would complete the Single Market. The basic idea was to produce positive rules that would push forward market opening (Fligstein and Mara-Drita 1996).

In 1986, the EU set out to 'complete the Single Market' by removing a whole variety of nontariff trade barriers. The ultimate shape of the Single Market

Program (hereafter, SMP) was deeply affected by the contradictory interests of member-state governments and their business and labor constituents. Governments did not want to build more organizations in Brussels or give more power to European institutions. Instead, they wanted to enforce European rules through their own bureaucracies. Governments were also wary of undercutting their own economic elites. They did not want to create a European market for corporate control and they were generally skeptical of making rules that would undermine their national champions. They were prepared to help their largest firms, firms who were already heavily involved in trading across Europe.

The main result of these concerns was reflected in the types of rules that were passed by the EU under the SMP. The SMP mainly made it easier for firms who were already exporting to engage in trade across Europe. It also preserved the power of states to control property rights and governance as one would expect given the theory of market institutions just proposed. The Single Market did not create Europe-wide regulatory capacity. Instead, it left the enforcement of European rules to the member-state governments. It opened markets in industries that could be logically connected to the completion of the Single Market: transportation, financial services, and professional and business services.

The original SMP consisted of 279 directives (each of which can be thought of as a rule or law) of which 264 (95%) were eventually passed by the European Council of Ministers. Some of the directives were quite simple. It is useful to consider a couple of the directives to show that they were heterogeneous in content and importance. Taxes on fuel differed across states. As a result, truck drivers would frequently fill their tanks when leaving a low-tax state to enter a high-tax state. The high-tax states tried to discourage this practice by taxing the fuel in gas tanks as trucks crossed borders. The first directive passed under the SMP eliminated these taxes. Another directive was more dramatic. It allowed all banks to set up shop in any country they chose. Banks who obtained this 'passport' had only to be in good standing with their national regulators.

Fligstein and Mara-Drita (1996) content-coded all directives with the idea of understanding what sort of market was being created. They used the *Official Journal* of the European Community to examine all of the directives in order to ascertain what kind of rule was reflected in the directive, the nature of enforcement, and the industry most affected by the directive. Table 3.1 shows the distributions for the SMP directives: 73.1 per cent of the directives were rules of exchange, 16.9 per cent were rules regarding governance structures, and only 10 per cent were rules regulating property rights. This confirms the argument I made above. Governments were not very interested in changing property rights or governance structures, but were mainly focused on creating rules for exchange to facilitate trade. In terms of enforcement, almost all the rules (87.4%) were going to be enforced by the member-state governments with only 12.6 per cent being in the purview of the EU Commission. This shows that the member-state governments were not interested in creating regulatory capacity at the EU level.

Table 3.2 presents data on the distribution of rules across industries by type. The greatest number of directives governed rules of exchange in food. A large

TABLE 3.1. *SMP directives: type, form of harmonization, and jurisdiction*

	No. of cases	%
Directive Type		
Rules of exchange	190	73.1
Governance structure	44	16.9
Property rights	26	10.0
Form of Harmonization		
Harmonized	185	79.1
Mutual recognition	37	15.8
Not harmonized	12	5.1
Bodies that Resolve Disputes		
Neither	120	58.9
Member states	65	27.0
Commission	30	12.4
Member states, then Commission	26	10.8

Source: Fligstein and Mara-Drita 1996, table 1.

number of directives also governed rules of exchange in chemicals, drugs, machines, and transportation equipment. These were industries that already enjoyed large amounts of trade, which is consistent with the argument that governments supported the creation of rules mainly to make it easier for their largest existing traders to increase trade still further.

Perhaps the most interesting result in Table 3.2 concerns the industries where governance structures and property rights directives were dominant. These rules were concentrated in three industries: finance, transportation, and professional services. The SMP made a serious attempt to open financial markets across Europe to competition from firms in all countries. They did so by changing the rules of competition (i.e. governance). They also tried to open up stock market exchanges and make it easier to finance new businesses either by selling stock or raising debt. In the transportation sector, many rules were written to promote competition in trucking, rail, and airlines. So, for example, before the Single Market, trucks that operated across borders could not make pick-ups and deliveries in a single country. The Single Market eliminated local monopolies over transportation. Professional services before the Single Market were also monopolized by local elites who were able to keep others out mainly by controlling certification. The Single Market pushed governments to recognize the credentials of most professionals. (I note there was one profession for which this was not true: lawyers!)

By 1993, there was an elaborate system of rules in place to facilitate trade by making exchange easier. There were also some efforts to open up certain new industries to trade by removing barriers caused by the use of restrictive governance structures or property rights. There had been an effort to create a general European system of property rights, mostly pushed by the British. But the French and German governments opposed that effort and argued that corporations should be firmly wedded to states. The shape of the SMP thus reflected the main interests and concerns of the governments. While there were real rule

TABLE 3.2. *Cross-tabulation of industry by directive type for Single Market*

Industry		Form of directive		
		Rules of exchange	Governance structure	Property rights
Food	no.	88	3	3
	%	46.8	7.3	11.5
Chemicals	no.	11	0	0
	%	5.9	0.0	0.0
Drugs	no.	19	0	2
	%	10.1	0.0	7.7
Machines	no.	10	0	1
	%	5.3	0.0	3.8
Finance	no.	1	18	9
	%	0.5	43.9	34.6
Transportation	no.	7	8	1
	%	3.7	19.5	3.8
Transportation vehicles	no.	10	0	0
	%	5.3	0.0	0.0
Professions and services	no.	3	5	7
	%	2.1	12.2	26.9
Telecommunications	no.	3	1	0
	%	1.6	2.4	0.0
Other	no.	15	1	1
	%	8.0	2.4	3.8
No single industry	no.	20	5	2
	%	10.6	12.2	7.7
No. of cases		187	41	26

Source: Fligstein and Mara-Drita 1996, table 6.

changes that made it easier to trade, restrictions to continue to keep national economic elites in charge of firms remained in place. Since 1993, there have been significant openings in a number of other industries including telecommunications, utilities, and eventually postal services. The logic of market opening in these industries has followed a similar pattern. Basically, governments have agreed to at least partially privatize their state-owned firms and to stop subsidizing them with state aid. They have also agreed to allow firms from other countries to compete. In practice, these market opening projects have worked in a complex way on the ground. The largest corporations have spread out their activities by entering new markets. But they frequently partner with the local firm by either setting up a joint venture or buying out smaller companies. It is useful to examine how things have played out on the ground in a more systematic way.

MARKET STRUCTURE IN EUROPE

In many ways, Europe is a single market in terms of market access, the ease of engaging in transactions across national borders, and competition policy. While there is still not a single market for property rights in Europe, the SMP was a substantial accomplishment that propelled forward the creation of European markets at the European level. To demonstrate the degree to which Europe is a single trade zone, it is useful to consider its relationship to broader trading patterns in the world economy. Table 3.3 presents data on the shares of world trade by region. There are several interesting and important features in this table. First, Western European countries accounted for between 40.2 and 48.3 per cent of world exports and 39.6 to 44.8 per cent of world imports over the period 1980–2005 even as world trade more than tripled in size over this period. Thus, nearly half of all world trade takes place in the EU zone. The share of world trade in which European countries were involved was extremely high and relatively stable over time. There are several other important features to note about this table.

More generally, the table shows that the largest amounts of trade in the world still begin and end in the developed countries. There is a great deal of continuity in the performance of the developed societies in the past twenty-five years. The developed world's (i.e. North America, Japan, and Western Europe) share of world exports and imports has remained relatively constant over time and still constitutes a little less than 70 per cent of world trade. The big losers in world trade have been the less-developed parts of the world, Latin America, Africa, and

TABLE 3.3. *Percentage of world merchandise exports and imports by region, 1980–2005*

	1980	1985	1990	1995	2000	2005
North America						
Exports	14.4	16.0	15.4	15.9	13.7	12.4
Imports	15.5	21.7	18.4	18.7	20.5	19.5
Latin America (with Mexico)						
Exports	5.4	5.6	4.3	4.6	5.2	5.6
Imports	5.9	4.2	3.6	4.9	4.8	5.0
Western Europe						
Exports	40.2	40.1	48.3	44.8	43.1	43.0
Imports	44.8	39.6	44.7	43.5	42.0	43.2
Eastern Europe (with CIS)						
Exports	7.8	8.1	3.1	3.1	5.5	5.7
Imports	7.5	7.4	3.3	2.9	5.0	3.3
Africa						
Exports	5.9	4.2	3.0	2.1	2.2	2.9
Imports	4.7	3.5	2.7	2.4	0.5	3.1
Middle East						
Exports	10.6	5.3	4.0	2.9	4.1	5.3
Imports	5.0	4.5	2.8	2.6	2.5	3.1
Japan						
Exports	6.4	9.1	8.5	9.1	6.5	5.9
Imports	6.8	6.5	6.8	6.7	5.1	3.1
Asia						
Exports	9.2	11.7	13.3	17.5	19.7	21.5
Imports	9.9	12.3	14.5	18.3	17.9	18.8

Source: World Trade Association Annual Report, 1996, tables III.1, III.2; 2004, table III.1; 2006, table III.1.

TABLE 3.4. *Regional structure of world merchandise trade in exports,*
1993 and 2005

| | Regional Destination | | | | | | | |
| | North America | | Western Europe | | Asia | | Rest of the world | |
Regional Origin	1993	2005	1993	2005	1993	2005	1993	2005
North America	35.6	55.8	20.2	16.1	25.0	18.3	19.2	9.8
Western Europe	8.0	9.1	68.9	73.2	8.8	7.6	14.3	10.1
Asia (incl. Japan)	26.4	21.9	17.0	17.9	46.5	51.2	14.2	10.0

Note: Rows sum to 100 within years.

Source: *World Trade Organization Annual Report* 1996, table II.1; 2006, table II.1.

the Middle East. These societies have not benefited as much from the huge expansion of trade or from the foreign investment that goes along with such advancement. The big winners (not surprisingly) have been the shares of imports and exports for non-Japanese Asia. Over the period, these increased from about 10 per cent to about 20 per cent, reflecting the rapid growth of first Taiwan, Singapore, Thailand, and South Korea, and later China and India.

Eastern Europe (without the former Soviet Union) saw their trade shares drop from about 8 per cent in 1985 to 3 per cent in 1995. But in the past eight years their trade share has increased to about 5.5 per cent. Most of the collapse was due to the fall of the Soviet Union and its Eastern European trading zone. But, as Eastern European countries reformed their economies and economic growth resumed, they have dramatically increased their share of world trade in the past ten years. As I shall show, much of this trade came about because of the decision of these societies to join the EU. Their trade share expanded as they became integrated into the EU zone.

Table 3.4 shows the ultimate destinations of trade in 1993 and 2005. One can clearly see that exports are divided into three regions: Asia (including Japan), Western Europe, and North America. These regions are often described as the 'triad' (Ohmae 1985), i.e. they create three large trading blocks in the world. The region with the strongest market concentration is Western Europe with 68.9 per cent of trade beginning and ending there in 1993, expanding to 73.2 per cent in 2003. Of Asia's exports, 46.5 per cent ended up in Asia in 1993 and this increased to 51.2 per cent in 2005. Of North America's exports, 35.6 per cent ended up in North America in 1993 and this increased to 55.8 per cent in 2003. The table suggests that in the recent past, the three blocks have become even more focused on trade between partners. Both the EU and NAFTA appear to have worked to increase the concentration of trade in their areas After NAFTA, the trade concentration in North America changed from 35 to 55.8 per cent. Taken together, these tables show that the largest part of world trade originates and ends up in Western Europe. The countries of Western Europe account for almost half of world trade and about 70 per cent of that trade ends up in Europe.

Figure 3.1 graphically portrays what has happened in European exporting between 1980 and 1999. The data in the graph portray the export destinations

Figure 3.1. Intra-European exports as percentage of all European exports.

Source: United Nations. *Annual Trade Statistics.* New York: United Nations. Various years.

of the fifteen countries that make up the EU through much of the period. I note that the Eastern European countries are counted as exports outside the EU (even though they begin to prepare for ascension into the EU in the late 1990s). Given the large increase in export activity between Eastern Europe and the EU after 1995, this makes our estimate of intra-EU trade even a little conservative. In 1980, about 60 per cent of EU exports were headed toward other EU countries. With the announcement of the SMP in 1985, the share of intra-European trade began to increase until 1990 when it peaked at about 71 per cent of EU trade. This number has remained relatively stable since then. I note that the share of world exports originating in the EU began this era at about 40 per cent and end the period at about 43 per cent, suggesting that Europe's share of trade did not change much. But there is clear evidence that most of this change came about as the result of the SMP which appears to have had the effect of redirecting European trade to the other countries of Europe.

Table 3.5 presents data on the share of manufacturing exports from various EU countries that end up in other EU countries. There are several interesting features of this table. Between 1970 and 1997, almost every country increased its share of their manufacturing exports that ended up in Europe. This is remarkable evidence that European manufacturers really saw Europe as their main market. The era where these numbers appeared to have increased the most was from 1980 until 1990. This was the period when the SMP was announced and implemented. This is evidence that European manufacturers were aided by the changes in EU rules in this period and responded to more trade opportunities by concentrating their trade on Europe.

The countries with the fewest European manufacturing exports include Ireland, Finland, and Great Britain. Finland is a recent entry into the EU. It also exports many

TABLE 3.5. *Total manufacturing trade of EU countries with others in the EU (%)*

	1970	1980	1990	1997
Austria	53	65	79	78
Belgium	77	86	83	89
Finland	21	35	41	51
France	82	84	86	90
Germany	70	75	79	81
Ireland	27	61	54	42
Italy	70	61	67	70
Netherlands	68	69	77	77
Portugal	28	41	53	64
Spain	43	69	75	81
UK		40	56	55

Source: OECD Outlook 64 (1998), 154.

telecommunications products into international markets. Ireland is a platform for many multinationals that use it both as an entry to the EU and also a manufacturing base for their world activities. Great Britain is the least Europe-focused of the large economies. This reflects its involvement with former colonies and the US market. The countries with over 80 per cent of their manufacturing exports going to the EU include France, Germany, Belgium, and Spain, while Austria, Italy, and the Netherlands have over 70 per cent of their manufacturing exports ending up in the EU. France and Germany have been the traditional leaders of the EU, because of the relative size of their economies and their relative economic interdependence. These statistics throw an interesting light on why some of the politics of the EU appear to ally France and Germany against Great Britain. The British depend the least on the EU for their trade while France and Germany are amongst the largest traders. It is not surprising that their governments have been the engine of advancing the European integration project while the British remain more skeptical.

Table 3.5 also gives us an opportunity to see how the decision by a country to join the EU effects the orientation of its manufacturing exporters. Ireland joined the EU in 1973. In 1970, only 27 per cent of its manufacturing exports ended up in the EU, but by 1980, this increased to 61 per cent. Spain and Portugal joined in 1985 and their exports to the EU jumped during the decade. Finland joined in 1994, and during the 1990s its share of manufacturing exports with the EU also climbed sharply.

It is useful to explore how the EU has affected the Eastern European countries that have recently joined. Table 3.6 presents data on the dates of application for the ten newest members (all of whom attained official membership on 1 May 2004). Table 3.7 shows how Eastern European trade changed during the 1990s. The top line shows exports from Eastern European countries from 1994 until 2003. The amount of trade slowly increased during the 1990s and began to accelerate from 1999 onwards. The second line of the table shows how much of world trade was accounted for by the Eastern European countries. The share of

TABLE 3.6. *Dates of formal application to the EU for members joining on 1 May 2004*

Country	Application Date
Cyprus	2 July 1986
Czech Republic	16 January 2002
Estonia	12 November 1991
Hungary	30 March 1990
Latvia	12 October 1991
Lithuania	23 November 1991
Malta	16 July 1990
Poland	4 April 1990
Slovakia	26 June 1991
Slovenia	9 June 1992

Source: <http://europa.eu.int/comm./enlargement/negotiations/index.htm>, accessed May 2004.

TABLE 3.7. *Merchandise trade exports for Eastern Europe (excluding Russia), 1994–2003*

	1994	1995	1996	1997	1998	1999	2000	2001	2002	2003
Total trade ($ billion)	150.1	175.8	173.4	176.7	168.9	169.7	187.6	275.3	302.1	400.1
World trade (%)	3.5	3.8	3.9	4.0	3.8	4.0	4.3	4.6	4.9	5.5
Trade within EU (%)	33.7	36.4	38.9	41.2	46.5	47.2	52.6	54.6	56.6	56.8
Trade with other Eastern European countries (%)	37.4	32.3	30.2	28.4	27.7	28.9	29.2	29.5	26.5	26.5
EU25	71.1	68.7	69.1	71.6	75.2	76.1	81.8	84.1	83.1	83.3

Source: WTO (2004), tables III.3, III.37, Website: <www.wto.org>, accessed 25 September. 2007.

world trade was 3.5 per cent in 1994 and this grew slowly until 1999. Then Eastern Europe increased its share of world trade from 4.0 to 5.5 per cent an increase of over one-third.

The most interesting question is the destination of the trade from Eastern Europe. Beginning in 1994, as the Eastern European countries began to apply for EU membership, the share of their trade that went to the EU began at 33.7 per cent and climbed steadily to 47.2 per cent in 1999, and finally to 56.8 per cent in 2003. This shows that Eastern European countries began to redirect their trade substantially to the EU. The next line of the table shows how their trade with the rest of Eastern Europe declined over the period. In 1994, 37.4 per cent of Eastern European trade ended up in Eastern Europe. In 2003, this had dropped to 26.5 per cent. The last line of the table adds up the previous two lines. It shows that over the period, Eastern European trade was 71.1 per cent with the EU-25 rising to 83.3 per cent in 2003 even as intra-Eastern European trade dropped by a third. The Eastern European economies which began the 1990s in disarray and mainly focused on exporting to each other have now been firmly integrated into the EU trading zone.

It is useful to summarize the results of this section. The EU represents over 40 per cent of world trade over time and this share has risen slightly even as world trade has tripled in value in the past twenty years. It is the most integrated trade bloc in the world with over 70 per cent of EU trade beginning and ending internally. The SMP had the effect of intensifying EU trade. The intra-EU share of total EU trade increased about from 60 to 70 per cent during the 1980s. Data on the manufacturing sector shows that intra-EU trade in manufactures is high and increasing generally over time. The SMP appears to have caused manufacturers to expand their European activities. Joining the EU had a big effect on the direction of a country's exports. Every country that joined the EU saw its share of manufacturing exports to the EU increase. Finally, the ascension of the ten Eastern European countries to the EU has resulted in the revival of the exporting sectors of their economies. Their exports grew dramatically, particularly after 1999. The main shift in trade was from the other Eastern European countries to the EU. Indeed, by 2003, 82.5 per cent of exports in Eastern Europe ended up in the EU-25.

EUROPE AND THE STRATEGIES OF LARGE FIRMS

If trade across Europe has grown denser, it is interesting to consider exactly what this means for corporations. One can imagine that firms engaged in export would pursue one of two strategies as they expand their activities in Europe. First, they could decide to redistribute their activities across Europe. This would mean that they would make investment in plant capacity and buy up firms in other countries. They could do this to lower the costs of their wage bills or just to be closer to finished markets. Alternatively, since the Single Market means that European firms are theoretically free to ship goods anywhere in Europe with few barriers, firms could decide to stay at home. Indeed, as trade barriers and transportation and communications costs decrease, firms would feel less compelled to relocate facilities to other societies. To figure out what large European corporations are doing, it would be useful to have data on their activities as they change over time. Unfortunately, data of this sort just do not exist. So, instead, I will rely on available data and try and examine more indirect evidence to ascertain if changes are occurring over time.

The first data I consider come from a study of the world's largest multinational corporations in 1987 and 1997 (Stafford and Purkis 1989; 1999). This dataset is unique in that it contains information on the world's 450 largest multinational corporations. It attempts to disaggregate where firms have their main investments and assesses their major markets. The data allow a comparison of how multinationals changed their activities over time. One of the advantages about the dataset is that it captures some of the reaction of both European and non-European multinationals to the SMP. The SMP was announced in 1986, but it was not intended to take full effect until 1992. Multinational firms probably

TABLE 3.8. *Comparison of the world's largest multinationals, 1987 and 1997*

	EU firms			Non-EU firms		
	1987	1997	significance level	1987	1997	significance level
Assets in home country (%)	64 (28)	57 (42)	0.05	71 (160)	64 (176)	0.000
Assets in Europe, not home country (%)	17 (28)	25 (42)	0.05	20 (91)	24 (102)	0.01
Employees in home country (%)	53 (43)	47 (50)	0.05			
Employees in Europe, not home country (%)	25 (23)	32 (31)	0.05			
Sales in home country (%)	42 (87)	35 (87)	0.02	70 (186)	62 (188)	0.000
Sales in Europe, not home country (%)	30 (69)	35 (80)	0.04	19 (102)	24 (109)	0.01
Total assets in Europe (%)	81	82	n.s.	20	24	0.01
Total employees in Europe (%)	78	79	n.s.			
Total sales in Europe (%)	72	70	n.s.	19	24	0.01

Notes: Number of cases reported is in parentheses.
Significance level refers to the t-test between the means.

Source: Stafford and Purkis (1989; 1999).

began planning their reaction to the SMP as soon as it was announced, but redeployed assets, sales, and jobs over a long period. Thus, the 1987 data probably contain the beginnings of the reaction to the opportunities presented by the SMP and the 1997 data certainly capture the change in firms' deployment of their resources. The data also allows us to compare the activities of Europe-based multinationals to other firms of similar size and with similar aspirations. Thus, we can see the degree to which European firms are like or unlike the multi-national firms of other societies.

Table 3.8 presents data on investment of the world's largest multinationals broken down by whether or not the firms are headquartered in the EU or elsewhere at two points in time. I note that there were substantial missing data on many of the variables for firms. I report the number of firms in each of the categories of interest where data were available and also report whether or not the differences were statistically significant. I also note that the identities of firms also change over the ten-year period. This means that the data reflect two snapshots of a population that is not exactly the same, and suggests caution about the comparisons.

It is useful to begin by examining how EU firms changed their distribution of activities between 1987 and 1997. In 1987, EU-based multinationals had about 64 per cent of their assets in their home country. This decreased to about 57 per cent by 1997, a statistically significant reduction in assets. There was an increase in the percentage of assets in Europe but not in the home country from 17 to 25 per cent over the period. There were similar statistically significant decreases in employment in the home country. In 1987, 53 per cent of employees of European multinationals were in the home country and this dropped to 47 per cent by 1997. At the same time employees in other European countries increased from 25 to 32 per cent. These results imply that European multinationals redeployed their assets and employment across Europe in response to opportunities from the SMP. The shift in assets and employment was mirrored in sales figures. Home sales for European multinationals dropped from 42 to 35 per cent while sales in the rest of Europe rose from 30 to 35 per cent. Both these changes were statistically significant.

The last three rows of the table examine the degree to which the overall assets, employees, and sales in Europe changed for European multinationals from 1987 until 1997. European multinationals had 81 per cent of their assets in Europe in 1987 and 82 per cent in 1997. Of their employees, 78 per cent were in Europe in 1987 and 79 per cent in 1997. Finally, 72 per cent of their sales were in Europe in 1987 while 70 per cent were in Europe in 1997. None of these changes were statistically significant. It should be noted that European multinationals were already very oriented towards Europe in 1987 (i.e. assets and employees were around 80 per cent in Europe and about 70 per cent of sales were accounted for by Europe). The change in the decade was that European multinationals spread out their assets, employment, and sales across Europe and thereby decreased their dependency on the home country while increasing their presence in the EU.

It is interesting to compare European multinationals to the other large multinationals in the world. In 1987, non-EU multinationals had 71 per cent of their sales in their home country, which decreased to 64 per cent in 1997, a statistically significant reduction. They also decreased their dependence on home assets from 70 to 62 per cent. Thus, non-EU multinationals became more 'global' during 1987–97. One interesting question is how much of this redeployment was in Europe in response to the SMP. The bottom three rows of the table show that non-EU multinationals increased their sales in Europe from 19 to 24 per cent and increased their assets from 20 to 24 per cent (both statistically significant). This shows that Europe was a huge focus of non-EU multinationals. Half their shift in assets (4% of 8%) was toward the EU market during the decade 1987–97. Even more impressive is that 71 per cent (5% of 7%) of their shift in sales out of their home countries were accounted for by Europe. Non-EU multinationals may have been 'globalizing,' but most of their globalization in this period was accounted for by their move into Europe.

CHANGES IN INVESTMENT IN EUROPE IN THE 1990s

The data on the activities of multinationals presents us with a consistent picture of what happened in the European economy from 1987 to 1999. The largest European multinational corporations took advantage of the SMP to invest in other European countries and increase their overall employment and sales to those countries. Non-EU multinationals also saw the SMP as an opportunity and increased their investment in Europe relative to their home countries and dramatically increased their sales to Europe. Investments into Europe were generally made in one of two ways: through either mergers or investment in new plant and equipment. It is useful to explore both kinds of investments.

Figure 3.2 presents data on investment flows into Europe in 2002. It contains two kinds of data, those on the amount of inflow in 2002 and those on the composition of all foreign investment in 2002. In terms of all foreign investment in European countries, the data show that most of the foreign investment has European origins. The smallest amount of foreign investment that originated in Europe is in Denmark and Great Britain. But even here, Europe is the source of 69 and 72 per cent respectively of all foreign investment. Of all foreign investment, in France 89 per cent and in Germany 77 per cent originates in Europe. European firms in general lead the way in investment in other European countries. If one looks at the Eastern European countries for which we have data, the Czech Republic has 92 per cent of its foreign investment from Europe, Hungary has 76 per cent, Poland 91 per cent, and Slovakia 94 per cent. This shows that European firms have made most of the investments in Eastern Europe as well.

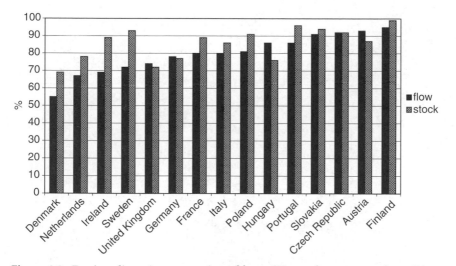

Figure 3.2. Foreign direct investment into fifteen EU member states and candidate countries, 2001.

The percentage of foreign investment in a single year is a less stable measure of foreign investment because flows in a year can fluctuate. Nevertheless, if we look at what happened in a single year, 2002, the percentage of foreign investment with European origins is also quite high. There is little indication from this data that European firms have lost their interest in investing in Europe as a place to organize their economic activities.

One of the main ways in which foreign investment occurs is through the use of mergers. There have been three periods of mergers in Europe since the 1980s. During 1985–92, there was a merger wave in anticipation of the SMP. During the period 1994–2001, there was a huge worldwide merger movement across the developed world. Finally, since 2003, merger activity across national borders has picked up substantially. My main conclusion is that in all three of these periods European firms were large players. I show that Europe-wide mergers occurred in large numbers in the run-up to the SMP while national mergers decreased in importance. During the second period, there were also active European markets of mergers. But, there was also substantial European investment in the US economy. Finally, the latest merger movement has been heavily focused on Europe with European firms buying each other out at a high rate.

Figure 3.3 presents data on the number of mergers and joint ventures that the 1,000 largest European firms engaged in on a year-to-year basis from 1982 to 1992. The graph clearly reveals the influence of the Single Market on mergers and to a lesser degree joint ventures. The largest European firms increased their merger activity between 1984 (the announcement of the Single Market) and 1990. Merger activity peaked in 1989 and fell off afterwards. Joint ventures follow a similar pattern.

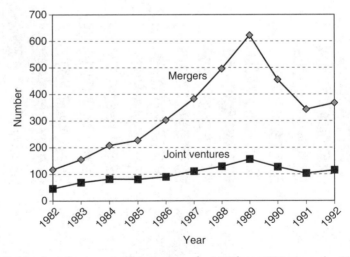

Figure 3.3. Number of mergers and joint ventures for 1,000 largest EU companies, 1982–1992.
Source: OECD 1996: table 1.12.

Figure 3.4 presents data on the country of origin of the merger targets. At the beginning of the merger wave of the 1980s, 60–70 per cent of the mergers were within national borders, but as the merger wave grew and peaked in 1989, cross-border mergers increased. In 1989, the peak year of merger activity, EU mergers made up a slightly higher percentage of all merger activity of the 1,000 largest EU firms. After 1989, however, national mergers became prominent once again. The number of mergers with non-EU firms fluctuated over the period. This graph shows that it decreases until 1986, then increases until it peaks in 1990. During the height of the merger movement, 20 per cent of the mergers involved non-EU firms (predominantly multinationals). There are two conclusions that one can come to about the merger strategies of large corporations of Europe in the 1980s. First, they increasingly engaged in mergers and joint ventures as a run-up to the completion of the Single Market. They were joined by non-EU firms who also increased their share of EU mergers in order to gain a toehold in Europe. Second, European firms continued to merge with their national counterparts. This made them larger and consolidated national production into a smaller number of large firms. The largest European corporations consolidated with their principal competitors within countries and pushed them to invest across countries.

It is useful to extend our analysis of mergers to the 1990s and the past few years when there has been an explosive international merger movement. If we consider the two merger waves separately we discover what is the same and what is different about them. Many analysts saw this movement as about globalization, but a simple look at the data reveals quite a different view of what happened. Table 3.9 presents data on international cross-border mergers from 1990 until

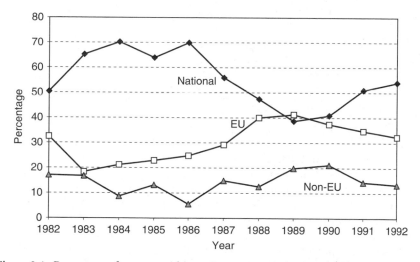

Figure 3.4. Percentage of mergers within nations, across nations, and with non-EU firms, 1982–1992.

Source: OECD 1996: table 1.12.

The Economic Transformation of Europe

TABLE 3.9. *Cross-border mergers by region, sales, and purchases, 1990–2005*

Region	Sales ($ billion)							
	1990	1995	1997	1998	1999	2003	2004	2005
EU	62.1	75.1	114.6	187.9	344.5	126.0	178.2	429.1
US	54.7	53.2	81.7	209.5	233.0	60.7	81.9	105.6
Japan	0.1	0.5	3.1	4.0	15.9	10.9	8.9	2.5
Rest of world	16.4	21.9	70.1	85.8	73.7	85.4	84.6	178.6
TOTAL	150.6	186.6	304.8	531.6	720.1	297.0	380.6	716.3

Region	Purchases ($ billion)							
	1990	1995	1997	1998	1999	2003	2004	2005
EU	86.5	81.4	142.1	284.4	497.7	121.2	164.7	386.8
US	27.6	57.3	80.9	137.4	112.4	82.4	110.0	147.5
Japan	14.0	3.9	2.7	1.3	9.8	8.4	3.8	8.1
Rest of world	7.0	12.9	32.7	20.2	42.8	84.2	102.1	163.9
TOTAL	150.6	186.6	304.8	531.6	720.1	297.0	380.6	716.3

Region	Sales (%)							
	1990	1995	1997	1998	1999	2003	2004	2005
EU	41.2	40.2	37.6	35.3	47.8	42.4	46.8	59.9
US	36.3	28.5	26.8	39.4	32.4	23.5	21.5	14.7
Japan	0.0	0.0	1.0	0.8	2.2	3.7	2.3	0.3
Rest of world	23.5	31.7	34.6	24.5	17.6	30.4	29.4	25.9

Region	Purchases (%)							
	1990	1995	1997	1998	1999	2003	2004	2005
EU	57.4	43.6	46.6	53.4	69.1	40.8	43.7	53.9
US	18.3	30.7	26.5	25.8	15.6	27.7	29.0	20.6
Japan	9.2	2.1	0.9	0.0	5.7	2.8	1.0	1.1
Rest of world	15.1	23.6	36.0	20.8	9.6	28.7	26.3	24.4

Source: United Nations *World Investment Report* (2000), 15, table 5; (2006), appendices, table B6.

1999 (the peak of the merger movement) and the resumption of the newer merger movement in 2003. The first thing to note is that the initial movement involved cross-border mergers of $186.6 billion in 1995 and ended up peaking at $720.1 billion in 1999. It can also be seen that in the peak year, 82.4 per cent of sales and 90.4 per cent of purchases are accounted for by the EU, the US, and Japan, while most of the rest of the mergers involved Australia, Korea, and some other Asian societies. Almost none were with developing societies.

The table also shows that the EU was the major seller and purchaser of companies in other societies. In the peak of the merger movement in 1999, the EU accounted for 47.8 per cent of the sales and 69.1 per cent of the purchases. The US was the second largest market with 32.4 per cent of sales and 15.6 per cent of purchases.

Unfortunately, it is not possible to break out where the buyers and sellers were and who did the purchasing. It is clear from the overall pattern that there was much buying and selling in Europe, but less clear whether or not it was European or US firms who were doing the buying. Put another way, the EU accounted for 47.8 per cent of sales in 1999 and 69.1 per cent of purchases. This means that if no one but Europeans had bought firms in Europe, Europeans purchased 21.3 per cent of the total cross-border mergers in countries other than Western Europe. The UN *World Investment Report* (2000, table 6) implies that much of this outward investment from Europe was in the US. Because of the high growth of the American economy during this period and the existence of a market for corporate control, European firms invested heavily in the American market.

The pattern changed during the recent merger movement that began in 2003. Table 3.9 shows that cross-border mergers have increased worldwide from $297 billion in 2003 to $716.3 billion in 2005. During this three-year period the largest buyers and sellers were European firms. As the market heated up, European firms became even more dominant buyers and sellers. The US share of cross-border mergers dropped dramatically, suggesting that US multinationals were not the leading firms in this period. If the 1990s merger movement was centered more evenly on Europe and the US, the most recent merger wave has definitely tilted to a European focus.

It is helpful to get a sense of who the buyers and sellers were in the largest cross-border mergers. Table 3.10 presents data on the more than $1 billion cross-border mergers in 2005. There were 187 of these mergers. Firms from the EU purchased ninety-two companies of this size while those from the US purchased fifty. The most interesting aspect of the table is where the buyers and sellers came from. British firms led the way as buyers and sellers in Europe, because, as noted earlier in the chapter, in Britain there exists an active market for corporate control. British firms actively pursued merger targets in other countries, and

TABLE 3.10. *Cross-border mergers of $1 billion or more by buyer and seller country, 2005*

Buyer	Seller									
	US	UK	Germany	France	Netherlands	Other EU	Other Europe	Asia	Other	TOTAL
US	—	4	9	4	4	6	1	1	21	50
UK	4	—	4	3	0	14			11	36
Germany	1	4	—	0	0	3	0	0	0	8
France	0	1	0	—	0	5	0	0	1	7
Netherlands	1	3	0	0	—	1	1	0	1	7
Other EU	2	4	3	3	1	15	1	0	5	34
Other Europe	1	1	0	1	0	1	0	0	1	5
Asia	3	3	0	0	1	0	0	7	1	15
Other	5	4	1	0	1	3	1	1	9	25
TOTAL	17	24	17	11	7	48	5	9	49	187

Source: UN *World Investment Report* (2006), appendices, table A17.

they themselves were attractive targets. One surprising result is that German firms were the targets of twenty-four mergers but the buyers in only seven. This implies that German firms decided to partner with their international counterparts. One explanation of this is that mid-size German firms, mostly family owned and controlled, have decided to sell out their interest in the firm. Since foreign firms were the most likely to be able to raise money, they became the obvious buyers. Many observers believe that the German system of labor relations has been a disincentive to invest in Germany. However, it is evident that many multinational corporations did not support this view and invested heavily in German production.

The other interesting result in the table is the large amount of activity in EU countries outside the UK, France, Germany, and the Netherlands which have been the traditional leaders in building global companies. European firms from across the continent increasingly are using mergers to expand their influence in the region. This implies that there are still opportunities for more market integration (i.e. the participation of firms from across Europe in all the countries of Europe). It also shows a deepening of this process as firms from Spain, Italy, and other EU member states move to purchase firms in the region.

Table 3.11 summarizes Table 3.10 by considering the main patterns of investment in the world's largest multinational mergers. Of all of these mergers, 56.7 per cent took place in Europe, 34.2 per cent in the rest of the world, and only 9.1 per cent in the US. American companies were very active in buying firms in Europe, thereby continuing their historical investments in the European marketplace. European firms were particularly likely to buy businesses in Europe, as 68.5 per cent of their largest mergers were in that market. Even firms from other countries were big players in Europe. I conclude that in the past three years, Europe has become an even more attractive place for corporations to make investments. European firms are intensifying their European strategies by buying other companies. The US has become less of a market for such mergers compared to the 1990s.

TABLE 3.11. *Cross-border mergers of $1 billion or more by region, 2005*

| Buyer | Seller | | | |
	US	EU	Other	TOTAL
US	—	27 (54.0)*	23 (46.0)	50
EU	8 (8.7)	63 (68.5)	21 (22.8)	92
Other	9 (20.0)	16 (35.6)	20 (44.4)	45
TOTAL	17 (9.1)	106 (56.7)	64 (34.2)	187

*Row percentage.

Source: See Table 3.11.

CONCLUSION

This chapter started by posing several issues: first, how has the economic integration of the European economy proceeded compared to the rest of the world? Second, how did European corporations respond to the market openings presented by the SMP and subsequent market opening projects? Third, what does all this suggest about the convergence of European corporations on a single system of property rights, governance structures, rules of exchange, and labor market policies?

The European Union is the largest trading region in the world, and the most economically integrated. It accounts for around 43 per cent of world trade. Over 70 per cent of that total trade originates and ends up in the EU. While there is evidence that the North American and Asian economies have also become more self-contained over time, neither approaches the size or integration of the EU. As of 1992, Eurostat, the agency in charge of collating statistics for the EU started to describe this internal trade as the 'internal market.' It began to consider only trade outside the EU as foreign trade. This clearly is a somewhat symbolic gesture, but it captures a real truth: Europe, for all intents and purposes, is nearly a single market economy.

The Single Market Program pushed this pattern forward. During the 1980s, European trade as a percentage of all exports increased in the wake of the Single Market. European firms invested heavily in other European countries. European multinationals spread their assets, employment, and sales across Europe. Non-EU multinationals also increased their European investments. I demonstrated that as nations join the EU and adopt the EU rules, their economies grow more linked with Europe. Investment from across Europe increases and trade patterns change such that imports and exports are more focused on the EU.

There are two interesting exceptions to this. First, the United Kingdom is less economically integrated with Europe than the other countries. This means that their firms are more likely to focus on markets elsewhere, most obviously America. It helps explain why the British have been the most skeptical of the EU political project. Because they are less well integrated into the EU economically, they think they have less to gain by increased political integration. Second, despite the overall evidence suggesting that firms have focused on Europe, large European corporations continued to expand their economic activities in the developed world, particularly the US. During the late 1990s, European multinationals from the UK, the Netherlands, France, and Germany bought out many large American corporations. However, this pattern reversed in the most recent merger wave, which appears to be affecting more European corporations across more countries and may be leading to an even more integrated regional market.

The SMP and the monetary union have pushed forward legal and political integration in the realm of the economy. Resulting rule changes have induced European firms to expand nationally and invest in the rest of Europe, and have convinced non-EU multinational corporations to invest in Europe as well. My argument earlier in this chapter was that a single market economy required both rules and geographically integrated markets. With a few notable exceptions, Europe is such a market.

This high level of economic and legal integration can be juxtaposed to the jarring realization that governments continue to see themselves as sovereign states and the people of Europe generally remain loyal to their own nations, not to Europe. How can this be? One reason is that most economic activity within Europe still takes place within national borders. Most Europeans work for national firms or national governments. Even where their jobs depend on exports, their employment conditions depend on national law. They still view their main political allegiance as to their society.

European firms continue to have primarily national identities. Firms such as Daimler, British Telecom, and Philips remain predominantly associated with their headquarters' countries even though they do substantial business in other countries. While the largest European multinational corporations are big traders, they are also firmly wedded to national governments and labor markets. The Single Market encouraged firms to engage in more cross-border mergers than they had previously done. Since it is difficult to engage in hostile mergers in most of Europe, they have had to be done on friendly terms. It is my assertion that this means that national management teams have generally remained in power and that national labor market practices continue to organize the employees of these firms. So even where ownership has passed to firms headquartered in other countries, the identity of the subsidiary firms remains largely intact. The question remains as to the degree to which these mergers have created a European capitalist class that views itself in primarily cosmopolitan terms. In order to get a view of exactly how these mergers and changes have played out on the ground, I now turn to exploring how three industries have been reorganized in Europe as a result of EU initiatives.

4

The Creation of Markets:
The Cases of the Defense,
Telecommunications,
and Football Industries

INTRODUCTION

I have demonstrated that ability to trade across borders has increased dramatically in Europe in the past twenty-five years to a large degree as a result of actions taken in the EU to open up market opportunities. Many European firms have increasingly shifted their focus of attention from their home country to Europe as their main market. This building of the European economy is something that has happened one industry at a time. New market opportunities were aided by the creation of new products and technologies and entrepreneurial efforts on the part of owners, firms, and managers. But the opportunities themselves were influenced by what was going on in Brussels and the desire of member-state governments to encourage firms to expand across borders in order to create new jobs and satisfy consumers.

In this chapter, I consider three case studies of how this process proceeded in order to give a flavor to what occurred on the ground in Europe. I have chosen disparate case studies in order to illustrate some of the general principles of expansion. I am interested in how former nationally owned firms who were focused on national markets came to sell their products in other countries. I want to trace the role of EU and national government policies in these changes, and also to understand how national patterns of firm ownership shifted as a result of market opening.

The first case study is the defense industry. The defense industry is an unlikely site for creating a single European market. At the core of the idea of state sovereignty is the notion that a government should be in control of both police and military power, the powers that enable it to enforce laws within the country and to protect the citizenry from invasion. In Europe, traditionally, the largest defense companies have been owned by governments, because military planners have wanted captive producers in order not to be beholden to foreign firms in times of war.

The end of the Cold War changed all of that. The Cold War was the main justification for governments to keep their defense firms focused on their national markets. Without the Soviet threat, the rationale disappeared for having so many arms producers in an era when defense budgets in most countries were shrinking. In the early 1990s in America, the Defense Department encouraged the large US arms producers to consolidate to create fewer large suppliers. In the face of the fact that American producers were getting bigger and the Pentagon (one of the world's largest procurers of weapons) was getting smaller, European governments realized that some form of rationalization of the arms industry in Europe made sense. Defense contractors around Europe were prepared to join together in mergers in ways that would have made sense economically. But what complicated this was the fact that national governments still wanted to have captive producers in order to guarantee weapons in time of war.

This has produced a crazy quilt pattern of ownership relationships and joint product alliances of defense firms across Europe. Most defense firms are no longer wholly owned by governments; there has also been substantial consolidation such that there are three large firms in Europe and an even larger number of alliances that cross-cut the industry. But, governments, particularly the French, continue to be interested in controlling firms and mergers. Compounding the confusion and uncertainty about the future is the effort on the part of European governments to forge a common foreign and security policy, create a European defense force, and move to produce a single system of procurement for large weapon systems (Sperling and Kirchner 1997; Mörth 2003; Britz 2004; Mörth and Britz 2004). The industry, while partially consolidated, still waits to see which European governments actually produce agreements and what their shape will imply for the willingness of the governments to allow further rationalization of the industry.

The second case study is telecommunications. Here too, historically, the largest firms were government-owned bureaucracies. But beginning in the 1980s, the member-state governments, with prodding from large supplier firms and the EU, began to liberalize the industry. They agreed to extensive privatization and deregulation, and as the industry became revolutionized by new products during the 1980s and 1990s, governments sold off large shares of their national firms and opened their markets to competition. This has produced a set of large firms that span not just Europe, but also operate in the US and, to a lesser degree, Asia. But, here again, it is possible to see the continued influence of governments; the German and French continue to own large (if minority) shares of their telecom companies. Other governments, with the exception of Great Britain, have generally not wanted their national phone companies to fall into the hands of foreigners. It has only been a few of the small national phone companies which have been sold into larger firms. Instead, there has been the development of extensive alliances across countries whereby firms jointly own ventures particularly for wireless telephones. Most of the smaller national firms have not disappeared, but instead entered into ownership alliances with the larger firms, particularly in the cellphone field. So while the telecommunications sector has been reorganized at the European level, governments still sit closely by to insure that citizens will have access to phones, both landline and cellular.

The final case study is the reorganization of European football. Football began as a sport developed by British college students in the mid-nineteenth century. By the late nineteenth century the sport had begun to spread around most of Europe and the world. In Great Britain and elsewhere it became the sport of working-class men. Teams began to compete more strenuously and leagues were formed. Players, who were originally from the same city or town, began to be recruited on a wider basis. In 1904, the Federation of International Football Associations (FIFA) was formed. The first World Cup occurred in 1930. National teams were formed with the best players in each country. They would meet in a tournament that began as a round robin in divisions and ended with a winner advancing to the final rounds of the competition. In the post-war era, with the advent of television, the World Cup grew into a truly worldwide sporting event. Fans from around the world would follow the tournament, support their teams, and get to know the best players on the other teams. In this way, football was an international sport before the advent of the EU.

In each European country, football was organized into national leagues which would compete annually, allowing fans to focus on the best team in each country. These leagues were also embedded in larger European football competitions. In 1954, the Union of European Football Associations (UEFA) was founded mainly to coordinate a set of competitions across Europe between the best football clubs in each country and, on a biennial basis, a European national competition called the European Nations' Cup. Fans were the primary beneficiaries of this system. They rooted for their local teams in the national competitions. If their teams were successful, they would be invited to play in the European competitions, and every two years they would be able to see how their national teams fared against other national teams in either the European Nations' Cup or the World Cup. This system evolved and expanded in the next three decades.

In the past twenty years, two things have come about to undermine this system. First, the emergence of cable television meant that football teams could sign lucrative contracts that would produce additional revenues that would allow them to compete for players. This increased both the salaries and the movement of players within national leagues and had the effect of making the richer teams able to buy the best players and consistently outshine the poorer teams. From a fan's point of view, if one lived in a place with a small market, one's team was likely not to be successful over the mid-run because they would not be able to hold on to players they had developed. Second, in 1995, a Belgian player named Jean Marc Bosman was prevented from signing a contract with a team in France even though he was no longer under contract to his previous team. Bosman sued his team in the ECJ, claiming he had the right to work anywhere in Europe. The ECJ agreed. This created 'free agency' for football players who were now no longer tied to their national leagues; consequently the competition for the best players expanded from just the national leagues to the whole of Europe. Fans could find that their favorite players had moved, for example, from the British Premier

League to the Spanish League (as was the case with David Beckham). Cable television has also enabled fans in one country to have access to league play in other countries.

These changes increased the incentive to form a European football league. With free agency and the ability of fans to watch their favorite players wherever they played, the richest and most successful teams began to consider forming a European football league along the lines of American-style sports leagues. UEFA has strenuously resisted this effort and so far, it has not come to fruition. But the industry is now clearly more European. Cable and satellite television enable citizens in every country to watch games taking place across Europe. Individual players and teams from other countries are more well known than they were in the mid-1960s or 1970s. The largest teams have a formal association, the G-14, and they play one another annually. It is probably just a matter of time before a European league emerges.

These cases illustrate some general principles about how European markets are being created. First, the member-state governments and the EU have been involved either directly or indirectly in most market opening projects. In all the industries discussed, governments and the EU play major roles. Second, formerly nationally oriented firms have risen to the challenge of moving onto the European stage. They began by keeping a strong position in their national market while looking for new business in other countries. They frequently engaged in mergers with firms in other European societies. If mergers were not possible, they created lots of alliances and joint ventures. They have also developed a style of both competing and cooperating with other firms. Indeed, in the telecommunications and the defense industries, the alliances are so thick that it is difficult to figure out which firms are owned by which other firms. While the football teams have not engaged in mergers, the largest and richest have quickly taken up the challenge of marketing themselves on a Europe-wide basis and have formed an organization to work in their interests.

The cases are also messy. They show that processes of market integration are not straightforward. Rarely is a decision made by governments and firms, and then followed by the regional market. Instead, in each case there is a pre-existing set of firms, national concerns, and competing interests who might favor different models of organization. All three industries studied have had a back-and-forth quality of integration as firms, consumers, and governments weigh in at different historical moments with their differing interests in the 'final' structuring of these regional markets. Indeed, in all three cases there are now opposing forces in place. These forces produce tensions that reflect the potential winners and losers of a final market integration project. None of these industries, although integrated across Europe, is in a state of equilibrium.

In the past two chapters I have shown a market integration process at a high level of abstraction. In this chapter, I examine on the ground how governments, firms, consumers, workers (if you can call football players workers) have differing interests in creating a regional market for their products and services. The real processes of market integration are dynamic, ongoing, and unfinished. Yet, in the past twenty years, firms and governments have increasingly faced off against each other to balance conflicting goals and interests. Even as this conflict has gone on, they have moved more and more to the European level.

THE EUROPEAN DEFENSE INDUSTRY

It is necessary to consider the changes that have occurred in the European defense industry from a broad perspective (for recent discussions, see Mörth 2003; Mörth and Britz 2004). European governments have had different foreign policy goals reflecting their historical experiences, the size of the country, their view of threats to national sovereignty, and their current views on the appropriateness of intervention in the political affairs of other states. As a result of those policy differences, they held differing views on the role of their national militaries, the adequate sizing of those militaries, and their national defense industries.

For example, Great Britain and France have the largest militaries and in the post-war era have used them to intervene in places where they believe they have national interests at stake. On the other hand, Germany has armed forces that are restricted to fighting only for self-defense. This, of course, is a result of World War II and subsequent restrictions on Germany's rearmament. Germany and many of the smaller countries such as Denmark, Sweden, and Finland, prefer to view their role in international affairs as involved more with diplomacy and less with military intervention. These governments have been doing the bidding of the majority of the citizens of their countries who do not want their governments to pursue aggressive foreign policies and are happy with the small size of their militaries. Citizens across much of Europe favor soft diplomacy over hard military intervention.

The ability for European governments to have this choice has been greatly shaped by the relationship between the US and European countries in recent decades. Since World War II the US has maintained a large armed force with the most technologically sophisticated weapons systems in Western Europe. It has led the way in the development of new weapons systems and more recently, new ways to fight wars (Schake 2002). During the Cold War, the US provided Europe with a nuclear umbrella and a massive troop presence in Germany, and was the leader for the North Atlantic Treaty Organization (NATO) which coordinated defense for Western Europe. This American presence allowed European governments to spend less on their own defense. In turn, European governments had a partnership with the US on military issues that was usually cooperative but sometimes contentious (particularly between the French and the US).

These two contexts shaped the size of European military forces and the relationships between the suppliers of weapons systems and the national governments. During the Cold War, most of the European governments wanted to be able to protect their ability to go to war by keeping their national defense contractors in business, which caused the European defense industry to be fragmented in two important ways. There were a large number of national (or government) defense firms that were totally dependent on their governments for orders and who had limited markets outside their national government. Second, these firms tended to specialize in one weapons system or another and as a result were relatively small, so did not have the resources to engage in expensive research and development and were often behind the technological curve of the US and the Soviet Union. The end of the Cold War created a crisis for these defense firms. Governments in Europe and around the world more generally were reducing their consumption of armaments of all kinds (Schmitt 2003). In the relatively small markets of Germany, France, Great Britain, Spain, Italy, and Sweden, home to the largest of the European defense producers, the continued existence of already small national firms was clearly at risk (Engelbrekt 2002; Britz 2004).

The end of the Cold War caused European governments to reconsider their foreign policy goals more directly (Sperling and Kirchner 1997). Beginning with the Amsterdam Treaty in 1999, the European governments began to consider undertaking more cooperation on a foreign and security policy at the European level (Schmitt 2003). The exact forms of cooperation and how they might be exercised has been a contentious issue from the beginning. One lofty goal has been to try and construct a European foreign policy that would allow an EU representative to speak for all EU governments on some security issues. Success on this front has come slowly. Javier Solana was appointed High Representative of the Common Foreign and Security Policy for Europe in 1999. His ability to help forge a common European position was limited. This is because the member-state governments agreed that all joint decisions on foreign and security policies had to be undertaken by unanimous decision. The war in Iraq beginning in 2003 divided European governments and highlighted the difficulty in creating such a policy.

A second goal has been to rationalize defense procurement around Europe in order to use research and development funding more effectively and to spread the costs of new weapons systems over different member states. Here, national governments have tried to cooperate to build common weapons systems that their national forces would then use. This goal has been partially more successful mostly because it skirts the issue of consolidating armies or defense forces. Instead, it concentrates on maximizing research and development investments by pooling them and producing single weapons systems. At the firm level, it has generally prompted firms to form alliances across borders in order to bid successfully for projects (Mörth 2002; Britz 2004).

In 1993, the German and French defense ministers agreed to work towards cooperating on common defense procurement. They were joined by Great Britain and Italy in 1996 and formed the Organisation Conjointe de Coopération en Matière d'Armement (OCCAR). The purpose of OCCAR was to facilitate the joint production of defence equipment. In 2001, OCCAR became a legal entity established through joint resolutions in the main countries' parliaments. Belgium and Spain joined, and currently membership reflects 80 per cent of Europe's military expenditures (Schmitt 2003). OCCAR is currently managing seven weapons programs: the 400M transport plane, Boxer armored vehicle, Cobra radar system, FREMM frigate, FSAF surface-to-air missiles, Roland surface-to-air missiles, and the Tiger helicopter (OCCAR 2007).

The European governments have had a more complex attitude towards managing the consolidation of existing defense firms. In 1998, France, Germany, Great Britain, Italy, Sweden, and Spain signed a letter of intent, known as the LoI, that committed them to allow for the rationalization of the European defense industry. They agreed to accept cross-border mergers if the states where firms were located would agree to continue to sell armaments across Europe. They also agreed to share technical information, jointly fund research and development, and where possible share the costs of common weapons systems (LoI Agreement 1998, LoI website; Schmitt 2003). This agreement has been hard to put into practice precisely because, as mergers have been proposed, governments have had second thoughts about how far they intend to allow national weapons capacity to be under foreign ownership. In 2004, the EU agreed to create a European Defence Agency with a broad mandate. This organization provides an EU area to continue discussions about defense consolidation and interfaces with OCCAR, the LoI, and other European organizations dedicated to the same ends.

A third goal has been the construction of a European Defense force that would be able to provide military muscle for a European foreign policy. Such a force would theoretically be able to intervene quickly in a deteriorating situation in areas deemed of essential interest to European governments. The creation of this force has been fraught with difficulties: there has been much bickering about how such a force would be organized and how decisions would be undertaken to authorize its deployment. Member-state governments will need to provide a substantial increase in budgets for its formation (Schake 2002). As of January 2007, there exists a 60,000-person European defense force (at least on paper). The force exists as a virtual army made up of divisions of existing European armies. It is not clear how the agreements will work in practice until the force is deployed.

Scholars interested in these issues tend to take the attitude that concerning the reality of a common foreign and security policy, a European defense force to enforce it, and a common weapons production and procurement system, the glass is less than half full (see Merand 2003 for a review and Epstein 2004 for a recent argument about how difficult this will be). While there remain many obstacles to the implementation of such a set of policies, it is clear that there has been movement in that direction. The goal of the rest of this section is to discuss how these broader forces pushing towards defense consolidation have played out for the defense firms themselves.

The main uncertainty in the reorganization of the European defense industry has been the role of governments in feeling their way towards a method of restructuring their relationships with their weapons producers. There have been three possible models of firm consolidation of production under these clouds of uncertainty. The first was that governments could try to consolidate their national defense industries into a single national champion and thereby continue to control their ability to produce weapons systems and fight wars. The problem with this strategy was that the European national markets still remained too small to justify the level of expenditures to devise new weapons systems, even for a large diversified firm.

A second strategy was for governments to cooperate and decide that they would specialize in different weapons systems. So, all the tanks would be made by one country, the fighter planes by another, and cruise missiles by a third. The problem here was that it was difficult to see how this would happen in practice. Governments would have to decide which markets to specialize in and then agree with one another about how to do this. Since jobs, national pride, and techno-logical advancement that might have important economic spillover effects were at stake, cooperation was problematic. Moreover, firms—many of which were privately held—would have to decide to comply.

Finally, governments could pursue a market-driven solution: i.e. allow firms to decide which lines of business to be in and which other companies to buy. This had two disadvantages. Governments were ambivalent about losing control over de-fense production, and they had spent much of the past twenty years deciding what exactly they wanted to control. To release their national producers and allow them to merge with foreign firms would have meant risking the ability to procure the weapons they might need in a national emergency. Second, the problem of creating a merger movement in defense firms was compounded by the fact that the French government continued to own the core of its defense industry, making it hard for any consolidation to occur. They reduced some of their holdings in such firms, but have continued to pursue the strategies of using their shares to create national champions and add to them by the capture of firms from other countries.

In the face of all of these ambiguities, none of the models considered was totally viable and the result was a hybrid that combined features of all three. Govern-ments remained intimately involved in the consolidation of firms all along and were never totally willing to let them decide whom to partner. Firms who wanted to cooperate with one another did so mainly through the creation of joint ventures and the use of subsidiaries that were jointly owned across firms from different countries. So instead of engaging in direct mergers, two firms would jointly buy up a third and operate it as a subsidiary. When they actually bought out a firm from another society, they frequently left it intact and ran it as a separate company. While there has been cross-national consolidation into three large groups (British Aerospace, EADS, and Thales), enough of the original national firms survive as joint ventures and wholly owned subsidiaries that governments are assured that they have not disappeared. The overall effect, however, is a cross-national industry where three large firms interconnect and appear on the whole to cooperate in the allocation of the national markets. There is a single market for defense products in Europe, albeit one that keeps intact the national firms that produce separate products.

Even before the end of the Cold War there was a great deal of discussion about possible consolidation in the European defense industry. In 1988, GEC (a British-owned armaments manufacturer) and Siemens (a large, diversified German firm) tried to buy Plessy, a maker of military electronics. Alain Gomez, president of Thomson, a major French arms maker, said, 'The Plessy bid is the start of a big shake-out in European defense firms' (*Business Week*, 28 Nov. 1988: 50). At another large French firm, Matra, a senior official commented, 'This is a sign that there will be a major restructuring of the European defense industry. Everybody has to have a European strategy' (ibid.).

The Plessy deal looked like the beginning of a cross-border consolidation in the European defense industry. A set of larger players began to line up to take over firms. So, for example, during the 1980s, Daimler Benz, a German firm, began to buy up mostly German companies. These included AEG, Dornier Aerospace, Krauss-Maffei, and in 1988, Messerschmidt (*Financial Times*, 13 July 1988: 22). This gave them a presence in many defense fields including a large participation in Airbus, the commercial aircraft business. The French firm (partially government owned) Thomson-CSF began to go on a merger binge with companies from a number of different countries. They bought Link-Miles (a UK firm), a stake in Pilkington electronics (UK), and three businesses from Philips (Netherlands). The two largest British firms, GEC and British Aerospace (hereafter BAe), were also active in the merger market. But in spite of a many attempts at consolidation, the pace of mergers slowed during the 1990s.

The US Department of Defense gave the international defense industry a huge jolt when it began to encourage mergers of its principal suppliers. By 1996, the bulk of the American arms producers were absorbed into four firms: Raytheon, Lockheed Martin, Boeing, and Northup Grumman. In 1997, Lockheed and Northup were merged. This presented the European firms and governments with a real challenge. The large American firms would not only dominate the American market, but would be huge players in the global market for weapons. The only way for European firms to compete was for them to consolidate as well.

I have already alluded to the problems of pushing this consolidation forward. The creation of a Europe-wide market was in question. The Single Market provided a framework for the integration of the defense market by specifying rules by which firms could compete in one another's territory. But Article 296 of the Treaty of Rome (the Treaty that founded the EU) gave the governments total control over defense and security issues and allowed them to ignore Single Market rules. The EU could not undertake cooperation to open up the defense market without approval of all of the member states, so the attempt to write rules to that end had no legal basis (EU Commission, 3 Nov. 2003: 8). The governments vacillated between being in favor of defense consolidation and being against it, depending on what merger was proposed, which firms were involved, and who was in power. The Thatcher government, for example, was caught between its free market ideology, which would have pushed them towards supporting consolidation of the industry without regard to national origins of firms, and its desire to preserve British sovereignty by protecting national champions. The French government was in an even more complex position. It continued to own a large amount of its defense industry. In order for mergers or consolidation to occur, privately held firms would have to merge with state-owned companies, creating possibly unstable alliances. Privately owned firms were skeptical about entering into agreements with French firms as a result.

In order to overcome political concerns about mergers, firms pursued several strategies. The easiest targets were other national companies: if firms were going to enter into cross-border mergers, it was frequently by buying discrete businesses of existing firms or else small specialty firms. Not surprisingly, the most difficult mergers to pursue were those with the largest of their principal competitors from other countries. This caused most of the larger firms who wanted closer cooperation to enter into joint ventures or joint ownership of cross-border assets. It is useful to consider some of the machinations that played out and resulted in the formation of three large companies, BAe, Thales, and EADS.

In 1994, Thomson-CSF bought the defense electronics businesses of UK firm Thorn-EMI, continuing their pattern of picking up smaller firms, or parts thereof, from other countries. Some companies pursued the tactic of cooperating with partners from other countries by either merging existing operations into new subsidiaries or creating wholly new subsidiaries for specific projects. In 1996, BAe and Matra (one of the large French firms) agreed to merge their missile businesses and form a jointly owned subsidiary. In that same year, four European companies (GEC, Daimler Benz, Alenia (Italy), and Saab (Sweden)) formed a new company, Eurofighter, to build a new fighter plane for European governments. GEC and Thomson agreed to create a new company, Thomson Marconi Sonar, out of assets they both already had. GEC also had arrangements with Matra to build satellites and Siemens (Germany) to work on telecommunications.

Beginning in 1996, European governments began to overcome their reticence to allow mergers to occur. The UK joined Italy, France, and Germany to create a European Armaments Agency which would help coordinate the production of arms systems that would be bought by all European governments. In 1998, it was decided to push defense consolidation forward. The six largest producers agreed to remove official obstacles to ownership and transfers of sensitive technologies. They also directed the EU's Commission to produce documents that would lay down rules for a single market in defense goods and services.

The French government went back and forth about how it wanted the defense rationalization to proceed. On the one hand, France appeared to want to protect national firms by maintaining ownership over many of them. In 1996, for example, they convinced Serge Dassault to allow his firm to be bought out by Aerospatiale, a firm owned by the French government. They appeared to be trying to build a national champion at the time that the British and German governments were more committed to creating a smaller number of more efficient competitors. In 1998, the French government did eventually agree to begin to privatize its holdings in Thomson-CSF and Aerospatiale, but executives in BAe and Daimler-Benz were skeptical that they were serious (*Financial Times*, 6 July 1998: 3).

The *Financial Times* summed up the dilemma:

Yet while companies have itchy trigger fingers, government procurement policies across Europe have not shifted sufficiently to give the industry a clear target at which to aim.

France still seems to regard the idea of competitive procurement as a quaint Anglo-Saxon obsession; Germany says it wants more defense work to be allocated competitively, but has yet to make all the tough decisions to back that up; Britain still ponders the philosophical niceties of a perfectly competitive defense market in a manifestly political field. None of these countries has yet made the hard compromises which would make a single European defense equipment market a reality.   (22 Feb. 1996: 21)

These problems did not go away in the subsequent years. In 1996, the president of Thomson, Alain Gomez, tried to open negotiations with GEC to merge the firms. The French government did not approve of that and sacked Gomez. They began to privatize Thomson by offering the company instead to Alcatel and the Lagardere Group who owned Matra. GEC opened talks with Martin Marietta, an American firm (*Sunday Times*, 13 Apr. 1997). These talks eventually fell through and GEC began to discuss a merger with BAe (*Herald-Glasgow*, 7 July 1997). The British government decided to oppose this merger because of its anti-competitive effects. When this happened, discussions began to create the largest cross-border defense merger of all, between BAe, Aerospatiale-Dassault, and Daimler Benz who were the main partners in the Airbus consortium. The problem with this merger was that the French government had a 100 per cent stake in Aerospatiale and a 50 per cent stake in Dassault (*London Times*, 10 July 1997). BAe and Daimler Benz wanted the French government to reduce its interest while the government wanted to maintain control.

When the French Socialist government came to power in 1997, it seemed to pull away from selling off its stake in Aerospatiale and Dassault. Indeed, it appeared as if it was intent upon creating a single national champion by pushing Thomson, Aerospatiale, and Dassault into merging (*Financial Times*, 27 Sept. 1997: 2). The negotiations over how to structure the Airbus consortium bogged down. The government decided to continue its partial privatization efforts by selling large parts of Thomson to Alcatel. The French government continued to be the main obstacle to cross-border mergers.

In spite of these actions, privately held firms continued to buy parts of one another to push forward consolidation. Daimler Benz and BAe bought the defense business of Siemens in 1998 (*Wall Street Journal*, 15 Jan. 1998: 18). GEC created a joint venture with Alena (Italy) to produce radar and guided missiles (*Financial Times*, 18 Mar. 1998: 6). GKN (UK) merged its helicopter unit with Agusta (Italy) to create the world's second largest helicopter company (*Financial Times*, 6 Apr. 1998: 6). In 1998, the French government began to backtrack on privatizing defense firms. It agreed to sell some of Aerospatiale's assets to Matra, the main company of Lagardere (*Guardian*, 24 July 1998: 21). At the same time, it resumed talks to create a large European merger between Aerospatiale, BAe, and Daimler-Benz's defense business (*Financial Times*, 24 July 1998: 21).

Once again these negotiations broke down. In November, the French government seemed to insist that they wanted to keep a 'golden' share that would prevent the company from a hostile takeover. BAe and Daimler refused to grant the French government that power and decided to go ahead on their own and create a European Aerospace and Defence Company (EADC) (*Financial Times*, 8 Nov. 1998: 2). In retaliation, the French government began to discuss pushing Aerospatiale entirely into the hands of Matra. A large number of mergers were under discussion. Racal (UK) began conversations with Thomson-CSF and GEC continued discussions with Thomson as well. It appeared as if the whole industry was about to experience a wave of consolidation with or without the consent of governments, including that of France.

But the BAe and Daimler merger hit a roadblock. BAe wanted controlling interest in the new company. The German government and Daimler balked at this. Talks cooled. Then GEC decided to sell off its defense business entirely. It put its Marconi unit up for sale and BAe was immediately interested. So were Thomson and Daimler. This further cooled relations between BAe and Daimler (*London Times*, 15 Jan. 1999: 10). In the end, BAe bought Marconi.

Ironically, while it initially appeared as if the French were trying to create a national champion in a single firm, it was, in the end, the British who seemed to create a major enterprise that consisted of their two largest defense companies. But this analysis of what happened is not entirely accurate. GEC had a large number of joint ventures and subsidiaries with both French and Italian firms. BAe took over the GEC stakes in Matra-Marconi (France) as well as joint ventures with Alena (Italy) and Daimler. It is more accurate to see BAe as a British-led firm with French, Italian, and to a lesser extent German, ties.

Daimler began to consider a merger with Aerospatiale-Matra. It began to execute its vision of a European Aerospace and Defense Company by buying CASA, its Spanish partner in Airbus (*London Times*, 29 June 1999: 26). Eventually, it came together with Aerospatiale to form EADS (*Financial Times*, 24 July 2000: 2). Thomson-CSF re-entered the picture by proposing a merger with Racal, a UK electronics firm (*Financial Times*, 5 Jan. 2000: 22). It too began a series of mergers and eventually renamed itself Thales.

By 2004, three large consortiums of European defense firms emerged, EADS (made up mostly of Aerospatiale, Dassault, the assets of Daimler-Benz, and the assets of CASA, a Spanish firm)), BAe (which had bought the military assets of GEC, Marconi, Saab, and a number of other British companies), and Thales (made up of assets from Thompson, Racal (a large British firm), and bits of several Italian companies). In the media, these firms are often described as a French-British-Italian consortium (Thales), a French-British-German-Spanish consortium (EADS), and a British-Scandinavian consortium (BAe). The truth, however, is more complex. Figure 4.1 shows some of the interconnections between the three firms. BAe and EADS, for example, shared ownership of Airbus (until 2006 when BAe sold its share to EADS), the civilian airframe manufacturer, and MBDA, a joint venture that makes missiles. Thales and BAe share ownership of Thomson-Marconi, a large producer of radar and other military goods. Finally, Thales and EADS share ownership of Dassault and Thomson Dasa. The French government continues to own shares in Thales and EADS, even though over time it has wound down its holding. Indeed, the cross-ownership patterns between the three firms are very dense.

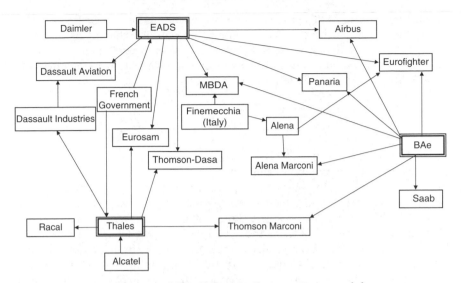

Figure 4.1. Some major ownership relationships between European defense contractors, *c*.2003.

Note: Arrows indicate direction of ownership.

Source: KMPG. 2003. *Defense Consolidation in Europe.* London: KMPG.

Observers of this situation believe that it is not stable and that further consolidation is in the offing (Ernst and Young 2002; KMPG 2003). Because so many of the arrangements are through joint ventures and fully owned subsidiaries, parent firms are not able to capitalize on scale economies or learning effects. Moreover, the three firms find themselves to be joint owners in some businesses and competitors in others. This would seem to make them less likely to be competitors and more likely to engage in market sharing. As a result of the complexities of these structures, these arrangements also make it difficult for European firms to compete for business in the US, the world's largest market for arms.

The story of the consolidation of the European defense industry is a microcosm of what has happened in industry after industry in Europe. Large national producers first merged with their counterparts; then, through a slow process of accretion, mergers occurred across borders. In the end, governments had the final say over what the ultimate shape of alliances would be. In the case of the defense sector, three large consortiums emerged, made up of pieces of firms from the main arms producers in each society. These large producers do not function strictly as competitors, but continue to operate joint ventures and subsidiaries. The end form of these firms will certainly depend on how far the member-state governments of the EU go in centralizing their weapons investments and expanding defense production because of commitments to a European defense force. While both these ideas are on the table and there is movement in the direction of centralizing production, the end state of these firms is not certain. Still, the remarkable feature of this process is that the defense industry, which one would have thought would have remained centred on national champions, has been reorganized on a European basis. What exists is a nascent military industrial complex, in spite of governments moving slowly and cautiously in their desire to maintain control over defense systems.

THE TELECOMMUNICATIONS INDUSTRY

In 1990, the telecommunications industry in Europe was even more centralized and government managed than the defense industry. In every country with the exception of Great Britain, the main telephone company was owned and controlled by the government. Of course, almost all the business was in landlines that were used for telephones. During the next fourteen years, the industry exploded in all ways: the emergence of new firms, the privatization of existing state champions, and the innovation of new products including the internet, the use of fixed lines and wireless for text and data, and the creation of wireless telephony.

It is easy now to look back and see that this process seemed obvious. But in the late 1980s, both the governments of the member states and their national phone companies were trying to resist any changes. Sandholtz (1993; 1998) argues that the eventual creation of an open telecommunications market required several stages, including persuading governments to counter the objections of their telephone companies.

There were four key elements to making these changes: the Single Market initiative being negotiated in Brussels; the general perception amongst EU governments that their high technology industries were in danger of being shut out of world markets because they were behind in product innovation; the support and lobbying of large technology industries who wanted new and growing markets and found themselves in conflict with the government-owned phone companies; and the European Commission, which was able to begin the process of market deregulation in telecommunications and, as it picked up steam, to persuade governments to agree to privatize their telephone companies.

The backdrop for both the Single Market and the eventual telecommunications deregulation was the general perception that the European economies were falling behind both the United States and Japan technologically (Sandholtz and Zysman 1989). In the US, the break up of ATT brought with it the creation of the 'Baby Bells' and the technological innovation that pushed forward new businesses. European corporations played an important role in all this by pioneering cellphone standards and figuring out how to market them to consumers, but national telephone companies resisted innovation that undermined their control over national phone networks.

European governments played a pivotal role in the creation of the telecommunications market. They decided that creating a single market for telecommunications services across Europe was a good way to spur innovation, increase competition, and give consumers more for their money. The EU wrote directives to liberalize the market. In the mid-1990s, the member-state governments agreed to privatize their telecommunications companies and open all their markets to competition. No one foresaw the internet explosion of the late 1990s and with it the move towards the convergence of telephones, television, and computers. The European governments freed up their telecommunications markets for these goods and services and gave their leading firms the opportunity to pioneer technologies.

The internet bust and the simultaneous downturn in telecommunications markets in 2001 have caused a shake-out in the industry. The survivors, not surprisingly, are mainly the heirs to the companies of the national telecommunications champions. British Telecom, France Télécom, and Deutsche Telekom continue to dominate their national fixed line markets and play a large role in wireless services. These companies also have pursued joint ventures and mergers with firms in America and the rest of the world. Several large free-standing wireless companies have emerged, notably ATT (US), Sprint (US), and Vodaphone (UK; Verizon in the US). The new European wireless companies such as Orange (now owned by France Télécom), Bouygues (owned partly by France Télécom and the Belgian government), T-Mobile (owned by Deutsche Telekom), and E-plus (owned by KPN, the Netherlands phone company) are either the offspring of the existing large telecommunications companies or joint ventures between companies in different countries.

So far, most of the smaller telecommunications companies in the smaller countries have maintained their independence. With the exception of Telia's (Sweden) link-up to Sonera (Finland) and the acquisition of Telecom Italia by Olivetti (Italy), there have been no major buyouts of former national champions. The smaller companies have partnered with larger firms from outside their countries to engage in joint ventures in wireless, cable, internet, and other services, and they have even sold off minority shares of their businesses. But generally national governments have been slow to allow their former state companies to be totally bought out by foreign firms.

The shift in the structure of the European telecommunications industry was a direct outgrowth of the political decision to create a single market for such services. While governments did not fully comprehend the nature of the technological innovations that were unleashed, they did understand that their national telephone companies were preventing innovative products from coming on to market. It turned out that building and marketing those innovations required lots of money. The incumbent phone companies had a huge advantage in having pots of money that was being reliably generated by their fixed landline businesses. They were in a position to organize the new businesses that sprung up in the 1990s around the digitalization of communications. It is not surprising that the largest of these—British Telecom, Deustche Telekom, and France Télécom—have survived and prospered. It is useful to consider these events more carefully.

During the 1980s, the main model of telecommunications was the large, state-owed telephone company. Such companies provided services and employment guarantees and acted as monopolies. They created barriers to entry by using proprietary equipment, and even when such equipment was made compatible across countries, they would not allow customers to attach equipment produced by other manufacturers to their system. They made it difficult to connect voice and data transmission across countries and they resisted new products such as cellphones and fax machines. They also controlled landlines into homes and charged high fees for long-distance phone calls.

Given that these were government-owned and -operated firms, it is interesting that, beginning with the Single Market Program of the EU in 1986, governments committed themselves to a market opening project, advancing in two waves. The first wave (1986–92) pushed the telecommunications companies to open their systems to other technology and make them more compatible with international standards. The second wave (1992–8) committed governments to privatizing their telecommunications firms, reducing their monopoly control over services, and allowing entry into national markets. Why did governments decide to open these markets up?

During the late 1970s, there was a great deal of technological change in the industry (Hills 1986; Cowhey 1990; Hart 1998). The microelectronics revolution made possible a new range of telecommunications equipment. As computers became hooked up to the telecommunications network and new forms of transmission media evolved (microwave, satellite, fiber optics), the possibility grew for new services such as data communications, data processing, database sharing and storage, electronic mail, teleconferencing, and of course, wireless phones and computers.

In Europe, producers and providers of these technologies found themselves increasingly at the mercy of national phone companies, who used their proprietary technologies to make it difficult for them to connect to the existing phone system; even if they could connect, makers of equipment were forced to conform to national standards. So even national manufacturers, who produced for only one national market, realized that if they were to survive they had to be able to sell their products across Europe. Companies interested in providing or using the new services had to deal with national phone companies who made it difficult to hook new equipment and services to existing systems, especially across national borders.

Sandholtz (1998) argues that American firms leapt ahead during the 1980s in a more open environment. Even where European phone companies tried to incorporate new markets and products, customers still had to face the problems of connectivity across countries; different standards for sending voice and data made costs high and the process difficult. Governments began to recognize that if such services were to be created and offered, national telephone companies would need to adjust. During the 1980s, the Thatcher government in Great Britain began the privatization of what became British Telecom. The government set up the firm in 1981 and sold a majority of the shares in 1984. It still protected the main business of the local landline phone service but gradually opened up the other telecommunications markets. Vodaphone and Cable & Wireless pioneered the wireless phone industry in Great Britain. In 1989, the French government allowed firms other than France Télécom to participate in all markets except for landline telephones, although it still made it somewhat difficult for them to do so. In 1989, Deutsche Telekom was separated from the postal service but maintained a monopoly over landlines as well (Sandholtz 1993). Italy, the Netherlands, Denmark, and Belgium followed suit to varying degrees.

As early as 1979, the European Commission began to propose the deregulation of the industry. Étienne Davignon, the EC Commissioner for industry, proposed a series of directives that would have deregulated most services across Europe. He was instrumental in bringing together executives of the largest telecommunications producers to form the European Business Roundtable. His rationale for this was that Europe was falling behind the high technology industries of the US and Japan, particularly in telecommunications. In 1983, Davignon drew on the European Business Roundtable and gathered a group of business and government leaders together to form a group called the Senior Officials Group for Telecommunications (SOGT). The group agreed to a set of proposals (which eventually became the official program of the EU) calling for an open EU telecommunications market where there would be common standards for connectivity and the opening of public procurement (European Commission 1983). They also agreed to introduce new networks and services and collaborate in producing new technologies. Table 4.1 provides a list of the main directives that dealt with issues opening up the telecommunications markets.

In 1987, the Commission published a Green Paper outlining its ideas for creating a standards-setting organization to insure compatibility across Europe, and calling for market liberalization (European Commission 1987). Several directives were passed to induce more cooperation between the telephone companies and equipment producers to set new standards for products. The goal was an end to public procurement policies that favored national champions and to phone company monopolies over services.

To push this along, the European Commission took unusual action. It invoked Article 90 of the Treaty of Rome to end the monopolies, and was able to put into effect directives that immediately opened up the modem, telex terminal, PABX, fax machine, mobile phone, and satellite markets to any firms. The French government tried to have the authority of the European Commission overturned and took them to the European Court of Justice. In 1991, the Court sided with the Commission. In 1991, the governments agreed to a directive that opened up all markets except for local land-based telephone markets. As part of the Single Market Program, the Commission was able to issue a directive that opened up equipment sales to competitive bidding in 1992.

The first wave of reform was met partly with a welcome and partially with resistance. The British government felt that their firms would do well in an open

TABLE 4.1. *Key European Union directives in telecommunications liberalization*

Sector	Key Directives	Year	Key Provisions	Source
Terminal equipment	Commission Directive of 16 May on competition in the markets in telecommunications terminal equipment	1988	Required member states to end restrictions on the sale of terminal equipment	(88/301/EEC) OJ L131/73, 27.05.88
Value added services; data services; services for closed user groups and corporate networks	Council Directive of 28 June on the establishment of the internal market for telecommunications services through the implementation of open network provision	1990	Established principle that incumbent operators should make capacity available on fair terms to new entrants to liberalized markets	(90/387/EEC) OJ L192/1, 24.07.90
	Commission Directive of 28 June on competition in the markets for telecommunications services	1990	Abolished the monopoly rights of incumbents over all services except public voice telephony and telex	(90/388/EEC) OJ L192/10, 24.07.90
Leased lines	Council Directive of 5 June on the application of open network provision to leased lines	1992	Required incumbents to publish terms and conditions for supplying leased lines to new entrants and established minimum set of leased line provisions throughout the EU	(92/44/EEC) OJ L165/27, 19.06.92
Alternative infrastructure	Commission Directive 95/51/EC of 18 October amending Directive 90/388/EEC with regard to the abolition of the restrictions on the use of cable television networks for the provision of already liberalized telecommunications services	1995	Required member states to lift restrictions on the use of cable TV networks for telecoms services, other than public voice telephony, by 1 January 1996	(95/51/EC) OJ L 256/49, 26.10.95
Mobile services	Commission Directive 96/2/EC of 16 January amending Directive 90/388/EEC with regard to mobile and personal communications	1996	Required member states to abolish monopoly rights over mobile services and allow operators to utilize existing alternative infrastructure	(96/2/EC) OJ L 20/59, 26.1.96

Open network provision	Directive 95/62/EC of the European Parliament and of the Council of 13 December 1995 on the application of open network provision (ONP) to voice telephony	1995	Requires fair and equal access to infrastructure under current regulatory conditions and provides for protection of consumer rights. Amendment will be needed to take account of full liberalization in 1998	(95/62/EC)
Full competition	Commission Directive 96/19/EC of 13 March amending Directive 90/388/EEC with regard to the implementation of full competition in telecommunications markets	1996	Requires member states to introduce legislation by 1 July 1996 to abolish special and exclusive rights over alternative infrastructure for telecoms services other than public switched telephony	(96/19/EC)
	Commission Directive (Directive 97/33/EC) establishes the framework for access to public telecom networks	1997	To abolish special and exclusive rights over telecoms services, including public switched voice telephony, by 1 January 1998, and to provide access to all firms	(97/33/EC)

Source: European Commission 2004.

market and did not oppose the liberalization that the Commission was pushing. The German government generally sided with the British, as their large telecommunications producers stood to gain in a deregulated market. They were concerned to preserve the national monopoly over line-based phone systems but were willing to open other markets. The French, Spanish, and Italian governments resisted liberalization the most and tried to preserve as much of the privilege of their local phone companies as possible.

By the 1990s, many of the technological breakthroughs began to create huge new market opportunities. The member-state governments realized that continued support of their national telecommunications companies was a rearguard action to defend the past. During the mid-1990s, they agreed to an even more ambitious market opening project—to privatize their national champions. They also agreed to allow firms to enter into joint ventures and alliances in order to exploit the new technologies. These changes were embedded in a series of directives that were to take effect on 1 January 1998.

Table 4.2 shows some key events in the process of privatization of national champions. Many of the firms remain at least partly owned by their governments, suggesting the governments still retain an interest in their success. This has meant that they are unlikely takeover targets unless government officials agree to sell their share. Initially the national companies used their monopolies over landlines to generate cash flow to expand into new markets. There has only been one merger of any consequence that combined former national champions, that between the Swedish and Finnish companies. The Italian government decided not to sell Telecom Italia to Deutsche Telekom and instead keep it within their borders by selling it to Olivetti. There have been attempts to sell off some of other companies in the smaller states, such as Austria (which sold a share of its state-owned company to Telecom Italia), Portugal, Spain, and the Netherlands, but so far governments have balked at losing control of them.

While much of the structure of the national champions has been preserved, there has been a huge growth in the number of companies and players in the market for wireless phones and other services. Many of these new entrants are spin-offs or partially owned subsidiaries of the former national champions. Table 4.3 shows some of the main subsidiaries of the largest firms. It can be seen that many of the subsidiaries are jointly held by more than one firm. British Telecom, Deutsche Telekom, Telia (Sweden), and France Télécom have been the most successful of the former national champions, suggesting that their national governments were correct in supporting deregulation. But the new market entrants from America and around Europe have been able to form alliances with the smaller firms in the other member states as well.

Entry into other European markets is mostly achieved at the national level, by means either of setting up a subsidiary in each country or else partnering with local firms. There are three layers of these developments that are worth describing. The new subsidiaries are mainly organized on the national market level. First, new entrants have emerged in the wireless, internet, and cable businesses. In

TABLE 4.2. *The state of liberalization in European Union telecommunications services markets, 1991–2001*

EU Country	Date of effective liberalization	National operator (former PTT)	Date and method of privatization of national operator
Austria	1998	Post & Telekom Austria	75% state owned, 25% owned by Telecom Italia
Belgium	1998	Belgacom	1995: sale of strategic stake
Denmark	1996/97	Tele Danmark	1994: international offering. State retains 51%
Ireland	Dec. 1998	Telecom Eireann	1996: sale of strategic stake
Finland	1994	Telecom Finland	Government sold 80% in 1990s, sold to Telia, 2003
France	1998	France Télécom	1997: international offering. State retains 80%; 2003, state share 55%
Germany	1998	Deutsche Telekom	1996: public offering. State retains 74%, 2003; state share in 2004
Greece	2001	OTE	1996, 1997: 20% of equity sold on Athens Stock Exchange over two years
Italy	1998	Telecom Italia	1997: privatization completed through second offering; sold to Olivetti
Luxembourg	1998 (July)	P&T Luxembourg	100% state owned
Netherlands	1998	KPN	1994, 1995: public offerings
Portugal	2000	Telecom Portugal	1995, 1996, 1997: public offerings. State retains 25%
Spain	Dec. 1998	Telefonica	Privately owned. State's remaining 20% equity sold in 1997
Sweden	1991	Telia	71% state owned in 2004
UK	1991	BT	1984–93: fully privatized over three international public offerings

Source: Standard and Poor's company reports.

Europe, firms such as Cable & Wireless, Vodaphone, and Viag have prospered. Second, many of the phone companies have opened up wholly owned subsidiaries in other countries. So, for example, Telia (the Swedish company) owned ventures in Denmark, Finland, and Eastern Europe. There has been a proliferation of joint ventures between existing national phone companies and foreign companies, particularly in producing wireless companies. For example, Wind in Italy was owned by Deutsche Telekom and France Télécom. Third, these ventures often include firms from outside the telecommunications industry, such as banks or manufacturers. An example is the Italian company Albacom which was owned by British Telecom and two local partners, BNL (a bank) and ENI (a government-owned manufacturing conglomerate).This has created a plethora of new companies that produce services within and across national boundaries.

TABLE 4.3. *Shareholdings of main European telecommunications companies, c.2003*

Deutsche Telekom (Germany: land, wireless, internet)	TMobil (wireless; US, France, Great Britain, Germany) Maxnmobil (wireless; Austria) Enel (wireless; Italy) Wind (wireless; Italy) Federa (wireless; Netherlands) Eurobell (cable; Great Britain)
France Télécom (France: land, wireless, internet)	Orange (wireless; Belgium, Great Britain, US, Switzerland, Germany, Netherlands, France) Mobistar (wireless; Belgium) Panafon (wireless; Greece) Wind (wireless; Italy) Airtel (land, wireless; Spain) Sonofon (land; Denmark) TeleDenmark (land; Denmark)
British Telecom (UK: land, wireless, internet)	9 Com (wireless; France) Viag (wireless; Germany) Albacom (wireless; Italy) Telfort (wireless; Netherlands) Telenordia (wireless; Norway, Sweden) Europolitan (fixed lines; Sweden) Airtel (land, wireless; Spain)
Vodaphone (UK: wireless, internet)	Verizon (wireless; US) Belgacom (wireless; Belgium) Mannesman (wireless; Germany) 9 Com (wireless; Italy) Libertel (wireless; Netherlands) Panafon (wireless; Greece) E-Plus (land, wireless; Germany) Omnitel (wireless; Italy) Sonofon (land; Denmark)
Telia (Sweden: land, wireless, internet)	Sonofon (wireless; Denmark) Telia Denmark (wireless; Denmark) Telia (wireless; Norway) Sonera (land, wireless; Finland) Telecom Eireann (land; Ireland)
Telecom Italia (Italy: land, wireless, internet)	Telekom Austria (land, wireless; Austria) Telestet (wireless; Greece) Retevision (land, wireless; Spain)
KPN (Netherlands: land, wireless, internet)	E-Plus (wireless; Germany) Base (wireless; Belgium) Hutchison3G (wireless; UK)

Source: Standard and Poor's company reports.

In 2004, the EU passed a set of directives (European Commission 2004) that tried to provide a combined set of rules to govern telecommunications markets, mergers, market entry, and standardization of equipment. These directives are the framework for building industry alliances. It now appears as if the wireless market has matured in Europe, 87 per cent of possible consumers having purchased phones. There remains the possibility for growth in internet and cable services. But the industry is rapidly maturing. It remains to be seen if this complex structure of firms will survive a slowing market. As long as national governments hold shares in their telephone companies, any consolidation is unlikely to involve the biggest players. More probable is the consolidation of subsidiaries or firms that are privately owned.

In many ways, the evolution of the telecommunications market mirrors the process of the evolution of the defense industry. Both industries moved from being highly regulated, with nationally owned and closed national markets, to having open markets that allowed participation of firms from other countries. The result has been to shift the players around, create larger firms, and complicate industry structure by producing a plethora of joint ventures and subsidiaries that operate across borders. While there has been some privatization of the industry, several of the largest players, including France Télécom and Deustche Telekom, remain partly government owned. National firms still exist and governments have been reluctant, with a few exceptions, to let their national telecommunications companies be merged with larger competitors. Still, the European telecommunications industry has been reorganized on a European basis. In the fastest growing market, wireless telephony, European firms have partnered to produce a Europe-wide industry.

EUROPEAN FOOTBALL

European football is undergoing a process of being organized on a European level in a similar way to the telecommunications and defense industries. The game of football has been around since the mid-nineteenth century, and was played internationally by the turn of the twentieth century. It is useful to have some history of the sport in order to understand how it has changed in Europe in the past twenty years.

Football was invented by the British in the middle of the nineteenth century. In 1863, the Football Association was formed and established the rules of the game. The first tournament of the Association took place in 1872 (Butler 1991). The game started out as an upper-class game played by college students at Oxford and Cambridge, but soon spread across English society, and was eventually taken up most vigorously by working-class men (Russell 1997). English clubs were attached to cities; they drew on local talent, and operated to create rivalry between communities (ibid.).

The game spread around the world, often following in the tracks of the British Empire and the Industrial Revolution. Missiroli (2002) has called football 'an export product—one can provocatively say—the most successful and durable one of the British empire.' One direct way in which the sport was spread was by employees of British companies who would introduce the sport locally by forming clubs. Most countries organized football in the same way that the British did. Local clubs would spring up, they would begin to compete with clubs from their neighboring towns, and eventually form leagues. Football in other countries was a sport adopted by working-class men (ibid.).

The current tendency toward the growing European organization of football has its roots in the international history of the game. While there have been many leagues organized on a national basis, which continue to capture the attention of many fans, football has had an international presence for much of the twentieth century. In 1904, the Federation of International Football Associations (FIFA) was formed in Paris (FIFA 2004, website). The first two international competitions occurred at the Olympic games in London in 1908 and Stockholm in 1912. National teams were fielded that represented the best players in each country. After World War I, the game spread into Eastern Europe and Latin America. European teams would go to Latin America to tour, thus introducing the game there. The first FIFA World Cup was held in Uruguay in 1930. It was organized by Jules Rimet, FIFA president at the time. Thirteen nations took part: six from South America, five from Europe and two from North America. Uruguay beat Argentina to become the first nation to win the trophy. These tournaments are now held every four years.

The modern era of football began in 1954, when television coverage of the World Cup began (Missiroli 2002). That same year, on 15 June 1954, the Union of European Football Associations (UEFA) was formed, making it the first regional association for football. The main purpose of UEFA was to coordinate the activities of Europe's various teams and leagues and to create a set of tournaments on a European scale. UEFA was set up with FIFA's blessing; they agreed that there was a need for a separate governing body devoted exclusively to European football given the amount of interest in football across Europe. UEFA and FIFA have since worked closely together. There were twenty-five national associations at the formation of UEFA and now, after the political changes in Eastern Europe, there are fifty-two.

There are thirteen separate competitions that are overseen by UEFA. The three most financially lucrative are the Champions League, the European Cup, and the UEFA cup (UEFA 2004, website). The UEFA Champions League consists of leading clubs from each country who are invited to participate in a tournament. The original version of the Champions League, then called the European Cup, was launched in March 1955, a year after UEFA was formed. From the beginning, the event was put together to attract the clubs which would have the most fan appeal. The tournament was organized by the French sports daily *L'Équipe* with the help of Jacques Ferran, the UEFA president. The tournament changed format in the 1992–3 season and increased the number of teams who participated. It changed its name from the European Cup to the Champions League. The UEFA Champions League created a round robin tournament that divided teams into divisions. The winners of each of the divisions of the tournament would advance to a final round. The final round was then a single elimination tournament. The competition has grown from eight to thirty-two teams.

The second competition sponsored by UEFA is the UEFA Cup, which began in the 1971/2 season, and is a tournament where teams who fail to make the Champions League are eligible to play. It is open to teams finishing in leading positions behind the champions in their domestic leagues as well as the winners of various other leagues and tournaments. In addition, the sixteen clubs eliminated from the UEFA Champions League in the third qualifying round switch to the UEFA Cup at the first-round stage, while the eight third-placed clubs at the end of the UEFA Champions League group stage also revert to the UEFA Cup.

The third competition, the current version of the UEFA European Nations Cup, is a tournament that consists of national teams from each country. The clubs loan their best players to the national teams to play in this tournament. The tournament is played every four years and the finals took place for the first time in 1960. It is timed to alternate with the FIFA World Cup at two-year intervals. In 1968, the European Nations Cup was renamed the European Football Championship. In 1977, the number of participants in the European Championship final round doubled to eight teams for the 1980 finals in Italy, and doubled again to sixteen in 1996 for the final round in England.

UEFA and FIFA exist to coordinate European and international tournaments. But the bedrock of the game, until twenty years ago, remained national. Most of the large European countries had multiple leagues that were sometimes competitors with each other, but frequently arrayed themselves as major and minor leagues. So, for example, in England there is a premier league made up of the largest and most successful teams and three lower divisions. The lower division teams remain more local and connected to place while the premier league teams recruit players from all over the world.

There is one other feature of European football that distinguishes the way that national leagues function and the various international competitions work. Teams switch leagues on the basis of their current performance. If they improve in a particular year, they can move up a league. If they have disappointing seasons, they can be moved down. This puts pressure on upper division teams to try and lock in their position by capturing more revenues and players. It also means that teams with a new infusion of cash can make a move up the ranks.

The sport has also become more organized at the European level. Lucrative television contracts have allowed some of the clubs to bid for the best players from all over the world. This makes them highly competitive both in their national league and in international competition. This, in turn, allows them to sell tickets and merchandise across Europe. As a result, these clubs have come to see that the future of their revenues is no longer national but European. They have increasingly been interested in creating a European super league that will play and broadcast games all over Europe. One of the motivations for this is that involvement in the Champions League depends on a club's current season's record. If a team has a bad year it may not qualify for the league and thereby misses out on a large percentage of its revenue. The largest clubs have been interested in preserving their revenue flow by insuring their participation in the Champions League.

While the attempt at a super league has so far failed and clubs have continued to play in their national leagues, they have also expanded their participation in the Champion's League, where they play their peers across Europe. A concentration of financial resources in the largest teams has put financial pressure on more locally oriented and less financially endowed clubs. Consequently many are in financial trouble. They have come to see their major role as finding and training talent which they subsequently trade to richer clubs. This process of creating a small core of successful teams and a large periphery of less well-off clubs becomes reinforced by the next round of television contracts which helps the rich get richer.

In 1995, the European Union began to get directly involved in European football. The European Court of Justice began this process when they helped create 'free agency' for European football players. Their decision in the Bosman case (European Court of Justice 1996) dramatically increased the geographic mobility of players (Jeanrenaud and Kesenne 1999; Caigner and Gardiner 2000). Teams are no longer restricted in how many foreign players they can employ. Players whose contracts have ended are no longer subject to transfer fees (money paid by a club for the rights to sign a player from another club). This decision has favored the largest and most successful football clubs who have had the revenue streams to buy the best players. It has also increased the incentives of lesser teams to sell the contracts of players before they run out in order to get something in return. After the Bosman decision, the European Commission became interested in the regulation of television contracts and the possibility for clubs and leagues to collude to create uncompetitive conditions in general. This has resulted in a series of negotiations between UEFA and the EU.

Football remains both national and international and the creation of a dominant European level league has so far not occurred. In 1999, there was an attempt to create a European football league. This attempt failed and left in place a compromise between the largest teams and UEFA, the Europe-wide federation that claims to regulate football. Teams still play in their national leagues even as they participate in the Champions League. In 2000, fourteen of the largest and most successful clubs formed a group called G-14 to represent their collective interests in Brussels and with UEFA and FIFA. This group has now expanded to representatives of eighteen teams. Figure 4.2 presents a list of these teams and their logos. Their ostensible goal of the organization is to balance off the needs of the clubs with the need to maintain national and European competitions (G-14 2004, website). UEFA has been somewhat hostile

Figure 4.2. List of G-14 football teams and their logos.
Source: G-14 website.

to the G-14 because it represents an attempt to create something outside the jurisdiction of the UEFA. The structure of European football is in flux. There is already a hierarchy of countries, leagues, and teams. But the final form of this structure is still a work in progress.

It is useful to consider the process over the past fifteen years in more detail. There is an ongoing tension between the national teams and their leagues and the pressure of the larger teams to be more European. This tension has been exacerbated mainly by the advent of cable and pay-TV. These systems required content and sport was an obvious choice for television. Cable and pay-TV systems would sign up rights for national games and international tournaments, which expanded the business dramatically as the possibility for making money increased exponentially.

Great Britain was the first country to experience these pressures directly. There were two major organizations that coordinated football: the Football League and the Football Association (FA). The Football League ran the game in the 1980s in a collectivist fashion. They sold television rights on behalf of the whole League and distributed revenue fairly equally among its members. But with the growth in commercial television increasing the competition for live broadcasting rights for top football matches, the big clubs became increasingly aware that a severing of this arrangement would allow them to take in a much bigger proportion of the revenue for themselves (Goldstein 2000).

From 1985 onwards, these major clubs began to press for a change. On a number of occasions they threatened to form a break-away league, which was only stopped by an increased share of TV revenue going to the top teams (Conn 1997; Russell 1997). In the late 1980s, the Football League and the FA began to discuss ways to reorganize the game, but while the Football League suggested a merger between themselves and the FA in order to stand united against the threat of a break-away league (Football League 1990; Tomlinson 1991), the FA took a rather different line, supporting a breakaway super league (Football Association 1991). In doing so, according to Conn (1997: 17) the FA was 'betraying its historic role as regulator, controller of commercialism for the wider good of football'.

At the start of the 1992/3 football season, the independent FA Premier League was created. The change was a watershed in English football and, crucially, it coincided with a similarly significant change in the British broadcasting industry. Two satellite television companies emerged: British Satellite Broadcasting (BSB) and Sky Broadcasting. The two companies merged (BSkyB), but continued to lose money. It was clear that they needed a product to persuade consumers to invest in both satellite equipment and the monthly subscription charges the service commanded. Premier League football became that product. Purchasing exclusive rights for the live broadcast of Premier League matches gave BSkyB the lever it needed in the marketplace, and the number of BSkyB subscriptions increased from under 2 million in 1993 to over 6 million in 1998. While this growth was not entirely due to football, the overwhelming majority of BSkyB subscribers take the company's sports channels (Murroni and Irvine 1998). But the rights to broadcast football came at a huge price for the broadcaster. A bidding war with ITV meant they had to pay $460 million to secure rights for the first five years of the Premier League, a huge increase on the $80 million over four years that ITV had previously paid for exclusive rights to the whole of the old Football League (Conn 1997; Russell 1997). In 1996, BSkyB extended this deal for a further four years, this time paying a $1 billion fee (Lee

TABLE 4.4. *Wages and revenues in the FA Premier
League* (£ millions)

Year	Wages	Revenues	Wages (%)
1995/6	163	346	47
1996/7	218	464	47
1997/8	305	582	52
1998/9	391	670	58
1999/2000	471	772	63

Source: Deloitte and Touche (2001: 16).

1997) and in 2000 they signed a $1.6 billion agreement for just three years of live rights (Deloitte and Touche 2001).

The Premier League began, therefore, with a huge influx of new money from satellite television. The increased revenue was mostly used to purchase the contracts of players. Competition for the top players increased, and both transfer fees and players' salaries rose as clubs raised their bidding in the transfer war. Indeed, the new cash set in chain a spiral of inflation, as each increase in the standard transfer fee or salary level sparked further increases from clubs seeking to gain competitive advantage over their rivals. Table 4.4 shows how both revenues and wages increased from 1995 until 2000. Even as revenues doubled, salaries almost tripled and came increasingly to consume budgets.

This chain of events resulted in a search for additional sources of finance. Despite the massive increase in TV revenues, clubs aggressively pursued four new avenues. First, they introduced huge increases in ticket prices. At Chelsea, for example, the average ticket price has risen from £7 in 1990 to over £30 in 1996 (see Conn 1997, for further examples). Such increases were largely justified on the grounds that teams were better as top foreign players were signed. Teams also claimed to have improved their stadiums (R. Taylor 1992). Second, clubs began to market merchandise related to their teams more aggressively, with many clubs expanding their stores. Third, teams actively sought out advertising sponsors for a whole range of venues and products, from stadiums to uniforms (see Deloitte and Touche 2001). Finally, a number of clubs began to float shares on the stock market in order to raise capital for investment in facilities and players (Lee 1997; Hoehn and Szymanski 1999).

In the 1990s, this process was being repeated in the main countries of Europe. In Italy, Spain, Germany, and France, the largest teams used cable and satellite TV to raise their revenues, then went out to purchase the contracts of the best players. Consequently teams were not only in competition with other national clubs, but also with clubs across Western Europe. The cable TV stations began to encourage the largest clubs to think about forming a European super league analogous to the American professional sports leagues (Kuypers and Szymanski 1999). The change in the rules in the European Champions League in 1992/3 was a gesture explicitly oriented toward heading off this possibility.

The EU involvement in football really begins with the Bosman case (Belgian FA *v.* Bosman ER (EC) 97 1996). A Belgian player, Jean Marc Bosman, played for a Belgium team called RFC Liège (Simmons 1997). At the end of his contract, he wanted to sign a new one with a French team, Dunkerque. RFC Liège claimed that he could not sign the contract unless they were compensated with a transfer fee, which Dunkerque refused to pay. Bosman sued RFC Liège under European law and claimed he possessed the right to 'freedom of movement' within the European Union under Article 48 of the Treaty of Rome. He argued that the transfer fee was illegal because he was already out of a contract. The European Court of Justice ruled in his favor; their ruling established two principles. First, players who were no longer under contract did not have to have transfer fees paid from their new team to their old; players who remained under contract with a team, however, could have transfer fees paid if they went to work for another team. Second, many leagues and teams had rules about the number of foreign players they could sign. The European Court of Justice ruled that this too was illegal because it prevented the free movement of labor, which opened up the cross-border market for players to take new contracts with the highest bidders for their services.

This was just the beginning of EU involvement. The European Commission became interested in football and decided that it was an economic activity and therefore needed to comply with European Union law, particularly as it pertained to competition policy and the free movement of labor. UEFA immediately tried to intervene in the Bosman case in order to preserve the right of teams to obtain some payment for players who left their service. Their claim was that football was different than other industries. In football, players often go through many years of training at the expense of smaller clubs. UEFA (and FIFA) argued that it was unfair for smaller clubs to bear the costs of development of players and then be unable to obtain compensation when they were out of contract and left for a larger club. Much of the scholarly literature adopts a similar perspective (Simmons 1997; Ericson 2000).

This argument did not stop the EU from continuing to act. In 2000, the Commission announced that it wanted to end transfer fees for players completely. The rationale was that football players were employees. Since any employee can leave a job in most industries with little penalty, football players ought to be treated in the same way. Both FIFA and UEFA put enormous pressures on the member-state governments to take up these issues. A clause was inserted in the Amsterdam Treaty in 1999 to argue that sport was a special case. A similar paragraph appears in the European Constitution. In 2001, a compromise between UEFA, FIFA, and the EU was reached (details are available at <www.FIFA.com>). It was agreed that clubs would be compensated with transfer fees for players under the age of 23, even those who were no longer under contract, in order to pay back the costs of training. It also set into place complex rules regarding long-term contracts and free agency that prevented players from unilaterally leaving existing contracts without notice. It remains to be seen if these rules will hold up under challenge at the European Court of Justice.

In September 1998, Media Partners supported by the audiovisual magnates Rupert Murdoch, Silvio Berlusconi, and Leo Kirch, proposed a project for a European Super League financed by TV rights and gathering the thirty-six richest clubs. Eighteen of these clubs would be selected on the basis of their performance over the previous ten years (notably Liverpool, Manchester United, Arsenal, Ajax Amsterdam, Borussia Dortmund, Bayern Munich, Paris St Germain, Olympic de Marseille, Inter Milan, Milan AC, Juventus of Turin, Real Madrid, FC Barcelona, Benfica of Lisbon, Panathinaikos Athens, Galatasaray Istanbul, clubs that are all in the G-14). The Super League was argued to be able to generate revenue more than thirty times that of the Champions League.

The response of UEFA was to forbid the selection for national teams in the European Cup of any players involved in the Super League. The European Commissioner for competition joined in by expressing concerns over the redistribution of TV rights. Eventually, in October 1998 UEFA proposed its own Super League project with thirty-two clubs. The major clubs eventually accepted this project (less profitable than that of Media Partners but more so than the Champions League), on the condition that UEFA gave them a say in the format of the European Cup, arrangements for TV rights, and the marketing of the competitions.

However, this has not laid the issue to rest. The G-14 continues to fight FIFA and UEFA. Football players are expected to play in exhibitions and with their national teams for no compensation to their regular employers. Recently a Belgian team, Royal Sporting Charleroi, initiated proceedings against FIFA for compensation for a player injured in such a match. The case has now been referred to the European Court of Justice. The G-14 has backed the team and there is another case wending its way towards the EU, involving G-14 member Olympique Lyon. The G-14 wants FIFA to set up an insurance pool to cover the cost of injuries to players in tournaments apart from regular league play. The G-14 is seeking 680 million Euros in damages from FIFA for the past ten years (Hobson and Edwards 2007).

Charleroi and G-14 are seeking guidance from the European Court of Justice on the question:

Do the FIFA rules which oblige clubs to release players under contract to national federations without payment to play in matches, as well as the unilateral and restrictive fixing of the international calendar of matches, constitute illegal restrictions of competition, or abuses of a dominant position, or obstacles to the exercise of fundamental freedoms conferred by the EU Treaty, which are thus contrary to Articles 81 and 82 of the Treaty, or to any provision of community law, in particular Articles 39 and 49 of the Treaty?   (Hobson and Edwards 2007)

Hobson and Edwards interpret the issues at stake as fundamentally about the relationships between football clubs and the federations that govern them. They argue that the G-14 is seeking out any edge it can in increasing the power of the clubs *vis-à-vis* the national and international federations. If the ECJ rules for the teams, then the whole relationship between the federations and the teams will be up for grabs. In March 2007, the G-14 leaked a document to *The Guardian*

(14 Mar. 2007) that proposed that members of the G-14 be allowed to participate in the European Cup each year no matter what their records were. The G-14 claimed that this was just a draft report. They have put out a ten-point plan that they say is oriented toward helping not just the biggest teams gain more control over the various federations, but all teams (see <www.g-14.com>).

There are deeper financial issues that remain unresolved. The smaller and financially weaker clubs over time will lose money and players and eventually be forced out of business. The national character of the sport has been undermined with free agency and the movement of foreign players onto teams. Whether these are good or bad things depends on how fans react. Football fans are quite passionate about their national teams, but such passion may die down if their teams are doomed by not having a chance to win regularly or enter the largest and most prestigious tournaments. If fans like the bigger teams with the best players from no matter where, then the efforts of FIFA and UEFA to protect smaller teams is destined to fail.

The current structure, however, also presents problems for the largest and richest teams. If they continue to obtain all the good players, fans will lose interest in contests where the strong continually win. No one will pay to see games where the better teams easily surpass the worse teams. Revenues would drop and even the biggest teams would suffer. Even worse, if the biggest and richest teams continue to compete against each other for players, their costs will continue to soar. It will become increasingly difficult to make enough revenue to cover those costs. It also remains to be seen whether or not fans in a particular country will in the long run support or be interested in teams in other countries.

Ironically, the best thing for the biggest and richest teams is for there to be some way to attain parity with each other in the purchase of the services of the best players and to maintain some competitive equilibrium. American sports leagues had these same problems at their formation before 1940. They have instituted minor and major leagues to divide the risk and reward of player development. They have solved their problems by getting exemption from antitrust laws and building draft systems that help the weak recruit new talent, and using salary caps to prevent any one team from stockpiling all the best talent.

European football is, in some sense, just beginning this process of consolidation. The pressures presented by Europe-wide play will encourage the debate over the solution. The question is whether the evolution of professional sport should follow the American pattern or try to find some other solution to the problems just discussed (Primault and Rouger 1997; Musso 1998; Hoehn and Syzmanski 1999). The end result of the Bosman case has been to contribute to the creation of a free market for the best players. This has led to the biggest and richest clubs buying the contracts of players from poorer and smaller clubs, and to the internationalization of the sport. *The Economist* (29 May 2003) reports that, on Tuesday and Wednesday evenings, most of the European male population is now watching the Champions League where the best players from all over Europe play for clubs that recruit national players from all around the world. European football has historically been a sport with both local and national focus.

Its future depends on how the local and national issues become intertwined with the issues of competition and a European basis.

CONCLUSION

European industries are increasingly becoming more organized at a European level. This means that firms have shifted their attentions from controlling national markets to becoming increasingly focused on their competitors from other countries. The three case studies presented here, defense, telecommunications, and football, reveal how nationally oriented firms were pushed toward becoming Europeanized as they perceived new challenges and opportunities. In the case of telecommunications and defense, governments encouraged their firms to reorganize on a European basis. It is useful to draw some general conclusions from these case studies.

First, European governments proved quite willing to push their former national champions to become larger players who would try and sell products across Europe, given shifts in technology and opportunities for new business. While there was some resistance on the part of governments at different points in the process, the French, British, and Germans in general saw mainly advantage in Europeanizing. The French government, for example, was intent on maintaining some control over its defense firms, but in the end, sold majority stakes of its industry into partnerships and joint ventures. The French and German governments sold off majority stakes in their telecommunications companies and urged them to become world-class competitors. The British government privatized both its defense and telecommunications industry early on. However, it prevented Manchester United, the most famous and richest British football company, from becoming owned by Rupert Murdoch's BSkyB, an Australian cable satellite TV company. In spite of these attempts by governments to maintain some control over these industries, they were by and large content to see the markets for these firms grow from national to European.

Creating European wide markets has mostly meant the preservation of the identities of national firms. While there were extensive mergers and the creation of joint ventures across national borders, national firm identities were preserved. So the three largest telecommunications companies before deregulation became European players by starting new companies as joint ventures and entering into partnerships across Europe with smaller phone companies. One can still recognize British Telecom, France Télécom, and Deutsche Telekom. The largest defense contractors maintained their identities and ownership even as they entered in consortium to produce arms across Europe. My map of ownership patterns in the defense industries (Fig. 4.1) shows clearly how the consortium firms that emerged remain ventures jointly owned by larger national corporate entities. In spite of increased cooperation between the largest and richest football teams across Europe, the ownership of these teams remains resolutely national (although rich tycoons from America and Russia have recently bought football teams in Great Britain). So far, no company has managed to buy out the largest teams across national borders. While they changed market orientation, they did so by finding partners in other countries or, if they bought those partners out, they maintained the identity of the national partner.

Finally, the EU has played a part in all these market changes. The push towards consolidation of the defense market was sparked by a similar consolidation in the US in the face of the end of the Cold War. But European governments also began to create a common foreign and security policy and recognized the need to coordinate arms production in order to foster both their industries and that effort. The EU became a place where these discussions took place. The deregulation of the telecommunications industry was given a great impetus by discussions in Brussels. Here again, technological change and challenges by American firms were part of the stimulus to act. But the common decisions required to open the telecommunications market were undertaken in a series of reforms in Brussels. European football was already well organized on a European and world level by the 1960s, but during the 1990s it was being transformed by the advent of cable and pay-TV. The European Court of Justice provided an important impetus to its advance by enforcing the rule that football players had freedom of contract and movement. Everyone agrees that whatever solution to European football's problems is crafted, it will occur in Brussels. The Commission recently agreed to a division of television rights, for example (EU 2003). The G-14, representative of the largest clubs, has set up shop in Brussels in recognition that this is how things will be.

The growth of European industries has a distinct flavor. National firms remain the main players, while the focus of competition and cooperation becomes transnational. European firms favor joint ownership ventures. When they buy out firms from other countries, they maintain the identity of those national firms. Collective governance of industries has also shifted focus from national regulators to the EU level. The ECJ and the European Commission play an important role in adjudicating and acting to solve joint governance problems. By and large, the member-state governments have been part of this effort as well.

The three case studies were chosen because they represent cases where European firms became organized on a European basis. They show clearly the dynamics by which previously nationally oriented firms turned toward a Europe-wide market as opportunities emerged, governments changed policy, and the EU intervened to create new collective governance. These processes have been messy and are not yet complete, but they demonstrate how organizing on a European wide basis provides for growth in firm size, revenues, and markets.

5

Who Are the Europeans?

INTRODUCTION

The European Union has produced a remarkable set of agreements to guide the political interactions of countries across Europe in the past forty-five years. These agreements have produced collective rules governing market transactions of all varieties, created a single currency, established a rule of law that includes a European court, and promoted increased interactions for people who live within the boundaries of Europe. Trade has increased dramatically; European corporations have greatly expanded their investments, production, sales, and employment; markets that were formerly fragmented across national lines have become regional; the largest corporations have redeployed their activities to profit from market opening projects. As firms have taken advantage of these opportunities, they have put more pressure on their governments, both in Brussels and at home, to continue such initiatives. Politicians have understood that the increased integration of the economy has worked to produce more trade, new jobs, and economic growth. This has created a kind of virtuous circle whereby more and more markets across Europe have become reorganized on a European basis.

The missing piece of this puzzle is how these changes have affected the lives of people who live in Europe beyond the mere fact that more goods and services are available. My central argument in this chapter and the next is that patterns of social interactions have changed, and now people from different societies are far more likely to interact with their counterparts for business and play. People who work for corporations, governments, and educational institutions (primary, secondary, and university levels) have been given increasing opportunities to get to know and socialize with people in other countries. They have formed organizations, held meetings, and acted collectively to create new social fields.

In Chs. 5 and 6 I document how the increase in social interaction in many fields has created denser relationships between people across countries. Here I consider how the opportunity to interact with people from different countries is differentially distributed across social classes. It is the educated, professionals, managers, and other white-collar workers who have the opportunity to travel, speak second languages, and interact with people like themselves in different countries. I show that these interactions have affected their national collective identities. Such people are more likely to call themselves Europeans than the elderly, the less educated, and blue-collar workers who have not had such opportunities.

In this way, I link together how the process of European political and economic integration has played out for the citizens of Europe. Those citizens who have been directly involved in this integration have changed in how they look at themselves and their neighbors. Those who have not, do not see their fate as shared with people from around Europe. Instead, they still view the nation and their own state as the appropriate unit to be defended against external forces, whether they are political enemies or forces of neoliberal globalization. They are also more likely to see the EU, not as an engine of positive social change, but instead as a distant place where business interests get served and the nation get undermined.

In order to make this argument coherently, it is necessary to put a set of theoretical building blocks together. There are a number of large issues at stake here. The first issue to consider is what is known about how people manage their identities in general. Then, it is important to take up the issue of national identity and nationalism as it relates to the issue of collective identity formation. The literature on national collective identities views nationalism as a kind of cultural story that unites disparate social groups. The mechanisms that produce this story are varied, and include: increased social interactions amongst groups in institutions such as the economy, the army, and schools (Deutsch 1966); shared communication through media and forms of culture (ibid.), state political elites using these societal institutions to produce or impose a national consensus (Rokkan 1973; Tilly 1975; Gellner 1983), and the resolution of the conflict between social groups that either imposes one view of collective identity on everyone or discovers a way to bring together a common identity under a political compromise between groups (Brubaker 1992; Breuilly 1994).

When applying the model of national identity formation to the possibility of the emergence of a European identity, one has already bought into the notion that the endpoint of European economic integration is to produce a nation-state. This idea is currently at dispute in Europe, among not only political elites but also the citizens of Europe. The opponents of a European state argue that the EU is not a proto-state but instead an intergovernmental organization focused only on issues of joint benefit to nation-states. They also argue that for a European nation-state to come into existence there would have to be Europeans, i.e. citizens of Europe, who would want this transition to occur.

But, the literature on the EU shows that it already has many of the features of a state and that over time these features have expanded (Sandholtz and Stone Sweet 2001). The EU could have a common foreign and security policy and an army in the near future, and already has a more coordinated education policy. Moreover, the historical literature demonstrates that states frequently precede nations or even impose them on populations (Tilly 1975; Rokkan 1973; Rokkan and Urwin 1983; Gellner 1983; Geary 2002). So the degree to which a European identity would precede the emergence of a European state or instead be an effect of its emergence, depends on the process of whether or not, and to what degree, the member-state governments pursue political integration.

While the issue of whether or not the EU is or should be a state remains in political contention amongst the citizens of Europe, it is clear that the people who have had great influence in the EU have been working to promote the EU as a state. Shore (2000) shows that the EU has created a flag, an anthem, license plates, money, citizenship, and passports in order to convince people that the EU deserves national allegiance. The educational workforce employed by governments, at all levels of schooling, have been amongst the main agents of teaching that students are Europeans, in much the way that Gellner (1983) suggests happened in industrial society in Europe in the nineteenth century.

The issue of European national identity can be separated from the issue of support for the EU (see Inglehast, Rabier, and Reif 1991; Gabel 1998; Hooghe and Marks 2001; Diez Medrano 2003; Citrin and Sides 2004; Hermann, Brewer, and Risse 2004; Hoehn and Lancefield 2005). Only a small percentage of citizens (12.7%) firmly identify with Europe, although general political support for the EU is relatively high with majorities supporting their country's membership in almost all the EU countries. Support for the EU of people who still have mainly a national identity, is based on their view of the EU as an intergovernmental organization by which their governments can cooperate with others in increasing trade, travel, and educational and employment opportunities (Eichenberg and Dalton 1993). These citizens hold firmly to their national identity but still appreciate the possibilities that EU cooperation can produce.

Given all its successes and the general levels of support for the EU amongst Europe's citizens, the EU is surprisingly misunderstood by most of them. Many scholars attribute these problems to the EU's lack of transparency in its procedures, its bureaucratic and technocratic approach to problems, and its lack of accountability to a larger democratic public (Baun 1996; Dinan 1999; McCormick 2002). The level of knowledge about how the EU works is poor (Gabel 1998). This lack of 'connectedness' of ordinary citizens to the EU has caused scholars to try to understand why a European identity (equivalent to a 'national' identity), a European 'civil society' (an arena where discussion of Europe-wide problems occurs), and a European politics have been so slow to emerge (Laffan et al. 2000). The main focus of these efforts is to ask why, after almost fifty years of the integration project, there is so little evidence of public attitudes that reflect a sense of solidarity within Europe.

The EU has been reorganized several times to try to make it more transparent to ordinary citizens. It has tried to deal with the democratic deficit by empowering the European Parliament, and has mobilized elite opinion to try and promulgate the idea that people are citizens not just of their own country but also of the European Union. One of the failures of the scholarly literature is that on the whole it bemoans the lack of a European identity and politics, placing that blame firmly on the EU apparatus in Brussels. I argue that the reason this is so, is that some of the current theories of nation-building focus mostly on a top-down process where states and elites are the main actors in convincing a population that they have a national identity (Rokkan 1979; Gellner 1983).

While I would agree that these top-down processes are important, they are only part of the story. Feelings of social solidarity are not just imposed upon populations. Instead, they must reflect bottom-up processes that involve education, socialization, political conflict, and social interaction (P. Taylor 1983; Deutsch 1966; Breuilly 1994). Obviously, before one can wonder why there are not more Europeans who might push their national politicians to create a European federal state, one must have a theory about how national identities and politics form in the first place. It is logical to believe that the main reason that there does not exist a widespread European identity is that the conditions under which national identities can form have not been met in Europe. This chapter presents an understanding of what those conditions would be. Then, it presents evidence that shows why they have not been met in Europe.

The main theoretical argument from the literature on the origins of nationalism views it as one kind of group identity. Group identities are based on commonly held meanings and values and they require face-to-face interaction with other members of the group in order to come into existence and persist. National identity is a peculiar kind of identity that implies that a group of people decide on some bases of pre-existing solidarities to express its collective identity in the context of creating a state to enforce rules to preserve that identity (Deutsch 1966). The key to the formation of a national identity depends on patterns of social interaction between pre-existing groups. In order for a European identity to emerge, one must consider which national groups are the most likely to interact with one another on a regular basis and thereby produce bonds with people from other European societies, bonds that suggest that these people are more alike than different and hence, Europeans.

In order to discover who these people are, it is useful to connect the possible patterns of interaction across European borders. I offer a simple hypothesis: as European economic, social, and political fields have developed, they imply the routine interaction of people from different societies. It is people who are involved in such interactions that are most likely to come to see themselves as Europeans and involved in a European national project. In essence, Europeans are going to be people who have the opportunity and inclination to travel to other countries, speak other languages, and routinely interact with people in other societies in the Europe-wide economic, social, and political fields. They are also going to be amongst the dominant material beneficiaries of European economic integration. They include owners of businesses, managers, professionals, and other white-collar workers who are involved in various aspects of commerce and government. These people travel for business, live in other countries for short periods of time, and engage in long-term social relationships with their counterparts, either in their firms or among their suppliers and customers, in their cohorts in other governments, or in the practice of their professions. Young people who travel across borders for schooling, tourism, and jobs (often for a few years after college) are also likely to be more European. Educated people who share common interests with educated people around Europe, such as similar professions, interests in charitable organizations, or social and cultural activities such as opera or art will be interested in travel and social interaction with people in other societies. Finally, people with higher income will travel more and participate in the diverse cultural life across Europe. They will have the money to spend time enjoying the good life in other places.

If these are likely to be the people who are most likely to interact in Europe-wide economic, social, and political fields, then it follows that their opposites lack either the opportunity or interest to interact with their counterparts across Europe. Most importantly, blue-collar and service workers are less likely than managers, professionals, and other white-collar workers to have work that will take them to other countries. Older people will be less adventurous than younger people, and less likely to have learned other languages, or to hold favorable views of their neighbors; moreover, they will probably remember who was on which side in World War II. They will be less likely to want to associate with or have curiosity about people from neighboring countries. People who hold conservative political views that value the 'nation' as the most important category will be less attracted to travel, or to know and interact with people who are 'not like them.' Finally, less educated and less rich people will lack attraction to the cultural diversity of Europe and be less able to afford to travel.

This chapter is structured thus: first, I consider the issue of identity more generally, and posit a mechanism by which new national identity could form. Then I consider how this applies to the issue of the possibility of a European collective identity. Next, I provide data that is consistent with the ideas just presented. In conclusion, I discuss the issue of the 'shallowness' of European identity and the problem of the advancement of the EU.

WHAT ARE COLLECTIVE IDENTITIES?

Sociologists, anthropologists, and political scientists have been interested in the formation of collective identities since the founding of their disciplines (for a critical review of the concept of identity in the post-war era, see Brubaker and Cooper 2000). Collective identities refer to the idea that a group of people accept a fundamental and consequential similarity that causes them to feel solidarity amongst themselves (Thernborn, 1995: ch. 12; Brubaker and Cooper 2000). This sense of collective identity is socially constructed, by which I mean that it emerges as the intentional or unintentional consequence of social interactions. Collective identity is also by definition about the construction of an 'other.' Our idea of who we are is usually framed as a response to some 'other' group (Barth 1969). Collective identities are anchored in sets of conscious and unconscious meanings that people share. People grow up in families and communities, and come to identify with the groups in which they are socially located. Gender, ethnicity, religion, nationality, social class, and age have all been the basis of people's main identities and their central relationship to various communities.

In the social psychology literature, it is argued that individuals come to identify with one group over another because they want to belong to a group that has the more positive identity (Turner 1975; Tajfel 1981). People who find themselves with a downgraded identity will try either to leave their group, to appear to be a member of another group, or to work to improve their group's collective identity in the minds of others (Goffman 1963). These social-psychological notions of collective identity would seem to imply that collective identities in a particular domain are hierarchically organized. So, for example, within the sphere of gender, men are valued and women are devalued. This hierarchical ordering of gender identities causes individual and collective conflicts between men and women.

People can have multiple collective identities—even ones that may seem to conflict—such as local, regional, and national identities (Brewer 1993; 1999; Brewer and Gardner 1996; Diez Medrano and Gutiérrez, 2001; Diez Medrano, 2003; Risse, 2005). A critical issue in exploring how individuals come to have collective identities is the degree to which such identities overlap, make exclusive demands on people, are situational, or are incompatible. There are three sorts of situation that are important to consider here. First, identities may be separate or exclusive. This means that they apply to actions in very different social fields and as such, their relationship is usually not very conflictive. So, for example, one's identity as a parent will frequently not clash with one's identity as a member of a political party.

More interestingly, identities can be nested or embedded (Lawlor 1992). Here, identities that are relevant to a particular domain may be kept separate. Calhoun (1994) and Brewer (1993; 1999) argue that identities within a particular domain may be complementary or activated under different circumstances. Diez Medrano and Gutiérrez (2001) argue that one can think of European identities as nested in national identities, regional identities, and even more local identities such as cities or neighborhoods. Since these identities require different kinds of activation, they may not be generally in conflict, but indeed complementary. Risse (2003), agreeing with Diez Medrano and Gutiérrez (2001), reviews the literature on the topic of European identity and concludes that strong national and European identities are not incompatible because they refer to different communities which are nested in relationship to one another and are activated under different social conditions.

Diez Medrano and Gutiérrez argue that the main psychological mechanism by which individuals are able to hold seemingly contradictory identities is the fact that in smaller groups, individuals will likely feel more control than in larger groups (Lawlor 1992). This will make them tend to identify strongly with their local groups. But it is also the case that larger groups might also, under the right conditions, be able to provide positive identities for individuals, particularly if the larger group's identity acts in a way to promote the smaller group's worth. This means that the larger group's identity comes into play under circumstances where it can prove useful. In the case of Spain, Diez Medrano and Gutiérrez (2001) show that Spanish national and regional identities are not only unthreatened by a European identity, but empowered by it. The Spanish view their membership in the EU and their identities as Europeans as proof that they are 'modern,' and have arrived as members of a functioning democratic society.

The third situation is the case where identities are either cross-cutting or overlapping and thus in potential conflict. In this situation, multiple group identities may involve overlapping but not equivalent sets of people. There are two sorts of strategy that are salient in this case: inclusion or exclusion. In the inclusionary circumstances, a group identity is enlarged to include members from both groups. So, for example, people of mixed racial and ethnic backgrounds might view themselves as 'hyphenated,' i.e. having inclusive mixed identities such as Afro-American or Irish-American (Waters 1990). In the exclusionary circumstances, identity in one group might be used to preclude members of other groups. So, for example, Inglehart's (1978) theory of European identity implies that people who are more cosmopolitan will be more European and less national in their identities. If one has to choose between a local or regional identity and the view that one is a member of a more enlightened cosmopolitan group, one will exclude those who try to maintain they can be both local and cosmopolitan.

This discussion implies that how identities are juggled or manipulated within and across groups will depend on some degree to what the identities are, how they might potentially come into conflict, and how individuals and groups will deal with those conflicts. It could be the case that in the same social field some groups will want to maintain their hold on a particular identity that overrides other identities and are exclusionary of those who do not share their group membership. Other groups in the same field may want to view their identities as either nested or inclusionary.

For example, some religious groups might want to claim that their path to salvation is the only true path, thereby setting them against all other religious groups in a particular society. Other religious groups could agree that while their theological differences were real, they could be ecumenical about them, being inclusionary, not exclusionary. Such a society would be rife with political conflicts and the resolution of those conflicts would have profound implications for people's religious identities. The real social conflicts between groups that make different identity claims, and their ultimate resolutions, are the source of the dynamics of much of social structure.

NATIONAL IDENTITIES

This brings us to the problem of national identity, one of the main features of which, historically, is that it could be used to legitimate the claim of a particular state over a particular territory by presenting the state as representative of the entire nation. From the point of view of the identity theory just presented, national identities have generally been thought of as exclusive collective identity claims that apply to all the people who live in a particular territory. The ways in which states and social conflict have resulted in a single such identity claim being used to control a territory is the subject of the literature on nation-building.

It is useful to begin with the ideas of Karl Deutsch, a major source of modern theorizing on national identities. Deutsch's argument is that societies are best conceived as based on a division of labor carried on through specific combinations of social institutions and technology. At the core of society is how particular occupational groups and classes have been the main architects and beneficiaries of the leading institutions and technologies. He describes these groups as forming 'a peculiar ruling class or elite, more or less united for their preservation by relatively stable cluster patterns formed in terms of family ties, interest, habit, organization, and ideology' (1966: 37). Culture, for Deutsch, is a 'common set of stable, habitual preferences and priorities in [people's] attention and behavior, as in their thoughts and feelings. Culture and community can be used interchangeably because they discuss a single complex of processes. When we say culture, we stress the configuration of preferences or values; when we say community we stress the aspects of communication' (ibid. 89).

Deutsch acknowledges a kind of tension between society and community. To the degree that a society contains inequalities of income, wealth, and status, the groups who control society must convince those who are not its main beneficiaries that they share some underlying goals. This involves creating a horizontal community united by these goals. Nationality is one kind of community than can be created by communicating common values and developing a sense that people share a common culture.

Nationality is 'a people striving to equip itself with power, with some machinery of compulsion strong enough to make the enforcement of its commands probable in order to aid in the spread of habits of voluntary compliance with them' (ibid. 104). But in order to attain this, there has to be an alliance between the members of disparate social groups. 'Nationality, then, means an alignment of large numbers of individuals from the lower and middle classes linked to regional centers and leading social groups by channels of social communication and economic discourse, both indirectly from link to link with the center' (ibid. 101).

Deutsch's approach helps makes sense of one of the most obvious difficulties with a theory of nationality. In different times and places, the basis of an appeal to a common culture can include language, religion, race, ethnicity, or common formative experience (e.g. in the US, immigration). Deutsch makes us understand that any of these common cultures can form the pre-existing basis of a national identity, and which one gets used in a particular society will depend on history. The historical 'trick' to the rise of a nation-state will be to find a horizontal solidarity that is appealing to wide groupings of people and offers both a justification for the existing stratification system and a rationale that using a state apparatus to protect the nation makes sense. So nationalism can have any cultural root, as long as that culture can be used to forge a cross-class alliance around a nation-building project.

Deutsch places the problem of communication and culture at the center of his theory of the emergence of a national identity. A nation-state will come into existence when such a national story exists, and once in existence the state apparatus will be used to reproduce the nation. At the core of this process is the need for there to be communication between disparate groups. These groups communicate through extensive networks made up of face-to-face interactions, the existence of organizations who communicate routinely in political, economic, and social fields, and, of course, other forms of communication such as the media.

One of the problems of the Deutschian analysis is that it can overestimate the role of consensus and legitimacy in creating nation-states. While the Deutschian view does introduce social divisions such as classes as the center of consideration, the emergence of nations was not exactly a peaceful process of political compromise. Nations were often imposed on regions or cities (Tilly 1975; Gellner 1983). The French and British governments used force to control their regions and suppressed local ethnic or regional identities. Italy and Germany used 'national myths to justify political projects that were mainly undertaken to protect smaller states from being swallowed by larger neighbors' (Moore 1966). Many of the elaborations on the rise of nation-states take up the issue of how an exclusionary collective identity on what constitutes the nation comes into existence and is enforced and inculcated by a state apparatus (Gellner 1983).

Benedict Anderson (1983: 5) follows Deutsch when he argues, 'In an anthropological spirit, then, I propose the following definition of the nation: it is an imagined political community—and imagined as both inherently limited and sovereign.' Nations are imagined because members of even the smallest state never know or meet every other member. They are limited by rules of membership and the idea that the nation has physical boundaries. There are citizens and, by definition, foreigners. Nations are sovereign in that they contain governments that claim to make the rules for the nation within a physical boundary. They are communities because, 'regardless of the actual inequality and exploitation that may prevail in each, the nation is always conceived as a deep, horizontal comradeship. Ultimately it is this fraternity that makes it possible, over the past two centuries, for so many millions of people, not so much to kill, as willingly to die for such limited imaginings' (ibid.).

Anderson argues that nationalism originated as a result of the decline of religion during the Middle Ages, the development of capitalism, and the technology of print. Before nationalism, there existed religiously 'imagined communities,' such as Christendom, which were based on shared languages such as Latin. With the rise of exploration, Europeans came to realize the insularity of their experience. The Reformation brought a split in religion in Europe. The printing press eventually brought about a decline in works published in Latin and the rise of new works that were published in other languages. Books, newspapers, and novels gave the idea to their readers that there existed a group of readers like themselves. These people did not need to know one another directly. Instead, common languages and shared culture that came through media provided common meanings for people. This upper- and upper-middle-class elite began to have a sense of national consciousness. They created unified fields of cultural exchange below Latin and above the 'common language.' They gave a new fixity to the language and helped give an idea of permanence to the nation. This caused them to produce a narrative about how they were connected.

For Anderson, the pivotal moment in the invention of the nation-state was not the French Revolution, but the revolts in North and South America which were justified as creating nations in the face of European domination (ibid. ch. 4). If nationalism is one kind of collective identity, then an intuitive question is, 'to whom is nationalism opposed?' Anderson views the natural opponent of the nation-state as first the colonial power and second the feudal dynasty. The nation-state's claim was to produce a state that would operate for all citizens, not just be the organization of society for the benefit of the monarch. The triumph of the nation-state as a social form occurred after World War I, when the remaining European empires were destroyed. After World War I, the nation-state became the dominant form of collective identity for states. New states proliferated after World War II and all of them pursued the idea that their boundaries were fixed by their nations.

There is a difference of emphasis in the theories of nation-building, one which might be called 'top-down' and the other 'bottom-up'. Top-down theories emphasize the role of state elites in the production of national identities (e.g. Rokkan 1973; Gellner 1983; Rokkan and Urwin 1983). The main mechanism by which a nationalist story is forged is through the coordination of efforts of elites who have coalesced around a particular national narrative. The opposing point of view is that nationalist projects instead reflect more bottom-up processes (e.g. Deutsch 1966; Brubaker 1992; Breuilly 1994).

There are two aspects of this kind of social process. Collective group formation can be produced through increased social interaction and the sharing of a common culture between disparate social groups; but, just as frequently, there are political conflicts between groups where interactional patterns are more conflictual and cultural differences are magnified. A nationalist project reflects the eventual solution to those conflicts either by one side imposing their vision of the national story on others, usually through revolution or some form of state-sponsored violence or through political compromise whereby disparate groups unite under the umbrella of a particular national narrative where they can collectively agree to coexist. In actuality, of course, both top-down and bottom-up processes can be observed.

Gellner (1983) offers a view of the rise of the nation-state that is complementary to that of Anderson. He sees the nation-state as the product of the functional needs of a modern society which depends on social mobility and communication between individuals, which in turn require a common view that all people in the society are part of a homogeneous culture. This common culture is propagated by an educational elite which socializes everyone in society to an understanding that they are members of a common group. For Gellner, it is the political elites of a society who come to propagate its nationalist message. They use the educational system, the military, and control over social communication to indoctrinate the message that people share a national identity.

Rokkan (1973) saw nation-state building as going through a set of phases. The first consisted of building a bureaucratic state apparatus that collected taxes, created labor markets, and created public order through the creation of public works, the police, and the army. The state also began to shape a system of rights that might be available for the population. The second phase, that of nation building, consisted of regulating the media and schools, and creating institutionalized symbols of the nation such as a flag, myths, and anthems. This phase attempted to create trust and loyalty in the population and was frequently accompanied by the extension of rights to traditionally oppressed groups. Finally, Rokkan saw that the consolidation of the nation-state ended up promoting more social justice through the use of social security, systems of progressive taxation, and the balancing of opportunities and risk across social groups.

Breuilly (1994) argues for a more bottom-up view of how nationalism emerges. He views the rise of nation-states as mostly about the internal political struggles within a given society. He argues that different social groups may or may not use nationalism as a political ideology to resolve the internal politics of their societies. Opposition groups can decide to use nationalism as a way to gain political advantage. They might argue that they are part of the nation and in order to create a more inclusive nation-state, they should be included in politics more directly. So, for example, the African-American civil rights movement in the US during the 1960s tried to use national identity around the issue of citizens' rights as a method of including them as full citizens. They might also use nationalism to propose secession from the nation as in the case of many of the ethnic groups who have fought in the post-war era in post-colonial countries. Some groups can also use the idea of the nation as a way to suppress other groups. The German fascist regime used nationalism to define who was not a member of the state and who therefore deserved to be eliminated. Political movements could decide not to pursue a nation-state and instead to transcend the nation-state altogether by creating a transnational community. This has been the tactic of some forms of political Islam. Breuilly's main point is to argue that the use of nationalism by certain groups will depend on their political and historical context, the nature of their opposition, and their understanding of their collective goals.

Brubaker's (1992) contribution is to investigate how particular conceptions of citizenship and nationhood that emerge in societies are a cultural product reflecting the history and conflicts of a given society. Here, the national story or narrative is what actually unites groups against their opposition and brings them together to form a nation-state (in exactly a Deutschian fashion). The nationalist narrative is important because it is a discourse that brings a particular people together. The nation-state that will be created will be inscribed with these unique cultural elements.

He demonstrates that in France, the concept of 'citizen' is universal and based on the idea that all members of society are part of the state. This conception of citizenship, which emerged out of the French Revolution, was opposed to the feudal conception of citizenship that privileged the king and nobility as citizens. The French conception of citizenship also enforced a strict separation of religion and state and viewed the goal of the state to be the protection of the rights of all its citizens. In return, it demanded that for people to have these rights and be

French citizens, they all needed to assimilate to the morals and values of the 'French.' Ironically, the French state was then put into the position of suppressing differences between groups and attempting to ensure that all citizens were socialized to be French. Brubaker points out that the modern French state has a universalistic conception of citizens that makes it difficult for multiculturalism to exist.

In Germany in contrast, the conception of nationhood was the *volk*, the people. Here, being of German descent was the most important marker of being worthy of citizenship. If one was not of German parentage or ancestry, citizenship was denied. Brubaker argues that it was this conception of citizenship that allowed the emergence of the German state in the nineteenth century. Without some conception that all the states that combined to form the German state shared some heritage and were indeed a common people with a common language and paternity, it would be difficult for the different groups in each state to unite. German unification turned on the myth of the German *volk*, an identity presumed to be primordial and mythically connected to the original Germanic language and tribes. Under this conception of citizenship, it was difficult if not impossible for people without parents or grandparents born in Germany to attain citizenship even if their forebears had lived in Germany for many generations. The concept also allowed people who had left Germany and lived elsewhere to return and claim citizenship because of their ability to claim membership of the *volk*. This conception of citizenship has been altered somewhat recently, but remains inscribed in the German state.

To summarize: the literature on the emergence of national collective identities follows quite closely the social psychological and collective mechanisms of closure implied by the general theories of collective identities. National collective identities are exclusive. When one comes into existence, it is frequently in opposition to another. The idea of the nation-state is that eventually one collective idea about the nation will emerge, become inscribed in the state, and be enforced through a bureaucratic apparatus that claims control over the means of violence in a territory. A distinguishing feature of nation-state collective identities then, is that one eventually wins out.

This can happen through three main mechanisms. First, a single group will defeat its opponents either peacefully or violently and can then enforce its view of society by taking over the state. Second, conflicting groups can find a collective identity that is inclusive and will allow them to agree to the contours of the nation-state. Here, they will decide that their differing collective identities can be combined in an inclusionary as opposed to an exclusionary way. Finally, the bureaucratic and political elite of a society will work to convince a population that they do indeed belong to the nation. They do so by using the state apparatus to socialize individuals through education, the production of collective symbols such as flags and anthems, and controlling the culture by regulating the media. They can also try to produce inclusionary social programs that include citizens' rights and a welfare state.

THE STRUGGLE AROUND A EUROPEAN
COLLECTIVE IDENTITY

In order to use these ideas to understand who might be a European, one needs to put what has happened in Europe into some historical context. Scholars of the emergence of the EU focus a great deal on the issue of how Europe's leaders after World War II came to think about their political situation (Parsons 2003). There was a great deal of discussion after the war about how to reorganize political arrangements across Europe in order to prevent another war. For example, in the late 1940s there was a movement to create a single European government. Churchill supported this movement, reasoning that if Europe had a single federated government, it would not have separate armies and would never go to war again (ibid.).

This idea failed for a number of reasons, not the least that there was no political groundswell from Europe's citizens for such an arrangement. If we put this in Deutsch's terms, there was not a national culture that could be harnessed to a Europe-wide political project. How could there be? There was little routine communication across European societies before World War II, and until after the war there was almost no connection between economic and political elites across societies. Moreover, in the wake of the devastation across Europe, the main possible linkage between countries was not a nationalist impulse. Instead, there were socialist and communist social movements oriented toward overthrowing capitalism and installing governments that would take over most of big business. Indeed, if one was going to look for a nationalism that might have produced a national European state in the post-war era (i.e. one that depended on some mass support), its main axis of solidarity would have been anti-capitalist.

Some of Europe's political elites began to have a different conversation about how to prevent renewed political conflict (Duchene 1994). They decided that they would try to increase economic interdependency; if they could engage in economic cooperation, countries would become richer through increased trade and the growing interdependence of their product markets. This would constrain politics in each country because jobs and continuing prosperity would depend on trade. It would also have the effect of bringing political elites together to govern a freer market and increase their communication. Countries that competed over producing goods and services and sold them to each other would be less likely to go to war. Part of the bonus would be increased communication and interaction across borders, thereby lessening nationalist impulses to view people in other countries as 'evil.'

There have always been those who thought that a process of economic integration would eventually lead to more political integration, i.e. some form of European nation-state. The theory underlying the model was that economic interdependence would eventually produce a European identity, which would then be grounds for political mobilization within and across the member states.

Eventually, this would form a transnational social movement to produce a groundswell of support for an expanded state. The Brussels complex would evolve into a federal organization where there was a division of power between the levels of government, supported by national populations who would partici-pate in both national and federal politics.

The main empirical problem with this model is that neither a European identity nor a groundswell of political support for an expansion of the EU has come into existence (Imig and Tarrow 2001). Political scientists have spent a great deal of time and energy trying to understand exactly why this is. Their answers have taken the form of trying to use the model of the emergence of the nation-state and seek out its analogy to the case of the possible emergence of a Europe nation-state. On the one hand are scholars who try to view the EU as a proto-state and then make arguments about how it might increase its legitimacy and expand its purview to become more of a European state (Hix 1999). For these scholars the EU's legitimacy with its citizens and their view of themselves as Europeans is of paramount importance. On the other hand are those who view the EU primarily as a particularly successful intergovernmental organization that man-ages to increase its ability to effect cooperation amongst the member states and engage in the pooling of sovereignty (Keohane and Hoffman 1993; Moravcsik 1998). If the EU is just an intergovernmental organization, then the issue of an EU identity is irrelevant to its future. The success or failure of the EU is instead linked to its being useful to the leaders of the member-state governments in their quests to be re-elected. It is here that much of the cacophony of the scholarly debate begins.

But this is not just a scholarly debate; it is also an ongoing political debate by the citizens of the various European nation-states about how best to manage their affairs. Citizens are concerned about their social welfare, health care, education, and economic growth and job security. How societies will be ordered and where decision-making for important issues will take place are core issues in the future of European welfare states. Governments have already given up power to the EU and they have been rewarded by increasing trade, economic growth, and job creation. But the future of economic growth and European welfare states, and the role of the EU in this, are being debated across Europe. National and European collective identities are playing a role in this debate. For the vast majority who hold primarily national identities, preserving their national welfare states is paramount. For those with more mixed identities, the value of trying to cooper-ate to do so at the European level is obvious.

Not surprisingly, such issues are contentious in many ways. It is possible to find groups within and across European societies who argue for disparate points of view on all these themes. In some countries, such as Great Britain, there is a fair amount of skepticism about moving additional policies to the EU level. Indeed, the dominant British point of view is that the EU is an intergovernmental organization oriented toward a free trade area that allows freedom to travel and invest, but not much more than that. Not surprisingly, the citizens of Great Britain are the most national in their political collective identity.

On the other side are citizens who want Europe to have a stronger set of social policies. Not surprisingly such points of view are frequently expressed in societies where there is more European collective identity, such as Germany, France, Italy, Belgium, the Netherlands, and Luxembourg. Jürgen Habermas, a leading intellectual in Germany, has expounded a set of arguments about why there should be a European constitution, a civil society or public space where there is ongoing political discourse about solving European problems, and a welfare state to guarantee that the European model of state and citizen is upheld (1992; 2001). German politicians have frequently been in the forefront of proposing more European political union. The political struggle over whether there will be or should be a European state, identity, and politics is ongoing.

But how is this struggle over the EU, its politics, and European identity being waged and who are its partisans? As I have already discussed, there is ample evidence that the EU bureaucracy and some of the Europe's political elites are trying to behave as if the EU is a proto-state. The empirical literature has produced interesting and somewhat consistent results. A large number of Europe's citizens remain mainly attached to their national identity. This attachment is a strong predictor of their attitudes toward European integration, regardless of other social characteristics (Hooghe and Marks 2005). Those who have some European identity are more favorable toward the EU.

One of the most interesting set of results concerns those individuals who have both a national and European identity. Risse (2005), in a review of the results on this issue, concludes that a strong European and a strong national identity are not in contradiction. Diez Medrano (2003) demonstrates how European identity means different things to people in different countries. He also shows that European identity is nested in national and regional identities. One interpretation of many people who have both European and national identities is that they view these not in exclusive terms but in hyphenated terms, i.e. they are German-Europeans. What being European means to them is situational and not in conflict with being German. There are relatively few people in Europe with only a European identity, so it is hard to tell if these people view their Europeanness in exclusive terms, i.e. that they no longer think of themselves as citizens of a country but only as citizens of Europe.

But, so far, this literature fails to situate these descriptions in a deeper sociology of who the groups are who have these identities and how this relates to their being potential winners and losers in European economic and political integration. If we return to Breuilly's or Brubaker's formulation, in order for there to be a European national identity, there needs to be people for whom that collective identity becomes a project and, by definition, people who will be opposed to that project. For Deutsch, the eventual success of that project would depend on building a cross-class alliance around a European collective identity.

There are two sorts of obvious opponents to a European collective identity project. First, the political elites who run the nation-states are potentially threatened by having their sovereignty removed to a larger political entity. The states with the strongest sense of that sovereignty, Great Britain, Denmark, Austria,

Sweden, and now some of the new member states from Eastern Europe are the most skeptical of increased political cooperation. From Gellner's point of view, if state elites do not back a nationalist collective identity—or indeed, oppose it—then the possibility of its success is not very good.

But even more important to the ultimate fate of the EU is how ordinary citizens view the role of Europe in their lives. After all, politicians in democratic societies generally follow voters' preferences. Those preferences will determine to a large degree the willingness of political elites who run governments to consider building more state capacity at the European level. So, the degree to which the people of Europe either accept or deny a European identity and favor it over a national identity will have the most profound effect on the future of Europe.

This brings me to the issue of the winners and losers in the economic integration project of the EU. Who in each country are going to see the nation as the protector of their rights? Who are going to be more likely to view themselves as interested in experiencing what the rest of Europe has to offer, both economically and culturally? Put another way, in the national political fields, political parties organize coalitions of groups who favor different programs depending on how those programs help or hurt their constituent members. Those who favor the national political collective identity are less in favor of the European project, while those who have some view of themselves as Europeans are in favor of it. It is now relevant to ask, who are the Europeans and, by implication, who are their opponents?

THE DETERMINANTS OF EUROPEAN IDENTITY

I use the rest of this chapter to show what kind of European collective identity has emerged and for whom. I unpack the link between economic interdependence and patterns of social interaction across Europe. I show that while there are groups of people across Europe who frequently interact, the vast majority of Europeans still remain tied firmly to the nation. Moreover, even for those who view themselves as Europeans, the meaning they attach to that depends upon which country they reside in. Diez Medrano (2003) has shown that for Germans being a European means atoning for their guilt from World War II. For Spaniards, being European is being 'modern.' And for the British, it means an identity that proves useful when contrasting oneself with others, such as Americans.

In some sense, it may be the case that it is too soon for a European identity or a Europe-wide politics to form. The EU has existed less than fifty years and its transformation into a more political organization (i.e. one with a foreign policy and a defense force) is just beginning (Merand 2003). National identities evolved over centuries, and even then have changed dramatically over time. So, however one thinks about the data to be presented, one must realize that the current state of a European identity and its link to a nation building project may alter over time.

One of the interesting features of national identities is their mixture of ideational and rational components. Easton (1974) argues that support for governments comes in two forms. First, if governments are perceived by individuals and groups to work in their interests, then they will be supported. This form of support can be more fleeting because as governments shift course or find themselves the victims of circumstances, public support might erode. A second form of support is ideational or affective. If people feel emotionally attached to governments or nations, then they are more tolerant of missteps by particular government officials. Sociologists tend to think that it is difficult to separate out the rational from the affective component of identity (Brubaker 1992). Indeed, people come to identify with a group of others often because they share common interests (material and otherwise).

Gabel (1998) has used Easton's distinction to analyze survey data on attitudes toward the EU. He has demonstrated that there are people in Western Europe who have a European identity. Not surprisingly, they are also in favor of the EU's activities. But he also demonstrates that people who have something to gain from the EU—professionals, managers, educated people, farmers, and the financially well-off—are also more likely to be in favor of the activities of the EU. I produce results that support Gabel's view.

My goal is to broaden Gabel's view of why these privileged groups are Europeans and why they support the EU. It is certainly the case that they have benefited materially. European integration has been first and foremost about creating a single market. However, the market integration project has had the unintended outcome of giving some the opportunity to interact with people from other societies. The people who are the most likely to be in a position to have that opportunity are those who are most likely to cross borders to engage in trade or other activities.

Business people, educators, academics, consultants, government employees, and lawyers are all likely to have traveled for business and to meet their counterparts across Europe. Young people are likely to travel, for pleasure and also for schooling. For example, almost 200,000 college students spend at least a semester abroad every year as part of the EU's Erasmus program. Young people are likely to know people from other European societies.

The issues of identity, interest, and interaction are difficult to untangle both theoretically and empirically. For example, if one is a business person who depends on trade for one's livelihood, one is likely to spend time in other countries and get to know people from those societies. This interaction will reveal common interests and a common set of understandings. People will develop friendships and get to know others with whom they will come to share a deeper identity. So an Italian businessman who befriends a French businessman will find they share a common interest in having more opportunity to interact. They will come to see each other less as Italian and French, and thus foreign, and more and more as sharing common interests, a process that will eventually lead to seeing themselves more as Europeans and less as having merely national identity. Of course, to the degree that these relationships are driven by material interest (i.e. selling and buying), affect may be difficult to separate from interest.

The problem is deeper than this. The question of what exactly a European identity might be is also unclear (Gabel 1998; Risse et al. 1999; Laffan, O'Donnell, and Smith 2000). Habermas (1992) argues that a European identity is part of the idea of completing the Enlightenment project. He argues that 'reason' and 'rationality' should guide people's interactions. Thus, being a European is about trying to settle differences peaceably with respect for differences and other's opinions. A European 'state' or 'polity' would be rational and allow for multiple discourses. Decision-making would be democratic and ideally follow the creation of a European civil society where such differences of opinion could be aired. Finally, he has recently argued that Europe should also stand for social justice and defense of the welfare state. Such an identity, of course, was associated during the Enlightenment with the rising middle classes and in contemporary Europe with social democracy.

The fictitious business people I describe above begin by interacting with one another for commerce. They discover that people from other societies who occupy similar social positions are not so different from themselves, which makes them see that national identities are limiting and that a European identity gives them more freedom to associate with others who are *really* like them in other societies. They are all educated, rational people who prefer to find win-win situations, who prefer compromise to conflict, and accept cultural differences as interesting and stimulating. It should not be surprising that the 'agents' of European identity should be the same upper and upper-middle classes who favored the Enlightenment: i.e. business people, professionals, and the educated. It is their identity project that underlies European integration.

One of the difficulties of proving the story that interaction between people from different European societies produces European identity is finding appropriate data. The data I use to demonstrate this linkage come from the Eurobarometer Surveys that are done twice a year in Europe. The Appendix for Ch. 5 contains information on the surveys and the measures reported in the tables. The surveys are intended to gauge public opinion across Europe on matters pertaining to the EU, but also in other issue areas. One of the problems in using the survey to prove the point I am trying to make here, is that no single survey asks all the relevant questions. So we do not have any means to obtain information simultaneously on socioeconomic characteristics, interaction patterns with people from other societies, and whether or not people have a European identity.

I therefore have to pursue an alternative approach to establish these linkages. All the surveys ask questions about socioeconomic variables such as occupation, education, and income as well as demographic variables such as age and gender. My strategy is to model the association between socioeconomic variables, demographic variables, and variables that index interactions between people in different European countries and their identity. I show that the socioeconomic and demographic variables predict interaction patterns *and* European identity. I use three separate surveys: one that asks questions on travel to another European country, one that enquires about second language use, and one that researches whether or not the respondents of the surveys have European identities. Travel is a direct measure of interaction with people from another country. A commitment to learn

TABLE 5.1. '*In the near future, will you think of yourself as a ... ?*'

	%
European only	3.9
European and own nationality	8.8
Own nationality and European	43.3
Own nationality only	44.0
TOTALS	
Mostly national	87.3
Mostly European	12.7
Sometimes European	56.0

Source: Eurobarometer 91, April 2004.

and use a second language reflects an interest in interacting with people from another country (either for work or pleasure).

Table 5.1 presents data from the Eurobarometer 2004. The question was, 'How often do you think of your self as a—European, European and [nationality], [nationality] and European, [nationality].' One can be skeptical about whether this is a very good measure of identity. It is hard to tell what anyone means by his or her answer, and for those who choose both a national and European identity, it is even more difficult to interpret how they view their allegiances. But often, simple questions can reveal a lot. So, for example, I show that the correlates of identity match quite closely the patterns of interaction. I also show a close link between feeling European and attitudes toward the European project. In this way, the measure has both face and predictive validity.

The data show that only 3.9 per cent of the European population think of themselves as exclusively European while another 8.8 per cent think of themselves as having European and some national identity. This means that only 12.7 of all Europeans think of themselves mostly as Europeans. Figure 5.1 tracks the response to this question from 1992 until 2004. It is clear from the figure that there is has been little change in the overall percentage of people across Europe who think of themselves as European. Indeed, there is remarkable stability in the answer to this question over time.

This result raises the issue of why European identities have not gained strength over time. One of the strongest predictors of being European is age. As the oldest cohorts have passed on and been replaced by younger cohorts, one would think that the number of Europeans would increase. I have looked at the survey in 1992 and 2004 and broken the responses down by age group. This reveals that indeed the oldest people in 2004 were more likely to be European than the oldest people in 1992. But the differences were not all that great and only one ten-year age cohort had passed from the scene between the two survey dates. Lutz, Kritzinger, and Skirbekk (2006) use the 2004 data to project European identities into the future based on the aging of the population. They conclude that the number of people in Europe with some European identity will rise from 56 per cent today to 69 per cent in 2030.

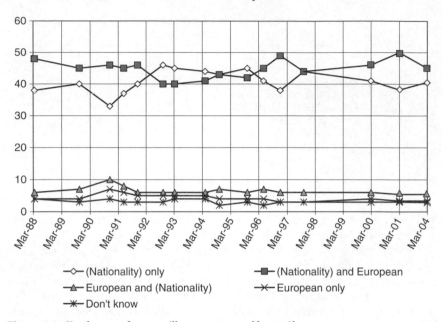

Figure 5.1. 'In the near future, will you see yourself as . . . ?'

Source: <http://ec.europa.eu/public_opinion/cf/subquestion_en.cfm>, Eurobarometer bl.

Scholars who have looked at this data conclude that the European identity has not spread very far (Deflem and Pampel 1996; Gabel 1998). However, this misses several interesting aspects of European identity. Of the people surveyed, 43.3 per cent think of themselves primarily as having a national identity, but also as partly European, while 44.0 per cent of the population think of themselves as having only a national identity. There are two ways to look at these results: 56 per cent of people living in Europe sometimes think of themselves as Europeans. This is a huge number of people. But, at the same time, 87.3 per cent of Europeans mostly think of themselves as have a dominant national identity. European identity is only deep for a limited set of people. However, for a large number of people, some European identity exists.

Table 5.2 presents the breakdown for the fifteen member states. I note that the surveys have not yet been done in the newly admitted member states in Eastern Europe. Not surprisingly, having a European identity varies considerably by country and its fits quite closely to the way that European politics plays out. Of the people surveyed in Great Britain, 62.8 per cent have only a national identity. This number shows that the British government's general skepticism about the European integration project reflects the deep-seated attitudes of the British public. Finland, Sweden, Greece, and Austria also have over 50 per cent of people who think of themselves only as nationals. The Swedes, Finns, and Austrians are more recent arrivals in the EU and their populations continue to view themselves primarily in nationalist terms. Therborn (1995) shows that in these societies, the majority of citizens would not be unhappy if their country left the EU.

TABLE 5.2. *European and national identity, by country, 2004* (%)

Country	National only	National and European	European and national	European only
Great Britain	64.7	27.1	4.0	4.2
Finland	59.9	36.8	2.3	1.0
Sweden	57.7	38.1	3.2	1.0
Greece	55.3	39.3	3.0	2.4
Austria	53.0	36.7	6.6	3.7
Ireland	50.1	44.5	2.4	3.1
Netherlands	49.0	43.8	5.1	2.1
Portugal	46.5	46.5	5.3	1.6
Denmark	43.0	51.6	4.2	1.2
Belgium	39.7	44.7	7.9	7.7
Germany	35.4	48.9	9.3	6.4
Spain	32.8	60.0	4.1	3.1
France	30.5	55.2	8.3	5.9
Italy	29.3	59.2	8.2	3.3
Luxembourg	27.8	40.7	12.5	19.0

Note: Some figures do not sum to 100 due to rounding.

Source: Eurobarometer 91, April 2004.

On the other side of the coin, the societies with the largest number of people who sometime think of themselves as European include Luxembourg (73.4%), Italy (72.2%), France (70.3%), Spain (68.2%), and Germany (65.5%). It is not surprising that France and Germany are frequently viewed as at the center of the European political project. Their populations are amongst the most likely to call themselves Europeans. The Italians and Spanish are also very European. Of the five largest member states amongst the European Fifteen, four have majority populations with some European identity and only one, Great Britain, has a majority of people who do not see themselves as European. Even where large majorities of the people sometimes think of themselves as Europeans, there is nowhere near a plurality of people in any of the member states who think of themselves as primarily Europeans. Luxembourg leads with 32.4 per cent, while Italy has 15 per cent, France has 16.5 per cent, Spain has 9 per cent, and Germany has 15.3 per cent.

It is useful to explore how a European identity is related to attitudes toward the EU. Table 5.3 presents answers to questions about attitudes generally toward the EU. A majority (56.2%) of people see Europe as a good thing for their country. Only 16.4 per cent see it as a bad thing. Another question was asked to gauge general attitudes toward the EU; 54.6 per cent of Europeans have a positive image of the EU while 20.2 per cent have a negative image. Taken together, these results suggest why the European governments continue to participate in the EU. People across Europe think that EU membership is a good thing and mostly they think that their countries have benefited from EU membership. This suggests that overall, even though large numbers of people do not think of themselves primarily as Europeans, they generally see EU membership as a good thing for their country.

TABLE 5.3. *Distribution of attitudes toward the EU*

	%
'Do you think that our country's membership in the EU is …?'	
A good thing	56.2
Neither good nor bad	27.4
A bad thing	16.4
'In general, what kind of image does the EU conjure up for you?'	
Very positive	19.3
Fairly positive	35.3
Neutral	26.2
Fairly negative	14.4
Very negative	4.8

Source: Eurobarometer 91, April 2004.

Being European does, however, have an effect on one's attitudes toward the EU. Table 5.4 presents breakdowns of attitudes toward the EU if a person has only a national identity or instead has some European identity. Here, quite clearly, people with some European identity have a much more favorable view of the EU, with 67.1 per cent of them viewing the EU as a good thing for their country, while only 36.8 per cent of people with only a national identity doing so. Only 8.5

TABLE 5.4. *Cross-tabulation of European identity and attitudes toward the EU* (%)

	Only national identity	Some European identity
'Do you think that our country's membership in the EU is…?'		
A good thing	36.8	67.1
Neither good nor bad	32.1	24.4
A bad thing	31.1	8.5
'In general, what kind of image does the EU conjure up for you?'		
Very positive	4.8	12.3
Fairly positive	24.3	53.4
Neutral	36.7	20.3
Fairly negative	21.3	10.4
Very negative	12.9	3.6

Source: Eurobarometer 91, April 2004.

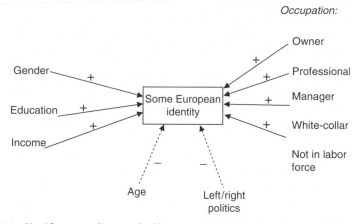

Figure 5.2. Significant predictors of self-perception as 'European.'

Note: Results control for home country.

Source: See Appendix, below.

per cent of people with some European identity think of the EU as a bad thing for their country, while 31.1 per cent of people with only a national identity think that. Similar results appear for the general image of the EU: 65.7 per cent of people with some European identity think of the EU in a positive way, while only 29.1 per cent of people with only a national identity do so.

It is interesting to explore what the social correlates are of people who think of themselves as Europeans. In order to do this, I ran a logit analysis where the dependent variable is whether or not people view themselves as ever being a European. Information on the coding of various variables, their means and standard deviations, and a presentation of the logit analysis is available in the Appendix to this chapter.

Figure 5.2 presents a diagram with the statistically significant determinants of whether or not people in the survey ever view themselves as being European. There is strong confirmation for my argument that the most privileged socioeconomic groups are the most European. Owners, managers, professionals, and other white-collar workers are more likely to think of themselves as Europeans than are blue-collar or service workers. Educated people, regardless of occupation, are also more likely to see themselves as European, and young people are more likely to do so than older people, as are people with higher incomes. All these groups have opportunities to interact with people from other European countries.

There are two interesting control variables that also affect European identity. Men are more likely than women to think of themselves as Europeans, and people who identify themselves as being more right-wing in their political views are less likely to be European. The gender gap in support for the EU is well known (Gabel 1998). The effect of political views is quite interesting. In Europe, people who identify themselves as on the right are more likely to be nationalist in their

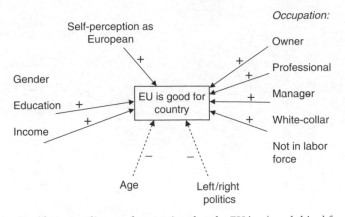

Figure 5.3. Significant predictors of preception that the EU is a 'good thing' for respondent's country.

Note: Results control for home country.

Source: See Appendix, below.

orientation than people on the left. Many right-wing parties favor, for example, restriction of immigration, to preserve jobs but also to preserve national identity. Since right-wing politics are more likely to be nationalist, it makes sense that people who are more to the right value their national identity over a European one.

It is useful to consider how well these variables predict attitudes toward the EU. Figure 5.3 presents the results from a logit model that predicts whether or not a respondent thinks the EU is a good thing for their country. The measures of social class perform as expected. Respondents with higher educations or higher incomes, or who are owners, managers, or white-collar workers have a more positive

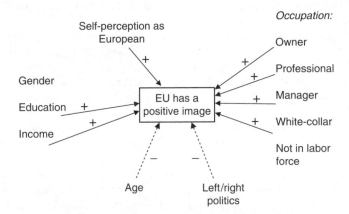

Figure 5.4. Significant predictors of positive perception of the EU.

Note: Results control for home country.

Source: See Appendix 5.1

attitude toward the EU. Older people are less favorable than younger people toward European integration. People who are more left-wing view the EU as more of a good thing than people who are more right-wing.

One of the largest effects in the model is the presence of a European identity. People who ever think of themselves as Europeans are very likely to have a positive attitude toward the EU regardless of social class variables. Figure 5.4 contains the results predicting whether or not respondents have a positive image of the EU. The model produces results virtually identical to the one predicting whether or not a person views the EU as a good thing for their country (I note that Hooghe and Marks (2005) also show similar results).

LANGUAGE USE AND TRAVEL AS MORE DIRECT MEASURES OF INTERACTION

One problem with the results is that it could be argued that the reason there is a class bias to these data is because people who are Europeans have disproportionately benefited from European integration (Gabel 1998). Their being Europeans is not a function of their interactional patterns, but instead of their self-interest. In order to argue that the class variables are also indicators of interaction, I will need to show that they also predict more direct measures of social interaction, like the use of second languages and travel. I use two other surveys here, one that measures the degree to which people speak second languages and the other whether or not people have traveled to other European countries in the past twelve months. Learning and keeping up a second language is a huge investment of time. If people are willing to make such an investment, it must be because they intend to use it. Speaking a second language is an indicator that a person is interacting with people from at least one other society. Obviously, travel to another European country is a strong behavioral indicator of whether or not someone has interacted with people from another country.

One of the problems is that I am limited by the questions asked on each survey. Unfortunately, the European identity question was not asked on either the language or travel survey, so in order to evaluate the overall hypothesis about the linkage between identity and social interaction, I will have to piece together results in a more indirect way. My argument is that the class variables predict identity. If I am right and identity is about interaction patterns, then the class variables ought to predict second language use and European travel as well. Since this is the case, it implies that the European project has predominantly been about the opportunities that upper- and upper-middle-class people have had to interact with their counterparts in other societies. This has made them more 'European'. I do know if respondents think the EU was a good or bad thing for their country on the travel survey. I will use European travel as a measure of interaction with people from other countries and see if it predicts having a

TABLE 5.5. *Second language use overall and by country* (%)

'Do you speak a second language?'	No	Yes
Overall	38.4	61.6
By country:		
Luxembourg	2.3	97.7
Denmark	12.6	87.4
Sweden	12.6	87.4
Netherlands	13.0	87.0
Finland	28.8	71.2
Belgium	37.6	62.4
Germany	41.3	58.7
Italy	44.7	55.3
Ireland	46.6	53.4
Greece	46.8	53.2
France	47.0	53.0
Spain	52.3	47.7
Austria	52.7	47.3
Portugal	53.5	46.5
Great Britain	64.3	35.7

Source: Eurobarometer 54LAN, December 2000.

positive attitude toward the EU. This will be some direct confirmation that interaction produces a more European attitude.

Table 5.5 shows that 61.6 per cent of people in Europe claim to speak a second language as reported in a Eurobarometer conducted in 2000. This result should be interpreted with some caution. The actual level of skill in a second language was not directly measured by the survey: instead, this was a self-report. Table 5.5 also shows that the use of second languages is unequally spread across countries. Citizens who live in the smaller EU countries, such as Luxembourg and the Netherlands, are much more likely to speak a second language than those who live in larger countries. People in the Scandinavian countries of Finland, Sweden, and Denmark are also quite likely to speak a second language. Majorities of the population claim to speak a second language in every country except Austria, Portugal, Spain, and Great Britain. The British are the least likely to speak a second language with 64.3 per cent of them speaking only English.

Table 5.6 explores second language use by country by presenting which languages are spoken the most. Not surprisingly, English is the second language that is spoken most frequently across Europe: 82.4 per cent of the people who claim to speak a second language in Germany speak English and in France the figure is 75 per cent. English is clearly the common language of business, government, and the academy. French is the second most frequently spoken second language, and German the third. Large numbers of Belgians, Italians, Luxembourgers, and British speak French as a second language. Large numbers of Danes, Luxembourgers, and Dutch speak German.

TABLE 5.6. *Distribution of second languages spoken, by country and language, 2000* (%)

	Second language spoken						
	English	French	German	Spanish	Dutch	Italian	Other
Overall	57.5	15.6	11.3	1.8	1.6	1.0	11.2
By country:							
Germany	82.4	5.7	4.5	2.5	0.7	0.2	4.0
Sweden	82.3	0.6	4.2	1.3	0.7	0.1	10.8
Greece	78.6	4.4	8.2	0.6	0.0	2.3	5.9
France	75.0	4.5	5.9	6.9	0.0	4.3	3.4
Denmark	74.6	0.7	20.3	0.0	0.0	0.1	4.3
Finland	70.9	0.1	2.6	0.2	0.0	0.3	25.9
Austria	66.1	3.3	2.1	0.2	0.0	0.0	28.3
Spain	66.0	20.8	1.5	4.2	0.0	1.9	5.6
Portugal	59.5	30.7	2.7	5.9	0.4	0.0	0.8
Italy	59.2	34.0	3.8	2.0	0.1	0.4	0.5
Netherlands	53.3	6.5	32.3	0.5	4.2	0.6	2.6
Belgium	26.2	45.4	6.9	2.5	14.4	2.5	2.1
Ireland	15.1	19.5	6.2	0.9	0.4	0.0	57.8
Great Britain	12.4	49.7	14.9	8.9	0.7	1.9	11.5
Luxembourg	8.0	41.9	38.4	0.5	1.2	2.0	8.0

Notes: In some countries, there are non-native speakers of the dominant language (4.5% for example in Germany). Of the Irish, 56.9% report Irish (or Gaelic) as their second language; of the Finns, 24.4% report Finnish.
Source: Eurobarometer 54LAN, December 2000.

TABLE 5.7. *How people use second languages and why they learn them*

	%
Use language at work	34.9
Use language for social reasons*	76.4
Are motivated to keep up language for work	47.1
Are motivated to keep up language for social reasons*	78.7

*Reasons include: holiday travel, reading, movies, talking to people from other countries and cultures.
Source: Eurobarometer 54LAN, 2000.

One interesting question concerns why people learn second languages. Table 5.7 presents the results of several questions on this issue. Respondents who knew second languages were asked the conditions under which they used them. Since they could respond to as many categories as they liked, people could check both work and social purposes. Of respondents who have a second language, 34.9 per cent report using a second language at work. In the data, there are only about 65 per cent of the respondents who were working. This implies that over half the people who work and know a second language have an opportunity to use their second language at work. This is a remarkable fact implying that many people routinely interact with others across borders for their job. An even larger percentage of people (76.4%) who

Table 5.8. *Cross-tabulation of age by second language use*

Second language	Age					
	15–24	25–34	35–44	45–54	55–64	65+
Yes	82.4%	72.9%	67.5%	58.2%	46.5%	34.1%
No	17.6%	27.1%	32.5%	41.8%	53.5%	65.9%

Source: Eurobarometer 54LAN, 2000.

know a second language report using it for social purposes, including holiday travel, reading, movies, and talking to people from other countries and cultures. Keeping up a second language implies both opportunity to use it and motivation to do so, and I present data on this. Here, 47.1 per cent say they do so for purposes of work while 78.7 per cent are motivated for social reasons.

It is useful to explore the linkage between age and second language use. There has been a great expansion of the EU, both politically and economically in the past twenty-five years. Education systems have responded to this expansion by teaching second languages more seriously. In small countries and in Scandinavia, students learn second languages (particularly English) from a very young age. Table 5.8 shows how strongly linked age is to second language use, 82.4 per cent of people aged 15–24 in the survey report having a second language while only 34.1 per cent of people over age 65 report using a second language. This survey suggests that as the population ages and the older cohorts die, the ability to use a second language will be almost universal across Europe.

It is useful to model the determinants of who speaks a second language in order to evaluate the degree to which second language use is connected to social class. Details of the logit model predicting whether or not a person claimed to speak a

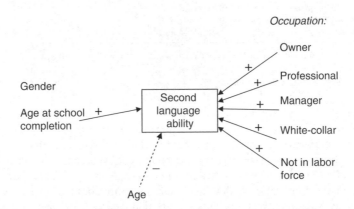

Figure 5.5. Significant predictors of second language ability.

Note: Results control for home country.

Source: See Appendix, below.

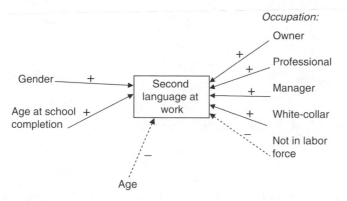

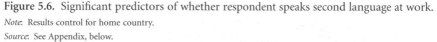

Age

Figure 5.6. Significant predictors of whether respondent speaks second language at work.
Note: Results control for home country.
Source: See Appendix, below.

second language appear in the Appendix to this chapter. Figure 5.5 presents the results in a diagram. Not surprisingly, age is one of the strongest predictors of whether or not a person speaks a second language. But second language use is highly related to social class as well. Education is a strong predictor of second language use. Owners, professionals, managers, and white-collar workers are all more likely to speak a second language than are blue-collar or service workers. Professionals and managers are particularly more likely to speak a second language. One result that deserves some attention is that people not in the labor force are also more likely to speak a second language than blue-collar or service workers. This is because respondents who are students are in this category, as are people who are unemployed, many of whom are young.

Figure 5.6 presents the determinants of whether or not people who speak a second language use it at work. The effect of age lessens on this variable. There is also a large gender difference with men much more likely to speak a second language at work than women. Again, the class variables dominate the equation. Educated people are more likely in general to use second languages at work. Owners, managers, professionals, and white-collar workers are all more likely to use a second language at work than are blue-collar or service workers. I note that people not in the labor force report not using a second language at work (implying that the measurement has at least face validity). Second language use at work would seem to be a good indicator of interaction with people from different societies. Since this usage is highly related to social class, it suggests that people who are more educated and have better jobs are more likely to interact with people in different societies.

Figure 5.7 shows the determinants of second language use for social purposes. These results are quite different than the earlier results and deserve some remarks. First, there is no gender gap in second language use for social purposes. Both men and women report using second languages for social purposes equally. None of the occupational variables predict whether or not people use a second language

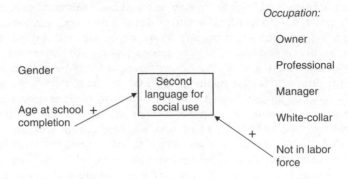

Figure 5.7. Significant predictors of whether respondent speaks second language for social purposes.

Note: Results control for home country.

Source: See Appendix, below.

for social purposes. Age also does not predict using a second language for social purposes. The strongest predictor in this sector is education. Here, educated people know second languages and like to use them to travel, read, and interact with people from different societies. It is also the case that people not in the labor force report using second languages for social purposes more than other workers. Again, this category includes students, who tend to travel.

The results of the determinants of second language use provide interesting confirmation for the idea that some Europeans are more likely to interact with people from other countries than others. In particular, the young and educated use second languages to travel and converse with people from other cultures. There is also strong evidence that owners, managers, professionals, and other white-collar workers have the opportunity to use second languages at work, which implies that they find themselves talking to people from other European countries, either face to face or on the phone, as a routine part of their jobs. Since these are the same people who are more likely to think of themselves as Europeans, it follows that part of the reason is their routine interactions with people from other countries.

The final indicator of whether or not people across Europe encounter one another is the most direct measure we have. Table 5.9 shows data on frequency of travel to other European countries in the past twelve months. These data come from a Eurobarometer conducted in 1997. The question asked was, 'Have you traveled outside of your home country in the past twelve months?' While this is a good measure of the possibility that people encounter citizens of other states, it is not a perfect measure. Much travel in Europe is for vacations, especially to sunny, warm beaches. Many travelers board a plane in their home country, go to resort areas dominated by their countrymen, and spend their entire vacations relatively unaware of the local culture and people. In most resort areas, it is possible to go to bars and restaurants where the staff speaks your language. Still, some travel is more centered on either business or cultural appreciation. Unfortunately, it is impossible with

TABLE 5.9. *Distribution of European travel 1997* (%)

'Have you traveled outside of your home country in the past twelve months?'	No	Yes
TOTAL	75.1	24.9
By country:		
Luxembourg	43.9	56.1
Netherlands	57.7	42.3
Germany	58.8	41.2
Denmark	65.2	34.8
Belgium	68.1	31.9
Sweden	68.4	31.6
Great Britain	76.3	23.7
Ireland	76.9	23.1
France	77.6	22.4
Austria	78.3	21.7
Finland	83.3	16.7
Italy	88.4	11.6
Spain	88.6	11.4
Greece	88.7	11.3
Portugal	94.5	5.5

Note: Figures do not sum to 100 due to rounding.

Source: Eurobarometer 48, Fall 1997.

these data to separate out travel where social interactions with people from a different country were more central to the visit versus pure tourism. In order to show the efficacy of this measure, I show that it is predicted by the variables which should be related to it. I also show that it is a good predictor of attitudes toward the EU implying that having traveled recently makes one more likely to see the other people in the EU as being part of something worthy of support.

Table 5.9 shows that 24.9 per cent of those surveyed said they had traveled to another country in the past twelve months. Travel varied quite a bit by country. Since it costs money to travel, one would expect that people in the richer countries are more likely to travel than people in the poorer countries. People from Greece, Spain, and Portugal are the least likely to travel (and of course, they have the least reason to travel to warm climates for vacations). People from the smaller countries such as Luxembourg and the Netherlands, are the most likely to travel, reflecting the ease with which one can move from one country to another. Of the big countries, the Germans are the most likely to travel.

Table 5.10 presents data on the destination of travel. The largest number of travelers visited Spain, followed almost equally by Germany, France, Italy, and

TABLE 5.10. *Main destinations of travelers in past twelve months* (%)

Main destinations in Europe						
Spain	Germany	France	Italy	Greece	Great Britain	Other
22.9	12.2	12.1	10.7	10.2	6.8	25.1

Source: Eurobarometer 48, 1997.

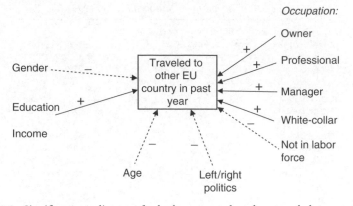

Figure 5.8. Significant predictors of whether respondent has traveled to another EU country in the past year.

Note: Results control for home country.

Source: See Appendix, below.

Greece. Since one cannot separate out the reasons for visits, one can assume that many of the visitors to Spain, Greece, and Italy went for vacations. The travel measure is picking up the degree to which people are going on vacation. Since the vacationers tend to interact with people from other countries in a mostly superficial way, the travel measure may be a flawed indicator of social interaction. The six biggest destinations (including Great Britain) account for 74.9 per cent of the visits.

Figure 5.8 presents results from a logit analysis where the dependent variable was whether or not a person had traveled outside their country in the past twelve months. The strongest predictors in the model are the class variables, i.e. education and income, and whether or not the person is an owner, professional, manager, or a white-collar worker. There are several other interesting effects in the model. People who have more right-wing politics are less likely to travel than people with more left-wing politics. This suggests that people who are more strongly committed to a national identity tend to stay home and not travel. Young people are also more likely to travel than older people. Regardless of age, people who are not employed are less likely to travel, indicating that travel costs money.

These results are direct evidence that the people most likely to interact with other Europeans are those who are educated and who hold higher-status occupations. It also shows that older people and more conservative people are less likely to interact with people from other countries. It should be noted that these variables also predict that such people do not have a European identity. Since they appear to travel less, one can infer that either they do not travel because they do not want to be around other Europeans or alternatively that because they have not been around other Europeans, they are less favorable toward them. While it is possible that the measure of travel is not a perfect measure of the desire to interact with people from other countries, it is clear that there is some evidence that people who do travel, do so because they want to encounter people from other countries.

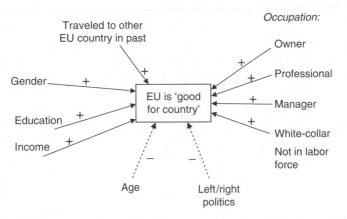

Figure 5.9. Significant predictors of whether respondent views EU as 'a good thing' for home country.

Note: Results control for home country.

Source: See Appendix, below.

If traveling abroad does expose one to people from another country, then such travel might affect a person's attitudes toward the EU. One would expect that those who travel and like it, would view the EU in a more favorable light than those who did not travel. Figure 5.9 presents the results of a regression predicting whether a person thinks the EU is a good or bad thing for their country. The results generally confirm my earlier analysis that showed that the class variables are the strongest predictors of support for the EU. I have included one additional variable, whether or not people have traveled to another European country in the past twelve months. It turns out that people who have interacted with other Europeans in the past twelve months are more likely to have a positive view of the EU than people who have not traveled outside of their home country regardless of the class variables. This implies that travel is indeed a predictor of how one feels about the European project. So, having had interaction with other Europeans recently, without account of the class variables, one's age, and one's political views, makes one feel more confident about the EU being a good thing. I conclude that while the measure of interaction (i.e. travel) may not be perfect, it is not a terrible measure. It has face validity as a measure and it has predictive validity (i.e. it is predicted by relevant causal factors and it affects a dependent variable it ought to predict).

CONCLUSION

Generally, there is little evidence that there is an outpouring of sentiment amongst the citizens of Europe for there to be a European nation. In spite of the obvious limits of survey data, the results presented here help make sense of a lot of reasons why this is the case. Only 12.7 per cent of the people living in Western Europe primarily think of themselves as Europeans. While all together, 56 per cent of people in Europe sometimes think of themselves as European, 44 per cent still have only a national identity. For the 43.3 per cent who sometimes think of themselves as European, their main allegiance is still in terms of being members of a nation-state first. In Great Britain, Finland, Sweden, and Austria, majorities of the population never think of themselves as Europeans.

The literature on national collective identities is helpful in understanding both the emergence of such identities and their ultimate use in building a nation-state. I show that citizens of Europe who interact with each other are more frequently likely to view themselves as Europeans. But, Europe so far has been a class project, a project that favors the educated, owners of businesses, managers, and professionals, and the young. The cross-class alliance that Deutsch argued was necessary for a nation-state to exist has not emerged. Instead, the economic integration project has produced patterns of interaction mainly amongst the young, educated, business owners, and managerial, professional, and white-collar workers. Ironically, those with a European identification clearly represent one set of social groups to the exclusion of others.

There are not enough people with strong European identities to push forward a Europe-wide political integration project. While there is a majority in most countries who sometimes think of themselves as European, this is a hyphenated identity that implies support for Europe under some situations but not others. Whether citizens will tend to think of themselves more as Europeans or of a national identity on any particular political issue is likely to be greatly affected by the issue at stake and their class position.

This suggests two futures for a potential European national identity project. First, I consider the scenario for why European national identity will not emerge. For the majority of the European population, the opportunity to interact with people across borders has been greatly circumscribed either by choice or by lack of opportunity. Blue-collar, service workers, and the less educated have not had the opportunity to learn second languages or interact for business or travel with their counterparts in other countries. As a result, they have lacked the impetus to see themselves as Europeans. Educated people and people with high-status occupations are more likely to become at least partly Europeans, but there are not enough of them to have a big effect on creating a mass European identity.

There are also opponents of a European collective identity. For blue-collar and service workers, the EU has not delivered more jobs and jobs with better pay. There is the suspicion that the EU is an elite project that has benefited mainly the educated, and our evidence bears out that this is what people experience. The elderly still remember World War II and its aftermath. They have less interest in knowing more about their neighbors and more in keeping a strong sense of national identity. Those politically on the right have decided to defend the nation. They view European identity and the EU with skepticism and are satisfied with the national story.

There are differences in how this has played out across countries. In Britain, national identity is the strongest and, not surprisingly, second language use is the lowest. National identity is still strong in Scandinavia as well and there is skepticism toward the European project as a result. In France, Italy, and Germany, European identity is the strongest and in all of these societies, support for the EU remains high.

It is possible to present a scenario that implies that the process of European identity building is just starting and that over time the forces to produce more European collective identity will rise. First, the European project has only really been going on since the mid-1960s. The biggest expansion of opportunities to interact with other people in Europe occurred beginning with the Single Market in the mid-1980s. It is the case that it just might be too early to see a majority emerging to create a European nation. After all, national identities took hundreds of years to evolve and Europeans have only been interacting in large numbers for between twenty and twenty-five years. Second, demography is working in the EU's favor. Young people are more likely to know second languages, be educated, travel, and be more open to the EU. As older people pass away and the young grow to take their place, there should be more people who think of themselves as Europeans. Third, as skill levels rise and education increases generally, people will be more interested in the cultural story of being with other Europeans. One of our more interesting results was the fact that educated people were the most likely to use a second language for travel and communication. As these people increase in numbers in the population, one would expect that the European identity would become more widespread.

As European markets continue to integrate, people will have more opportunities to interact with people in other countries. This could occur through work. But it could also be that awareness of media, tourism, and culture in other countries expands. So, for example, the creation of a European football league would spark more Europe-wide interest in games being played across Europe. Players from all countries would be playing on the different teams. Games would be televised, people would have the opportunity to watch their favorite national players even when they played on foreign teams, and they would travel more to support their teams.

It is useful to consider the implication of people having hyphenated identities (i.e. German-European). Generally, the fact that a majority of citizens sometimes think of themselves as Europeans implies that they are not likely to go to war with their neighbors because they view their counterparts in other societies as being part of a larger social group, i.e. Europeans. In the core of Europe where people hold such views most strongly, governments decided to remove border controls completely, accepting the idea that there should be free movement for all Europeans. It follows that if the right political issues were on the table, solidarity with citizens across Europe might lead to increased cooperation with national neighbors.

In many countries the rise of European identity has been accompanied by a resurgence in regional identity (Risse 2005). Regional groups are likely to view the EU as an ally, not an opponent, in their struggle for autonomy from their national governments (Diez Medrano and Gutiérrez 2001). European identity makes citizens more readily accepting of trade-offs their governments might make concerning issues of common interest across countries. This is because citizens will not see every EU issue as a zero-sum game, but instead will understand that their governments' actions in Brussels are part of a repeated set of interactions with like-minded states. This repeated interaction is built on the trust that because everyone is interested in the EU in the long run, over time everyone will be a net winner.

It is clear that the process has not reached a kind of Deutschian tipping point that might produce a groundswell of support for a European nation-state. In the next chapter, I explore the theme of the emergence of a European identity by considering more carefully the types of social field that have evolved in Europe. While business is one kind of interaction that occurs in Europe, people also interact to discuss a great many common issues of interest. I present some case studies of the building of social fields across Europe that show some of the ways in which people routinely interact by looking at the creation of organizations, and the degree to which they share education, media, and culture.

APPENDIX

The data analyzed in Ch. 5 originate from a series of surveys called Eurobarometers, which are financed by the European Commission and carried out simultaneously in the European Union member countries. They study the social and political opinions of persons living in the member countries. The material is collected by specialized organizations in each country. For example, in Finland, the material is collected by Gallup. The collection is coordinated by INRA Europe (International Research Associates Europe).

The first series was published in 1974. As a rule the surveys are carried out twice a year, in spring and in the fall. They consist of regularly repeated questions, and additional questions on topics considered important at the time of the survey. The regularly asked questions deal with the European Community/European Union, the European Parliament, and the functioning of democracy in respondents' native countries. The alternating questions have focused, for example, on the following issues: employment, unemployment, the roles of sexes, ecology and energy policy, position of children and adolescents, poverty, health, biotechnology, regional development, consumer behavior, and education.

The surveys are archived at data centers around the world and are available to researchers everywhere. The surveys used here were provided through the Survey Research Center at the University of California and were accessed through the Interuniversity Consortium for Political and Social Research (ICPSR) at the University of Michigan. The identity questions were asked in Eurobarometer 61, taken in February–March of 2004. It is useful to review the questions (where they were not reviewed in text) and how the data was coded for the data analysis.

For the data analysis, variables were coded thus:

Some EU Identity: 0 = national identity only, 1 = European only, European and nationality, nationality and European.
EU good/bad thing: 0 = neither good nor bad, bad thing, 1 = good thing.
EU positive/negative image: 0 = very negative, fairly negative, neutral, 1 = fairly positive, very positive
Gender: 0 = female, 1 = male.

Age: Age in years.

Age at school completion: age in years during last year of school.

Income scale: income from all sources was reported. It was converted into local currency. It was then converted into five groups for each country based on the income distribution. Number '1' is the lowest income group and '5' the highest.

Left/right politics. The question asked was, 'People talk about politics as being left and right. How would you place yourself on this scale?' Respondents were asked to place themselves on a five-point scale where 1 indicated the furthest left and 5 was the furthest right.

The occupational variables were coded based on the response to the question: 'What is your current occupation?' Respondents were given nineteen choices. I created a series of dummy variables whereby a person was coded 0 if they were in the category and 1 if they were not. The following groups were coded as 1 for each of the dummy variables.

Owners: 1 = self-employed, categories 5–9: farmer, fisherman, professional, owner of a shop, craftsmen, other self-employed, business proprietor, partner in a business.

Managers: 1 = general management, middle management, supervisor, categories 11, 12, 16.

Professionals: 1 = employed professional, category 10.

Other white-collar: 1 = employed, working at desk, salesperson, categories 14, 15.

Blue-collar and service; left-out category, categories 15, 17, 18.

Not in the labor force: 1 = house caretaker, student, unemployed, retired, temporarily ill, categories 1–4.

Country dummy variables; 0 = if respondent not in the country, 1 = respondent in the country. Left-out category for all the analyses is Great Britain.

The means and standard deviations used in the data analyses reported in the chapter are contained in Table 5A.1. The dummy variables are intrepreted thus: 52% of the people in the gender variable were men, while 8% of the occupations were owners, etc. Average age in the studies was 44.83 years. Fifty-four per cent of the people have some European identity, 56% viewed the EU as a good thing for their country, and 54% had a positive image of the EU.

TABLE 5A.1. *Means and standard deviations for logit analysis of determinants of European identity*

Variable	Mean	SD
Gender	.52	.50
Left/right politics	2.32	1.06
Age at school completion	18.44	1.96
Age	44.83	10.57
Income scale	3.29	1.49
Owner	.08	.27
Manager	.10	.28
Professional	.13	.12
White-collar	.11	.30
Service/blue-collar	.21	.41
Not in the labor force	.37	.50
Some EU identity	.54	.49
EU good/bad thing	.56	.46
EU positive/negative image	.54	.48

All the data analyses were carried out using logit models in the computer program SPSS. Logit analysis is the appropriate technique when the dependent variable in a data analysis is 'limited' (discrete not continuous). Researchers often want to analyze whether some event, such as voting, participation in a public program, business success or failure, morbidity, or mortality, occurred or not. In my case, I am interested as to whether a person does or does not have some European identity. More details on logit analysis and its interpretation are available from Ameniya (1985). For nontechnical readers, a positive statistically significant coefficient implies that more of variable X makes it more likely that the respondent will be in category '1' rather than category 0. So a positive coeffient for gender implies that men are more likely than women to think of themselves as Europeans. A negative coefficient implies that as X increases, the probability that the respondent will be in category 0 increases. So, for example, in the case of European identity, age is negatively related to having a European identity. This means that older people are less likely to see themselves as Europeans.

Table 5A.2 presents the results from the logit analysis predicting whether or not a respondent is more or less likely to view him- or herself as a European. In the text, I discuss

TABLE 5A.2. *Results of a logit analysis predicting whether or not respondents ever viewed themselves as a European*

Variables	B	SE(B)
Gender	.20**	.05
Age at school completion	.04**	.00
Income	.06**	.02
Age	−.004**	.002
Left/right politics	−.06**	.01
Occupation:		
Owner	.25**	.11
Professional	.74**	.23
Manager	.51**	.10
White-collar	.35**	.09
Not in the labor force	−.01	.07
Belgium	.73**	.13
Denmark	.60**	.13
Germany	.71**	.11
Greece	.18	.13
Spain	1.09**	.13
France	1.32**	.13
Ireland	.60**	.13
Italy	1.59**	.13
Netherlands	.32**	.12
Luxembourg	.83**	.16
Portugal	.87**	.12
Finland	−.28*	.13
Sweden	.08	.12
Austria	.32**	.12
Constant	−1.19**	.16

*p < .05.
**p < .01.

TABLE 5A.3. *Results of a logit analysis predicting attitudes toward the EU*

Variables	'Is EU a good/bad thing?'		'Overall does EU have positive/negative image?'	
	B	SE(B)	B	SE(B)
Gender	.06	.06	−.07	.05
Age at school completion	.02**	.00	.04**	.00
Income	.01*	.00	.02*	.01
Age	−.019**	.001	−.03**	.00
Left/right politics	−.01*	.003	−.02**	.00
Occupation:				
Owner	.07*	.02	.02*	.01
Professional	.12	.08	.05	.05
Manager	.09**	.03	.09*	.04
White-collar	.05*	.02	.03	.02
Not in labor force	.05	.02	.04	.03
Belgium	.14**	.05	.29**	.06
Denmark	.08	.05	−.01	.06
Germany	.05	.04	.03	.06
Greece	.18**	.05	.60**	.06
Spain	.17**	.04	.45	.06
France	−.09*	.05	.01	.06
Ireland	.34**	.05	.60**	.06
Italy	.20**	.06	.32**	.06
Netherlands	.06	.05	−.01	.06
Luxembourg	.35**	.06	.39**	.08
Portugal	.16**	.05	.43**	.06
Finland	−.03	.05	.01	.06
Sweden	−.28**	.05	−.43**	.06
Austria	−.32**	.05	−.11*	.05
European identity	.35**	.02	.42**	.03
Constant	2.18**	.06	3.01**	.07

*p < .05.
**p < .01.

the statistically significant and insignificant results. Table 5A.3 presents the results for the logit analysis on whether or not the respondent thinks the EU is good or bad for his or her country and the logit analysis for his or her overall view of the EU.

The Eurobarometer used for the language data was 54.2, taken in the fall of 2000. It concerned knowledge of second languages. It surveyed language (multiple responses, second and third language); self-assessment of language proficiency; frequency and manner of use of foreign languages; manner of acquisition of foreign languages; motives for learning a new foreign language; and possible reasons against acquisition of a foreign language. All the demographic variables were based on the same questions used in Eurobarometer 61. The only variables that were unique concerned the language variables. The data analysis uses the question 'Do you speak a second language?' The dependent variable in the analysis is coded 0 if the respondent does not speak a second language and 1 if they do.

In order to assess the conditions under which people who had second languages used them, I created two other dependent variables for the speakers of second languages. One of

TABLE 5A.4. *Means and standard deviations for variables used in data analysis*

Variable	Mean	SD
Gender	.51	.49
Age at school completion	17.44	4.96
Age	43.46	17.47
Owner	.09	.27
Manager	.11	.28
Professional	.10	.13
White-collar	.14	.30
Service/blue-collar	.23	.41
Not in labor force	.33	.50
Second language	.62	.48
Use language at work	.34	.50
Use language for social reasons	.76	.28

Source: Eurobarometer 54LAN, 2000.

the variables was based on the question, 'Do you use a second language for work?' The dependent variable was coded 0 for people who did not use their second language at work and 1 for people who did. A series of questions were also asked about other conditions where people might use their second language. These include communicating with family and friends, reading books, seeing movies, travel, and 'to get to know people from other cultures'. If the respondent answered 'no' to all these questions, they were coded 0 and if they answered 'yes' to any of these questions, they were coded 1.

Table 5A.4 contains the means and standard deviations for the variables used in the analysis. Fifty-one per cent of the sample is male, the average age at school completion is 17.44, and the average age in the sample is 43.46. Of the sample 62% claim to speak a foreign language. It is useful to compare Table 5A.4 to Table 5A.1 on the socio-demographic variables. The samples are quite comparable: they have similar numbers of men and women, similar educational levels, and similar occupational distributions.

Table 5A.5 contains the results of the logit analyses of the three dependent variables. The statistically significant variables are discussed in the text.

Eurobarometer 48.0 was conducted in the fall of 1997. This round of Eurobarometer surveys queried respondents on standard Eurobarometer measures such as public awareness of and attitudes toward the European Union, and also focused on issues surrounding travel. Respondents were asked whether they had taken a trip in 1997 and, if not, the reason they did not travel. Respondents were allowed to mention up to five trips they had taken. They were also asked which countries and locales they visited, who accompanied them, and how they traveled to their destinations. I used these questions to construct a measure of whether or not a respondent had traveled to another European country. A variable was coded 0 if the respondent had not visited another EU country in the past twelve months and 1 if they had. I note that people could have traveled to a non-EU country and be coded 0 on this variable.

Table 5A.6 presents the descriptive statistics for the dataset. If one compares this sample to Tables 5A.1 and 5A.4, one sees that the samples have similar socio-demographic characteristics. Table 5A.7 presents the results of the logit analyses. These results are discussed in the text.

TABLE 5A.5. *Logit analysis predicting second language use overall, at work, and for social purposes*

Variables	Second language use		Work use		Social use	
	B	SE(B)	B	SE(B)	B	SE(B)
Gender	.03	.04	.34**	.05	−.01	.05
Age at school completion	.04**	.00	.01**	.00	.02**	.00
Age	−.06**	.00	−.01**	.00	.00	.00
Occupation:						
Owner	.68*	.08	.68**	.09	.13	.10
Professional	1.63**	.24	1.06**	.19	.28	.23
Manager	1.41**	.09	.92**	.08	.15	.09
White-collar	.96**	.08	.74**	.08	.14	.08
Not in labor force	.60**	.06	−.70**	.05	.23**	.07
Belgium	−.22**	.09	.30**	.10	−.07	.10
Denmark	1.99**	.11	.56**	.10	1.35**	.12
Germany	.31**	.09	.19	.10	.69**	.11
Greece	−.08**	.08	−.10	.12	.35**	.12
Spain	−.31**	.09	−.28**	.13	.02	.11
France	−.32**	.09	−.06	.11	.25**	.10
Ireland	.36	.19	.99**	.25	.39	.22
Italy	.16	.09	−.22	.13	−.16	.15
Netherlands	.21**	.08	.25**	.11	.14	.12
Luxembourg	4.96**	.57	.83**	.13	1.46**	.18
Portugal	-.07	.08	.13	.11	.09	.10
Finland	.70**	.09	.71**	.10	.93**	.11
Sweden	1.89**	.11	.55**	.10	1.89**	.14
Austria	−1.04**	.08	−.07	.11	.54**	.13
Constant	1.39**	.09	−.84**	.10	.21*	.10

*p < .05.
**p < .01.
Source: Eurobarometer 54LAN, 2000.

TABLE 5A.6. *Means and standard deviations for analysis of European travel data*

Variable	Mean	SD
Gender	.48	.50
Age at school completion	17.04	4.46
Age	43.54	17.92
Owner	.09	.27
Manager	.09	.28
Professional	.15	.13
White-collar	.13	.30
Service/blue-collar	.20	.41
Not in labor force	.34	.50
Left/right politics	3.21	2.02
Income (harmonized)	31.71	40.72
Europe travel	.26	.44
EU good/bad thing	2.46	1.23

Source: Eurobarometer 47, 1997.

TABLE 5A.7. *Logit analysis for determinants of European travel and question, 'Is EU good or bad for your country?'*

Variables	European travel		EU good/bad	
	B	SE(B)	B	SE(B)
Gender	−.17**	.04	.09**	.01
Age at school completion	.01**	.00	.02**	.00
Income	.00	.00	.01*	.00
Age	−.019**	.01	−.03**	.00
Left/right politics	−.01**	.003	−.02**	.00
Occupation:				
Owner	.07*	.02	.02*	.01
Professional	.26**	.08	.13**	.03
Manager	.66**	.07	.15**	.03
White-collar	.46**	.07	.14**	.02
Not in labor force	−.32**	.06	.02	.02
Belgium	.44**	.09	−.02	.04
Denmark	.36**	.10	.15**	.04
Germany	.87**	.09	−.16	.03
Greece	−.97**	.12	.25**	.04
Spain	−.89**	.13	.20**	.04
France	−.17**	.11	.00	.04
Ireland	−.18**	.10	.68**	.04
Italy	−.99**	.13	.43**	.03
Netherlands	.75**	.12	.48**	.04
Luxembourg	1.32**	.11	.39**	.04
Portugal	−1.67**	.11	.19**	.04
Finland	−.54**	.12	−.01	.04
Sweden	.26**	.11	−.06	.04
Austria	−.17	.11	−.17**	.03
European travel			.12**	.01
Constant	−1.73**	.12	1.98**	.04

$p < .05.$
$**p < .01.$

Source: Eurobarometer 47, 1997.

6

What is European Society?

As a result of changes in European politics and the European economy, the likelihood of social interaction between people who live in different countries in Europe has expanded dramatically over the past twenty-five years. While business creates a large number of social fields in which people from different countries can interact, it is only one area in which the frequency of encounters between such people has changed. People travel to attend meetings of European organizations; live, work, and study abroad for shorter or longer periods of time; sometimes retire abroad; and consume news, television, movies, music, and books which make them aware of what is going on in other countries. Documenting these patterns is difficult; it is hard to figure out how many such social fields exist, and harder to sample from them; it is even more challenging to study how these fields have changed over time.

My strategy in this chapter is to consider various ways in which to index the creation of European social fields. I consider it a preliminary attempt to establish the degree to which a Europe-wide society and culture might exist, how widespread it might be, and how it differentially affects people from around Europe. I do not consider my cases to be exhaustive, or even a sample of all possible fields. Instead I hope that the consistency of my results inspires others to work more on this issue.

From the identity data in the last chapter, one can argue that there are three sorts of people in Europe: a relatively small number of people deeply immersed in social interactions across Europe on a daily basis and who are thus Europeans; people who occasionally travel abroad for work or vacation, may know some people from other societies, and consume some common popular European culture by means of movies, television, music, or books, but still remain wedded to a national perspective on events and the national vernacular for culture; and people who remain firmly wedded to the national vernacular, travel little, don't speak second languages, and consume only the national popular culture. When I consider who participates the most in Europe-wide social fields, my general conclusion is consistent with what was presented in the previous chapter. The groups who are the most active in European society are the educated, owners, managers, professionals, other white-collar workers, and the young.

One of the strongest forms of social integration is migration (Favell 2005; 2007). When EU residents leave their country and move to another they are creating ties to the host country culture and at the same time maintaining ties to their home country. From the 1950s until the 1980s, migration within Europe was mostly from southern to northern Europe, the main reason for this being the move of less skilled people to higher-paid jobs. Beginning in the mid-1980s, contemporary European migration changed to reflect the EU's opening of travel, educational, and work opportunities (R. King 2002) across national borders. Citizens from one EU member state began to move to others in greater numbers. At the top of the skill distribution, Europeans migrate for the best jobs (Favell (forthcoming) calls these people 'Eurostars'). Europeans now go to university in other countries, more frequently marry foreigners as a result of their travels, and retire abroad. The people who are most likely to migrate are professionals, managers, educated people, the financially better-off, and the young.

Another direct way to look for a European society is to consider the evolution of Europe-wide voluntary associations. Such organizations exist to provide fields where like-minded people from different countries can meet to discuss issues of common interest. My analysis reveals that most of the nongovernmental organizations operating on a European basis serve professions and business associations. There are also a significant number of organizations that are involved in popular charities, political issues such as the environment, or particular sports and hobbies. All have significantly expanded in number since the announcement of the Single Market in the mid-1980s.

This result, again, is quite consistent with my analysis of who is a European. Professionals, academics, and managers not only travel for their work, but have formed trans-European associations to support and encourage interactions. The growth in the number of traditional nonprofits such as charities, political action groups, and trans-European associations dedicated to sports and hobbies are probably also biased by social class. Building such organizations requires time, money, and interest, and middle- and upper-middle-class people are more likely to have these.

People who work in the education establishments in all countries of the EU are probably the leading actors explicitly engaged in building European society. In the previous chapter, I showed that education is one of the strongest predictors of having a European identity, speaking a second language, and being interested in communicating with people who live in another society. I argue that the educated elites are at the forefront of European society-building, because in many ways the European identity project is theirs.

I explore the ways in which European social fields have been constructed by educators interested in promoting an agenda of creating Europeans. School superintendents of primary and secondary schools meet yearly from across Europe to discuss what might be a 'European' education. Language training is one of the core elements of such an education. An other has been a subtle rewriting of history textbooks to tell a more European version of national history.

At the university level, the Erasmus program, sponsored by the EU, allows college students to spend a semester or year abroad. I examine in some detail how students experience this program and how it affects their futures. The literature shows that students who go abroad tend to come from upper-middle-class families. It also shows that the experience changes their attitude toward people from other countries and makes them more likely to see themselves as European. Students who spent time abroad are significantly more likely to work abroad after college.

Education ministers from all European member-state countries have embarked on a project to create what is called the 'European Higher Education Space.' The Bologna process is pushing European universities to converge in the degrees they offer and the ways in which they count course credits. The goal of these reforms is to allow students to study anywhere in Europe and transfer credits easily. Such a system would also produce transparency in qualifications and allow employers to compare degrees from different university systems. All levels of educational elites are actively trying to socialize students to be Europeans.

While all these experiences tend to produce 'Europeans,' the fact is that very small numbers of people participate. Only 2–3 per cent of European nationals currently live across borders. Only 3–4 per cent of all college students spend significant time abroad. While everyone does go to school and most young people speak second languages, over all, experience in other societies is likely to be limited to vacation travel, discussing business issues with colleagues from other societies over the phone, and the occasional business trip. Of course, the people who have even these experiences are generally those with higher education and who hold higher skilled jobs.

There is another way to view how European society is forming. Deutsch and other theorists of national identity argued that the media and the emergence of a common culture are pivotal to the creation of a national identity. Given the high level of at least partial identification with being a European across Europe, it is plausible to look for some elements of an emergent European culture, and to that end it is useful to look more closely at popular culture. Here, I consider the degree to which media organizations are owned and operated by a small set of corporations. I also consider the origins of music, television, movies, and books being consumed across Europe in order to see if at any given time the same things are being viewed or read across national borders.

Media companies sell some of the same content in many places. But, they also tailor some of what they produce for local consumption. National media companies continue to produce media for local consumption only, but there are elements of a European culture in all forms of media. There is an international business press that writes in English and is read by top executives. In terms of the content of popular culture, it is not uncommon for books, music or films to cross over European borders and become popular in different societies. The advent of cable television and the proliferation of cable channels have made it possible to watch shows originating from all around Europe. Ironically, one source of cultural convergence across European societies is US-produced media. American movies, television, pop stars, and authors are present in European media; but in all the largest countries in Europe, national language and culture persist. So, for example, in popular music, there are German, French, Italian, and British pop stars that do not cross over to other countries, although there are some exceptions. I consider the emergence of a Europe-wide pop song in the summer of 2005 called 'Axel F,' a dance song that had its roots in several countries.

Taken together, my analysis of European social fields parallels my analysis of European identity. The most educated people in Europe who hold the highest occupational positions (managers, professionals, and academics) are more likely to migrate to other countries and be members of pan-European organizations; they consume media from different countries; they have the time, opportunity, money, and inclination to absorb culture from other countries. Educators involved with all levels of education endeavor to socialize young people to be more European. There exist some European popular culture and certainly European news media. These are available to many people. But even here, people often have to pay to have access to cable, satellite, or internet, and this favors the young, educated, and financially better-off.

A large part of the rest of the population occasionally travels for work and vacations, but an equally large part does not participate in Europe-wide social fields, which are dominated by middle- and upper-middle-class people. While the numbers of people who are routinely engaged in these activities is not trivial, my results demonstrate that a small number of Europe's citizens are deeply involved in cultural and social fields across Europe, while the largest numbers are either less involved, or not involved at all.

PATTERNS OF EUROPEAN MIGRATION

From the 1950s until the 1980s, most migration in Europe was from the south to the north (Rodriguez-Pose 2002), reflecting the poor economic conditions in Italy, Spain, Portugal, Greece, Algeria, Morocco, and Turkey and the need for unskilled labor in the booming economies of Germany, France, and the rest of northern Europe. Most movement of labor was heavily regulated by government-sponsored programs that established quotas and viewed migrants as 'guest workers,' i.e. people who were not going to stay. In Germany, in 1980, there were estimated to be 1 million Turks (A. King 1988).

During the 1980s, migration patterns began to change. Governments began to crack down on migration from poorer countries. With the Single Market there began to be a dramatic increase in the migration of highly skilled people within Western Europe (ibid.), and at the same time an increase in illegal migration caused by governments trying to stop migration of less-skilled workers. Finally, the many violent conflicts around the world brought a surge in migrants seeking asylum in Europe.

Rodriguez-Pose (2002: 98) argues that these patterns of migration intensified in the 1990s. Between 1990 and 2000, the number of non-EU foreigners grew from 9,473,800 to 12,9013,000, an increase of almost 40 per cent (OECD 2002). At the same time, the number of total EU foreigners living across national borders

TABLE 6.1. *Foreign-born populations in select European countries,*
1995 and 2004

Country	Foreign-born (%)	
	1995	2004
Austria	8.5	9.5
Belgium	9.0	8.4
Czech Republic	1.5	2.5
Denmark	4.2	4.9
Finland	1.3	2.1
Germany	8.8	8.9
Ireland	2.7	5.5
Italy	1.7	3.9
Luxembourg	33.4	39.0
Netherlands	4.7	4.3
Portugal	1.7	4.3
Spain	1.3	4.6
Sweden	5.2	5.1
United Kingdom	3.4	4.9

Source: OECD, SOPEMI 2006, table A.5.

increased from 5,501,700 to 6,014,300, an increase of about 10 per cent. It is also the case that, generally, EU nationals represent only about one-third of all foreign-born people in different countries. This varies from country to country, with Italy having the fewest EU nationals amongst its foreign-born (about 10% in 2000) while in Luxembourg, Belgium, and Ireland a majority of the foreign-born are EU nationals. About one-third of the foreign-born in France, Great Britain, and Germany are of European origin. The EU nationals living abroad represent only 2–3 per cent of the total European population.

Most of the increase in population in Europe in the past twenty years has been due to the cross-border travel of migrants from Eastern Europe, Africa, and Asia. Table 6.1 presents data on the increases in the levels of foreign-born populations in many of the EU countries. Between 1995 and 2004, the most extensive increases in foreign-born populations were in Italy, Spain, and Portugal. The main source of migrants for these countries was Eastern Europe, particularly Romania, and North Africa, particularly Morocco. But there were also substantial numbers of people from the United Kingdom and Germany who moved to these countries to retire. The leading source of in-migration in Portugal was from Brazil. Luxembourg, the United Kingdom, and Ireland also experienced large waves of immigration. In the case of Ireland, the largest source of migrants was people from the United Kingdom who migrated to take advantage of the booming job market. The UK witnessed migration from many places including Australia, China, Germany, and France (OECD 2006).

One can see the social selectivity of these migration streams in Table 6.2. In Europe, the percentage of the population holding tertiary degrees (what might be considered university degrees of all types) in European countries ranges from 10 to 20 per cent. The social selectively of migrants to most European countries is

What is European Society?

TABLE 6.2. *Foreign-born populations with tertiary*
(university) diploma, 2004

Country	Tertiary diploma (%)
Austria	30.6
Belgium	34.6
Czech Republic	25.2
Denmark	37.4
Finland	26.3
Germany	30.4
Ireland	27.8
Italy	13.0
Luxembourg	27.9
Netherlands	36.1
Portugal	6.7
Spain	18.7
Sweden	40.1
United Kingdom	41.2

Source: OECD, SOPEMI 2006, table 3.

evident. Over 40 per cent of the migrants to the United Kingdom and Sweden have tertiary diplomas, while over 30 per cent of the migrants to Austria, Belgium, Denmark, Germany, and the Netherlands hold such degrees. These data illustrate how the general expansion of European trade and the growing presence of formerly national firms spreading their activities across Europe presented the most-educated citizens of Europe with opportunities in other countries. The most noticeable exception to this rule occurred in Italy, Spain, and Portugal where foreign-born people who arrived were less well educated. Job seekers entered these economies to take low-skill work.

It is useful to delve a bit deeper into these statistics in order to understand the reasons why people moved. Clearly the migration of EU nationals to other EU countries is related to the increase in work opportunities across Europe, but the patterns of migration reveal that there are differences across countries suggesting varieties of motives for moving. In a theoretical piece, R. King (2002) proposed that the nature of European migration had changed in the past ten to fifteen years as a result of the Single Market, the Erasmus program that encourages college students to spend time abroad, and the increase in tourism. King identifies several interesting new kinds of migration that appear to have emerged as a result of the increased European interactions. One of the largest flows is the phenomena that Favell (forthcoming) calls 'Eurostars,' i.e. migrants who work for large corporations and move for opportunities that utilize their specialized skills. There has been an increase in what King calls 'shuttle migration,' whereby people move somewhere for a sojourn and then return home, only to move again. Student migrations are one kind of shuttle migration, and large numbers of college students are on the move each year. King suggests that more interaction across Europe has resulted in an increase of marriage between couples of different EU nationalities, which has caused migration for one of the spouses. Finally, Europeans have taken to moving or retiring to places that are naturally beautiful, i.e. the mountains or the beaches of southern Europe.

King does not provide any data on these types of move. The most systematic data available on the motives of migrants come from the study sponsored by the EU entitled 'Pioneers of European Integration "from below" (PIONEUR)' which was done by an international team of scholars led by Ettore Recchi and his colleagues. The core of their work was a survey of 5,000 European citizens who were residing in member states other than their country of origin. The results showed that Europeans who moved gave the following reasons for their moves: family or love (29.7%), work opportunities (25.2%), quality of life (24%), retirement (7%), study (7%), and other reasons (6.1%) (Recchi et al. 2003). The PIONEUR study also presents some data on migrants' social backgrounds. They demonstrate that many of the migrants are highly educated and are drawn from upper-middle-class backgrounds, corroborating the OECD data presented in Table 6.2. This study offers evidence to support King's arguments about the changing nature of European migration.

One of the most interesting aspects of this survey is the degree to which migration is about people moving their families for different reasons and other relatives following in order to keep the family intact. Women, in particular, were more likely to report that they moved to be with their spouses rather than for work or retirement. Some 37.4 per cent of women gave the reason for moving as family and love while only 21.8 per cent of men gave this reason. Only 17.6 per cent of women as against 33.1 per cent of men gave work as the reason for their move. This implies that male breadwinners generally brought their wives and families with them to their new homes.

Moving had a profound effect on the national identities of migrants. They found themselves having to juggle a national identity, a host country identity, and in most cases, a European identity. Of the respondents, 68.9 per cent report having a European identity; 67.4 per cent of migrants reported both a national identity and a host country identity. These people viewed themselves as having a 'hyphenated identity.' Most of the remaining migrants reported feeling conflict between their national and host identity, and as a result chose one or the other. The most common situation was the 49.7 per cent of respondents who claimed to have a country of origin, country of residence, and a European identity. This survey corroborates the view expressed in the previous chapter that, for many people, holding national and EU identities is not incompatible.

The study also shows that EU migrants are strong supporters of continued political and economic integration. They follow political issues closely and are more likely to vote in European elections than is the general populace in the states where they reside (Recchi et al. 2004). The report concludes by arguing, 'In sum, EU movers contribute to reinforce the legitimacy of the EU. They form a "carrier group" of European identity, the living testimonials of an ever closer Union' (ibid. 11).

In addition to the 'Eurostars,' students, and retirees, there has been a recent wave of migration from the ten eastern Europe states that joined the EU in 2004.

Most EU member-state governments severely restricted migration from these member states for some period of adjustment. However, a few of the member states allowed some immigration. Great Britain has accepted almost 400,000 migrants, Ireland 232,000, Italy, 110,000, the Netherlands about 20,000, and Sweden, a little over 11,000 (OECD 2006: table I.22). The greatest number of migrants originated from Poland, followed by Lithuania and Slovakia. Less is known about the social selectivity of these migrants. In Great Britain, most of the migrants were young and single, suggesting that they were probably going to be sojourners and eventually return home. The occupational distribution of these migrants in Great Britain was very close to the overall distribution. Migrants who came were more skilled than those left at home because of the generally lower skill levels of citizens of the new member-state countries, but equal in skill to those in their places of arrival. This implies some social selectivity of migrants who clearly moved for economic opportunities.

Taken together, the recent migration patterns in Europe reflect two factors: the continued arrival from non-European countries of skilled and unskilled job seekers, and the more differentiated motives of European nationals who move to other countries. As Europe has become a single market and as national firms have Europeanized, European nationals have taken new jobs around Europe. The general picture of European national migration very much confirms our results in the last chapter. Not very many people have moved across national borders. Those who have are predominantly better educated and tend to come from middle- and upper-middle-class backgrounds. Those who have moved are the literal creators of a European society by interacting with people in both their countries of origin and their countries of residence; they exhibit more of a European identity and act as ambassadors for a more unified Europe.

EUROPE-WIDE CIVIC ASSOCIATIONS

One measure of the existence of a European society would be the existence of Europe-wide associations. These associations would bring together people from different societies who had common interests. Their interactions would also facilitate a spreading of information about people from other European countries that would make people in the home country more likely to see their European counterparts as part of a common project. As a result of their interactions, they would learn from each other and perhaps come to engage in collective action in their home countries or in Brussels.

In order to study this question, I collected data from the *Yearbook of International Organizations* (Union of International Organizations 2000). I created a database with every organization that had Europe as its primary zone of activity. There were 989 organizations that fit this description. Organizations were eliminated that lobbied only in Brussels. Since my interest is in Europe-wide associations with members who might engage in dialogue with each other across

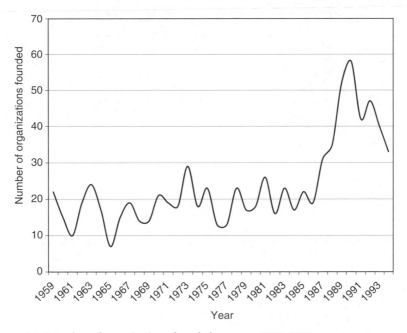

Figure 6.1. Number of organizations founded per year, 1958–2000.

countries in order to create a European society, it made sense to eliminate organizations that existed to lobby the European Commission. Brussels lobbying groups are not in the business of creating interactions of like-minded people from around Europe, but rather of protecting their members' political interests in Brussels.

Figure 6.1 shows the founding of the organizations by year. From the inception of the EU until 1985 there was no discernible pattern in the founding of Europe-wide associations with the average being about twenty new organizations per year. With the announcement of the Single Market, the number of newly founded organizations climbed steeply to a peak of sixty-eight in 1989. The number of organizations then decreased back to its historic level. Thus the Single Market was an opportunity for organizations to be founded. I note that the data source was published in 2000, which means that it tends to undercount the newest organizations. The drop-off in organizations at the end of the series is due to the undercounting of new organizations by the *Handbook*.

Figure 6.2 shows the cumulative percentage total of organizations over time. About half of them were founded from 1957 until 1985, and the rest between 1986 and 1994. It is interesting to speculate why the Single Market presented groups with such an opportunity to form new ones. It is well known that the launching of the Single Market Program brought about more interactions between groups across Europe in the economy, politics, and in the legal system (Fligstein and

What is European Society?

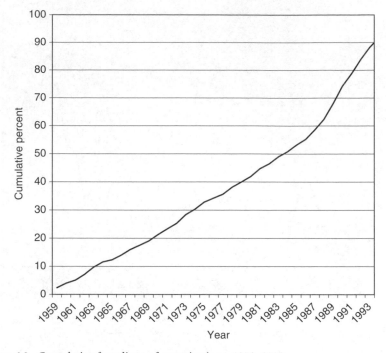

Figure 6.2. Cumulative foundings of organizations, 1958–2000.

Source: International Handbook of Nonprofit Organizations

Stone Sweet 2002). These interactions brought people to found organizations that enhanced their own interests and also to bring people together to discuss issues they held in common. This outburst of founding is support for the idea that the opportunities for interaction did increase after the announcement of the Single Market and organizations were founded owing to that momentum.

The interesting issue is the kinds of organization that have been created. The conclusions of the previous chapter were that people who tend to think of themselves as Europeans are managers, professionals, the young, and the educated. One would expect that the purposes of the groups that are founded will reflect the interests of the same people who interact across Europe. So, professionals and upper-middle-class people will create organizations that show their occupational, political, and cultural interests. These will include professional and scientific organizations, and those dedicated to hobbies, cultural interests, and common causes such as the environment.

In order to assess whether or not this is true, I coded the identity of each organization into four categories: professional associations, business/trade associations, nonprofit groups oriented toward charities or common causes such as the environment, and groups organized for hobbies or sports. Examples of professional associations include the European Accounting Association and the

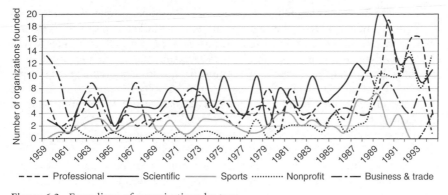

Figure 6.3. Foundings of organizations by type.

Source: International Handbook of Nonprofit Organizations.

European Association of Chiropractors. Examples of business and trade associations include the European Forum for Electronic Business and the European Alliance for Advertising Agencies. Charitable groups include the European Arteriosclerosis Society and the Cetacean Society. The European Federation of National Youth Orchestras and the European Croquet Federation are examples of sports and hobby groups.

Figure 6.3 presents the number of organizations by type that are founded each year. Societies organized for professionals and scientists comprise by far the largest number. In almost every year since the founding of the EU, most new organizations were in this category. Beginning in 1985, the number of these kinds of organization that were formed spiked and went from about ten per year to a peak of thirty-six in 1989. It is interesting to consider why such organizations proliferate even if their members do not obviously benefit by the creation of a single market. Most professional and scientific organizations have annual meetings where their main goal is to educate members about new ideas and techniques in their fields. The European Sociological Association brings together sociologists from all over Europe to discuss not just European issues, but also changes in the state of knowledge about many social issues. Similarly, the European Association of Dentists holds meetings to discuss advances in dental techniques. Of course, all the professional meetings offer the opportunity to mix socially and the meetings are frequently held in pleasant resorts. Many universities, and in some cases the European Union, pay for professors to attend such meetings. Many professionals, such as physicians, can declare attendance at these meetings as a business expense. Professional and scientific communities view their activities as being about the exchange of knowledge and information, which presumably can affect the practice of participants. The dialog between professionals and scientific communities is an important feature of the creation of European society. If the identities of the people in these groups transcend national borders, then they will be inclined to view more political and economic cooperation in a positive light.

The second largest number of groups was founded in the business/trade association category. Here, the logic of the Single Market is more of a driving force in the creation of new Europe-wide business associations as markets across Europe become more Europeanized. These organizations also increased their numbers dramatically after 1985. The nonprofits groups oriented toward charity were the third largest group, followed by sports/hobby organizations. Both of these categories also increased their numbers dramatically after the Single Market was expanded.

Such results are very consistent with our underlying argument. The people who were the most likely to interact in Europe routinely were business people and professionals. After 1985, their opportunities for interchange occurred more frequently and they often felt compelled to start an organization to promote meetings. Professional organizations were formed in large numbers across Europe and, post-1985, Europe-wide professional associations exploded in number.

There was a huge increase in the number of organizations that can rightly be called nonprofits, i.e. charities, political groups oriented toward good causes, and groups oriented toward sports and hobbies. There is certainly a class bias at work in the founding of these organizations. Since upper-middle- and middle-class people were the most likely to travel and get to know their counterparts in other

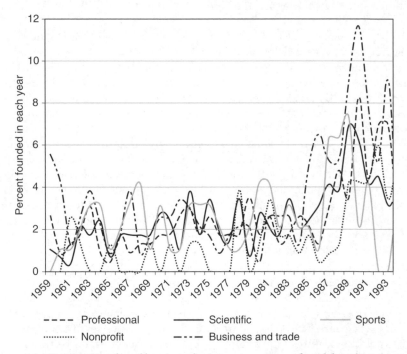

Figure 6.4. Organization foundings in each year as percentage of total foundings by type.

Source: International Handbook of Nonprofit Organizations.

countries, it is not surprising that they also worked to create Europe-wide organizations oriented toward good causes, sports, and hobbies. Since it would take both money and effort to fund and run such organizations, it is likely that these organizations would reflect the interests of the most educated and richest sections of the European population. Still, the great increase in the number of these organizations suggests the emergence of a Europe-wide nonprofit sector, a nascent European society.

Figure 6.4 presents the percentage of all organizations that were founded within each type in a particular year. The most interesting finding of this graph is that a large percentage of all five types of organization were founded post-1985. The group that expanded the most in the last period was nonprofits oriented toward good causes. Thus, if there is a European 'civil society' reflected in Europe-wide organizations dedicated to the discussion of social issues, it clearly accelerated after 1985. Figure 6.4 presents this same information in a slightly different fashion: it shows the cumulative total of organizations in a given category over time. Until 1970, there were almost equal numbers of organizations in the professions and business/trade association categories. But beginning in the 1970s, the professional category took off and rose steeply after 1985. Again, one can see that post-1985, all organizations increased dramatically. The category that really increased the most was that of the nonprofits.

What does this say about the formation of a European society? Sports, hobby, and nonprofit organizations focused on good causes are the purest form of organizations that reflect the growth of a European society devoted to activities without a material interest. While these organizations comprise a relatively small percentage of all organizations (they account for about 15% of all cases), they show clearly that some European society is emerging. But most of the Europe-wide associations are not focused on creating European society per se. The 85 per cent of the organizations founded across European boundaries are really oriented toward the interests of professionals, scientists, and managers. The vast majority of civil society organizations do not bring together people across class and ethnic lines, but rather those who share a profession or work in a particular industry. This is evidence that the nonprofit organizations that exist are creating a European society that does not cut across class lines but instead reflects the interests of educated groups.

THE ROLE OF EDUCATORS AND EDUCATION IN THE CREATION OF EUROPEAN SOCIETY

One of the consistent themes in this and the previous chapter has been the role of educated people in the construction of Europe. I have documented how professionals and managers who travel and speak second languages are more European. European nationals who are living in other countries tend to be better educated, and they too are more European. The data on the founding of Europe-wide associations show that the bulk of them are professional and trade organizations that exist to bring together managers, professionals, scientific workers, and white-collar workers from across Europe to discuss issues of common concern. Much of this is clearly driven by an expanded European economy which benefits people with more education.

I would like to explore another aspect of why it is that educated people want to learn second languages and are inclined to want to have closer interactions with people from other countries. There is an extensive literature that shows that educated people are in general more tolerant of others and accepting of difference (Inglehart 1997; Inglehart and Baker 2000; 2003). They believe in democracy and peacefully adjudicating political issues. They are also more likely to value reason, rational discourse, the rule of law, and science, and believe in the possibility of some form of material progress.

This should not be surprising. Since the English and French Enlightenments began, education and educated people have stood for these things. Indeed, the Enlightenment's main project was to educate people precisely to hold such values. The German philosopher Immanuel Kant thought that the whole project of the Enlightenment was a process whereby the individual would develop personal and social maturity and a sense of responsibility. Philosophers interested in the Enlightenment project came to see the possibility of the pivotal role of education in producing a tolerant, rational society.

I would like to make a provocative claim. At its core, one of the reasons that educated people support the European project is because the European values they espouse are identical with the Enlightenment values that have been a hallmark of educated people for over two hundred years. Indeed, if Europe stands for anything, it is the completion of the Enlightenment project of democracy, rule of law, respect for the differences of others, and the principles of rational discourse and science (Habermas 1992; 2001; Thernborn 1995; Swedberg 1994; Offe 1996).

To show this continuity, 1 quote from the preamble to the Draft Version of the European Constitution:

This constitution draws inspiration from the cultural, religious, and humanist tradition of Europe. The Union is founded on the values of respect for human dignity, freedom, democracy, equality, the rule of law and respect for human rights including the rights of persons belonging to minorities. These values are common to the Member States in a society in which pluralism, nondiscrimination, tolerance, justice, solidarity and equality between men and women prevail.   (Article I-2)

A strong claim can be made that educated people and their ideals are the real moral engine of the EU. They see not just economic advantage in opening up Europe to a single market, but also consider that the joining together of Europe helps create a zone that pushes forward Immanuel Kant's dream of an enlightened Europe. This explains why educated people are at the forefront of European integration. They view interacting with their counterparts across countries as a kind of fulfillment of the important task of disseminating new ideas, knowledge, and information and the free exchange of those ideas across national borders. They also care about rational debate, having tolerance for other people's points of view, and using discourse to settle grievances.

My purpose here is to document some of the ways that the educated elites in Europe have pushed their Enlightenment project forward with the help and support of both the EU apparatus in Brussels and the national governments. Educated elites are in the forefront of trying to create a European society by transforming their curricula and engaging in collective dialog to put forward a European educational space. I consider three sorts of initiative: the attempt to create a 'European education' by schoolteachers, school administrators, and academics, the Erasmus program which provides financial aid for college students who wish to spend time in another country studying, and the Bologna process which seeks to create a 'European Higher Education Space' (European University Association 1999).

TEACHING LANGUAGES AND REWRITING HISTORY

One of the main issues in primary and secondary education has been how to educate students to be Europeans (Soysal 2002; Schissler and Soysal 2005). Many of the Europe-wide professional associations have taken up this topic. Two concrete sorts of program have emerged. First, there has been a major attempt to promote the learning of second and third languages. Learning and using a second language gives students exposure to other cultures and literatures, and presumably will prove useful in traveling for work or pleasure. In the previous chapter, I showed that almost 80 per cent of young people claim to speak another language. In 1995, the EU issued a White Paper arguing that the goal ought to be that every European would speak *three* languages (EU 1995). Every year, the European Commission produces a report on language teaching in all the member states (see EU 2005 for an example of this report). In every country except Ireland, learning a second language is compulsory and all EU countries begin teaching a second language in primary schools (EU 2005). The push to teach languages has obviously succeeded as the vast majority of young people report they know a second language. One caveat to this general pattern is that students in Great Britain tend not to speak second languages. The growth of English as the language of business across Europe has made it easy for people from Great Britain to travel and not speak second languages.

A more subtle approach to socializing people to become European has to do with what gets taught in primary, secondary, and university curricula. Tradition-ally, students learned the national history and literary traditions. The purpose was to give students an understanding of how the nation emerged, what it stood for, and how they should view themselves as citizens (Gellner 1983). There are now annual meetings of various groups of European educators that consider how students should not just be taught the national narrative, but also how the nation historically related to Europe. These groups include teachers' unions and associations, advocacy groups, and international organizations such as the Council of Europe. They are not formally sponsored by the EU and some member-state governments resist their activities, which have produced a rewriting of textbooks and a rethinking of the literary canon across Europe.

Hanna Schissler, Yasemin Soysal, and their colleagues have produced a set of studies that examine the content of these new books and curricula. Soysal, Bertolotti, and Mannitz (2005) show that the teaching of history and literature in primary and secondary schools has changed substantially across Europe. Europe has a diffuse identity in these texts. It is a diffuse identity with diffuse boundaries and a loose set of civic ideals such as democracy, equality, progress, and human rights. It is sometimes associated with the idea of social justice. Europe is less of a narrative story about how it has come to emerge historically, and more a search for the implementation of these ideals in practice. The message to students is that there is a kind of trajectory to the history of Europe whereby, if people work together, they can produce a more just society.

Favoring Europe does not mean denying the existence of the national narrative. Instead it means situating the national narrative in the context of both European history and the ideals of the Enlightenment. So, for example, national heroes still exist in the writing of history, but the national story is now often presented in the context of the European story. This means, for example, that French history is not just the story of the rise of modern French society, but how France evolved in concert with the general economic, political, and social development of Europe. History has also been sanitized so that the more odious events of medieval and modern Europe are played down and the more positive events, like the production and sharing of modern trading, culture, art, and science are pushed forward. This attempt at rereading history is to celebrate the good things that European civilization and cooperation have produced.

Some countries have moved further along this dimension, as in Germany where the national history is invoked only to teach the lesson that the 'imagined' Europe is a better thing to strive for. (In other countries, for example Great Britain, the teaching of 'Europe' has been explicitly resisted by the government.) There is a general attempt in these texts to get students to see themselves more as Europeans and less as citizens just of nation-states. What is clear is that European educators are trying to promote a more European view of who students are in primary and secondary schools, a view that emphasizes a set of common values.

ERASMUS AND THE MIGRATION OF COLLEGE STUDENTS

In 1987, the European Union began several programs that were designed to allow the exchange of students and teachers and facilitate meetings amongst educators across countries. The most important of these was the Erasmus program, whose purpose was to provide grants for university students to spend three to nine months in a different country. The most important effect of Erasmus was to change the direction of exchange programs from students going to the US to students going to universities in other parts of Europe. Erasmus also created a system of credit transfers and brought about a network of European students. By 2004, 1,000,000 students had taken part in the program (EU 2005).

Table 6.3 presents the actual number of students who went abroad every year. The program started modestly with only 3,244 students in 1987 and rose steadily until 2002 when 123,957 students studied in other countries. Not surprisingly, the largest countries in population (Germany, France, Italy, and the UK) had the most students involved in the exchanges. Spain also had a large number of students who traveled. In almost every country, the number of students who go abroad has increased every year. One notable exception is the UK where the total going abroad peaked in 1994 and has declined subsequently to 7,972 in 2002. Given that the British generally report lower levels of second language use and given the general skepticism of the British toward the European project, it is not surprising that students from Britain chose to go aboard less frequently.

Table 6.4 presents data on where students went on their exchanges in 2002–3. The largest number of students ended up in Spain, followed by France, the UK, Germany, and Italy. Clearly, students from many of the northern countries chose Spain as a destination reflecting their desire to enjoy better weather. Again the largest countries were not only the senders of students, but the main receivers of students as well.

There are almost 12 million college students in Europe. Since Erasmus enrolls about 120,000 per year, this means that only 1 per cent of the college students in a given year studies abroad. Given students are eligible for going abroad for at least four years, it is probably the case that the total number of any university cohort who spends a semester abroad might be as high as 3–4 per cent. A UNESCO study in 1998 confirms this number. Teichler (2004) and King and Ruiz-Gelices (2003) show that these students tend to come from the wealthiest households because the Erasmus grants are not large enough to cover people's entire expenses. This has been corroborated in studies by Teichler (2004) and King and Ruiz-Gelices (2003), both of whom used different data sources.

There has been a set of interesting studies on how the experiences students had living abroad affected their attitudes toward other people across Europe and their ultimate choices of career. Students who go abroad often get a good experience of the local culture of the host country and have the opportunity to mingle with young people from these other societies. Their experiences ought to make them more European and eventually make them more likely to consider taking a job in another country.

Teichler (2004) reports on a study by the Erasmus program whereby students who went abroad were questioned about their experiences. Students reported wanting to go abroad for a number of reasons: to learn a foreign language, to travel, to meet people from other countries, to develop themselves, to take a break from their home country studies, and to improve career prospects. Two-thirds of

TABLE 6.3. *Actual number of Erasmus students by country of home institution, 1987/8–2003/4*

Country of home institution	1987/8	1988/9	1989/90	1990/1	1991/2	1992/3	1993/4	1994/5	1995/6	1996/7	1997/8	1998/9	1999/2000	2000/1	2001/2	2002/3	2003/4	TOTAL
BE	58	404	795	1,154	1,837	2,314	2,809	3,480	3,978	4,101	4,233	4,446	4,404	4,427	4,521	4,620	4,789	52,370
DK	57	189	417	729	950	1,282	1,561	1,771	1,930	1,730	1,795	1,751	1,764	1,750	1,752	1,845	1,686	22,959
DE	649	1,727	3,744	4,933	6,858	9,011	11,118	12,633	13,638	13,070	13,785	14,693	15,715	15,872	16,626	18,482	20,688	193,242
GR	39	195	459	566	926	1,266	1,454	1,928	1,897	1,601	1,431	1,765	1,910	1,868	1,974	2,115	2,385	23,779
ES	95	1,063	2,201	3,442	4,353	5,697	7,043	8,537	10,547	10,841	12,468	14,381	16,297	17,158	17,403	18,258	20,034	169,818
FR	895	1,785	4,059	5,524	6,360	8,983	8,782	9,844	13,336	12,505	14,821	16,351	16,824	17,161	18,149	19,365	20,981	195,725
IE	112	167	351	644	894	1,214	1,493	1,632	1,618	1,584	1,564	1,504	1,689	1,648	1,707	1,627	1,705	21,153
IT	220	1,365	2,295	3,355	4,202	5,308	6,808	7,217	8,969	8,907	9,271	10,875	12,421	13,253	13,950	15,225	16,829	140,470
LU	30	13						47	68	61	66	82	87	126	104	119	138	941
NL	169	650	1,261	1,969	2,554	3,290	4,387	4,853	5,180	4,132	4,190	4,332	4,418	4,162	4,244	4,241	4,388	58,420
AT						855	982	1,801	2,301	2,384	2,442	2,711	2,952	3,024	3,024	3,325	3,721	29,522
PT		158	276	543	760	1,025	1,333	1,903	1,609	1,674	1,834	2,179	2,472	2,569	2,825	3,172	3,782	28,139
FI						779	976	1,641	2,530	2,538	3,052	3,441	3,486	3,286	3,291	3,402	3,951	32,373
SE						1,101	1,792	2,302	2,912	2,915	3,264	3,321	3,087	2,726	2,633	2,656	2,667	31,376
UK	925	2,181	3,585	5,047	6,620	8,872	10,519	11,988	11,735	10,537	10,582	9,994	10,056	9,020	8,475	7,973	7,539	135,648
CH						223	480	717	1,048									2,468
LI								3	3	0	3	2	3	18	17	7	19	75
IS						33	58	83	103	117	113	147	138	134	147	163	221	1,457
NO						441	767	980	1,212	1,165	1,071	1,101	1,107	1,007	970	1,010	1,156	11,987
EUR*								47	28	12	14	20	12	8	10	12	10	173
BG													134	398	605	612	751	2,500
CY												35	42		72	91	64	304

																		Total
CZ												879	1,249	2,001	2,533	3,002	3,589	13,253
EE													183	255	274	304	305	1,321
HU												856	1,627	2,001	1,736	1,830	2,058	10,108
LV													166	182	209	232	308	1,097
LT													361	624	823	1,002	1,194	4,004
MT														92	129	72	119	412
PL												1,426	2,813	3,691	4,323	5,419	6,276	23,948
RO												1,250	1,699	1,899	1,964	2,701	3,005	12,518
SI													170	227	364	422	546	1,729
SK												59	380	505	578	653	682	2,857
TOTAL	3,244	9,914	19,456	27,906	36,314	51,694	62,362	73,407	84,642	79,874	85,999	97,601	107,666	111,092	115,432	123,957	135,586	1,226,146

Notes: AT Austria; BE Belgium (Fr = French-speaking, Fl = Flemish-speaking); BG Bulgaria; CH Switzerland; CY Cyprus; CZ Czech Republic; DE Germany; DK Denmark; EE Estonia; ES Spain; FI Finland; FR France; GR Greece; HU Hungary; IE Ireland; IS Iceland; IT Italy; LI Liechtenstein; LT Lithuania; LU Luxembourg; LV Latvia; MT Malta; NL Netherlands; NO Norway; PL Poland; PT Portugal; RO Romania; SE Sweden; SI Slovenia; SK Slovakia; UK United Kingdom.

Figures for 1988/89–1993/4 are estimates based on National Agency reports pro-rated to match global estimates for total number of students.

*EUR denotes the three intergovernmental institutions in Arlon, Florence, and Reims.

Source: National Agency final reports.

Table 6.4. *Erasmus student mobility*

Country of home institution	Host country																														TOTAL
	BE	DK	DE	GR	ES	FR	IE	IT	LU	NL	AT	PT	FI	SE	UK	IS	LI	NO	BG	CY	CZ	EE	HU	LV	LT	MT	PL	RO	SI	SK	
BE (Fr)		43	129	26	615	235	77	255	0	189	41	71	70	62	185	0	0	16	1	18	4	1	0	3	11	5	35	16	2	4	2,114
BE (Fl)		41	177	49	672	533	44	212	3	188	64	136	148	87	156	3	0	24	10	33	1	0	4	4	17	8	34	14	7	6	2,675
BE (all)		84	306	75	1,287	768	121	467	3	377	105	207	218	149	341	3	0	40	11	51	5	1	4	7	28	13	69	30	9	10	4,789
DK	44		302	13	259	260	36	111	0	117	70	15	5	30	330	12	0	27	0	19	2	2	0	3	3	4	12	5	5	0	1,686
DE	330	410		165	4,325	3,997	926	1,755	1	862	387	283	918	1,653	3,159	47	8	463	17	207	25	7	23	49	171	28	395	27	24	26	20,688
GR	140	45	356		374	420	27	248	1	106	71	90	116	109	139	2	0	17	6	63	1	8	1	1	20	5	14	3	2	0	2,385
ES	1,054	573	2,553	178		3,412	513	4,250	0	1,263	298	992	501	670	2,974	21	0	200	11	169	12	0	1	24	67	9	176	59	22	32	20,034
FR	420	500	2,804	218	5,115		1,081	1,550	6	891	361	288	727	1,062	4,652	23	0	246	9	206	21	10	3	25	169	43	314	167	40	30	20,981
IE	47	30	292	12	291	557		109	0	110	35	18	40	57	14	23	0	8	6	26	2	1	0	4	5	5	10	0	3	0	1,705
IT	633	357	1,994	180	5,688	2,859	230		0	607	339	766	367	399	1,511	29	1	156	8	86	28	7	4	28	129	71	174	129	20	29	16,829
LU	1	2	39	0	14	27	0	9		0	17	6	1	3	15	0	0	0	0	2	0	0	0	0	0	0	1	0	0	0	138
NL	184	158	391	42	907	543	88	256	0		98	93	275	389	635	11	0	140	1	44	7	5	6	10	49	13	21	14	5	3	4,388
AT	79	104	262	30	631	528	132	461	0	215		60	227	305	410	15	1	82	3	51	7	5	5	12	30	14	22	8	16	6	3,721
PT	250	63	295	53	920	325	19	713	0	250	53		95	95	178	4	1	38	8	103	3	8	5	26	59	4	125	68	14	7	3,782
FI	148	37	654	72	479	413	111	190	0	377	229	58		101	552	14	0	15	5	126	35	9	9	15	162	16	60	13	29	22	3,951
SE	42	25	426	17	370	484	80	137	0	236	142	25	24		494	9	0	22	0	38	10	0	3	11	28	11	24	3	6	0	2,667
UK	117	136	1,127	60	1,636	2,303	21	740	0	365	143	97	233	238		9	0	69	5	107	8	4	1	3	31	12	42	10	6	16	7,539
EUT*	0	0	1	0	0	4	0	0	0	0	2	0	0	1	2	0	0	0	0	0	0	0	0	0	0	0	0	0	0	0	10

																Total
IS	4	54	40	3	36	26	2	16	0	13	10	1	1	2	13	221
LI	0	2	1	0	0	0	1	0	0	4	0	2	3	1	5	19
NO	29	53	190	15	231	156	17	85	0	78	50	36	15	42	159	1,156
EUR 18	3,522	2,633	12,033	1,133	22,563	17,082	3,405	11,097	11	5,871	2,410	3,037	3,766	5,306	15,606	116,689
BG	46	14	227	62	43	136	6	39	0	23	52	34	16	9	44	751
CY	0	2	4	13	9	9	0	3	0	0	1	2	14	5	8	64
CZ	134	103	931	78	286	510	43	180	0	203	211	189	241	163	317	3,589
EE	10	19	59	6	30	42	2	26	0	10	16	4	47	26	8	305
HU	98	44	566	42	125	276	15	227	0	145	110	42	201	58	109	2,058
LV	27	13	111	2	9	18	2	9	0	24	8	4	42	32	7	308
LT	70	145	294	18	61	77	10	67	0	30	49	51	180	120	22	1,194
MT	5	2	6	0	3	3	6	52	0	7	4	2	6	1	22	119
PL	358	362	1,870	122	546	855	74	481	0	294	159	222	310	286	337	6,276
RO	163	29	457	87	285	1,125	21	448	0	72	38	119	33	42	86	3,005
SI	30	19	125	6	63	62	1	56	0	25	59	30	24	17	29	546
SK	50	11	191	24	59	80	2	58	3	29	44	30	52	17	32	682
A/C**	991	763	4,841	460	1,513	3,193	182	1,646	3	862	751	729	1,166	776	1,021	18,897
TOTAL	4,513	3,396	16,874	1,593	24,076	20,275	3,587	12,743	14	6,733	3,161	3,766	4,932	6,082	16,627	135,586

Note: AT Austria; BE Belgium (Fr = French-speaking, Fl = Flemish-speaking); BG Bulgaria; CY Cyprus; CZ Czech Republic; DE Germany; DK Denmark; EE Estonia; ES Spain; FI Finland; FR France; GR Greece; HU Hungary; IE Ireland; IS Iceland; IT Italy; LI Liechtenstein; LT Lithuania; LU Luxembourg; LV Latvia; MT Malta; NL Netherlands; NO Norway; PL Poland; PT Portugal; RO Romania; SE Sweden; SI Slovenia; SK Slovakia; UK United Kingdom.

*European University Institute, Florence

**Accession countries (CY, CZ, EE, HU, LV, LT, MT, PL, SI, SK)/Candidate countries (BG, RO) in 2003/4.

Source: European Union (2005), Erasmus Statistics.

Erasmus students took courses in the language of the country they were visiting. They mostly studied alongside their counterparts from other countries. Students tended to take courses different from their fields of study at home and to take fewer courses. This implies that for many students, travel to another country was as much for the adventure of living somewhere else as it was to attend a university. More than two-thirds reported engaging in organized activities such as going to the theater, museums, sports events, and the cinema. A similar number reported traveling in the host country. Students generally felt well integrated into the social activities of the host countries although a small number (13%) reported they wished they had had better contacts with host country students.

It is interesting to consider the longer-term effects of spending time abroad. King and Ruiz-Gelices (2003) did a study of former Sussex University students who did and did not choose to go abroad for a year in order to compare their experiences. These students live in Great Britain which has been the most skeptical of the value of Europe and, as I demonstrated in the previous chapter, has among the fewest people who think of themselves as Europeans. Their experiences are particularly interesting to consider. In general, the students who went abroad were very happy about their experiences. They thought that it had made them more aware of their host country and its culture and history. Most reported that they formed an emotional attachment to the country they visited. Of those interviewed, 59 per cent agreed that living abroad had increased their sense of belonging to a European cultural space. The comparisons to students who did not go abroad are instructive. Students who went abroad had stronger European identities. They also had better knowledge about the EU and claimed to follow EU political affairs more than students who did not go abroad. They generally had a more positive attitude toward the EU and they were more likely to be disappointed if Great Britain pulled out of the EU.

The experience of having spent time abroad in college also had a profound effect on people's career paths. King and Ruiz-Gelices (2003) and Teichler and Jahr (2001) report that students who spent time in another country were more likely to take a job in another country. Of the Sussex sample who went to another country, 44 per cent reported applying for a job abroad, compared to 12 per cent of those who did not. Of the same sample, 46 per cent of those who went abroad report traveling to other countries in their current job, compared to 26 per cent of those who did not. Those who went abroad were three times as likely as those who did not to report that they would be interested in taking a job in another country sometime in the future.

Teichler and Jahr (2001) report on a sample of students from across Europe who went into the Erasmus program in 1993–4 and were surveyed in 1998–9. Of these students, 75 per cent report that their Erasmus experience helped them find a job and half considered their experiences relevant in their current jobs. Even more striking was the rate of international mobility for those who were formerly in the Erasmus program five years later: 25 per cent reported having received an offer to work abroad; 20 per cent report having worked abroad; and 22 per cent reported traveling abroad frequently for their current job. Currently less than 3 per cent of EU nationals work in another EU country. This means that people who were in Erasmus were almost seven times more likely to work abroad.

The Erasmus program fits neatly into our discussion of the class biases of the European project. Those who participated appear to have come from an upper-middle-class background. Participating in Erasmus increased their European identity and made them more aware of and more fond of other cultures. It also made them more interested in EU politics and affairs. Most importantly, students who participated in Erasmus were much more willing to consider employment outside their home country, and they appear to have accepted such employment at a much higher rate than their counterparts. But the Erasmus program affects a relatively small number of college students and hence its Europeanizing effects, while impressive, are limited.

THE BOLOGNA PROCESS AND THE CREATION OF THE EUROPEAN HIGHER EDUCATION SPACE

Currently, there is a big effort underway to create a 'European Higher Education Space.' This project is the remarkable outcome of two meetings, one held in Paris in 1998 and the other held in Bologna in 1999. The Bolgona Declaration (or what has come to be called the 'Bologna process') gathered together all the education ministers of EU countries. The European Higher Education Space has brought about an agreement that all universities will enact a series of reforms to harmonize attainment of a college degree, and in doing so make it easier for credits to be easily transferred across universities.

One of the most interesting features of this agreement is that it was carried out entirely outside the context of the EU. The agreement was initiated by education ministers and relies entirely on their mutual consent to push the project forward. That they all agreed to transform their universities' degree structure to produce a harmonized system is an amazing act of consensus and coordination. Indeed, the education ministers who came up with the idea intentionally avoided going through the EU to advance their agenda. They wanted to avoid Brussels because they felt that it would take even longer to harmonize education systems if they spent years in slow negotiations.

The Bologna process was set in motion by Claude Allègre, the education minister of France in 1998. M. Allègre invited the education ministers of Germany (Jürgen Ruettgers), Italy (Luigi Berlinguer), and Great Britain (Tessa Blackstone) to France to celebrate the 800th anniversary of the founding of the Sorbonne. M. Allègre proposed to his counterparts that they sign an agreement committing them to a harmonization of the European higher education system that would focus on producing a 'two cycle structure' of degrees, in essence a system of degrees that would be a Bachelor of Arts and a Masters/Ph.D. level.

The 'Joint Declaration on harmonization of the architecture of the European higher education system' argued:

Universities were born in Europe, some three quarters of a millennium ago. In those times, students and academics would freely circulate and rapidly disseminate knowledge throughout the continent. Nowadays, many of our students still graduate without having had the benefit of a study period outside of national boundaries. An open European area for higher learning carries a wealth of positive perspectives, of course respecting our diversities, but requires on the other hand continuous efforts to remove barriers and to develop a framework for teaching and learning, which would enhance mobility and an ever closer cooperation. The international recognition and attractive potential of our systems are directly related to their external and internal readabilities. A system for all universities, in which two main cycles, undergraduate and graduate exist, enhances this readability. We thereby commit ourselves to encouraging this common frame of reference, aimed at improving external recognition and facilitating student mobility as well as employability.

Ravinet (2005) has studied the machinations that led up to this meeting. She has interviewed many of the principals and offers the following argument as to their motives. She suggests that M. Allègre wanted to make some reforms to the French education system. He was interested in making the French system more coherent by combining elements of the university system with the Grand Écoles (the elite French universities). But, in order to push these forward, he felt he needed some outside legitimacy, so he decided to try and produce a Europe-wide project that would give him the leverage to move forward with his reforms in France. At the outset of the process, Ravinet argues that M. Allègre did not have a particular set of reforms in mind.

M. Allègre knew his German and Italian counterparts quite well. They had attended conferences together and spent time discussing the situation of higher education in Europe. He trusted that they would be interested in constructing such an agenda which might help all of them in encouraging university reform in their countries. The idea to go to a two-track degree system seems to have originated with Jürgen Ruettgers, the education minister of Germany. He had been engaging in reform of the German universities for some time and was about to push a piece of legislation through the German parliament to do so. One of the main features of his reform was an attempt to create a more uniform degree system in Germany that more closely resembled both the British and American models. M. Allègre saw that one of the main problems of the French system was its proliferation of degrees and diplomas. Moving to a two-cycle system would help solve that problem and make the meaning of degrees in France more transparent. The English were the least involved in the process, but they had the least at stake. They already had a two-cycle system in place and therefore the reform would just make sure their system of credits would transfer easily across countries. The person who took the biggest political risk in this situation was Luigi Berlinguer. He had also been trying to negotiate a reform of the Italian system. While the two-cycle idea was not part of that reform, he came to see that it had some merit and he supported the declaration.

As a result of the Sorbonne declaration, the four ministers proposed to convene a Europe-wide conference of education ministers a year later in Bologna. They proposed a more detailed set of reforms that all the ministers would commit to at that meeting. What they had in mind was a kind of harmonization of degrees so that employers from around Europe could evaluate their content. For example, a bachelor's degree in accounting in England would imply the same amount of coursework as the same degree in Italy. This harmonization would also make it easier for students to study in other countries as their credits would more easily be brought back to their home university. As I mentioned earlier, the ministers intentionally did not want this process to occur through the EU or Brussels, but instead wanted their agreement to be a pact between themselves. They felt that if they tried to engage in this kind of massive cooperation through the EU, the process would be slow and the output uncertain. By producing a document, asking people to sign it, and setting out goals to attain the ends of the document, they would push the process forward much more quickly.

The Bolgona Declaration was signed in 1999 by the education ministers of twenty-nine countries. It argued:

A Europe of Knowledge is now widely recognized as an irreplaceable factor for social and human growth and as an indispensable component to consolidate and enrich the European citizenship, capable of giving its citizens the necessary competences to face the challenges of the new millennium, together with an awareness of shared values and belonging to a common social and cultural space. We must in particular look at the objective of increasing the international competitiveness of the European system of higher education. The vitality and efficiency of any civilization can be measured by the appeal that its culture has for other countries. We need to ensure that the European higher education system acquires a world-wide degree of attraction equal to our extraordinary cultural and scientific traditions.

In order to attain these goals, the Bologna Declaration agreed to the following principles of harmonization:

While affirming our support to the general principles laid down in the Sorbonne declaration, we engage in co-coordinating our policies to reach in the short term, and in any case within the first decade of the third millennium, the following objectives, which we consider to be of primary relevance in order to establish the European area of higher education and to promote the European system of higher education world-wide:

Adoption of a system of easily readable and comparable degrees, also through the implementation of the Diploma Supplement, in order to promote European citizens' employability and the international competitiveness of the European higher education system.

Adoption of a system essentially based on two main cycles, undergraduate and graduate. Access to the second cycle shall require successful completion of first cycle studies, lasting a minimum of three years. The degree awarded after the first cycle shall also be relevant to the European labor market as an appropriate level of qualification. The second cycle should lead to the master and/or doctorate degree as in many European countries.

Establishment of a system of credits as a proper means of promoting the most widespread student mobility. Credits could also be acquired in non-higher education contexts, including lifelong learning, provided they are recognized by receiving Universities concerned.

Promotion of mobility by overcoming obstacles to the effective exercise of free movement with particular attention to:
- for students, access to study and training opportunities and to related services;
- for teachers, researchers and administrative staff, recognition and valorization of periods spent in a European context researching, teaching and training, without prejudicing their statutory rights.

They agreed to complete this task by 2010. They laid out a timetable for universities to work toward to comply with these goals, and they agreed to a set of procedures to monitor the progress toward them. They met again in 2001 in Prague, in 2003 in Berlin, and in 2005 in Bergen. By 2005, the number of countries who had signed on to the Bologna process had increased to twenty-nine and the group had added several new tasks to their efforts.

It should be noted that harmonizing university degrees required a huge amount of work. First, since every country had a different set of degrees and diplomas and these had evolved over long periods, there were a great many entrenched interests at work. Moreover, the technical problem of comparing programs in particular fields of study is enormous. Since some universities were on quarters and others on semesters, credit hours were also counted in different ways in different systems. Finally, some systems used exams exclusively to award degrees and others used the completion of courses and credits. So, if a student came from a system with credits to a system with exams, they might find themselves unable to get a degree. In the summer of 2000, representatives of the different countries met to create a set of standards to make the venture possible; these standards have evolved over the past few years.

Given that this initiative came from 'above,' one could imagine that universities, departments, and individual faculty members would have ample opportunity to resist its implementation. There is certainly evidence that faculty, students, and administrators have resisted implementing the Bologna process. This has led to a whole series of attempts to quantify if universities are making progress toward the new degree structure or not. It is useful to review the evidence of this convergence as of 2005. I use two sources of data. First, I have the results of a survey undertaken in the fall of 2002 by Bogdan Voich (2003) for the European University Association. Second, Reichert and Tauch (2005) have put together an in-depth study of sixty-two universities in 2004 in order to assess how the reforms are playing out on the ground. These reports are at the basis of the education ministers' meetings that have occurred and thus they provide 'official' assessment of how far progress has been made in implementing the goals of the Bologna process.

The 2003 Survey was sent to the presidents of all European institutions of higher education. It has a 42 per cent response rate (very respectable for a mail-out survey) and 760 completed questionnaires were collected. It is useful to report some of the results of the survey. Of those surveyed, 88.8 per cent felt that the idea of a European Higher Education Area was good and should be implemented. By 2003, 53.2 per cent of the universities had already implemented the Bachelor/Masters/Ph.D. levels of degree and another 36.2 per cent were in the process of doing so. Only 11 per cent of those surveyed did not plan to participate. The main problems that respondents reported were that national governments had not provided enough resources to undertake the necessary reforms. Of the respondents, 45.8 per cent report that national legal frameworks work against changing the degree structure and 45.3 per cent report that the lack of higher education financing makes reforms difficult. This appears to be a rather high level of cooperation and participation.

Of course, there are problems in using the results of this survey. Since respondents knew the questionnaire was being gathered to monitor their performance, universities administrators had an incentive to report more positive views of the implementation than they might otherwise have done. The Reichert and Tauch report used site-based interviews that included discussions not just with higher level administrators but also faculty. Its alternative methodology is quite relevant to making sense of what is going on.

Reichert and Tauch (2005:8) report that 'the overwhelming perception from the site visits is that actors in institutions are now facing and tackling the challenges of implementation with commitment and energy.' They go on to suggest that almost all the countries concerned have now changed their laws to make the new degree system possible. They show that considerable progress is being made toward the implementation of the degree cycles. There remains the large challenge that national administrations have provided few resources for the changes in curricula that are necessitated by changes in degrees. So, for example, if a university has shifted from a five-year degree program to a three-year one, it can have done so only be redesigning its curriculum. Departments have generally underestimated the difficulty of redoing their programs and rethinking their curricula to fit into the two-cycle system. Moreover, universities and departments have to cope with their need to change programs within already constrained budgets. But what is remarkable is that in spite of problems of implementation, the overall goals of the reforms have more or less been accepted on the ground. Reichert and Tauch report that there is little resistance to the overall idea of the reforms and the emergence of the European Higher Education Area, but only difficulties associated with making the transition to a new system. If the process keeps going at its current rate, it will be completed by 2010.

One of the most interesting questions is whether or not a large number of students will ultimately choose to study or work in other countries given that their diplomas will be harmonized. Currently, 1 per cent of college students are studying abroad in any given year and only 2–3 per cent of European nationals are working in other EU countries. Thus, while all the universities will have harmonized degrees that will facilitate the exchange of students and the ability of graduates to work in other countries, so far only a small number of people have taken these opportunities.

This brings us to a conclusion. The education establishments of all European societies have embraced reforms that orient primary, secondary, and tertiary educations toward producing students who know different languages, are taught a common history and heritage, and now, who are given opportunities to study and work abroad and have their credits and degrees recognized. European educators are certainly part of what constitutes European society. This shows how one set of elites, those of education, have played a remarkable role in advancing European social integration. For those who availed themselves of the opportunity to travel and live abroad, the effects were profound. It changed their identity and their career paths and made them likely candidates to become Europeans. But, for all the effort, apart from the educators, students, and highly skilled workers who have gone overseas, most citizens of Europe so far have not availed themselves of these opportunities.

EUROPEAN POPULAR CULTURE

One of the main ways in which national identities are formed is through the sharing of culture. Television, newspapers, books, movies, and now the internet (which combines features of all forms of media) produce a common idiom by which people reinforce and discover new identities. While much of what popular culture offers is about entertainment, it also contains images of what people want for themselves and others. If there existed a Europe-wide culture, that would suggest that everyone in Europe was consuming similar messages and themes at the same time and this could be a source of 'Europeanness.' In this section, I explore this theme in several ways. First, I consider the degree to which European media are integrated, and second, I consider the degree to which the media messages originate in various countries in Europe.

One would hypothesize that if there is a European culture, there ought to be European media. This would be expressed by ownership of the main media outlets across societies by a small set of companies, each of whom owned and operated across national borders. The degree to which such media exist is a matter of some controversy. On the one hand, McChesney (2004) argues that the largest media conglomerates in the world control a vast amount of media. He estimates that the top 70–80 companies own 80 per cent of the media in the world. On the other hand, Campaine (2001) suggests that while the largest media companies indeed control an impressive amount of activity, their market shares have been in great flux over the past twenty years as new forms of media have evolved. The number of media outlets (i.e. television channels, the internet, movies, magazines, and books) has exploded. My concern is less whether or not there is too much media control and more the degree to which one might point to the existence of European media.

Table 6.5 presents data on the holdings of the six largest media companies in the world, accounting for about $260 billion in revenues in 2000. For my purposes, it is useful to note that three of the companies are American (AOL Time Warner, Disney, and Viacom) and the others are French (Vivendi Universal), German (Bertelsmann), and Australian (News Corporation). One of the

TABLE 6.5. *Descriptive data on top six media companies, 2000*

Company	Revenue ($ billion)	Market value (000)	Employees (no.)	Officers (no.)	Directors (no.)
AOL Time Warner	36.2	165,945,078	88,500	14	16
Bertelsmann AG	18	70,000,000	82,162	11	8
News Corporation	13.8	15,636,000	33,800	14	16
Vivendi Universal	24.3	59,415,059	253,000	11	19
Viacom	20	80,600,000	57,840	8	18
Walt Disney & Co.	25.4	53,232,568	120,000	10	16

Source: Albarran and Moellinger (2002).

distinctive features of these companies is that they have holdings in many kinds of media and across the entire world.

Figure 6.5 shows graphically some of these holdings. Disney, Viacom (Viacom owns MTV, a network that I will discuss a bit more in a moment), and AOL Time Warner have holdings all over the world, but their primary market is still the US. News Corp. has extensive US holdings in newspapers, television, and movies (Fox), and also in the UK in newspapers and television. It has holdings across Europe and is the largest satellite television operator in Europe. Vivendi Universal has extensive US holdings, but is also a major player in French books, magazines, television, and movies. It produces television, movies, and music for the European (and world) markets and owns mobile phone systems and cable networks across the world. Bertelsmann owns many media properties in Europe and worldwide and is the world's largest book publisher. This is evidence to suggest that some major European media companies exist and certainly that all of the largest media companies have some European presence.

In spite of the emergence of multinational media companies, there still exists much national ownership of European media (Cavillin 2001; Harcourt 2002). So, for example, Silvio Berlusconi still owns and controls much of the Italian media. Small and medium-sized enterprises still often control newspapers and other media outlets within particular societies (Cavillin 2001). Across Europe, the national governments still own television stations (Djankov et al. 2003).

It should be noted that the EU has been a force for media openness in Europe. Harcourt (2002) documents how the EU has pushed the member-state governments to harmonize their media policies. In general, firms from any country can operate across Europe and with a few notable exceptions, mergers and acquisitions can occur. Even where there has been resistance, as in France, the overall effect has been to make all European countries open to media firms from other countries.

I conclude that while there are clearly media conglomerates that work across borders, there is also some dispersion of ownership of various parts of the media. What is probably more interesting is the content of the media and the degree to which that content is shared across national borders. There are three possibilities. First, while media outlets have proliferated, because of the centralization of

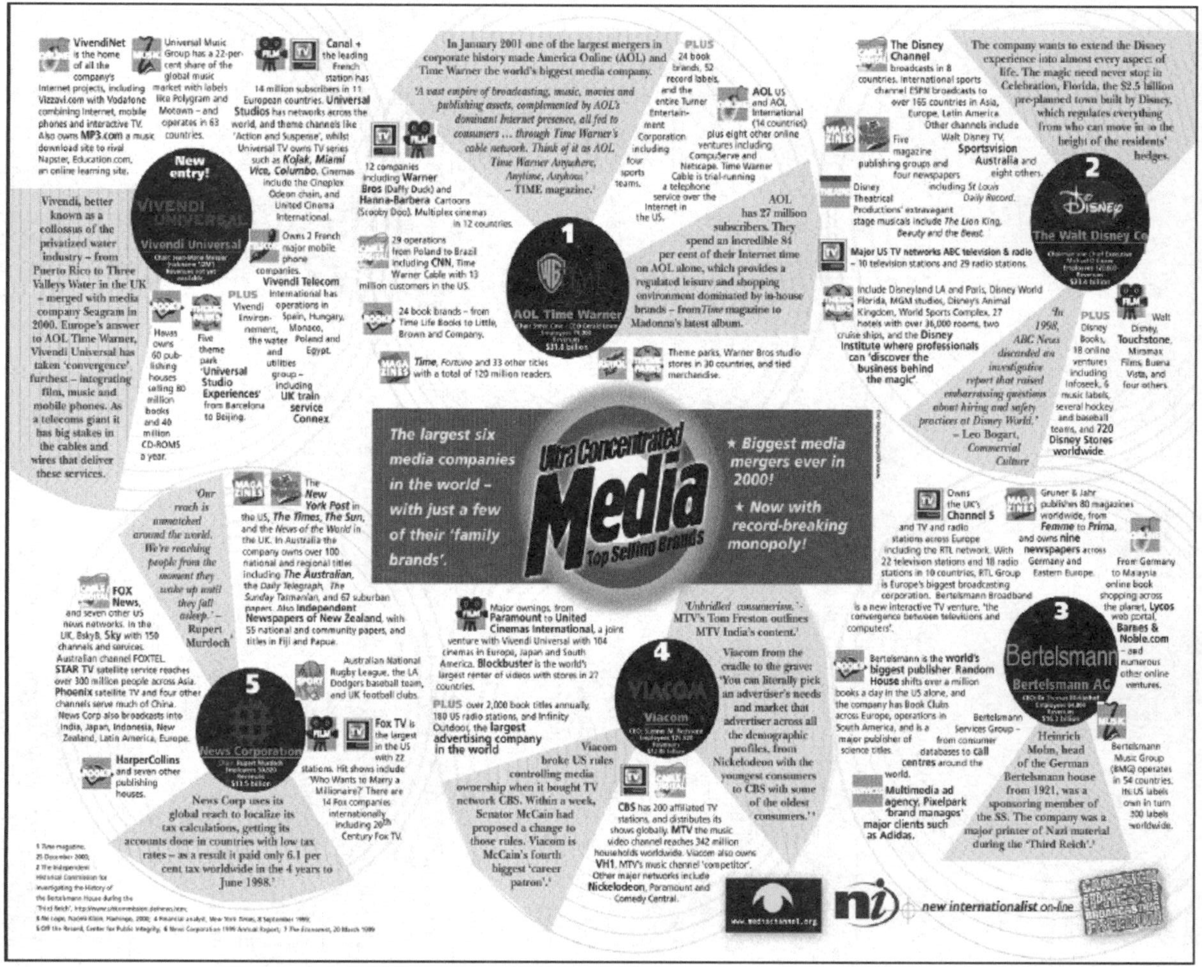

Figure 6.5. 'Ultra concentrated media.'

Source: <http://www.mediachannel.org/ownerships>, accessed 17 April 2007.

ownership they could be the same outlets in every country. This would imply that everyone is consuming the same content regardless of where they live. Second, because of differences of language and national culture, both global and local media companies could tailor their content to local audiences. Third, the ownership patterns of various media might make local content both more global and more local. The largest media companies would move the same content to every country while their local counterparts would concentrate on media that involved the local culture.

My review will conclude by arguing that there exists evidence for all three. Large media companies do sell the same content across many markets. This is most true in the case of movies and television, although there is evidence of crossover for both music and books. In some markets, media companies do specialize in international information and the local producers report on national issues. A good case in point for this model is the business press, which I will consider in more detail in a moment. Finally, there is also evidence that media conglomerates are able to target national markets by producing their content in the national language and focusing on national culture. The most prominent case identity of this process is Music Television (MTV) Europe, the music cable station.

Given the growing integration of European business, one natural place to look for 'European' media is the business press. Schlesinger (1999) looks at the growth of publications such as the *Financial Times*, the *Wall Street Journal-Europe*, *The Economist*, and the *International Herald Tribune*, and cable stations such as CNN and BSkyB and concludes that there has been some emergence of Europe-wide media. Business people all over Europe pay attention to these media outlets when they are interested in European business news.

But there is also evidence that business people continue to read their national business press. The 2004 European Business Readership Survey (EBRS) looked more carefully at all the business publications read by business people. This survey was sponsored by the *Financial Times*, was conducted in seventeen countries, and had 10,000 respondents drawing from a sample of 431,000 executives in 58,000 companies. It was carried out by Ipsos-RSL. The survey shows that the most senior business people read magazines and newspapers for their information on international events (79%), well ahead of TV (36%), radio (20%), and the internet (18%). Not surprisingly, the survey shows the dominance of English-language publications. The business magazines with the highest pan-European readership rates are *The Economist* (7.7%), *Harvard Business Review* (5.6%), and *Forbes* (5.5%). The international newspapers with the highest penetration are the *Financial Times* (13.1%) and the *International Herald Tribune* (3.4%). The TV channels with the highest daily reach are Sky News (6.6%), CNN International (6.1%), and EuroNews (3.7%). The most widely accessed websites (visited in last four weeks) are BBC News (12.7%) and ft.com, the home of the *Financial Times* (8.0%).

This would seem to indicate that executives across Europe are reading many of the same publications. But, these same executives are also reading their local business presses. So, in France, *Le Echos*, the French business newspaper, has twice as many readers as the *Financial Times*. In Germany, the *Borsen Zeitung* (a newspaper specializing in financial issues) has a substantially higher level of circulation than the *Financial Times* and the *Corriere Della Sera* has almost four times the circulation of the *Financial Times* amongst business leaders in Italy. This shows that even business people pick and choose their sources of information and many probably read multiple newspapers and magazines for different kinds of information. One can also conclude that there are some pan-European business media, almost all in English. In the case of the business press, the large multinational content producers concentrate on the international market while the national business press continues to specialize in national stories.

It is useful to consider the content and sourcing of popular culture more widely. David Laitin (2002) has shown that movies and popular songs in Europe in the late 1990s reflect two sorts of forces. First, American films dominated European films in box office returns across Europe. Only in France and Great Britain were there even any movies in the top twenty that were produced nationally. Second, there was also a clear influence of America in music, but here there was a great deal more national music. My purpose is to update Laitin's analysis to more recent data and look not just at movies and music, but also at TV and books.

It turns out that the American presence is most greatly felt in movies, followed by TV, music, and books. I show that the media conglomerates' power is driven by their control over content. Such content is relatively expensive to produce but once produced is relatively cheap to market in another country. The proliferation of movie cineplexes and cable and satellite television channels increases the demand for content dramatically. National media comes second to American. In all countries, national content continues to be distributed, sometimes by the large media conglomerates, sometimes by national companies. There is some evidence that European national popular culture crosses over borders, mostly distributed by the media conglomerates. Across media, it is likely that Europeans have access to many similar movies, television shows, sporting events, news stories, music, and books. But they also continue to consume popular culture in their national languages and frequently in content prepared by national companies.

Figure 6.6 presents the breakdown of box office admissions to films produced by different countries in western Europe in 2004. Of European box office admissions, 59.7 per cent were accounted for by American film companies, and if one includes joint productions between American and European companies, this rises to 71.4 per cent. France (9.5%), the UK (6.1%), and Germany (4.5%) had the next three highest box office takings. Table 6.6 presents data on the twenty largest grossing films in 2004. Seventeen of these twenty films were produced by American companies. France, Germany, and the UK are represented by one film on the list.

Even while American films dominated European markets, there were a large number of films produced across Europe. The European Audiovisual Observatory estimates that 625 feature films were produced in Europe in 2001. France produced 172 films, Germany 50, Spain 86, Italy 90, and the UK 11. Half the box office receipts for Great Britain's films came from outside the national market. French films accounted for 25 per cent of their total box office receipts outside France, German films made 20 per cent outside Germany, and Italian and Spanish

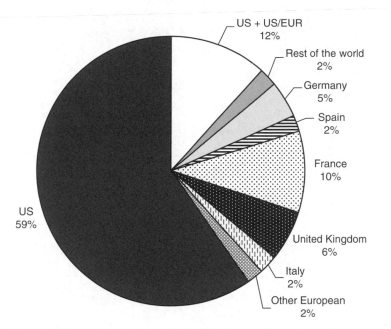

US + US/EUR
12%

Rest of the world
2%

Germany
5%

Spain
2%

France
10%

United Kingdom
6%

Italy
2%

Other European
2%

US
59%

Figure 6.6. Breakdown of adimissions in the EU 25 according to the national origins of film (2004 figures).

Note: Admissions of European films on their national markets are included in the calculation of percentages.

Source: European Audiovisual Observatory—LUMIERE database <http://lumiere.ods.coe.int>.

films about 10 per cent of their total outside their home countries. While the movie industry is dominated by American films, there are a substantial number of films made in Europe. Most of these are consumed nationally, but there is some European market for European, particularly British, French, and German, films.

The situation in television is quite similar, although there are some interesting variations. Figure 6.7 presents the national origin of total TV hours in Europe from 1997 to 2001. American productions account for a huge number of European television hours and this has increased over time. European productions have not increased to match the total number of television hours produced. Indeed, the fastest-growing category is that of co-productions between American and European partners. Figure 6.8 shows the percentage of programs broadcast on all channels and their source over time. The US share has increased from about 73 to about 75 per cent if one counts co-productions. The European share of production has decreased from about 18 to about 16 per cent. The good news for European television producers is that if one counts their shares in the co-productions with the US companies, their market share has increased from 19 to about 23 per cent.

Table 6.7 contains data for only the major networks in the five largest television markets in Europe in 2000. The table breaks down the geographical origin of

TABLE 6.6. *Admissions to top twenty films in distribution in Europe, 2003 and 2004*

Rank	Original title	Country of Origin	Year	Director(s)	Admissions
1	Shrek 2	US	2004	A. Adamson, K. Asbury, and C. Vernon	43,107,277
2	Harry Potter and the Prisoner of Azkaban	US/GB	2004	Alfonso Cuarón	40,232,461
3	Troy	US/GB/MT	2004	Wolfgang Petersen	26,938,980
4	The Lord of the Rings: The Return of the King[a]	US/NZ/DE	2003	Peter Jackson	26,531,171
5	Spider-Man 2	US	2004	Sam Raimi	26,199,978
6	The Day After Tomorrow	US	2004	Roland Emmerich	23,601,695
7	The Incredibles	US	2004	Brad Bird	23,176,201
8	The Last Samurai	US/NZ/JP	2003	Edward Zwick	18,819,511
9	The Passion of the Christ	US	2004	Mel Gibson	18,585,975
		GB/US/FR/IE/D			
10	Bridget Jones: The Edge of Reason[b]	E	2004	Beeban Kidron	17,421,322
11	Brother Bear[c]	US	2003	Aaron Blaise and Robert Walker	15,774,824
12	Shark Tale	US	2004	B. Bergeron, V. Jenson, and R. Letterman	15,304,178
13	I, Robot	US	2004	Alex Proyas	14,367,114
14	Van Helsing	US/CZ	2004	Stephen Sommers	12,744,935
15	The Village	US	2004	M. Night Shyamalan	12,485,662
16	Something's Gotta Give	US	2003	Nancy Meyers	11,408,376
17	Les Choristes	FR/CH/DE	2004	Christophe Barratier	11,406,139
18	King Arthur	US/GB/IE	2004	Antoine Fuqua	10,931,434
19	Garfield	US	2004	Peter Hewitt	10,854,041
20	(T)Raumschiff Surprise—Periode 1	DE	2004	Michael Herbig	10,731,881

Note: Provisional ranking on the basis of available data from 24 European countries, including Turkey. Around 88% of admissions in the 25 EU countries are analyzed.

[a] 27,670,398 admission in Europe in 2003.

[b] Still on release in 2005.

[c] 718,534 admissions in Europe in 2003.

Source: European Audiovisual Observatory—LUMIÈRE database <http://lumiere.obs.coe.int>.

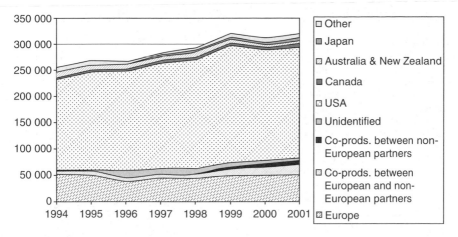

Figure 6.7. Origin of imported fiction broadcast by TV channels in Western Europe, 1994–2001.

Source: ETS/European Audiovisual Observatory.

programming by times of day for these networks into domestic, US, European, and other. The general pattern in the table is that US productions appear less in prime time than they do during the rest of the day. This is consistent with the idea that producing programs is expensive and filling air time is more difficult. The major European networks obviously concentrate their programming efforts on prime time

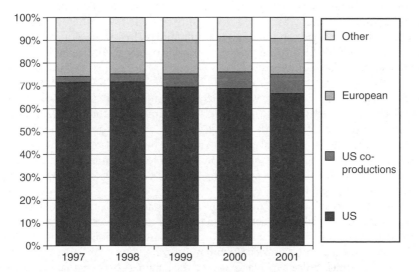

Figure 6.8. Imported American, European, and other broadcasts on television channels in Western Europe, 1997–2001.

TABLE 6.7. *Geographical origin of TV fiction programmed by major networks, 2000* (%)

		Domestic	US	European	Other
United Kingdom	Whole day	47	43	0	10
	Prime time only	51	49	0	0
Germany	Whole day	36	57	5	2
	Prime time only	56	44	0	0
France	Whole day	25	56	15	5
	Prime time only	75	25	0	0
Italy	Whole day	19	64	4	13
	Prime time only	43	51	6	0
Spain	Whole day	20	56	7	17
	Prime time only	51	37	12	0

Note: Sample week 12–18 March 2000.

Source: European Audiovisual Laboratory, *Eurofiction* (2001).

and use mainly domestic production for this. There is evidence in the table that in the larger countries, programming from other European and non-European countries play a role in programming, particularly during the day. It is useful to look at some of the differences here as well. The UK main networks use US programs during both prime time and the rest of the day to an equal amount. The French main networks are the most extreme in the use of US programming all day (56%), but less (25%) in prime time. The Germans, Spanish, and Italians have a similar pattern to the French, but a little less extreme.

Cable and pay-TV have grown dramatically across Western Europe since 1990. This has been one of the main destinations for American imports. After all, if one has to fill programming for 100 cable channels, finding television shows to fill all that air time will cause TV producers to buy content from wherever they can. Since the US pioneered cable and has many channels already developed, they have exported many of them to Europe. It is useful to examine how cable channels have changed what Europeans watch.

The explosion in cable networks is illustrated in Table 6.8. In 1990 there were 103 stations and by 2003 there were 1132, an elevenfold increase. In 1990, general channels comprised 75 per cent of the total number of channels. These were mostly the dominant network channels in each country, and frequently these channels were, and still are, government-owned. The number of channels in every other category has exploded. Channels devoted to sport went from 0 in 1990 to 92 in 2003, movie channels went from 7 in 1990 to 143 in 2003, and news channels went from 5 in 1990 to 88 in 2003.

In the US, the cable market contains, on the one hand, the content providers who run general and specialty channels, and on the other hand, the cable companies. The picture is similar in Europe, but there, because of language differences, many of the cable channels are not exported to other markets. Thus the large number of European channels reflects to a large degree the language barriers that continue to exist in Europe. Table 6.9 presents data on the main cable companies in each

TABLE 6.8. *Number of television channels by channel genre in Europe, 1990 to May 2003*

	1990	1991	1992	1993	1994	1995	1996	1997	1998	1999	2000	2001	2002	2003
General	75	77	93	103	109	117	129	147	177	192	210	222	249	261
Children's	1	2	2	5	6	8	13	21	26	45	64	66	77	78
Movie	7	9	11	19	22	26	34	70	93	109	120	128	142	143
Music	3	3	3	4	7	11	17	28	35	42	56	64	74	75
News, business, parliamentary	5	5	6	12	13	16	25	39	49	54	60	70	85	88
Sport	0	12	12	15	15	18	22	26	42	53	68	82	92	92
Shopping	1	1	1	3	3	3	5	5	7	7	15	33	47	52
Entertainment, computer, games	7	9	11	14	14	19	23	34	43	50	59	66	73	74
Culture, documentary	3	5	6	8	8	11	23	33	55	75	82	86	94	94
Health, lifestyle, weather, travel	0	0	0	0	0	0	3	4	8	8	11	16	20	22
Other	1	1	4	7	7	12	21	46	59	83	104	124	149	153
TOTAL	103	124	149	190	204	241	315	453	594	718	849	957	1,102	1,132

Source: European Audiovisual Laboratory, *Eurofiction* (2001).

TABLE 6.9. *Number of TV channels made available as part of offer by main cable-operators and satellite packagers in the European Union (February 2004)*

			National	Foreign	TOTAL	Foreign (%)
AT	UPC Telekabel	Cable	8	27	35	77.1
	Premiere Austria	Satellite	1	27	28	96.4
BE (CFR)	Coditel	Cable	20	24	44	54.5
	Le Bouquet	Satellite	0	37	37	100.0
BE (VLG)	Coditel	Cable	20	24	44	54.5
	Canal Digitaal	Satellite	1	113	114	99.1
DE	Kabel Deutschland	Cable	80	56	136	41.2
	Premiere	Satellite	28	0	28	0.0
DK	TDC Kabel TV	Cable	11	92	103	89.3
	Canal Digital Danmark	Satellite	8	35	43	81.4
	Viacat	Satellite	2	32	34	94.1
ES	ONO	Cable	58	43	101	42.6
	Digital+	Satellite	52	14	66	21.2
FI	Helsinki Television	Cable	9	52	61	85.2
	Canal Digital Finland	Satellite	3	37	40	92.5
FR	Noog	Cable	93	27	120	22.5
	Canal Satellite	Satellite	75	22	97	22.7
	TPS	Satellite	62	10	72	13.9
GB	NTL	Cable	125	5	130	3.8
	Sky	Satellite	131	3	134	2.2
GR	Nova	Satellite	14	16	30	53.3
IE	NTL	Cable	3	12	15	80.0
	Sky	Satellite	1	133	134	99.3
IT	Sky Italia	Satellite	106	22	128	17.2

(*Continued*)

TABLE 6.9. (*Continued*)

			National	Foreign	TOTAL	Foreign (%)
NL	UPC	Cable	15	17	32	53.1
	Canal Digitaal	Satellite	14	100	114	87.7
PT	TV Cabo	Cable	n.a.	n.a.	0	n.a.
	TV Cabo	Satellite	21	27	48	56.3
SE	ComHem	Cable	15	46	61	75.4
	Canal Digital	Satellite	11	37	48	77.1
	Viacat	Satellite	20	16	36	44.4

Note: Due to differences in marketing practices, these figures should be considered as indicative. Channels are considered as national once they are established in the targeted market whatever the nationality of their majority shareholding. In the case of Premier (Germany), for example, Germany Disney Channel is considered to be of national origin.

Source: European Audiovisual Observatory, *Eurofiction* (2001).

country, the number of channels on each cable network, and their national origins. There are a great number of interesting issues raised by this table. First, cable TV in every country does show channels from foreign countries. This means that, potentially, Europeans are watching similar things across countries.

However, there is a great deal of variation in this table. In the smaller countries such as Belgium, Finland, Ireland, and the Netherlands, a large number of foreign channels are available. This makes sense because programming cable TV is relatively expensive and small countries are just less likely to have large industries devoted to it. Moreover, cable content producers in the large countries have an incentive to sell their product wherever they can. Once produced, it is very cheap to reproduce in another country.

The larger countries, France, the UK, Germany, Spain, and Italy have many more cable channels that are produced nationally. The UK is one of the leading exporters of cable TV channels. It has a large number of indigenous cable channels and a very small number of foreign networks. The Italians and French import the next fewest number of foreign stations. The Germans and Spanish import the most channels from the large countries.

An important issue is the size of the audience for the different types of television. As of 2000, European publicly owned television stations still controlled 36 per cent of the market. Private commercial television stations that are free but contain commercials accounted for an additional 38 per cent of the market. Pay cable and satellite systems accounted for only 26 per cent of the market. So, while cable and satellite television contains the most European content, it probably draws the smallest audiences because it costs money to purchase. Access to more European content is restricted to those who are inclined to buy satellite or cable systems. Consuming television produced in other European countries is more likely to be done by those in the middle or upper-middle classes.

Popular music is an arena in which there is more cultural integration across Europe. Young people are the main consumers of popular music; youth culture travels through the media of television, the internet, and radio. The evolution of MTV in Europe makes an interesting general context in which to understand cultural diffusion, difference, and convergence. When MTV first entered the European market, it did so with a single program that originated in Great Britain and was broadcast in English. But, after a rough start, the people who ran the network realized that language and musical tastes differed across societies. The MTV format was relatively cheap to produce; it involved a young person standing on a set, making sardonic comments, and introducing videos. So MTV began to expand its cable offerings across Europe in different languages. They developed play lists that contained songs from both national and international sources. MTV now produces shows in eighteen European countries. It has proliferated channels in many countries in order to introduce music for different audiences, and also engages in original programming in many of its largest European markets. In this way, it is both European and national.

In order to get a feel for the degree to which popular music is shared across Western Europe, I gathered data on the top ten popular music songs (by sales) in each of the five largest European countries during the week of 24–31 July 2005. A reader might wonder if a single week on the European popular charts is very representative of overall patterns, and of course, focusing only on the top ten songs is arbitrary as well. But, if one looks at these charts week in and week out, one will see that the patterns are fairly stable. This represents an example of what people are listening to at any single moment. The data is presented in Table 6.10.

The first thing that is obvious from the table is that for all five countries, national artists are important. Four Spanish songs are in the top ten in Spain, five songs from national artists are in the top ten in the UK, Germany, and Italy, and eight French songs are in the top ten in France. There is also an American presence on all these lists, although American production does not dominate European popular

TABLE 6.10. *Home country of artists for the top ten popular songs, 24–30 July 2005*

Country of song	UK	SE	NL	IT	IE	FR	ES	DE	BE	AT
US	2	4	5	2	4	1	3	3	2	1
UK/US	1									1
UK/DE	2	1	1	1	1	1	1	1	1	1
UK	5			1	2		2		1	
SE		2								
NL			3						1	
IT				5						
IE					2					
FR						8		1		1
ES							4			1
DE		1						5		2
BE			1						4	
AT										
Other		2		1	1			1		

Note: UK United Kingdom; FR France; SE Sweden; ES Spain; NL Netherlands; DE Germany; IT Italy; BE Belgium; IE Ireland; AT Austria.

Source: Official Charts and Box Office Ratings <www.allcharts.org>.

music in the same way that American movies and television do in their fields. Popular music remains fairly national, with some notable crossovers.

It is interesting to look at the same lists for some of the smaller countries. Table 6.10 also gives the origins of artists for Austria, Sweden, Ireland, Belgium, and the Netherlands. In general it is the case that there are fewer national artists in these countries on the Top Ten lists and more artists from other countries. There are no songs from Austria, two from Sweden, two from Ireland, three from the Netherlands, and four from Belgium on their own lists. The smaller countries have more US songs on all their lists than do the larger countries. One interesting feature is that the tastes of people in these countries appear to be more eclectic, as there is a sprinkling of songs from many other countries on all their lists.

It is of great interest to consider the one song that did cross over in the summer of 2005, a German song, 'Axel F,' by a group called Crazy Frog. The evolution of 'Axel F' offers a vignette of the existence of a European youth culture. In 1997, a 17-year-old Swede named Daniel Malmedahl recorded himself impersonating the sounds produced by a car. Eventually, he was persuaded by a friend to record a live version on air, and this circulated around the internet. In late 2000, Erik Wernquist, another Swede, got the idea of using the sound track with a character of a frog that was named 'The Annoying Thing.' He put this on his website. Malmedahl was told of this, and convinced Wernquist that he was the author of the original soundtrack. They began to collaborate on expanding both the video and sound portion of the film clip.

'The Annoying Thing' was broadcast for the first time on Belgian television in a commercial for Ringtone Europe, a Belgian company. Ringtone Europe became part of Jamba!, a British company, in 2001. An executive at Jamba! got the idea of using the animal figure against the background of the automobile sound as a ringtone. It soon became the most downloaded ringtone in the UK and eventually in all Europe. 'The Annoying Thing' was renamed Crazy Frog, and was used in a series of ringtones.

In early 2005, two members of a German band called the Bass Bumpers were commissioned to record a dance song using the Crazy Frog ringtone. They produced a remix of the song based on the 1984 instrumental song 'Axel F,' written by American Harold Faltermeyer for the movie, *Beverly Hills Cop*. The 'Axel F' in the title referred to the character, Axel Foley, played in the movie by Eddie Murphy. The song was released on 23 May 2005 and rose to the top of the charts in Great Britain and eventually all over Europe. 'Axel F' is a general exception to the idea that European popular music is mostly either national or American. It shows the power of the internet and the connectedness of people around Europe. Under the right conditions, a European popular culture artifact can be created.

These results suggest that popular music has national, European, and American aspects. American popular music is represented in all the countries, and all continue to have a national popular music scene where artists record in the national language—and here the French are an extreme case in point. But there is some crossover from one European country to another. There was at least one song that in the summer of 2005 was common to all the charts that originated in Europe, and represented a collaboration between Swedish, British, Belgian, and German citizens.

The final form of popular culture to be considered is novels. Here, I will do the most cursory job of comparison. I present data for only the UK, France, and Germany for the ten bestselling novels as reported by Amazon.com during the month of July 2005. There are separate websites for France and Germany that are in the national languages, and all of the novels considered were published in the national languages. Seven of the ten bestsellers in Britain were by British authors and the remaining three were by Americans. In France, four of the ten were British, three were French, two from the US, and one from Italy. In Germany, three were from Britain, four from Germany, and three from the US There was enormous overlap across the list. Three of the British novels on all three lists were from the Harry Potter series written by J. K. Rowling. Two of the US novels were written by Dan Brown, author of *The Da Vinci Code* and *Gods and Demons*. I investigated other sources of information, but was unable to find any systematic sources that would allow a comparison of bestseller lists across countries. Obviously, there is some bias in using Amazon.com, a company based in the US and one that requires people to use the internet to order books. This list shows that there is a surprising degree of crossover in books. While books written by national authors are represented on the lists, there are some international bestsellers, mostly represented by the American author Dan Brown and the British author J. K. Rowling.

This overview of European popular culture suggests a complex interplay of popular culture in Europe. American presence in movies, television, music, and to a lesser extent books means that people across Europe are exposed to similar cultural content presented to them by large media conglomerates. A second important conclusion is that national languages continue to be the idiom for some popular culture, particularly in music, books, and television. At least half of prime-time television broadcasts across Europe on the main 'free' television networks are produced for the national market in the national language. There is evidence that where the media conglomerates are involved, they do sell the same content across Europe. But they also are sensitive to the national language and culture and where possible tailor their products to local audiences. There are nationally owned media outlets that continue predominantly to record pop music and sell books written for national audiences.

There are hints of some crossover in European culture. There is a Europe-wide business press read by managers and executives. Cable and satellite television have brought channels from the rest of Europe into the households of every society. Popular music does occasionally cross borders and there are Europe-wide hits that originate in Europe. Finally, some novels travel across borders as well.

The ability to consume European popular culture has a class bias to it as well. The people who are the most likely to pay attention to what is going on in other European countries are managers who read the business press, people who are better off, can afford access to cable, and might be aware of and attend foreign films, and young people who share a music-oriented youth culture. Older and less-well-off people lack the money to buy expensive cable channels, tend to consume their free public and commercial television, listen to the radio, and read newspapers, books, and magazines in their native tongues. They are most likely to see only two cultures: those offered them by American television content and those presented to them by national media. While there are some elements of a European culture, the aspects of popular culture that most bring people together are their common consumption of Hollywood movies and American television.

CONCLUSION

This chapter provides evidence that there exists a European society for the group of educated, mobile people who are middle or upper-middle class. The European economic integration project has produced opportunities for people to work, travel, and study abroad. I demonstrate that those Europeans who are living in another country are those with high skills who can profit by working abroad, students who spend a short time abroad to study, or people who decide to retire to or live in unspoilt places such as the mountains or beach towns.

Managers, professionals and other white-collar workers have taken advantage of their chances to travel by setting up European organizations where they meet their counterparts across national borders to talk about common issues. Managers and professionals have founded many organizations on a Europe-wide basis, particularly in response to increased social interaction in the wake of the Single Market.

The education elite across national societies have been in the forefront of trying to push the creation of a larger, more all-encompassing European society and identity. They have done so by encouraging the teaching of languages, changing the way that the national history is taught to sensitize students to their place in Europe, and to teach the values of an 'enlightened, rational, tolerant' Europe. Exchanges of college students have been organized on a large scale. Those who have taken advantage of these exchanges have tended to come from upper-middle-class backgrounds. Their experiences do appear to change them by making them more European, more aware and fond of other cultures, and more likely to migrate to work in another country. Universities are now pushing forward a project to create a European Higher Education Space.

There now exists a Europe-wide business press that writes in English. There are also a great number of cable and satellite networks that produce news, sports, and specialty channels for consumption across Europe. There are occasional elements of exchange of popular culture across Europe through television, films, music, and books. Identities have shifted for those who live, work, study, and play with people from other European countries. They are also more interested in the EU and its success. They are aware of European politics and business and keep up on cultural goods that might be being produced in other countries.

Untouched by pan-Europe developments are the vast majority of people. They do not belong to European associations or work in positions where they travel across Europe. Most of the European college students do not choose to engage in college exchanges and only 2–3 per cent of Europeans are working in other countries. 'Average' people do not consume international media on a systematic basis, but instead read national newspapers with national stories. Either by interest or cost, national markets for TV, films, music, and books persist. To the degree that there is some convergence in popular culture, it is at least partially generated by the use of American content in films, TV, music, and books. This does not mean that Europeans do not share some common popular forms of culture or are not aware of what people in other countries are like. Many people do travel in Europe for vacations and access to information about Europe is widely available. What it does mean, is that a European identity and interest are much shallower and more fleeting.

The organization of trans-European social fields mirrors the survey results on who is a European. European society is heavily dependent on the selective interactions of members of different social classes. The people with the strongest European identities are young, educated, and with highly valued labor market skills. They engage not just in work across national borders, but other forms of professional and social association with their peers from across Europe. They read the European press and consume popular culture from national, American, and European sources. They are part of and connected to social fields and help form European society.

The large group of people with mostly national identities but who occasionally thinks of themselves as Europeans occasionally travel for business and pleasure. They may consume some culture from other countries through films, music, books, and television. Those with only a national identity are less prone to travel and associate with people from other societies and consume mainly national media. While they may occasionally find themselves in European social fields, they are mostly enmeshed in their national networks and culture. They tend to be less educated, older, and have fewer job market skills valued by the largest European firms.

Finally, the least educated, the elderly, the less well-off, and the less skilled remain wedded to the national worldview. They do not travel and do not work with colleagues from other countries. They continue to associate only within their national social circles. They consume culture through the national vernacular, read local newspapers, listen to music provided by national artists, and read books written by national authors. They cannot afford cable television, but instead watch public and commercial television focused on their society. Their identities remain wedded to the nation.

7

The Structure of European Politics

INTRODUCTION: EUROPEAN AND NATIONAL IDENTITY AND THE LAYERING OF EUROPEAN POLITICS

The debate over the relationship between the EU and national politics hinges on the underlying model one has of the linkages between the EU, the member-state governments, and national politics. Some scholars view the EU as primarily an intergovernmental organization where governments agree to pool their sovereignty to create rules in circumscribed arenas of joint benefit such as trade and monetary policy (Majone 1998; Moravcscik 2002). The EU obtains its political legitimacy by virtue of the political legitimacy of the member-state governments. Since those governments are freely elected, citizens who disapprove of their government's policies in Europe can vote for other parties. In this way, the EU is ultimately within the power of citizens and does not suffer a 'democratic deficit'.

Other scholars view the EU as an existing political community that affects citizens in myriad ways without their direct input (Scharpf 1999; Follesdal and Hix 2006). From this perspective, EU politics remain distant from citizens in spite of the expanded powers of the EU Parliament. This lack of direct political accountability of the EU apparatus in Brussels makes it inherently undemocratic and less legitimate, particularly when an EU directive hurts some group in one of the member states. Some argue that the EU produces public policies that favor business and undermine social democracy (Streeck and Schmitter 1992; Scharpf 1999). They suggest that these policies are out of line with the preferences of Europe's voters, which tend toward the center left. So when EU directives appear that favor business over workers, they work to undermine EU legitimacy. The discussion over the 'democratic deficit' in the EU is generally theoretical, without empirical reference to either what citizens want or how they actually vote.

There exists a related literature in political science on the degree to which there exists a European public sphere or civil society where political discussion on a Europe-wide level occurs (Schlesinger and Kevin 2000; Risse 2002; 2003; Koopmans and Erbe 2003; Downey and Koenig 2004; Koopmans, Neidhart, and Pfetsch 2004; Koopmans 2005, for examples). This literature starts with the assumption that having some such an arena would be a good thing for Europe. A large part of the literature is definitional, i.e. it depends on what one means by such a public space as to the degree to which one thinks it exists. At one extreme, scholars who think that Europe has need of such a thing postulate that in order for a European politics to exist, it must be constituted as a layer above national politics (Gerhards

1993; 2000). It must form fields where participants from many European societies are simultaneously debating an issue and responding to one another's arguments. The result of such politics is public policy that takes into account all Europeans (for a critique of this view, see Van de Steeg 2002).

Scholars more interested in the degree to which there actually is a European politics critique this position. They suggest that the criteria are too stringent for evaluating the degree to which a successful and active European politics exists. The public sphere envisaged is an idealized version of democratic politics that does not even describe national politics in any of the member states. Instead, these scholars try to examine exactly how particular European issues are being discussed across Europe through media coverage (Van de Steeg 2002; Van de Steeg et al. 2003). Media attention to European issues is extensive and frequently informs and shapes national debate on European topics (Koopmans, Neidhart, and Pfetsch 2004). There is evidence that the media report similar stories across Europe and sometimes groups in one country react to groups in another. The reactions across countries vary with the issue. Sometimes issues produce cooperative solidarity, but at others such events create conflict. Scholars have also documented the role of interest group and social movement organizations in protests made about Europe to national and European authorities (Imig and Tarrow 2001a; Koopmans 2005). Here, they find that most social movement activity is focused on national governments, although there are occasionally attempts to cooperate across national borders. When groups protest EU policies, they tend to be working to protect their national privileges against EU imperatives.

The purpose of this chapter is to untangle some of the features of these politics and then link them more closely to the issue of European identity. This is done first by discussion of a theoretical model of the linkages between various political actors and fields across Europe and the dynamics inherent in these kinds of political process. Such linkages have been institutionalized through the various treaties and the national constitutions that provide for the existing division of labor in policymaking across political fields. One of the main issues that is ignored in the debate over whether or not a civil society with a public sphere exists in Europe is the exact division of political issues between the EU and the member-state governments. The EU has wide jurisdiction over issues related to trade, commerce, and, for those who have the Euro, monetary policy. The governments have retained almost all issues concerning the welfare state, including pensions, labor relations, welfare, unemployment insurance, job training, health care, and education, under their jurisdiction. They do so because public opinion polls show that citizens are against governments allowing these kinds of decision to be made in Brussels (Dalton and Eichenberg 1998; Eichenberg and Dalton 1998), being afraid that changes in welfare state policies made at the EU level will be against their interests.

Then, I consider evidence on how EU and national politics intersect. I show that EU-level politics is highly institutionalized around a fixed set of policy fields located in Brussels. National governments are the most powerful actors in these fields as they ultimately have to agree to the passage of directives, but their decisions are influenced by organized interest groups, the European Parliament, and the European Commission. I then turn my attention to national political processes. The literature shows that most politics within nation-states is oriented nationally, and particularly with regard to the welfare states. Because of the division of labor between European and national politics, it follows that political groups who are interested in welfare state issues will not waste resources going to Brussels to lobby, but instead will engage in national politics. Most political coverage in the media is national in focus.

Citizens, interest groups, and social movement organizations have a number of avenues by which to express their opinions to their governments about the EU. In Ch. 5 I showed that most citizens of Europe support their country's EU membership and most citizens have a favorable attitude toward the EU. In this chapter, I show that this is reflected in the stances of the main political parties across Europe. Center-left and center-right parties in France, Great Britain, and Germany have converged on a pro-European stance in the past forty years. In all three countries, political parties have experimented with running for national office on an anti-EU campaign. This has not been a winning issue and over time, all center-right and center-left parties eventually have come around to being strong supporters of the EU. While fringe left- and right-wing parties have tried to run against the European project, they have never been able to use an anti-EU position to take over a government. This reflects the overwhelmingly positive support for the EU from middle- and upper-middle-class citizens across Europe. No political party can build a majority vote in the largest European societies, even in Great Britain, and get elected with an openly anti-European stance.

This does not mean that all policies decided at the European level are accepted passively by citizens. There is a high level of coverage of European politics in the national media in most societies, so citizens have a great deal of information about contemporary issues that are being played out at the European level. Interest groups or social movement organization express their grievances over a particular EU policy mainly by directly lobbying their national governments. They can also take their grievances to Brussels and attempt to influence a policy there. There is evidence that such groups often do both (Rucht 2000; Helfferich and Kolb 2001).

The weakest linkages in European politics are coordination of political grievances across nation-states. Firms, interest groups, and social movement groups rarely try to coordinate with their counterparts in other countries to put collective pressure on their governments. Instead, they engage with them directly or go to Brussels. I documented the lack of such politically oriented groups in Ch. 5. There are very few Europe-wide associations that are civil society groups oriented toward coordinating political action across states. Instead, these groups represent the interests of professional and managerial groups.

This lack of horizontal connection is partly an intentional result of the organizational design of the EU on the part of the member-state governments and partly an unintended consequence of the citizens of Europe who favor a limited EU. Member-state governments have carefully controlled the issues on the agenda for EU-level policy fields (Milward 1997). Some have opposed discussions that transfer taxing power to the EU and all forms of social policies, such as labor relations, social welfare provisions, healthcare, education, and pensions. This division of political fields means that national politics and EU political fields are quite separate. Governments play different roles in national and EU political fields, but they remain central to both.

Citizens across Europe have accepted just such a division of labor in political fields. While they have been happy with the results of shifting trade issues to Brussels, they have not wanted their governments to shift welfare state issues to the European level. Even if they generally support their government's participation in EU-level political fields, they are able to disagree with European-level policies by appealing directly to their governments through the medium of national politics. This has the unintended consequence of focusing national political groups on their governments and keeping national citizens from interacting politically with citizens from other countries to organize on a European basis. Most of these complaints involve protecting national interest groups, so such groups simply do not think that their particular national interest in opposing some EU directive will be best served by looking for allies in other societies, because they have conflicting interests.

The current constitution of European identity works into this institutional separation of politics in important ways. The small but economically privileged group of citizens who think of themselves as Europeans favors EU-level solutions to common problems and would be open to more EU coordination of welfare state issues. They are pleased with the existing nature of Brussels politics and happy with their interactions with other Europeans.

The part of the population that still sees itself as national in identity is the less privileged part of society: the poor, the less educated, the blue-collar workers, and the elderly. They look to their governments to protect them against the forces of 'globalization' or 'unbridled market capitalism,' or 'neoliberalism.' They seek social protection from the market. Governments have maintained power over issues of social protection and so national politics remains the site to contest these issues. For other less privileged citizens who remain firmly wedded to the idea of the nation, the EU appears as a threat to national sovereignty. They look to their governments to protect them from 'outsiders' and 'foreigners.' These citizens are already skeptical of their government's participation in the EU.

The third group, those with mostly a national identity but sometimes a European one, are middle class. They are in the middle of the income and skill distributions. Their politics *vis-à-vis* the EU are more complex. On the one hand, they are in favor of their governments creating market opening projects that will provide new jobs and job stability. On the other hand, they feel comfortable with the existing division of European political fields. They want their governments to continue to control the welfare state and are happy to use the national political system to express grievances over particular EU policies. They are the most susceptible to changing political events. On the right issue framed the right way, they might be open to European solutions to problems. But, they are as likely to favor national solutions to political problems as EU solutions. Much of the dynamics of European politics can be directly traced to the mood of these swing voters.

One example of how these dynamics played out explicitly is the debate over the European constitution and in particular the vote in France in May 2005. As noted in Ch. 5, the French have a very high level of European identification in general. As a result, the center-left and center-right political parties have generally been supportive of the European project and both sides supported the European constitution. Indeed, both the main political parties in France supported passage of the constitution. But parties on the far left and some members of the Socialist Party argued that the European constitution did not make any provision for Europe-wide social protection against the onslaught of 'globalization' and 'neo-liberalism.' They called for a rewriting of the document to create a floor under European social benefit systems. The National Front, a party on the far right, argued that the constitution was a further erosion of the power of the national government. They wanted to reject the document to keep the French government and by inference the French people from losing their national identity.

Many middle-class citizens who had both a French and European identity voted 'no' on the constitution. They were the swing voters who accepted the argument that an EU constitution without social protection was going to present an attack on both the sovereignty of the French state, and also the welfare state. The result was a victory for the anti-EU forces who were able to attract voters in the middle ground and form a political coalition to defeat the passage of the European constitution.

The case of the failure of the European constitution in France illustrates vividly two of the main dynamics of European politics. First, the citizens of different countries have a very different idea about what the EU should be. Many French citizens prefer a more 'social Europe,' i.e. one where social protections are inscribed at the European level. Because many citizens in other countries, particularly Great Britain, do not want a 'social Europe,' that entire conversation is off the political agenda. What remains is what the member-state governments can agree to. This means that policies that might actually be favored by a majority of Europe's citizens are easily blocked by a minority of member-state governments that do not want to implement them.

In this case, the interests of the citizens of different countries in Europe are pitted against one another in a very indirect way. The EU constitution could not contain much effort at transnational cooperation on a 'social Europe' because of the opposition of some of the member states, so the document that was produced could include agreements only on things that did not engender opposition. The citizens of France did not get an opportunity to vote on a 'social Europe' because other member-state governments would not let that be on the agenda.

Second, center-left and center-right governments have pursued more economic integration through the EU. They do so because polls tell them that the median voter in Europe is pretty happy with their country's membership and participation in the EU. But, because EU politics is pretty much removed from national decision-making, when citizens are asked to weigh in on a particular issue they are as likely to oppose the EU as to support it. This is because the swing voters sometimes see their interests and identities as tied up with Europe and sometimes as tied up with the nation. Where they settle on any particular issue depends greatly on its content and how it is framed. If they become convinced that the EU is not working for them, they will oppose their government supporting whatever issue is on the table.

HOW ARE EUROPEAN AND NATIONAL POLITICAL FIELDS ORGANIZED?

Scholars who are interested in the ultimate trajectory of the EU often start out with idealized models of what a European polity might look like. One of the most important normative views of such a polity begins with Jürgen Habermas's idea (1989) that a democratic society needs a public sphere populated by civil society organizations. These groups operate outside the institutions of the state. In such arenas, a wide range of views and opinions can be developed in relation to matters of public concern. Discussion should occur in this sphere, involving a free and open range of opinions. The desired outcome of such discussion is presumably public policy in the public interest. Implicit in this idea is that there exists a single public sphere that encompasses all relevant political issues, that all actors in society have equal access to it, and that its activities are oriented toward a single state.

Such a conception of the public sphere and civil society has engendered much debate, questioning all assumptions both theoretically and empirically (Fraser 1992; Calhoun 1994; Keane 1998; Schlesinger 1999; Van de Steeg 2002). Scholars have been interested in the question of the degree to which Europe has such a public sphere. They have recognized that the existence of the EU poses a problem for national political discourses and they wonder if it is possible for a Europe-wide public sphere to emerge. One way in which the EU is critiqued is to note that ordinary citizens are not directly privy to EU-level debates. As such, this implies that the EU lacks a public space and this produces a 'democratic deficit.' The critics of the EU assume that it lacks a public space and considers this a serious source of illegitimacy.

The debate over the European public sphere has been both conceptual and empirical. Obviously, how one defines such a public sphere is crucial to whether one thinks it exists or not. On the one side of the debate have been scholars who have such a stringent definition of what a sphere should look like that it is difficult to imagine how one could exist. Their basic idea is that Europe must reproduce a public sphere much like those that supposedly exist within national boundaries (Grimm 1995; Kielmansegg 1996). Since there is no community of communication on a Europe-wide level based on a common language and genuinely European media, there can be no public sphere. Gerhards (1993; 2000) goes even further and argues that a European public sphere should be populated with

Europe-wide interest groups, parties, and social protest movements. Such a sphere must be concerned about taking a European and not a national perspective on any given event. With this kind of definition, it is clear that there does not exist a European public sphere.

The other point of view begins with the critique of Habermas's central ideas. Policy spheres are not unitary but plural in any given society. Public issues are inherently fragmented into different communities of interest because not every citizen or every citizen group is interested in every issue (Schlesinger 1999). The groups interested in environmental pollution in any given society are generally not the same as those interested in pensions. This fragmentation of policy arenas means that collective interests are not always accurately represented in policy formation. Small, highly motivated interest groups can capture policy fields and have an inordinate effect. A good example of this is the role of the gun lobby in the US. The National Rifle Association (NRA) is able to have a great deal of effect on the regulation of firearms in American society, in spite of a public that consistently would be interested in having more gun control.

Groups do not share equal access to policy fields. The less powerful groups in society have neither the organization nor the money necessary to participate actively in policy fields which affect them. The winners of debates are not those with the most rational ideas that will help the public good, but instead those who have the most resources and who are the best organized. In most democratic societies, national politics is about the relative power of groups and the ability of political parties to build governing majorities by combining such groups. Groups with less resources and capital and who have traditionally been downtrodden (women, immigrants, the working class, ethnic and racial minorities) do not have access to power (Calhoun 1994; 2003). Consequently, even within a given society, it does not make sense to assert the existence of a public sphere. Habermas (1989) has acknowledged many of these criticisms. But he has gone on record as proposing that in order to remove the democratic deficit in the EU, an EU public sphere with civil society organizations and a European politics should be formed (2001).

It is useful to consider more closely exactly what does exist in Europe in terms of what people call multilevel governance (Hooghe and Marks 2001) before one considers how this relates to the public sphere debate. My main point here is that scholars who accept the terms of the public sphere debate begin with trying to make a conceptual distinction about what such a sphere should look like. Even those who are trying to use a more realistic definition of that sphere (Van de Steeg et al. 2003) still accept the importance of such a sphere. I want to argue that it is more useful to try to make conceptual sense of exactly how political units across the EU interact before one concludes how politics happen in the EU. The real politics that does go on in Europe is highly structured across policy fields, some of which are regional (i.e. subnational), some national, and still others European.

I begin with the abstract idea that political fields are social spaces where various kinds of political actors interact. These fields can be characterized in terms of who are the participants (who the players are), what positions they occupy (who has resources that can be converted to power), which policy outcome is at stake, and how policy outcomes are attained (the rules of the game). In discussing politics in the EU, one can view these fields are being composed either at the EU or the national level. So, at the EU level, policy fields consist of representatives of the member-state governments and members of the European Commission, the European Parliament, the European Court of Justice, and lobbying groups located in Brussels whose interactions are governed by rules in the various treaties (Fligstein and McNichol 1998 provides an overview of the political fields in the EU). The national political fields contain citizens who vote, bureaucracies, political parties, courts, organized interest groups including organizations claiming to represent the various branches of business and labor, and social movement organizations. Figure 7.1 presents a stylized version of how such fields are constructed in Europe.

The question of multilevel governance concerns the degree and methods by which the national political fields are linked to those of the EU. One argument is that political fields of the EU and the nation-states were intentionally set up to be independent of and complementary to one another (Moravscik 2002). The

Figure 7.1. Theoretical linkages between political actors and political fields across Europe.

various treaties specify what issues can be considered at the European level and the rules by which agreements are reached. The member-state governments agree collectively to policies decided at the EU level, then implement these policies at the national level. This view implies that what is national politics remains national and what is EU-level politics is decided in Brussels. The main direct mechanism that citizens have to monitor EU politics is by participating via an EU lobbying group. More indirectly, citizens can vote for or against how their current governments have been acting with regard to EU politics. Citizens can participate in their national politics more directly by being members of interest groups, social movement organizations, or political parties and thereby trying to affect their government's position on particular EU issues.

Such a view of the political fields in Europe is both a kind of ideal type and a not totally inaccurate representation of how politics works in Europe. Moravscik (2002) presents an interesting interpretation of this position by arguing that the relationship between the EU and national politics is now in some kind of equilibrium. Citizens through their governments have spoken on the issues that they are willing to let migrate to Brussels and are now happy with the division of labor between the two. In order to believe that the arrangements between the EU and member-state governments is in equilibrium, one has to believe that the preferences of citizens on these issues are fixed and unchanging. That is, citizens are happy with the current division of policy fields and the mechanisms by which they are able to have input. Thus there is little reason to believe that this will change.

The main problem with this stance is that it ignores the possible dynamics that created the division of power and could equally upset the equilibrium. One such is the issue of European identity. Figure 7.2 presents an idealized version of how EU competencies could be ratcheted up. As the EU creates more rules, more European trade and more interaction with other Europeans is produced, through work, play, and culture. If European identity is primarily a function of interaction with other Europeans, then if more people become involved in economic and social fields, more people will start to think of themselves as Europeans, and be prepared to have more national policies coordinated at the EU level. In this way, as people become more Europeanized, their preferences for policy coordination might shift to the European level.

While this is one plausible scenario that would upset the current balance between EU and national government policies, it could be problematic. Identities become activated by real political events and the way that people come to see where they stand in terms of a particular political conflict. A large percentage of citizens of Europe have a national and European identity; if the right political issue comes along, then a European identity might be activated amongst citizens—but another political issue could play out in exactly the opposite way.

Figure 7.3 presents a view that focuses on how continued European economic and social integration might create an opposition to continued integration processes. The dynamics of European economic and social integration do not just produce Europeans. Given the class nature of who is a European and who is not, the losers of market opening projects tend to be the less educated and less

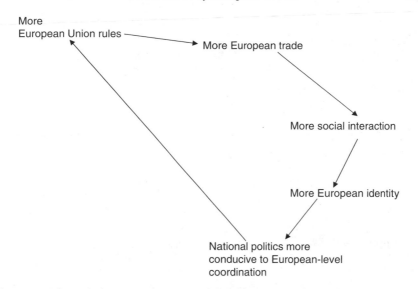

Figure 7.2. Theoretical process of European political integration that builds more European cooperation.

skilled, and they are likely to experience an intensification of their national sentiments. How citizens with a national and European identity and education and skills in the middle of the distribution will experience continued integration is an open question. One might expect that European economic and social integration could polarize opinion as easily as it would promote more support for integration. This sets up a national political debate over the future of EU cooperation, a potential for what I term 'Euroclash'. The evidence shows, for example, that the EU has become more of a target for social movement organizations at the national level precisely in reaction to integration processes (Imig and Tarrow 2001*a*).

Moreover, political field dynamics at the EU and national levels are not always so easy to separate. It is entirely possible that national-level dynamics can activate European-level activities. So, for example, during the late 1990s, European governments realized that their economies were not growing as fast as America. One way they could have reacted to this, was to try and undertake reforms to stimulate economic growth in their societies. Because of the internet boom in the US, European governments were interested in how to promote high technology in general, and technology transfer between universities and business in particular. Since education is a national issue, governments could have easily worked to craft national solutions to their competitiveness problems conceived this way. Instead, they chose to try and coordinate their policies at the EU level. European leaders met at a summit in Lisbon in March 2000 and they set the European Union the goal of becoming 'the most dynamic and competitive knowledge-based economy in the world.' The Lisbon process committed governments to a set of policy reforms that

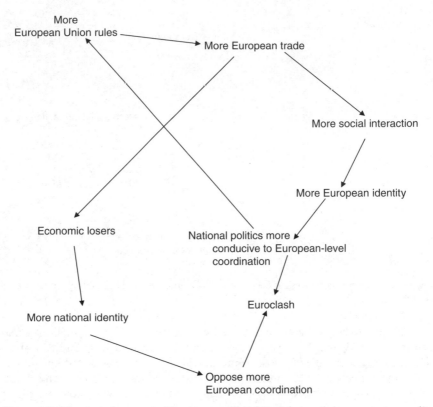

Figure 7.3. Theoretical process of European political integration that creates more political opposition to the EU and results in 'Euroclash.'

are to be implemented by 2010. By pushing for European solutions to these problems, politicians agreed that every country was in the same boat and they needed to work together.

Similarly, the degree to which European politics can be entirely segregated from national politics is not complete. One of the unintended consequences of the creation of the Schengen area is that now it is easier to cross national borders without any passport control. So, controlling illegal immigration across Europe becomes difficult as migrants can choose points of entry that are relatively undefended in order to end up eventually in a place where they might be employed. As this becomes a national issue, then political parties can push one of two solutions: close the borders, or work to heighten security by adopting an EU-wide policy. Again, how this kind of debate will play out in national politics will reflect the political situation in each member state, their history of dealing with migration, and the role of interest groups, social movements, and political parties in framing such an issue.

The last issue to consider in terms of the layering of European politics is the existence of possible horizontal linkages between policy fields across member states. The main mechanisms I have identified for input into EU policy for citizens and groups is either through their national politics or through direct lobbying in Brussels. The weakest mechanisms in the emergence of a European politics are the horizontal linkages between citizens across countries. Currently, the main way that such coordination might occur is through the connection of people in different societies via media such as newspapers, television, and the internet. Koopmans (2005; Koopmans and Erbe 2003) argues that there are two forms of this communication. A weak form exists when events in one country are covered in another and possibly reacted to, but there is little direct communication or coordination amongst groups in each country. A stronger form could occur if groups begin directly to discuss issues of common interest across countries after finding out about each other through media coverage.

Imig and Tarrow (2001*b*; *c*) push this view along by arguing that these types of coordination vary along two dimensions: whether there is more or less coordination between groups across societies, and whether or not the groups are cooperative or competitive in their actions. Cooperative transnationalism involves 'parallel protests which make claims on different national targets in cooperative but recognizably separate acts of contention' (2001*a*: 17). Competitive transnationalism is where 'private actors from one member state protest against and may target private actors from another member state' (ibid.). Collective European protest is where 'groups from different member states combine and take action against the same national or international target' (ibid.). When Imig and Tarrow examine protest events aimed at the EU in Europe, the largest number reflect competitive transnationalism and the smallest number reflect collective European protest.

One can conclude that there exist two sorts of European politics, one that goes on in Brussels and another that goes on in the member states. The latter politics is the more complex. National interest groups can try directly to influence their national government's policies in the EU by lobbying and demonstrating, thereby putting pressure on political parties and sitting governments. The weakest form of European politics is the degree to which national interest groups cooperate directly or indirectly with their counterparts in other countries. The most important reason for this is that they are quite likely to find themselves opposed to what their counterparts in other countries might want. But, even where groups might find themselves on the same side on an issue, coordination is difficult because it requires national interest groups to know what their counterparts in other countries are doing. This can be learned somewhat through the media. But to actually reach out to their counterparts in other countries in order to coordinate actions is quite costly in time and effort and difficult to negotiate.

The model of existing European politics that I am proposing starts with the institutional features of the division of political fields between Brussels and the member states. Then, it considers how citizens participate in these politics. They have multiple direct and indirect means to affect EU politics, including voting for political parties, direct lobbying in Brussels, and engaging in national politics via interest groups and social movement organizations to affect their government's position on a particular European issue. The dynamics of European politics can be introduced by political contestation at the national level whereby citizens in one or several countries can help enact or derail EU policies. EU policies can also impact national political debates. At the core of national and EU debates are the social class and identity divisions between those who are the most direct beneficiaries of the EU economic and social integration project and those who are likely to suffer as a result of those projects. The positioning of these groups in their national debates will greatly affect their outcome. Finally, while there is quite a bit of information flow through member states via the media, there is less opportunity for collective mobilization across interest groups and social movement organizations across countries. Frequently, these groups find themselves on different sides of the debate and so their focus is on causing their national governments to intervene on their behalf. But even where these groups share interests, it is difficult to get Europe-wide coordination.

Hooghe and Marks (2001) have argued that the best way to think about the EU is as a system of multilevel governance. What they have in mind is a set of distinct competences given to different levels of government and a pattern of relationships between those levels. So, the EU has a political architecture that defines the role of governments, the Commission, Parliament, and the Court, and the procedures by which it reaches decisions. It has also specified the policy domains in which such agreements are possible. In the political processes of the EU, the national governments remain the most important actors. All other powers not specified in the treaties are still in the purview of the governments. In every society there are rules that define the relationship between their own parliaments, political parties, legal systems, and voters. Many European countries have federal structures in place (as in Germany and to a certain degree Spain, Italy, and Great Britain) and these also define competences and relationships (Offe 1996).

I am sympathetic to their account but I consider it to be incomplete in several ways. First, it lacks the sense of dynamics of politics within countries, within the EU, and between the states and the EU that I have just outlined. While the idea that politics in Europe takes place at different levels depending on the issue at stake makes sense, their view does not imply how potential conflicts might play out. A second critique of their approach is that this model of politics needs to be connected more closely with the winners and losers of the European social and economic project. Much of their discussion focuses on the formal political links between the EU, member-state governments, and national politics, their shape, and the degree to which they are legitimate. It is less about the groups and interests that are stake. The more economic integration occurs, the more likely that the beneficiaries of that integration will see the wisdom of increased political cooperation. But that integration will also produce losers who will become more vehement in their rejection of European solutions. They will want to focus more on national solutions to economic problems and less on European ones. The lack of horizontal relationships between groups across societies will tend to push groups with grievances to settle those grievances in a national political context. This will put pressure on governments either to roll back or to hold constant their efforts at European-level coordination. I argue that in order really to understand how Europe works as a system of multilevel governance, one needs to conceptualize how national interest groups and national political systems interact both with Brussels and with their neighbors.

I look at three sorts of evidence for considering the degree to which a European politics that fits the outline I have just provided has emerged. The first is represented by the politics that takes place in Brussels. Here, there is quite a well-developed political sphere. The main conclusion is that the European governments have created a set of institutions to produce monetary policy and common policies regarding the free movement of capital, goods, and labor. They have begun to cooperate on common foreign and security policy and the EU frequently acts as a bargaining agent for the member states in international arenas; but governments remain the most important actors in the ongoing negotiations around common issues. In this way, they represent the national interest in Brussels deliberations. National political opinion thus is expressed in Brussels in two ways: first, citizens vote for political parties which represent their interests in Brussels. Second, interest groups, primarily those reflecting the interests of business, work in Brussels to insure that changing market rules will either do them no harm or prove to be beneficial.

Second, I want to consider the overall evidence for the degree to which national politics is concerned with European issues. I consider evidence that the major political parties in Germany, France, and Great Britain have reacted to the EU. I show that over time, various parties have tried to take an EU stand. It turns out that such a stand has not worked to provide parties with the ability to sustain political majorities. As a result, the large center-left and center-right parties in Europe have converged on a pro-EU stance. Thus, the national civic publics have consistently approved of their governments cooperating in Brussels on issues of trade and commerce.

Next, I consider how groups in the member states express their approval or disapproval of particular European policies and the possibility for the creation of a European political sphere where a conversation could occur across societies about policies affecting people in different countries. The ability of groups to organize and mobilize across countries is one possible way in which a more integrated European polity might emerge. I show that such groups do not yet exist.

However, there are two sorts of evidence that shows that there does exist at least a weak form of European politics and in some cases, a strong form. First, I consider the studies of protest events and the coverage of the EU by the European press. Second, I present evidence from a set of case studies within and across countries about both competitive and cooperative European-level politics. Many of these studies focus on media coverage of events and try to discover the degree to which the media converge around the presentation of issues as being about Europe, or instead interpret the issues through a national lens.

THE POLITICAL FIELD IN BRUSSELS

The political fields in Brussels are very institutionalized. The governments repre-sented in the Council of Ministers, the European Commission, the European Parliament, the European Court of Justice, and lobbying groups operate under a framework of rules and informal practices that produce a highly structured set of policy fields. The most important actors in the policy fields are the member-state governments and the lobbying groups. It has been estimated that there may be as many as 3,000 lobbying groups in Brussels (Andersen and Eliassen 1991; 1993). Fligstein and McNichol (1998) have examined the largest of these groups and demonstrated that 80 per cent of them are representatives of firms or industry groups. The interest representation in EU-level deliberations is dominated by business.

The scholarly literature has used a great number of metaphors to explain the Brussels complex, including: intergovernmentalist bargain (Moravscik 1991; Garrett 1995); supranational governance (Sandholtz and Stone Sweet 1998); multilevel governance (Marks, Hooghe, and Blank 1996; Hooghe and Marks 2001); pooling of sovereignty (Keohane and Hoffmann 1991); condominia (amongst others, Schmitter 1996); consociationalism (P. Taylor 1983); postmod-ernist state (Caporaso 1996); regulatory state (Majone 1996); Europe as a set of policy networks (Peterson 2004); and fusionist state (Wessels 1997).

These perspectives point to different features for understanding the relation-ships between the various actors in the EU. The main differences of opinion stem from alternative views as to how many actors get involved in policymaking and the degree to which policymaking remains firmly intergovernmental as a result (for an exchange, see Moravscik 1995; Wincott 1995). Scholars who favor inter-governmental approaches tend to see governments as the only important actors and common policies only possible when all the main governments agree. Scholars who work with other models view other potential actors, particularly the European Commission, the European Parliament, and organized interest groups, as important to the process of negotiation. Intergovernmentalists stress that the process by which policy is made is not consequential for outcomes: the lining up of national interests is still all that counts. Scholars who study the processes of Europeanization think that the process of decision-making can bring about unexpected outcomes.

I view the member states as the central actors in the EU and of course, in their national politics. But governments' interactions in the EU political fields reflect both a highly developed set of political institutions and ongoing relationships that are both cooperative and competitive. The governments are involved in a repeated effort to find cooperative solutions. This does not mean that they will always find them, but it does mean that they are inclined to treat the negotiations with civility. Newly elected governments are heavily constrained by the previous political agreements in the EU. Given the complexity, and breadth, governments have to work out what their interests are in a myriad of situations. In Ch. 2 I described the mechanics of how the EU worked. In this chapter, I want only to highlight some aspects of how politics in Brussels works in practice.

One of the most surprising features of the political fields in Brussels is the emergence of interest groups. The original organizational design of the EU called for a decision-making apparatus that was corporatist. There was supposed to be formal interest representation of firms, workers, and governments; but this never worked in practice, and instead, the structure evolved in a more haphazard fashion. Instead of formal consultation between representatives of industry and labor, a lobbying scene has emerged in Brussels that more resembles American-style politics. Lobbying groups are overwhelmingly representatives of business; they directly address members of the European Commission, the European Parliament, and their member-state governments.

In order to get a sense of the dynamics of policymaking in the EU, it is useful to start with Keohane and Hoffman's (1991) argument that the Brussels complex is best characterized as a place where sovereignty is pooled by the governments, but agreements are enforced by national governments. This conclusion is based on two facts about which most scholars are in agreement. First, the number of people who work in Brussels is very small. There are only about 2,000 senior staff in the European Commission who are in policymaking positions. With so few staff, it would be impossible for the European Commission to do much direct regulation.

Second, the Brussels complex is not a regulatory apparatus like the normal bureaucratic structure of a state because of conscious decisions made by the member states (Majone 1996). What the Brussels personnel mostly do is facilitate the production of agreements. Those agreements are then transposed into national law and enforced by national bureaucracies. The pooling of sovereignty refers to the idea that governments agree to negotiate a wide range of relatively detailed issues collectively. The policy domains that I described in Ch. 2 contain actors from the European Commission, the member states, and interested organized lobbying groups. It is instructive to consider the roles that the three groups play in the policymaking process.

There has been a great deal of dispute about who dominates the decision-making in EU political fields. The empirical evidence on these questions is surprisingly clear. If some subset of governments is strenuously opposed to a particular policy initiative, it will not pass. The governments remain the most powerful voices in Brussels precisely because, in the end, they have to agree to vote for directives (Wallace and Young 1997; Wallace 2000). The empirical evidence is also clear that interest groups matter a great deal to these processes. Corporations and lobbying groups that represent industry play important roles in expressing themselves to their governments, the Commission, and the Parliament.

But this is an incomplete and static view of policymaking in the EU. It suggests that governments, interest groups, and the European Parliament know what they want, that they meet in Brussels and Strasbourg, and the European Commission plays only an arbitrating function. The basic interesting problem of policymaking is discovering what is in the interests of governments and organized interest groups. The problem can be thought of thus: the member states have committed themselves to certain large-scale projects such as the Single Market and monetary union, but carrying out such projects requires that someone has to decide the principles important to those projects and to try and generate agreements on a great number of issues.

At any given moment in Brussels, there are a large number of proposals being considered for directives. Which ones end up being passed depends on who the opposition is, how organized they are, and the ability of the Commission to find political compromises suitable to most of the parties. The power of the Commission is mainly in making sure issues do not get over looked, are aired, and have support mobilized. Since a priori, it may be difficult to assess whether or not an issue is a 'winner,' many initiatives are pushed forward simultaneously, with the further complication that many of the issues involved are technical and involve standard-setting and matters of health and safety. Because of the small size of the Commission and the lack of expertise on technical issues, they often farm out technical work to either consultants or committees made up of representatives of business and the governments.

This is where the Commission plays its most important role as collective strategic actor (Peters 1992). The European Commission has no 'interests' except to promote political Europeanization. The Commission aggressively tries to find arenas for agreement, both in terms of issues that are well understood and, particularly, in new areas. The basic problem is one of 'cultural framing' (Goffman 1974; Snow and Benford 1992). In order to get governments and interest groups to agree, they must find a way to attach what is going to be done to their interests. So, if governments become convinced that a particular policy initiative is connected to an issue about which they care a great deal, they are more likely to support it.

The relative role of national governments and the representatives of interest groups in these processes is in dispute as well, but the empirical literature shows that in different cases, different sides predominate. So, for example, concerning some issues business is absolutely influential, while in others representatives of governments hold sway. There are several related factors at work here. First, is the degree to which governments consider the issue important, because they mainly use their influence to shape the issues most relevant to them (Scharpf 1999). Interest groups face similar dilemmas: they must not only work narrowly for themselves, but more broadly with other potential opposition groups and representatives of governments. It is useful to consider how this process works in different empirical contexts. I show how in different situations governments lead the way or block action, interest groups make proposals that are adopted, and the Commission keeps processes going that might otherwise expire.

Eichener (1997) has considered this process in great detail in the context of initiatives in the sector of health and safety in the workplace. He argues that the Single Market set up the possibility of a lack of regulation of health and safety standards at work. Countries where there is low regulation of health and safety standards would not be interested in having regulations that would raise the costs of doing business. Their labor representatives would weigh in on the side of employers in order to maintain jobs. High-regulation societies would be forced either to lose business to lower-cost producers or lower their own standards, causing what might be called a regulatory 'race to the bottom' (what Scharpf 1996 calls 'negative integration'). But in fact this is not what happened. Europe-wide standards of workplace health and safety were introduced and they embodied principles from the most highly regulated states such as Denmark and Sweden (which at the time was not a member of the EU).

The question, is how did the political process evolve to produce higher, not lower regulations? Eichener carefully considers various hypotheses from both the intergovernmentalist and neofunctionalist perspectives. He concludes that intergovernmentalist perspectives would have predicted lowest common denominator solutions whereby there would have been little or no regulation agreed to. A more sophisticated intergovernmentalist argument could be made that the more powerful EU actors, France and Germany, who cared about the issues, might be able to push their agendas. This hypothesis was not true: the directives ended up with regulation well above both of those countries.

Eichener's complex answer is that it was the process by which consensus was built around the directives that, in the end, produced winning coalitions. The directives were first of all generated by committees convened by the Commission. These were made up of technical experts and representatives of governments from around Europe. They felt compelled to find consensus solutions to their problems, and the results were directives with a high level of social protection.

Eichener (1993: 39–50) suggests that this worked mainly through a process of framing the issue. The winning arguments made the following appeal: low levels of regulation undermined European cooperation by using regulation to make one society the beneficiary at another's cost. By using higher standards, workers were safer and more protected and this would increase the legitimacy of the European project. The higher regulations imposed costs on everyone equally and therefore were viewed as fair. Eichener argues that the costs of vetoing the legislation were high for all governments. Business, surprisingly, did not weigh in strongly against the directives; it appeared to have been excluded from the negotiations.

Scharpf (1996: 19–20) has contested Eichener's account of these events. He argues that blockage of regulations will only occur when conflicting interests are at stake. That the negotiations moved forward proves that none of the member states were seriously opposed to raising health and safety standards. This kind of objection is common in the literature (see Moravscik 1995; Garrett 1996). One assumes that the existence of an agreement implies the outcome of a rationally interest-driven, bargained game. The way that scholars usually try to prove this perspective is to reconstruct the original interests on the basis of the outcomes (Garrett 1995).

It is possible that on some issues rational bargaining does find lowest common denominator solutions. It is also the case that sometimes governments or interest groups have sufficient clout to block agreement (what Scharpf 1988 calls 'bargaining traps'). But this misunderstands the point that Eichener is trying to make. Eichener is not arguing that the Commission gets governments to do things that are not in their interest. Instead, he is arguing that the process of negotiation using committees, experts, and representatives of lobbying groups helps build a consensus about what are appropriate arguments concerning the interests at stake. He is suggesting that the process of negotiation matters precisely because governments figure out what interests they have in a particular case. They also hear from various constituencies both within the government (from different ministries) and from organized political groups, in order to arrive at a decision about what is their interest in a particular situation.

Windhoff-Héretier (1999) considers the progress of a set of directives oriented toward environmental protection during the early 1990s; their outcome supports Eichener's conclusions in several ways. First, the Commission played an important role in organizing and framing the issues; however, in cases of environmental regulation they must also see that governments play a more active and crucial role. In this case the German and British governments had already a set of environmental regulations in place, which they proposed should be the basis of negotiation in a particular arena. Héretier demonstrates that the 'first mover' on a particular directive has the greatest chance of having its approach approved by other member-state governments. In this case, once environmental regulations came to the negotiating table, governments played leading roles in writing and framing the eventual shape of the directive.

Pollack (1997; 1998) has selected cases that show more clearly how governments have controlled the Commission's attempts to be more 'European'. He considers the case of regional and structural funds. As part of the Single Market initiative, the member states decided to provide funds to help less-developed regions. The European Commission moved aggressively to make alliances with regional or other subnational governments. In 1993, the authority of the Commission in this area was up for renewal, during which process additional rules were set in place to constrain the latitude of the Commission in defining acceptable projects for these awards (1998: 228). Pollack argues that this and other cases show that while the Commission has some autonomy, it must be aware that the member states can monitor and constrain its actions.

Sandholtz (1998) considers the expansion of EU competencies in the field of telecommunications. Before the Single Market initiative, telecommunications were essentially state monopolies, and governments were reluctant to engage in pooling their sovereignty over the sector. Sandholtz argues that over time two things changed this. First, the Single Market produced the idea that more competition in markets was a good thing. The European Commission used the Single Market to argue that the telecommunications sector was a good place to try and increase European competitiveness. Second, telecommunications equipment manufacturers were encountering competition from their Japanese and American counterparts. They felt it was essential to deregulate European markets in order for products to sell in Europe and overseas. They were willing to join up with the Commission and go to their governments to argue for such an agenda.

Together, they were able to convince the governments to engage in writing directives to open these markets across borders. Sandholtz emphasizes that this case demonstrates the entrepreneurship of the Commission, however, the pivotal move in this case appears to have been the large telecommunications equipment manufacturers themselves coming over to the Commission's side. They convinced their governments that their interests favored deregulation. The national governments changed their minds when their largest firms lobbied for a different approach.

These few cases should give the reader insight into why the fundamental nature of the Brussels complex is a matter for so much controversy. Depending on which cases one selects and how one puts together the evidence, one can conclude that policymaking is dominated by states or by interest groups, or is affected by the entrepreneurship of the Commission. I think there is more agreement than disagreement here. Who wins and who loses on a particular issue depends on the salience of the issue to various actors, the existence of strong preferences or established practices in some of the member states, the organization and mobilization of interest groups, and the ability of the Commission to help find a common frame and allies to promote it.

Moreover, part of the European political process is about governments figuring out what their interests are in a particular policy field. For some issues, they may have clear preferences and highly organized interests. For others, the mobilization of interest groups and the Commission around an issue helps governments decide what their interests are. Blocking can occur where many states have strong preferences even in the face of intense interest-group pressure. Alternatively, compromises can be reached and motivated member states and interest groups can have profound effects on outcomes. Through it all, the European Commission constantly searches to expand cooperation.

EU-level politics is both organized and explicable. The relationships between the various actors, the member-state governments, and the organizations of the EU are relatively well defined. Lobbying groups fit into the Brussels policymaking fields by joining particular policy discussions and talking directly to their governments, members of the European Parliament, and the European Commission. The ultimate decision-making power in Brussels lies with the governments, but the process of producing legislation often gives other actors, the European Commission, the European Court of Justice, the European Parliament, and the various lobbying groups an important role in producing consensual legislation.

POLITICS AT THE NATIONAL LEVEL: POLITICAL PARTIES AND NATIONAL POSITIONS ON THE EU

It is clear that there is strong evidence of a heavily institutionalized political sphere in Brussels, of which there are two related criticisms. The first is that the main interests represented in Brussels are business-oriented (Streeck and Schmitter 1992; Schmitter 1996). This is a problem because business uses Brussels as a way to put national policies into place that circumvent national politics; such pro-business policies are then implemented to help business to the detriment of labor and other societal interests. A second criticism of the existence of Brussels is that the decision-making that occurs there is far removed from ordinary citizens, making them feel that it is happening behind their backs, and therefore policy-making in Brussels is illegitimate because it does not have enough democratic openness.

It is useful to make some criticisms of both of these points of view from the perspective of the model, developed earlier, of political fields. The governments founded the EU and have expanded its activities mainly to remove tariff and nontariff barriers to trade within Europe, develop a common currency, and create a single market. The main reason that business organizations dominate lobbying in Brussels is because these topics are inherently of interest to businesses. The issues of European social rights, the rights of labor to organize, welfare states, pensions, and healthcare have all stayed under the purview of governments, with the result that most citizens and national level interest groups who are not interested in issues around trade have simply not gone to Brussels to participate.

Business interests are not unitary. They are divided along national lines, industries, size of firms, and the degree to which they want to increase trade and open the home market. Some sectors of business will be for market openings and others will be against. One can find business groups on both sides of any issue in Brussels. They are as likely as anyone else to prevent the passing of legislation. Finally, on the few social issues that have migrated to Brussels, particularly the environment and, to a lesser degree, women's issues, social movement groups have had a great deal of effect on their outcomes. Brussels is a place where the governments have agreed to cooperate on issues of trade, commerce, and monetary policy, not the structure and functioning of their systems of labor relations or welfare states. The European lobbies most concerned with these issues, mainly business groups, have flocked to Brussels to express their opinions.

The degree to which the politics of Brussels is remote from citizens needs some unpacking. Citizens have a number of ways in which to express their opinions on their government's participation in the EU. One is the way they vote in national elections. Parties are the main political actors in the democracies of Europe, and win elections by building coalitions of citizens around particular policy issues. As it turns out, all the main political parties in Europe have taken a stand on European issues. At different historical moments, political parties of both the center-left and center-right have experimented with anti-EU positions. By the mid-1990s, all these parties had converged on a pro-EU position. This is because the majority of European voters have consistently rejected political parties that are anti-EU, even in Great Britain. This is an issue to which I will now devote some attention.

Ernest Haas (1958) argued that in the 1950s, European integration had no salience for voters across Europe. He analyzed the political positions of various parties and observed little support or opposition for the European project. Haas thought that if the project was ever to go anywhere, it would be necessary for this to change. Subsequent research has revealed that most people have almost no knowledge of the EU and its workings (for a review, see Gabel 1998). But, even here, large and important minorities of people across Europe find European issues salient to their voting. (For an interesting set of arguments that locate support for the EU in national politics, see Diez Medrano 2003.)

It is useful to make an argument about why this might be. It follows from the analysis of who is most European, that middle- and upper-middle-class voters benefit directly from Europe either materially or because they have formed ways of life whereby they relate to their peers across societies. These are certainly people who tend to vote, and it follows that political parties would want to take positions on the EU that might attract such voters. While the EU is not going to be the only issue on which voters choose to support a party, it might be one of them (Featherstone 1988).

In order to assess how political parties in the largest European societies have evolved their policies toward the EU over time, I present data from a study by Budge et al. (2001). The data consist of an analysis of the platforms of political parties across Europe. I present two sorts of data on the major political party platforms in England, France, and Germany. I first include the number of total mentions of the EU in the platforms of the parties. This gives a rough indication of how salient the issue is for parties. Then, I look at the difference between positive and negative mentions of the EU. If parties have a wholly negative or positive attitude toward the EU, their mentions will reflect this. If parties are trying to occupy somewhere in between, they will balance positive and negative mentions of the EU.

The data for Germany is presented in Figs. 7.4 and 7.5. Table 7.4 shows that all three major German political parties increase their mention of the EU over time. During the 1950s and 1960s there were few mentions of the EU confirming Haas's argument. During the 1980s and 1990s, these mentions increased dramatically for all three parties. Figure 7.5 shows the degree to which these mentions were positive or negative. With the exception of the 1987 and 1990 elections, the general trend in the table is for all three major political parties to converge

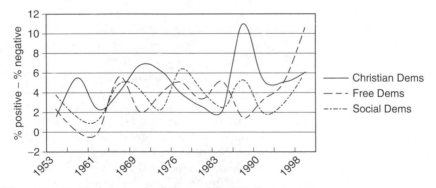

Figure 7.4. Positive party attitudes toward the EU, Germany.

Source: Budge et al. 2001, *Mapping Party Preferences.* Author calculations.

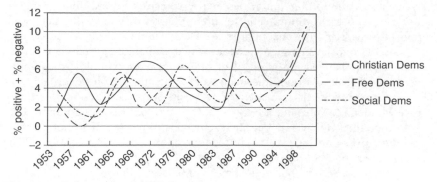

Figure 7.5. References to the EU, Germany.

Source: Budge et al. 2001, *Mapping Party Preferences.* Author calculations.

around a positive view of the EU. In 1987, the Social Democratic Party decided to run against the EU in protest at the Single Market which it argued would undermine workers' interests. The Christian Democratic Party maintained a more positive attitude toward the EU, and, in the 1987 election, retained political power even though they were forced to form a coalition government.

The 1990 election was the first to cover the newly unified Germany. The Social Democratic Party decided that being against the building of Europe was a losing political issue, and shifted its position on the EU. Even though it was in opposition to the Single Market, it felt that by supporting European integration, it would make clear to voters and the rest of Europe that a post-unification Germany would be an engaged member of Europe. The Christian Democrats (who shifted their rhetoric about Europe in that election campaign) were re-elected, although their re-election mainly hinged on the appreciative support of the newly joined East German voters. The Free Democrats were always a free market party. When the EU turned toward the completion of the Single Market, the Free Democrats were strong and consistent supporters. After 1990, the EU was a frequent topic on party platforms and all three parties had converged to a positive position.

Figures 7.6 and 7.7 present similar data for Great Britain. Europe has not been a terrifically salient issue on British party platforms except during a few select elections. Support for the EU by British political parties shifted as the parties developed ideas about what the EU would mean for their constituents. The Labour and Conservative parties both had a negative stand on the EU at different historical moments in order to try and garner votes. Great Britain joined the EU in 1973 under a Conservative Party government led by Edward Heath. In the 1974 election, the Labour Party ran in opposition to joining the EU. It argued that workers would be the likely losers in a European free trade area. The Conservative Party supported the EU precisely because it thought that joining the free trade area would improve the fortunes of British business. During the 1980s the political parties switched positions. Labour favored the EU as it became clear

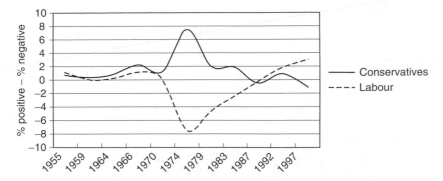

Figure 7.6. Positive party attitudes toward the EU, Great Britain,
Source: Budge et al. 2001, *Mapping Party Preferences.* Author calculations.

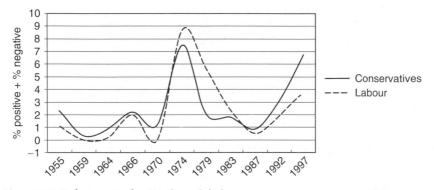

Figure 7.7. References to the EU, Great Britain.
Source: Budge et al. 2001, *Mapping Party Preferences.* Author calculations.

that the Single Market would help produce more jobs and perhaps persuade the British government to adopt labor market reforms that would make Britain more like the rest of the continent. The Conservative Party began more and more to see the EU as a threat to national sovereignty, and by 1987, they turned against it. In the 1990s, both parties took a more moderate European stand. The Conservative Party realized that it risked alienating middle- and upper-middle-class voters who were benefiting from the EU materially if they continued to take a radically Euroskeptic stand.

Figures 7.8 and 7.9 present the data for France. Again, Europe had low political salience during the 1950s through 1980s. Beginning with the Single Market, it became a more important issue for all three political parties and in the 1990s, the Gaullist and Socialist Parties had frequent mentions of the EU. French political parties were mostly favorable toward the EU in the 1950s–1970s. But, as the EU became more of a possible political issue, the attitudes toward it shifted, and both

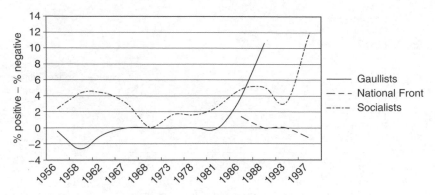

Figure 7.8. Positive party attitudes toward the EU, France.
Source: Budge et al. 2001, *Mapping Party Preferences.* Author calculations.

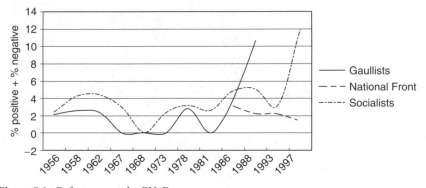

Figure 7.9. References to the EU, France.
Source: Budge et al. 2001, *Mapping Party Preferences.* Author calculations.

Gaullist and Socialist Parties became very positive. The motives for this were twofold: first, the EU was a positive vehicle by which the French could exert political leadership in Europe. Second, French business benefited greatly from the opening of European markets. The only French party of any significance to take an anti-EU stand was the National Front (a far right-wing party). They decided to take a negative stance in the 1990s as part of their attempt to find voters. Their argument was that the EU undermined national sovereignty. This position allowed them to pick up substantial support, but they have not been able to build a majority.

In the three biggest EU polities we see a remarkably similar pattern. Over time, the EU has become a more salient issue for political parties and the center-left/center-right parties have converged in their support for the EU. During the 1970s and 1980s, the Labour and Conservative Parties in Great Britain shifted their positions on the EU in order to attract middle-class voters. The defeat of the Conservative Party with their strongly anti-EU stance caused them to shift their position in the 1990s and both Labour and the Conservatives now favor the EU. German political parties have generally supported the EU, but even here, political parties did experiment with an anti-EU position only to discover that this was not a popular policy to run on. In France, the only political party to try and run on an anti-EU agenda is the National Front, but since their votes have tended to be in protest against both immigrants and foreign trade, it is not surprising that they have taken an anti-EU stand.

This brings me to an important conclusion: no major center-left/center-right European political party in the three largest countries is likely to run against the EU precisely because it is unpopular to do so. Middle- and upper-middle-class voters benefit from the EU and identify with it sufficiently that there has been no pay-off in opposing Europe. Citizens who have a committed European identity and citizens who are mostly national, but sometimes European, have had a generally positive attitude toward the EU. Political parties have therefore not gained much traction by being anti-EU.

A EUROPEAN POLITICAL FIELD?

The fact that European center-left and center-right political parties have converged on a pro-EU stance in order to court middle- and upper-middle-class voters implies that the EU remains salient and popular with these voters. But, voting in national elections is only one way in which European citizens can express their opinions to their governments about EU policies. It is a blunt instrument in that it appears to give governments carte blanche to pursue as many policies as it likes at the EU level.

Particular policies of the EU have generated winners and losers in each of the societies of Europe. One of the main ways in which citizens who have felt excluded from EU-level decision-making express their feelings to their governments is to protest directly to those governments. It is useful to explore both how national groups become aware of EU-level decisions and how they organize to protest those decisions they do not like. It is possible that the losers from EU policies could organize a Europe-wide coordination of such protests. It is useful to examine the existence and limits of what can be called the European political field.

Koopmans (2005) reports on a set of studies of six EU countries (Germany, France, Italy, Spain, and the Netherlands). They examine seven political fields (agriculture, monetary policy, defense issues including the recent 'war on terror-ism', immigration policies, pensions, education, and general issues of European integration). They had several data collection strategies. First, they collected articles from newspapers in each country that concerned these political fields in five different years, 1990, 1995, 2000, 2001, and 2002, and examined them for mention of the EU. They were interested in coding information about who the important actors were in the articles and what particular claim the actor was making (i.e. the political position that the actor took). They also analyzed editorials from these same newspapers in each political field in order to see if the media had a bias in the stories. Finally, they conducted interviews with various civil society groups such as interest groups, nongovernmental organizations, and social movement groups active in each area in each country.

Their data collection is the largest and most systematic done so far on the links between European and national politics. Their main results are consistent with all that has been said so far in this chapter. The most important determinant of the degree to which a political field contains discourse with a European content is whether or not policy is made in that field at the European level. Agriculture, monetary policy, and issues of European integration are discussed in terms of European partners. Defense, pensions, immigration, and education are mostly discussed at the national level. The most important substantive result is that within policy fields, governments have been the most important actors in European affairs. Koopmans (2005: 3) discovered that over time, executive members of sitting governments are the most frequently interviewed and they generally have a pro-European stand. This makes sense given that the political parties controlling governments all have a pro-EU platform. Their policies toward Europe reflect the commitments that political parties have made to support the activities in Europe.

Koopmans (2005) also shows that business groups and corporations are also likely to have their views aired in the press. He interprets this to imply that it reflects the dominance of these actors in political processes. One of the problems of interpreting this result is that most of the policy fields dominated by the EU are oriented toward business. It should not be surprising that media accounts tend to interview national representatives of business when writing about EU concerns. What is clear is that media coverage of these politics favors those who are closest to decision-making. The least represented in all of discussions are civil society organizations such as national interest or social movement groups. This is confirmed not just in the media analyses of articles, but also in interviews with the leaders of such organizations.

In order to understand better how interest and social movement groups are able to express their opinions on EU matters to their national governments, it is useful to consider the dataset gathered by Imig and Tarrow (2001*b*; *c*) on protest events in Europe from 1984 until 1997. Their goal is to use such national protest events as indicators of the degree to which national politics have become Europeanized. They identified 9,872 protest events over this period of which 490 appear to contain elements of EU protest. This means that the vast majority (about 95%) of European protest events concern strictly domestic issues and are directed against national or regional governments. This would seem to be evidence that most politics across Europe remain domestic and there is little European political sphere. I note that this makes sense as national groups would be mainly focused on the fiscal politics of the welfare state.

But, there are several interesting caveats to this thesis. Over time, the number of EU-level protests has increased in frequency and as a percentage of total events. So, in 1997, 147 EU protests took place and these constituted almost 30 per cent of all protest events that year. So, the interest of national groups in staging protests against the EU has increased, as has also the ability to cooperate across societies.

Tarrow (2001: 249–50) sees both the possibility and limits of the emergence of a European public sphere. Since many issues of politics remain within the purview of national governments, there is a natural limit to the degree to which national groups will organize for or against EU policies. For the time being, most protest events will be about national issues. This recognition is a healthy corrective to the view that member-state governments are losing control over their policies (particularly policies related to welfare states and employment) and national publics are being excluded from important national political decisions.

Tarrow also argues that national groups have learned how to cooperate with their counterparts in other countries to protest EU policies in Brussels and at home when they have reason to. But, these protests are as likely to be competitive as cooperative. National protest groups are trying to protect their own turf and are pushing their governments to restrict the EU's ability to affect their privileges (Helfferich and Kolb 2001). So, for example, farmers and fishermen have produced the largest number of protest events and their main concern is getting their national governments to preserve their livelihoods (Bush and Simi 2001). They view their counterparts in other societies in a negative way and are not cooperating but competing.

The overall picture one sees is that most European politics is domestic politics. When the EU policies are relevant, national groups express their opinions mainly by protesting to their national governments. Given that protest events have increased over time and as a percentage of all such events, this suggests that at least part of the national public sphere is given over to European-level politics. This sphere is likely to be contentious as sitting governments will be pressured by national groups to not cooperate with the EU on particular policy issues.

One of the more interesting aspects of the Koopmans study was the attempt to assess the degree to which European issues were salient in the media. He concludes, 'There is a remarkable level of Europeanized debate in the print media. Moreover, the evaluations of European issues and actors show that European integration is supported by most newspapers' (Koopmans 2005: 3; Pfetsch 2004). The only noticeable exception in their data is the case of the British press, which is unrelentingly negative about European issues: it consistently portrays them from the narrow perspective of British politics and consistently objects to British involvement in Europe.

There have been a number of other studies done on different cases, countries, policy fields, and time-frames. They are worth reviewing because they produce corroborating results. Trenz (2004) has done an extensive survey of the types of political articles written in ten of the main European newspapers plus the *New York Times* during the period September–January 2000. His results show that there is already a huge amount of European news reported in the media. Of all articles with a political content across all of the newspapers, 35.2 per cent had something to do with European issues. There was some variation across newspapers with, at the low end, 26.1 per cent of the articles mentioning Europe in *La*

Republica, an Italian newspaper, and, at the high end, 55.2 per cent, for the *Frankfurter Allemeiner*, a German newspaper. He also tried to analyze how the issues in these articles were framed. About half the articles were attempts to report some aspect of what was going on in 'Europe.' Another 20 per cent were mainly concerned with national issues and took up European issues only as a backdrop. The rest of the articles conceptualized Europe as an actor. Trenz (2004: 311) concludes, 'On the basis of these quantitative data on extensive newspaper coverage about Europe, it is difficult to uphold the thesis of a persistent communication deficit of the EU.' Trenz's conclusions corroborate Koopmans (2005).

One of the main issues is the degree to which European newspapers are taking one another into account in their coverage. So, for example, are German newspapers referring to French debates and vice versa? And most important for those looking for a European sphere, do those debates end up creating a 'European' position on a political issue? In order to consider whether or not this is occurring, it is useful to survey several studies that have covered particular events. The main conclusion that can be drawn is that 'it depends.' There is evidence that often issues are being discussed simultaneously in the European press. But a European point of view does not always emerge, and frequently the debate is carried out in terms of protecting some conception of the national interest.

Van de Steeg (2002) considers how the issue of European enlargement is carried out across four weekly magazines in Europe from 1989 until 1998. The magazines include *Cambio 16* (Spanish), *Elsevier* (Dutch), *New Statesman* (British), and *Der Speigel* (German). She analyzes the articles on enlargement with an eye toward the degree to which they reference events or perspectives from other societies. She is also interested in the degree to which the articles take a national versus a European point of view on enlargement. She discovers a continuum of opinion. *Cambio 16* is the most Europeanized, going so far as to reprint articles from other publications in other languages. The *New Statesman* and *Der Speigel* are somewhere in the middle. While about half the articles analyze what people in other countries think about enlargement and take a European point of view, the other half report the events from a strictly national angle. *Elsevier* is the only one of the four publications where events are passed almost entirely through a national filter with no mention of how other European countries view enlargement. She concludes that while there is some evidence for an emerging European public sphere, there is also evidence that this sphere is uneven.

Rendeiro (2003) undertakes a newspaper analysis of coverage of the European Constitutional Convention between 1 January 2003 and 28 February 2003. He does a content analysis of the coverage in two countries, France and Portugal, and uses two newspapers in each country, *La Liberation* and *Le Monde* in France and *Publico* and *Diaro de Noticias* in Portugal. He discovers that all the newspapers covered the main events of the Convention. He also argues that most of the discussion is informative rather than evaluative. That is, the articles focused on what happened and not on how that might affect each country. He concludes that there exists media awareness of European events equally in France and Portugal. He also argues that both offer similar coverage that does not reflect the national filtering.

Van de Steeg et al. (2003) reports how the European press covered the debate over the so-called sanctions that EU governments used against the Austrian government, formed by the People's Party (OVP) and the Freedom Party (FPO) and led by Jörg Haider, in 1999. They examine how the events were discussed across thirteen newspapers representing a wide political spectrum in Austria, Germany, Belgium, France, Italy, and the US. They use the US coverage as a kind of 'control' group in order to see if there is a different kind of coverage in the US and Europe. They conclude that the debate across societies was focused on how Haider did not embody European values of tolerance. The coverage took a moral stance against Haider and he was quickly labeled a 'neo-Nazi.' In 2000, the EU took concerted action to force him out of the ruling coalition. Van de Steeg et al. conclude, 'We see here the emergence of a community that treats the Haider issue as an affair that concerns "us" as Europeans. In short, the Haider debate was about core principles of a European identity' (ibid. 15).

Another case where there appears to have been substantial coordination of transnational political groups is the European conflict over genetically engineered foods during 1995–7. The issue was the attempt to introduce genetically modified organisms (GMOs) into the production of crops in Europe. At the time, the EU was considering a set of directives oriented toward insuring the safety of GMOs. Kettnaker (2001) presents data on how protests were organized across Europe and aimed at national governments, the EU, and the corporations that were involved. She shows that the protests were coordinated across countries, mostly by transnational social movement organizations. The results of the movement were that the campaign 'seems to have deterred food producers and retailers from the mass marketing of genetically modified food in Europe' (ibid. 226).

While the Haider debate and the GMO case seem to be the clearest evidence yet of the emergence of some kind of European political sphere, there is ample proof that many European political discussions are not nearly so harmonious. Bush and Simi (2001) examine in some detail the case of protests of European farmers during 1992–7. Generally, what they found is that farmers mobilized at the regional or national level to protest national officials implementing EU regulations. A typical response was a French farmers' protest in December 1992 where farmers 'blocked the cross-Channel ferry port of Calais, vowing to "throw the English into the sea"' (ibid. 119). Here, there was little agreement between civil society organizations across national boundaries to cooperate and there was no collective discussion of a joint European agriculture policy.

Downey and Koenig (2004) consider another case: the media coverage in Europe of a speech given by Italian Prime Minister Silvio Berlusconi to the European Parliament in July 2003 where he compared a German MP, Martin Schulz, to a *kapo* (i.e. a concentration camp guard). They examined the coverage in twenty-five European newspapers where they examined 782 articles. They discovered that the reporting of the incident had wide variation within and across countries. In Germany, for example, left-wing newspapers defended Berlusconi and right-wing newspapers decried him, while in Italy it was exactly the opposite. Much of the framing of the discussion was about universal values such as primordial ethnic ties. Downey and

Koenig conclude that there is little evidence for a 'strong' European perspective to suggest the discussion was undertaken in terms of 'European values.' Instead, the discussion very much reflected the national and political stance of each publication.

It is useful to draw some conclusions about the kind of European political sphere that actually exists within the member states. Most political discussion within European countries remains focused on national politics, and most political activities organized by national groups are focused on national governments. But there is plenty of evidence that European political stories are also part of the national discourse. Generally, national government officials appear in these stories and their usual stance is pro-European. Business people are also frequently interviewed and their positions are usually infavor of market reform. Newspapers, with the exception of those in Great Britain, are also pro-EU on the policy fields in which the EU dominates.

But that does not mean that European-level issues are not politically contentious. The way these stories play out depends very much on the issue and the groups who are affected by the issue. There is some transnational organization occurring of social movement groups oriented toward protesting policies undertaken at the EU level. There is evidence that the frequency of protests against European policies is growing. But, there is also evidence that much of this protest reflects national groups trying to get their governments to protect them from EU policies that undermine their positions.

If one takes a strictly Habermasian view of what a political sphere in Europe should look like, one would conclude that such a sphere does not exist. European politics most of all reflect the jurisdictional differentiation between issues decided in Brussels and in national capitals, but in both these spheres political parties and representatives of sitting governments participate and dominate. Interest groups represented by lobbyists and social movement groups present their grievances in whatever venue they can and sometimes in multiple venues. None of these politics seem oriented toward evolving rational discourses and consensual politics that involve all citizens, but are instead chaotic, anarchic maneuverings where groups vie for resources, votes, and attention using whatever framing of events will help them. European issues are reported across countries and frequently national media are in dialog with one another, but they are often debated in a way that will not promote a European viewpoint. National political cultures and group interests provide framing for all political debates; consequently there are multiple arenas of European politics rather than just a single one that the advocates of an idealized democracy and civil society would recognize.

CONCLUSIONS

The economic and social construction that has accompanied the growth of the European Union since its inception in 1957 has produced a complex, if explicable politics. The goal of the member-state governments has consistently been to create a single market in Western Europe, one that would eliminate tariff and nontariff barriers and eventually open all industries to competitors from other countries. This goal has created a huge increase in cross-border economic activity, trade, investment, and the creation of Europe-wide corporations. On the social side, the people who have been most involved in this market opening project have been managers, professionals and other white-collar workers, and the young, who have the opportunity to travel and work with their counterparts in other countries. These groups have benefited financially, but also have had the pleasure of discovering that people in other countries could be friends, and, through travel for leisure or work, the discovery of new and interesting places. Meeting people from other societies has been a good thing that has encouraged people to see themselves as both similar and different.

At the same time, through the whole process, member-state governments have restricted the issues that the European Union can take up. They have kept the EU from intervening in national labor markets, labor relations, and all policies tied up with welfare states. They have done so for two reasons. First, there are huge national differences in such systems, reflecting underlying values and preferences that are not easy to harmonize. But, more important, popular public opinion has opposed transferring sovereignty over these issues to the EU for fear of interference in national social models.

These features of the EU and national politics and the growth of a Europeanized middle and upper-middle class have created several interesting levels of politics. First, of course, is the highly institutionalized politics in Brussels where governments continue to dominate, but the lobbying groups, Commission, Court, and Parliament all play roles. Second, national political parties over time have adopted different political positions to try and attract voters. The middle- and upper-middle-class voters who have benefited from the EU have generally voted for parties with a pro-EU stance. This has produced a pro-EU platform for all the main European political parties.

The most interesting and subtle effect of all this economic and social interaction is the creation of interest in European affairs in national political discourse. There is strong evidence that European matters are covered in national papers and that national groups organize to protest to their governments about EU policies they don't like. There is also some evidence that on occasion, these discussions can be trans-European and result in policy coordination. But there are real barriers to coordination across national borders. Groups are used to directing their protests toward their national governments in order to get some redress for their grievances or to force their governments to shift policies. Frequently the interests at stake pit groups in different countries against one another. So, the losers of a particular market opening project will not have obvious allies in other countries where the winners live.

Since the vast majority of people who live in Europe have a predominantly national identity, it should not be surprising that many European political issues end up appealing to national as opposed to Europe-wide interests. This means that as issues confronting Europeans are discussed within national media, they are more likely to be filtered through national debates and self-images than through European ones. So while there is certainly a wide awareness of European issues, the ability to produce European policies is always going to be difficult because of the institutional limits on the EU and the conflicting political demands that citizens place on their governments.

Key to the support of the EU project is that of national center-left and center-right parties. As they take turns governing across Europe, they maintain their overall commitment to European solutions of some of their collective action projects. They also maintain their control over those projects by limiting issues to be discussed at the European level.

Usually, when scholars discuss the democratic deficit, they imply that average citizens have little direct input into EU-level decisions. Our review suggests that European citizens have good access to information about those issues and opportunities, which they have increasingly taken up, to express their grievances to their governments. Their governments can respond to these protests in several ways: if the aggrieved groups are constituents of the party in power, that party can oppose a particular European-level rule. It can also try to mitigate the effects of that rule on potential losers in their society. Finally, if the protesters do not get any satisfaction, they can support alternative political parties that will implement policies more to their liking.

If one asks in whose interests a democratic deficit operates, it is those of sitting governments. They control what they agree to in Brussels. They listen most carefully to those of their citizens for whom these policies are significant, i.e. business people. At home, they can selectively respond to constituent protests. They may be able to compensate groups in their political coalition or even expand that coalition by changing policies on a particular issue in order to satisfy some organized interest. Governments are probably least interested in having a horizontal European politics emerge. If European interest groups and social movement organizations began to organize on a European basis, they would both surround and circumvent states. Political parties might then feel compelled to organize more effectively on a Europe-wide basis. But this is not likely to happen as long as citizens' identities remain firmly national in orientation, and their natural place to organize, even to discuss European issues, is national politics.

This does not mean that the EU project is one by which all are equally treated. Indeed, the main political parties are representative of middle- and upper-middle-class interests. The EU, by expanding economic opportunities for firms, does so for those with the highest education and best occupations. That the dominant political discourse at the national level is pro-EU means that the discourse is also pro-middle and upper-middle class. These have been the principal beneficiaries of the EU and, as I have shown, the ones most likely to be involved with their counterparts across Europe. The poorest, least-educated, and oldest citizens in any society by definition are the most likely to be losers in the EU project. It is these groups that are the hardest to organize. When they manage to protest to their governments, the response can be in proportion to the size of the group and its ability to mobilize public support.

In Europe, the middle class which sometimes thinks of itself as European but mostly thinks of itself as having a national identity, is going to see its government's commitment to the EU in qualified terms. They will be in favor of such things as increasing the Single Market, and making it easier to travel, trade, and go overseas for education; but they will also want their national welfare state privileges to remain intact. Large parts of the European middle class see themselves as firmly social-democratic and in favor of social justice and equity claims. If the EU looks, on any particular issue, to be the villain, national politics can trump the commitment to be more 'European.' If the issue spreads more deeply into middle-class interests, such as free education, low-cost healthcare, and fixed pension benefits, then the middle class's sense of itself as European dissipates and national politics rule.

The layers of politics in Europe reflect both intention and accident. EU politics in Brussels is well organized; the relationship between member-state governments and their citizens is also highly organized. What is complex is how particular European policies bring people together in each of the member states and how it potentially pits them against each other. As European economic and social integration intensifies, the winners and losers of these processes will harden their positions. The future of European integration thus hinges on how those in the middle will end up voting. Will they support a greater Europe or will they want to protect the nation? This potential clash is the subject of my concluding chapter.

8

Conclusions

At the beginning of this book, I posed the question of how it could be that people from around Europe have come to live in peace with each other, given their long history of war and conflict. After World War II there were proposals in Europe geared toward controlling future conflicts; for a brief period, there was even a proposal to unite Western Europe under one state (Parsons 2003). Winston Churchill was one of its proponents. But the idea of creating a United States of Europe never got wide acceptance from Europe's citizens. Grandiose schemes of a political Europe were of less concern to citizens than the very real problem of rebuilding their lives after the war.

The European Union was founded by people who had a much less utopian vision of what might be possible to bring Europeans together. Jean Monnet, one of the EU's founding fathers, argued that if the European economies became more integrated, it would make it harder for governments and citizens to consider going to war with each other (Duchene 1994). Economic integration would increase interdependence and this would in turn make countries allies rather than enemies. In this way, people's economic self-interest would trump their hostile view of their neighbors. The forerunner to the EU was the European Coal and Steel Community (ECSC). The main project of this effort was to integrate the markets for coal and steel, particularly in France and Germany. This was done in several ways. Governments eliminated tariff barriers in order that companies from one country could compete in others. But, in order to prevent ruinous competition, the ECSC was able to protect firms that were losing money by setting and monitoring prices. This project worked magnificently and gave governments confidence that they could cooperate on economic matters of common interest.

The Treaty of Rome envisioned setting up a permanent organization to cooperate on creating a single market across all industrial sectors of Europe by eliminating all forms of trade barrier. The model for the European Economic Community (later, the European Union) was the ECSC. As I have shown in Ch. 2, the EU created laws to advance the Single Market. These in turn helped the market grow, and as it did so, firms and governments pushed for an increase in laws. This process worked in fits and starts. On many occasions the EU looked as though it was hopelessly bogged down, but in every situation member-state governments found the EU a useful vehicle to encourage economic cooperation. They found a way to settle their differences through compromise, and the market integration project went forward. It was this self-perpetuating cycle that ultimately has driven economic interdependence across Europe for the past forty years, in line with Lindberg and Scheingold's (1970) argument about how integration might proceed.

I have shown how this played out across the European economy. Many European industries have moved from being organized on a national basis by national firms to being organized on a European basis by firms from many countries. Now, the largest firms face one another across borders where they compete (and sometimes cooperate) in ventures that know no national borders. Chapter 3 demonstrated how the largest European corporations have reorganized themselves on a European basis. There have been many mergers within countries to create larger and more efficient firms across many industries. There has also been increasing numbers of cross-border mergers. Frequently, large firms in one country partner with smaller counterparts in other countries in order to gain a toehold. European firms invest heavily in other European countries. There is also evidence that as countries join the EU their firms begin to focus more of their attention on the European market. This has been true for the countries in Western Europe that joined the original six countries of the EU. It has been spectacularly true for the Eastern European countries that joined in May 2004.

In Ch. 4 I considered how the process of European market integration was undertaken in the defense, telecommunications, and football industries. The defense and telecommunications industries were highly regulated and in many cases, the firms were owned by their national governments. In the wake of decisions made by governments to open up their markets for these products, firms were privatized and these industries reorganized to take advantage of new opportunities for cross-border trade. Mergers and joint ventures were used to consolidate and facilitate cooperation between national and regional firms. The typical European telecommunications and defense firm reflects a set of alliances and cross-ownership between formerly national companies. While European governments remain involved with their largest corporations in many ways, firms no longer view just the national market as their main source of revenue and growth.

The example of football shows a different kind of European integration. Football has been an international sport for most of the twentieth century. The World Cup was first played in 1930 and the European Champions League began in 1956. But the 1980s and 1990s brought sweeping changes to the sport. The advent of cable TV meant that teams could use their TV revenues to hire top players. The more successful teams became, the more likely they were to participate in the Champion's Cup (the Europe-wide club competition) and the higher their revenues would subsequently be. Such financial growth encouraged teams to hire players from other clubs, and they began to look abroad to hire the best players they could afford. As a result, the largest and most successful teams improved and prospered at the expense of the smaller teams.

The European Court of Justice's decision in the Bosnan case legalized the free movement of football players across national borders. Before long, the largest teams with the most revenues, calling themselves the G-14, began to consider forming their own league. They were ultimately discouraged from doing so by UEFA, the governing body of the sport in Europe. But there now remains an uneasy relationship between cable companies, the biggest teams, and the smaller teams. Fans can now watch the top teams on cable and satellite TV from any country, and can follow their favorite national players and the best players in general. The largest budget and best teams now play one another during their regular seasons, setting up TV matches with large audiences. If a European league emerges, this would create a form of truly European popular culture.

From the point of view of what the founders of the EU hoped to accomplish, one can only conclude that the economic interdependence they set out to achieve has occurred. The EU is a functioning polity that regulates the largest economic region in the world with a court, a single currency with a European Central Bank, and an institutionalized politics oriented toward creating a single set of rules to govern markets. The member-state governments maintain contact with each other on a permanent basis and use the EU to cooperate on both economic and non-economic matters such as defense and security. It is impossible to conceive that European countries would once again go to war with one another. Indeed, the reorganization of the European defense industry implies that armaments production is now no longer set up on a purely national basis, so even if one country tried to arm itself against the others, they would be unable to produce the necessary armaments by themselves. The decisions by European governments to set up a single market and a single currency, to integrate Eastern Europe into the Single Market, and to continue to cooperate routinely on economic and security matters, is surely one of the most remarkable and important positive developments in the world in the past fifty years.

European economic integration has produced many benefits. It has increased trade and employment; it has proliferated the variety and decreased the costs of goods and services to consumers; it has brought large numbers of people from different countries together to interact on a routine basis. Whether it is for work, school, play, or the sharing of common interests, citizens across Europe have increased their social interaction with their neighbors dramatically, which has brought them to see citizens from other countries in a more positive way. It has caused large numbers of people to view themselves as having not just a national identity, but also a European one. There now exists a European politics. Newspapers are filled with European political stories and social movements organize to protest European-level political issues. In every society, it is possible to view media and consume popular culture from other societies. Given the density of social interaction and the willingness of a majority of citizens to say they sometimes have a European identity, it is possible to say that there now exists a European society.

But, in the face of all of this success, the future of the EU seems uncertain. With its enlargement to twenty-seven member states, the problems of decision-making in Brussels have multiplied. The EU tried to deal with this situation by producing a European Constitution beginning in 2001. The Laeken declaration of December 2001 committed the EU to improving democracy, transparency, and efficiency, and set out the process by which a constitution could be produced. The European Convention was established, presided over by former French president Valéry Giscard d'Estaing. A draft of the constitution was produced and put forward to votes by the member-state governments beginning in 2004. But in 2005, both Dutch and French citizens voted 'no' on the constitution. The member-state governments have agreed to take parts of the constitution and produce a new treaty in the summer of 2007. In spite of this current agreement, the deeper conflicts across Europe over the direction and end state of the EU will not go away. What does my analysis say about the root causes of these conflicts and what might happen next?

The expansion of markets and the accompanying economic growth have produced Europe-wide economic, social, and political fields. The creation of these fields has had effects on people's identities. The most-well-off citizens now think of themselves as Europeans. Substantial numbers of middle-class citizens have at least some European identity. This has meant high levels of support for the EU amongst the middle- and upper-middle-class citizens of Europe. However, these changes have also produced a backlash. Less-well-off citizens oppose the EU as they have not shared the fruits of economic integration. Many middle-class citizens, even those who sometimes think of themselves as Europeans, are skeptical that the EU is the right level of government for social policy. Put simply, most citizens in different countries want their nation-states to protect them from the vagaries of the economy, illness, and old age. This sets up a potential clash in each nation-state between the winners of economic integration, many of whom identify themselves as Europeans, and the losers of economic integration, many of whom remain wedded to national identities.

These differences of opinion vary across member states. So, for example, the strong national identity in Great Britain goes hand in hand with a skepticism about the value of EU integration. In Germany, where European identity is much stronger, the EU is viewed as a vehicle to attain cooperation and maintain peace in Europe. When governments meet in Brussels, they aggregate these opinions and their conflicts frequently reflect the underlying attitudes of their citizens.

I would like to return to Ernest Haas's magisterial work, *The Uniting of Europe?* (1958) before considering the future path of this conflict. Haas founded EU studies as a discipline and made important contributions to the fields of international relations and theories of regional integration. Haas was present at the founding of the European Coal and Steel Community, the precursor organization to the European Economic Community and later the European Union. He knew all the major players involved with planning the ECSC and was privy to the inside machinations during the first five years of that organization.

Haas's book was an exploration of how the ECSC, which started out as an organization with little public awareness or support, ultimately became the impetus for the creation of the European Union. The book explores how the process of integration gained momentum as the ECSC began its work. Haas's central thesis was that at the beginning of the integration of the ECSC, there was little enthusiasm for supranational regulation of the coal and steel industries. But after five years, national trade unions, trade associations, firms, and political parties became part of the political process of the ECSC and came to favor its efforts at regulating the steel and coal industry at a supranational level.

One of the central preoccupations of Haas's book, however, was the fact that for almost all the citizens of Europe and their representative political parties, European economic and political integration were not significant issues in and of themselves. The book documents how in every country, political parties and citizens lacked of knowledge of the ECSC and were mostly indifferent to its importance. When political parties had to take a stand on European issues, they did so with the narrow view of what was in the short-run interest of their members. Haas readily acknowledged that while Monnet's plan to unite Europe economically appeared to work spectacularly, the project to unite Europe politically trailed far behind.

Haas's central mechanism for how the EU would become important for European politics (and publics) was through what he called 'spillover' (Haas 1961). The basic idea was that as Europeans came to cooperate on certain market issues in Brussels, they would discover the need to expand their cooperation to others. So, for example, European-level rules allow for the free movement of labor across Europe. But, if people choose to live and work in other countries for part of their lives, then the issue of where people would qualify and collect pensions becomes a potential political issue. Haas thought that these sorts of problems would force member-state governments and the European Commission in Brussels to extend and expand their arenas of cooperation. I note that Haas saw 'spillover' as a political process that would occur within the political arenas of Brussels.

Stanley Hoffmann directly confronted Haas's argument in a famous paper written in 1966. Hoffmann's main point was that European integration would never produce strong enough spillover forces to overcome the diversity of points of views of the governments. The national identities, conceptions of national interest, and the focus of most organized political groups at the national level would mean that national politics would always trump EU politics. Governments would never be able to agree to positions whereby some of their citizen's interests were harmed. They would also jealously guard their ability to defend the 'nation.' Thus, the logic of spillover would be severely restricted in two ways: first, governments would resist increasing the policy fields of cooperation at the EU level; second, they would use national-level political fields to help resolve the tensions caused by the process of creating winners and losers through market integration projects. Hoffmann saw that governments would be reluctant to give up more power to the EU than they needed to in order to promote joint gains from cooperation. They would do so to preserve the nation, but also because citizens of the member-state countries would be reluctant to support too much EU political integration.

Haas (1976) would later recant his view that spillover would be sufficient to overcome the political goals of national leaders. In 1966, Charles de Gaulle began to realize that EEC rules would come to constrain the actions of the French government. He staged a walk-out in Brussels that is known as the 'empty chair crisis.' His main stipulation to return to the bargaining table was that all actions taken in the EU have unanimous votes. This meant that if he disagreed with any possible directive, he could successfully prevent it from becoming law. This put a damper on the ability of the EU to attain agreements. There was a general sense during the 1970s that the EU was bogging down and going nowhere. Haas came to argue that the process of spillover in the EU was now unlikely. He suggested that there were too many variables at work to make spillover happen. In essence, the narrow interests that might be brought together to favor liberalization or regulation of trade in some industrial sector could be easily overcome by national concerns expressed by particular political leaders that overrode the possible gains of integration.

In hindsight, both Hoffmann writing in 1966 and Haas writing in 1958 were right and wrong. Hoffmann was right that governments would severely resist Haasian spillover. Governments have kept issues regarding social welfare exclusively to themselves and have resisted calls to produce a social Europe. This is mainly because the citizens of the different member states have major differences in their expectations of government social protection. The British favor less social protection and government intervention into the economy than do the French, Germans, or Scandinavians. Citizens have not wanted their governments to bargain away national forms of social protection because of their fear that they would get stuck with someone else's system. As a result, governments have agreed to keep these issues out of discussion in Brussels.

But Haas was right that EU-level coordination would expand as a result of increasing economic integration. The early market opening projects of the EU were resisted by national governments, but the European Court of Justice ruled that the governments had to stand by the Treaty of Rome. As corporations expanded their activities across borders, they produced new jobs and economic growth. Governments began to see the advantage of increased trade. While they remained wary about producing citizens who were winners and losers, they eventually succumbed to the pressure of their largest and best organized corporations to expand this cooperation into new market opening projects. The Single Market project and the monetary union pushed economic cooperation in entirely new directions. There was also some spillover into the promotion of the free movement of labor and the growth of the environment as an issue in the EU.

But even granted the general problem of getting governments to expand their arenas of cooperation, Hoffmann in 1966 and Haas in 1976 would have had a difficult time predicting that a monetary union would occur, and of course, an even harder time in predicting that Europeans would seriously consider any attempt to forge a common foreign and security policy. The monetary union removes monetary policy from governments' tools of economic management. It is hard to see, in a world of national diversity, why governments would be willing to cede such a potent economic weapon to a supranational authority. It is also difficult to see what governments might get from extensive merging of their military and foreign policy apparatuses. Even if one believed that Haas's spillover

mechanism existed, it is impossible to discern any obvious way in which economic integration would cause cooperation in foreign policy and defense.

The main drawback of Haas and Hoffmann was their theoretical fixation on a
state-centric view of integration. Both had an international relations perspective
on what was going on in Brussels, causing them to focus narrowly on states as the
main actors in the integration process. For them, it would be states who would
agree to new issue arenas opening up in Brussels; spillover would occur when the
states agreed to let it happen; if government officials came to see these issue
linkages, they might be compelled to act. This state-centric view left little role for
citizens, lobbyists, courts, and national politics in the possible expansion of EU
political cooperation.

This book has presented evidence that the success of the EU is only partly
attributable to the actions of the member states cooperating in Brussels. My
central argument is that if the actions taken in Brussels did not positively affect
the lives of many people across Europe, then the organization would have died. It
was firms and citizens who took advantage of the opportunities presented by the
market opening projects of the EU: they reorganized their economic, social, and
political activities on a Europe-wide basis. They were the ones who went to
Brussels to litigate against governments who wanted to protect national firms
from competition; they lobbied for more European cooperation and more market opening. One of the main contributions of this book is to attempt to
document some of the ways in which life has changed in Europe.

Here, I return to Karl Deutsch. European economic integration is quite far
advanced, but, as I have shown, the part of the population that has been most
involved in directly encountering its counterparts in other countries is a small
fraction of the whole. It also contains the most privileged members of society. For
these citizens, more and more of their lives are organized on a European basis.
However, most of the citizens of Europe still feel attached to the nation as the
main political anchor. It is when one considers how this process has worked that
one can make sense of the central conflict in European integration.

European integration is not limited by the states themselves and their 'need' to
maintain sovereignty. Instead, it is limited by the citizens who vote for their
governments across Europe. These citizens decide what issues their governments
will allow to be resolved in Brussels and what issues will be kept to the national
capitals and subregional governments. It is only if the citizens of European
nations decide that they want more of their affairs coordinated in Brussels that
they will be. Governments attempting to press unpopular integration would soon
find themselves voted out of office. In Great Britain, for example, the Blair Labour
government at the turn of the twenty-first century would probably have preferred
to join the Euro, but the unpopularity of the idea forced the Labour Party to agree
to hold a referendum. This is not an isolated issue. In many European societies,
citizens fear more cooperation around issues of social welfare; they tend to prefer
their national welfare arrangements. Any attempt to create a European welfare
state would certainly run into citizen opposition if they felt that their privileges
were likely to disappear.

From a Deutschian perspective, the most interesting clue to understanding the possible conflicts around European integration is to discover why there are not more 'Europeans.' Deutsch had two ideas about how such an identity could form: first, by direct face-to-face interaction between people of different social backgrounds; second, through the emergence of a common culture, propagated through communication, mainly via the media.

As I documented in Ch. 5, majorities of the European population sometimes think of themselves as European. Large numbers of Europeans have been in other countries in the past twelve months, and very large numbers of Europeans claim to speak a second language. But, this identity is quite shallow for most. My central argument for why this is so turns on Deutsch's idea that the most 'European' people will be those who have the most opportunities to interact with people from other European countries. The economic integration of the EU has offered a large, but significant, minority of its citizens the opportunity to interact routinely across member states. People who do so consist of managers, professionals, government personnel, people with higher incomes, the young, and the educated more generally. They have benefited materially and culturally from these interactions and clearly have responded by coming to see themselves as more members of a common Europe and less as members merely of nation-states. But this hard core of Europeans is a very small percentage of the population, and the number of people who are in this camp varies widely across Europe. So Great Britain, Sweden, and Finland are the least, and Germany, France, Italy, and the Benelux countries the most, 'European.'

In Ch. 6 I extended this study of identity in two ways. First, I looked more carefully at migration and the various non-work-related arenas where citizens of various European countries might encounter one another. Then I considered Deutsch's second mechanism by which integration could occur: the integration of culture through the media. I showed that only 2–3 per cent of Europeans live and work in other European countries. Those that do are more likely to have European identities and favor more EU-level cooperation. I confirmed that most of the trans-European organizations were trade associations where managers might meet and professional associations where professionals would gather. There exist a substantial number of groups oriented toward various charities and some oriented toward sports and hobbies. But for people in different countries to find these groups requires time and money. It can be argued that these groups also draw their members disproportionately from the wealthier and more educated parts of the population.

I show that the establishments who run the education system in Europe are driving European integration in a number of ways. For primary and secondary students, there is an emphasis on second-language use. There have been systematic attempts to retell the 'national' history and literature by situating them in a broader Europe. For colleges and universities, there exists the Erasmus program to promote students spending at least a semester abroad. The education ministries across Europe are now encouraging their universities to harmonize degrees across Europe and create a European higher education space. This evidence suggests that those who think of themselves as Europeans have acted to create social relationships with their counterparts in other countries.

I also considered the degree to which European culture has converged. I demonstrated that while there was some shared culture and communication across Europe, it is still the case that national popular culture dominates. To the degree that European popular culture has converged, it is less because there is a European media than because American movies and television are everywhere. American music and books dominate less but are also present in all societies. There still remains a large market for nationally produced music and literature, and to a lesser degree movies and television. These markets remain segmented by language in spite of the large number of citizens who claim to speak a second language. There are the occasional crossovers of music, literature, and movies that are produced in one country and make it to another. And it is possible in every society to sample popular culture from other societies directly through film, television, music, books, and now the internet. However, most popular culture in Europe is national (or American) and there is very little recognizable Europe-wide culture except for some 'high culture' that is consumed by the educated, managers, and professionals.

Taken together, this suggests a rough division of people in Europe into three camps. One camp (10–15% of the population) has deep economic and social ties with their counterparts across Europe. This sector benefits from Europe materially and culturally. There is also a European youth culture that engages some part of the young population who are more likely to travel for fun, work, and education. These opportunities are not generally available to the whole population. The second camp (40–50%) has a more shallow relationship to Europe. Their employment may bring them into contact with people in other countries; they may even be aware of the fact that their jobs depend on European trade. While they may occasionally travel for holidays or share some aspects of popular culture and be interested in such things as football across borders, they are still wedded to national language, culture, and politics. Finally, in the third camp are people (40–50%, and higher in countries such as Great Britain) who speak the national language and do not travel or consume culture from other societies. This part of the population is older, less educated, and more likely to be poor. It is more firmly wedded to the nation and more fearful of European integration.

Chapter 7 took up the question of making sense of the structuring of European and national politics. The institutional division of labor between the EU and member-state governments creates a European politics in Brussels that is mainly affected by the interests of business. But this does not mean that citizens do not have input into what their government's policies are. Citizens have several ways of expressing opinions about EU politics to national governments. First, they can vote for political parties who have espoused positions toward the EU with which they agree. Second, they can join organizations that lobby their national governments both at home and in Brussels. Third, they can participate in social movements and protest issues both to their national governments and the EU. I show that over time, the major center-left and center-right political parties in Great Britain,

Germany, and France have converged on a pro-European policy reflecting the preferences of the vast majority of middle- and upper-middle-class citizens.

What people don't have is easy access to citizen groups from other countries and political fields to support Europe-wide political discussions on a given issue. There is evidence that there is a kind of public policy field where Europe-wide issues are considered and debated, mostly through concurrent media coverage of events, but these debates have been more likely to be confrontational than they are to lead to more European cooperation. Because of the shallowness of European identity, debates over particular issues can easily swing toward citizens viewing their national groups and national interest as more relevant than a common European interest. National politics continues to be more important than EU politics.

'Europe' as a social and cultural project is clearly a social class project. The class aspects of European economic and social integration explain some of the anti-EU national politics that have emerged. On the political right, the EU is viewed as elitist and against the nation. On the political left, the EU's lack of a social policy provides ammunition for the view that the EU is the enemy of the 'average' man. In countries with strong social-democratic systems, much of the current dissatisfaction with the European project amongst electorates builds on the perception that the Brussels project is not one that will protect people from the market. In countries with more liberal traditions, the worry is that the EU is not sufficiently committed to the market. It goes without saying that the people who need such protection are not the educated, professionals, and managers. My inquiries into the social basis of who is a European explain quite clearly why Europe is so popular with those who benefit and less popular for those who experience those benefits less directly.

This problem is made even more obvious in the new member states; they are both poorer and have had a shorter involvement in Europe. It follows that they have fewer managers, professionals, and government officials who have been traveling and interacting across Europe for the past twenty years, and that they have more citizens who can potentially lose from the market integration project. That the new member states are more skeptical about how much advantage membership will have follows from this analysis. It makes sense that national voters in these countries are more likely to line up for anti-EU political parties.

It should be remembered that European cooperation through the creation of the EU has been going on only for about fifty years. The modern nation-states emerged over a very long period of time. The sense of national identity came late to most societies, well after the consolidation of the state. Given the long history of the nation-state, it is remarkable that in such a short period of time so much has changed. The fact that so many people in Europe feel 'European' at all suggests how powerful the mass increase in social interaction has been.

From my sociological perspective, the changes in solidarities amongst Europeans that have occurred have followed predictable lines. The future of those solidarities will depend on increasing and deepening them and bringing them more broadly to the citizens of Europe. If the rest of Europe's citizens do not have the positive feelings generated from systematic social interaction or perception of shared culture, the EU will remain institutionally where it is. Subsequent rounds of integration will depend on drawing more citizens into finding virtue in increasing their interdependencies on their neighbors. One can tell two stories about the future of these solidarities. One suggests how European identity might expand and the other relates how the current make-up of identities is in equilibrium—or perhaps even in danger of falling apart.

What might increase European identity? First, the fact that young people favor more European integration implies that over time, as the population ages and is replaced, Europe will be more popular. It is the case that 80 per cent of people under the age of 30 speak more than one language. By 2030, most Europeans will be bilingual and nearly 70 per cent will sometimes think of themselves as Europeans. The continued shift from a manufacturing to a service economy will mean there are more white-collar and fewer blue-collar workers. This will put more people in jobs where they will be more likely to interact with people from other countries. The general increase in the part of the population that is college educated will produce more people who will be interested in interacting with their counterparts across borders. Second language use, frequent travel (either for tourism or business), and greater cultural contact through movies, music, and other forms of popular culture mean that there will be more personal knowledge of people from other societies. European football, for example, is already close to being organized across the continent. Fans frequently watch games from other leagues and if a European football league emerges, this will produce further solidarity.

But one can tell the story the other way as well. The positive effects of trade and routine social interaction are offset by the fact that most Europeans remain resolutely national in their outlook precisely because they are not as deeply enmeshed in European economic, social, or political affairs. They continue to rely mostly on their national governments for social protection and do not want increased political integration with the rest of Europe. Majorities of people consume culture in their national language and in line with national cultural traditions. Their reflex in a national crisis is to want their governments to intervene on their behalf. In Great Britain, Finland, Greece, Austria, and Ireland (and nearly the Netherlands), majorities of the population have only a national identity. Great Britain is the clear leader in efforts to prevent an extension of EU authority; but in many other countries also nationally oriented oppositions exist to stand against more European cooperation.

Increased integration will have to rely on the expansion of Europe's citizens' feelings that a European politics will provide better solutions to their political concerns than the national politics that currently exists. This is not likely to occur given the current distribution of European identities and connections to European society. In no country (with the exception of Luxembourg) does the proportion of citizens who think of themselves as mainly European rise above 16 per cent. There is also the problem that the interests of a particular group in one society are at variance with the same group in another. This means Europe's citizens will tend to see themselves in competition rather than cooperation with their counterparts in other countries.

Political issues will continue to divide citizens in different countries. Immigration is one of the most inflammatory issues that pushes national identity to the fore. The possibility of immigration from Eastern Europe has caused much consternation in Western Europe. Large majorities of European populations feel even more negatively about continuing immigration from the Middle East and Africa. Ironically, the European identity which seems to have taken hold in many places is one that emphasizes not tolerance and enlightenment, but racial, ethnic, and religious differences between people who are thought of as Europeans and those who are 'others.'

A continued emphasis on national identity reflects not just cultural concerns but also economic ones. The aging of the population will put more pressure on governments to continue to support welfare state structures and use the national government to protect employment, healthcare, and pensions. Citizens will expect their national governments to protect them, their pensions, and their healthcare systems. Citizens tend to have a zero-sum conception of job loss such that if a plant closes and reopens elsewhere it is perceived as a national loss. These economic concerns cause people to rely on their national governments more, not less. It would require an extreme and common political or economic crisis to widen and deepen a sense of being a European among a larger population of the citizenry.

The swing group for the future of Europe are those middle-class voters who view much of the EU economic integration project as a good thing but are worried about its effects on their welfare states and their jobs. It is for these voters that the battleground issues are going to be debated. There is already a clash between citizens who clearly are in favor of more European economic, social, and political integration and those who view this as a bad thing. In every country, the real politics will be played out amongst the middle-class voters in the center of these discussions. Both the left and the right will appeal to their interests and identities. How this happens within each of the member states will define the EU in the twenty-first century. If citizens in enough states come eventually to favor more European integration through the mechanisms I have described, then the project might move forward to create more cooperation. But, if enough of the citizens in the biggest states become convinced that integration has proceeded far enough, then the project will stall. Clearly, the EU and European society have developed well beyond what Haas (1976) and Hoffmann (1966) thought possible. Nonetheless, the drama that Haas and Hoffmann saw playing out in the 1960s is continuing today.

References

Articles and Books

ALBARRAN, A. B., and T. MOELLINGER. 2002. 'The Top Six Communication Industry Firms: Structure, Performance and Strategy.' Paper presented at the 5th World Media Economics Conference, University of Turku, Finland, 9–10 May, 2002.

ALTER, K. J., and MEUNIER-AITSAHALIA, S. 1994. 'Judicial Politics in the European Community: European Integration and the Path-Breaking Cassis de Dijon Decision.' *Comparative Political Studies* 26/4: 535–61.

AMABLE, B. 2003. *The Diversity of Modern Capitalism.* New York: Oxford University Press.

AMEMIYA, T. 1985. *Advanced Econometrics.* Cambridge, Mass.: Harvard University Press.

ANDERSEN, S. S., and ELIASSEN, K. 1991. 'European Community Lobbying.' *European Journal of Political Research* 20/2: 173–87.

—— 1993. *Making Policy in Europe.* London: Sage.

ANDERSON, B. 1983. *Imagined Communities.* London: Verso.

BAIROCH, P. 1996. 'Globalization, Myths and Realities: One Century of External Trade and Foreign Investment,' in R. Boyer and D. Drache (eds.), *States against Markets.* London: Routledge.

BARTH, F. 1969. *Ethnic Groups and Boundaries.* Long Grove, Ill.: Waveland.

BAUN, M. 1996. *An Imperfect Union.* New York: Westview.

BERGER, S., and DORE, R. 1996. *National Diversity and Global Capitalism.* Ithaca, NY: Cornell University Press.

BOURDIEU, P., and WACQUANT, L. 1992. *An Invitation to a Reflexive Sociology.* Chicago: University of Chicago Press.

BOYER, R., and DRACHE, D. 1996. *States Against Markets.* London: Routledge.

BREUILLY, J. 1994. *Nationalism and the State.* 2nd edn. Chicago: University of Chicago Press.

BREWER, M. B. 1993. 'Social Identity, Distinctiveness, and In-Group Homogeneity.' *Social Cognition* 11/1: 150–64.

—— 1999. 'Multiple Identities and Identity Transition.' *International Journal of Intercultural Relations* 23/2: 187–97.

—— and GARDNER, W. 1996. 'Who is this "We"?: Levels of Collective Identity and Self-Representation.' *Journal of Personality and Social Psychology* 71: 83–93.

BRITZ, M. 2004. 'The Europeanization of Defence Industry Policy.' *Stockholm Studies in Politics* 103. Stockholm: Department of Politics, Stockholm University.

BRUBAKER, R. 1992. *Citizenship and Nationhood in France and Germany.* Cambridge, Mass.: Harvard University Press.

—— and COOPER, F. 2000. 'Beyond Identity.' *Theory and Society* 29/1: 1–47.

BUDGE, I., KLINGEMANN, H.-D., VOLKENS, A., BARA, J., and TANENBAUM, E. 2001. *Mapping Policy Preferences.* New York: Oxford University Press.

BULMER, S., and WESSELS, W. 1987. *The European Council.* Basingstoke: Macmillan.

BURLEY, A. M., and MATTLI, W. 1993. 'Europe Before the Court: A Political Theory of Legal Integration.' *International Organization* 47/1: 41–76.

BUSH, E., and SIMI, P. 2001. 'European Farmers and their Protests.' in Imig and Tarrow (eds.) (2001*a*), 97–124.

BUTLER, B. 1991. *The Official History of the Football Association*. London: Macdonald.

CAIGNER, A., and GARDINER, S. 2000. *Professional Sport in the European Union*. The Hague: T. M. C. Asser.

CALHOUN, C. 1992. *Habermas and the Public Sphere*. Cambridge, Mass.: MIT.

—— 1994. 'Social Theory and the Politics of Identity,' in C. Calhoun (ed.), *Social Theory and the Politics of Identity*. Cambridge, Mass.: Blackwell.

—— 2003. 'The Democratic Integration of Europe: Interests, Identity, and the Public Sphere,' in M. Berezin and M. Schain (eds.) *Europe without Borders*. Baltimore, Md.: Johns Hopkins University Press.

CAMPAINE, B. M: 2001. 'The Myth of Encroaching Media Ownership.' Paper presented at the Association for Education in Journalism and Mass Communication Convention, August 2001.

CAPORASO, J. A. 1996. 'The European Union and Forms of State: Westphalian, Regulatory, or Post-Modern?' *Journal of Common Market Studies* 34/1: 29–52.

CASTELLS, M. 1996. *The Rise of the Network Society*. Cambridge, Mass.: Blackwell.

CAVILLIN, J. 2001. 'European Policies and Regulation on Media Concentration.' Report produced by the Swedish Council for Pluralism in the Media, Ministry of Culture, Stockholm Sweden.

CICHOWSKI, R. 2001. 'Judicial Rulemaking and the Institutionalization of European Union Sex Equality Policy,' in Stone Sweet, Sandholtz, and Fligstein (eds.) (2001).

CITRIN, J. and SIDES, J. 2004. 'Can there be a Europe without Europeans?', in R. Hermann, M. Brewer, and T. Risse (eds.), *Transnational Identities: Becoming European in the EU*. Lanham, Md.: Rowman & Littlefield.

CONN, D. 1997. *The Football Business: English Football in the 90's*. London: Mainstream.

COWHEY, P. 1990. 'The International Telecommunications Regime.' *International Organization* 44/2: 169–99.

CROUCH, C., and STREECK, W. 1997. *Political Economy of Modern Capitalism*. London: Sage.

DALTON, R. J., and EICHENBERG, R. C. 1998. 'Citizen Support for Policy Integration,' in Sandholtz and Stone Sweet (eds.) (1998).

DEFLEM, M., and PAMPEL, F. C. 1996. 'The Myth of Post National Identity: Popular Support for European Unification.' *Social Forces* 75: 119–43.

DEHOUSSE, R. 1997. *La Cour de justice des Communautés Européennes*. Paris: Montchrestien.

DE LA MARE, T. 1999. 'Article 177 in Social and Political Context,' in P. Craig and G. De Burca (eds.), *The Evolution of EU Law*. Oxford: Oxford University Press.

DELOITTE and TOUCHE. 2001. *Annual Report on Football Finance*. London: Deloitte and Touche.

DE VREESE, C. H. 2002. *Framing Europe: Television News and European Integration*. Amsterdam: Aksant.

DEUTSCH, K. W. 1966 (1953). *Nationalism and Social Communication*. Cambridge, Mass.: MIT.

DIEZ MEDRANO, J. 2003. *Framing Europe: Attitudes to European Integration in Germany, Spain, and the United Kingdom*. Princeton, NJ: Princeton University Press.

—— and GUTIÉRREZ, P. 2001. 'Nested Identities: National and European Identity in Spain.' *Ethnic and Racial* 24/5: 753–78.

DiMaggio, P., and Powell, W. (1983). ' "The Iron Cage Revisited," Institutional Isomorphism and Collective Rationality in Organizational Fields.' *American Sociological Review* 48: 147–60.

Dinan, D. 1999. *Ever Closer Union.* Basingstoke: Macmillan.

Djankov, S., McLiesh, C., Nenova, T., and Shleifer, A. 2003. 'Who Owns the Media?' *Journal of Law and Economics* 46: 341–81.

Djelic, M. L. 1998. *Exporting the American Model.* Oxford: Oxford University Press.

Dogan, R. 1997. 'Comitology: Little Procedures with Big Implications.' *West European Politics* 20: 31–60.

Downey, J., and Koenig, T. 2004. 'Nationalization vs. Europeanization vs. Globalization of Issues That Should Belong to the European Public Sphere.' Paper presented at the ESA Conference, Thessaloniki, Greece, 5–7 November 2004.

Duchêne, F. 1994. *Jean Monnet: The First Statesman of Interdependence.* New York: Norton.

DuChesne, S., and Frognier, A-P. 1995. 'Is there a European Identity?' in O. Niedermayer and R. Sinnott (eds.), *Public Opinion and Internationalized Governance.* Oxford: Oxford University Press.

Epstein, R. 'Structural Impediments to European Defense Reform.' Paper presented at the annual meeting of the International Studies Association, Le Centre Sheraton Hotel, Montreal, Quebec, Canada, 17 March 2004.

Easton, D. 1974. 'A Re-assessment of the Concept of Political Support.' *British Journal of Political Science* 5: 435–57.

Eichenberg, R., and Dalton, R. J. 1993. 'Europeans and the European Community: The Dynamics of Public Support for European Integration.' *International Organization* 47/4: 507–34.

Eichener, V. 1997. 'Effective European Problem-Solving: Lessons from the Regulation of Occupational Safety and Environmental Protection.' *Journal of European Public Policy* 4: 591–608.

Engelbrekt, K. 2002. *Security Policy Re-orientation in Peripheral Europe: A Comparative-Perspective Approach.* London: Ashgate.

Epstein, R. 2004. 'Structural Impediments to European Defense Reform.' Paper presented at the International Studies Association Meeting, March 2004.

Ericson, T. 2000. 'The Bosman Case.' *Journal of Sports Economics* 1/3: 203–18.

Ernst & Young. 2002. 'Europe's Aerospace and Defense Sectors: An Industry at a Crossroads.' London: Ernst & Young.

European Audiovisual Laboratory 2001. *Eurofiction.* Strasburg: EAL.

——2004. *Lumière Database.* Strasburg: EAL.

European University Association (EUA). 1998. *Sorbonne Joint Declaration on the Harmonization of the Architecture of the European University System.* Brussels: EUA.

——1999. *The European Higher Education Space: The Joint Bologna Declaration of the European Ministers of Education.* Brussels: EUA.

Farrell, D. M., and Scully, R. 2007. *Representing Europe's Citizens?* Oxford: Oxford University Press.

Favell, A. 2005. 'Europe's Identity Problem.' *West European Politics* 28/5: 1009–16.

——2007. 'The Sociology of EU Politics,' in K. E. Jørgensen, M. A. Pollack, and B. Rosamond (eds.), *The Handbook of EU Politics.* London: Sage.

——forthcoming. *Eurostars and Eurocities.* Oxford: Blackwell.

Featherstone, K. 1988. *Socialist Parties and European Integration.* Manchester: Manchester University Press.

Financial times. 2004. *European Business Readership Survey 2004.* London: Financial Times.

FLIGSTEIN, N. 1996. 'Markets as Politics: A Political-Cultural Approach to Market Institutions.' *American Sociological Review* 61/4: 656–73.

—— 2001. *The Architecture of Markets.* Princeton, NJ: Princeton University Press.

—— and BRANTLEY, P. 1995. 'The Single Market Program and the Interests of Business,' in B. Eichengreen and J. Frieden (eds.), *Politics and Institutions in an Integrated Europe.* Berlin: Verlag-Springer.

—— and CHOO, J. 2005. 'Law and Corporate Governance.' *Annual Review of Law and Social Science* 1: 61–84.

—— and FREELAND, R. 1995. 'Theoretical and Comparative Perspectives on Corporate Organization.' *Annual Review of Sociology* 21: 21–43. Palo Alto, Calif.: Annual Reviews.

—— and MCNICHOL, J. 1998. 'The Institutional Terrain of the European Union,' in Sandholtz and Stone Sweet (eds.) (1998).

—— and MARA-DRITA, I. 1996. 'How to Make a Market.' *American Journal of Sociology* 102/1: 1–33.

—— and STONE SWEET, A. 2002. 'Constructing Polities and Markets: An Institutionalist Account of European Integration.' *American Journal of Sociology.*

FOLLESDAL, A., and HIX, S. 2006. 'Why There Is a Democratic Deficit in the EU: A Response to Majone and Moravcsik.' *Journal of Common Market Studies* 44/3: 533–62.

FOOTBALL ASSOCIATION. 1991. *Blueprint for Football.* London: Football Association.

FOOTBALL LEAGUE. 1990. *One Game, One Team, One Voice.* Lytham St Annes: Football League.

FRASER, N. 1992. 'Rethinking the Public Sphere: A Contribution to the Critique of Actually Existing Democracy,' in Calhoun (ed.) (1992), 127–47.

GABEL, M. 1998. *Interests and Integration.* Ann Arbor: University of Michigan Press.

GARRETT, G. 1995. 'The Politics of Legal Integration in the European Union.' *International Organization* 49/1: 171–81.

—— 1998. *Partisan Politics in the Global Economy.* New York: Cambridge University Press.

GEARY, P. 2002. *The Myth of Nations.* Princeton, NJ: Princeton University Press.

GEERTZ, C. 1983. *Local Knowledge.* New York: Basic Books.

GELLNER, E. 1983. *Nations and Nationalism.* Ithaca, NY: Cornell University Press.

GERHARDS, J. 1993. 'Westeuropäische Integration und die Schwierigkeiten der Entstehung einer Europäischen öffentlichkeit.' *Zeitschrift für Soziologie* 22: 96–110.

—— 2000. Europaisierung von Ökonomie und Politik und die Trägheit der Entstehung einer Europäischen öffentlichkeit,' in M. Bach (ed.), *Die Europäisierung nationaler Gesellschaften.* Opladen: Westdeutscher Verlag, 277–305.

GOFFMAN, E. 1963. *Stigma.* New York: Simon & Schuster.

—— 1974. *Frame Analysis.* New York: Harper & Row.

GOLDSTEIN, D. 2000. *English Football.* London: Rough Guides.

GREENWOOD, J., and ASPINWALL, M. (eds.) 1998. *Collective Action in the European Union: Interests and the New Politics of Associability.* London: Routledge.

GRIMM, D. 1995. 'Does Europe Need a Constitution?' *European Law Journal* 1/3: 282–302.

GROEBEN, H. 1982. *The European Community: The Formative Years.* Luxembourg: Office for Official Publications of the European Community.

HAAS, E. B. 1958. *The Uniting of Europe.* Stanford, Calif.: Stanford University Press.

—— 1961. 'International Integration: The European and the Universal Process.' *International Organization* 15/3: 366–92.

—— 1976. 'Turbulent Fields and the Theory of Regional Integration.' *International Organization* 30/2: 173–212.

HABERMAS, J. 1989. *The Structural Transformation of the Public Sphere*. London: Polity.

—— 1992. 'Citizenship and Identity: Some Reflections of the Future of Europe.' *Praxis International* 12/1: 1–19.

—— 2001. 'Why Europe needs a Constitution.' *New Left Review* 11: 5–26.

HALL, P. A., and SOSKICE, D. W. 2001. *Varieties of Capitalism: The Institutional Foundations of Comparative Advantage*. Oxford: Oxford University Press.

HARCOURT, A. 2002. 'Engineering Europeanization: The Role of the European Institutions in Shaping National Media Regulation.' *Journal of European Public Policy* 9/5: 736–55.

HART, J. 1998. 'The Politics of Global Competition in the Telecommunications Industry.' *Information Society* 15/3: 115–29.

HELFFERICH, B., and KOLB, F. 2001. 'Multilevel Action Coordination in European Contentious Politics: The Case of the European's Women's Lobby,' in Imig and Tarrow (eds.), (2001*a*), 143–63.

HERRMANN, R., BREWER, M. and RISSE, T. 2004. Transnational *Identities: Becoming European in the EU*. Lanham, Md.: Rowman & Littlefield.

HICKS, A. 1999. *Social Democracy and Welfare Capitalism*. Ithaca, NY: Cornell University Press.

HILLS, J. 1986. *Deregulating Telecoms*. London: Frances Pinter.

HIX, S. 1999. *The Political System of the European Union*. New York: St Martin's Press.

HOBSON, A., and EDWARDS, P. 2007. 'G-14 scores against FIFA.' *International Sports Law Review* 10: 313–16.

HOEHN, T., and SZYMANSKI, S. 1999. 'The Americanization of European Football.' *Economic Policy* 14/28: 203–40.

—— and LANCEFIELD, D. 2003. 'Broadcasting and Sport.' *Oxford Review of Economic Policy* 19/4: 552–68.

—— —— 2005. 'Calculation, Community, and Cues: Public Opinion on European Integration.' *European Union Politics* 6/4: 421–45.

HOFFMANN, S. 1966. 'Obstinate or Obsolete: The Fate of the Nation State and the Case of Western Europe.' *Daedalus* 95/3: 862–915.

HOOGHE, L., and MARKS, G. 2001. *Multilevel Governance and European Integration*. New York: Rowman & Littlefield.

IMIG, D., and TARROW, S. (eds.) 2001*a*. *Contentious Europeans*. Lanham, Md.: Rowman & Littlefield.

—— —— 2001*b*. 'Studying Contention in an Emerging Polity,' in Imig and Tarrow (eds.) (2001*a*), 3–26.

—— —— 2001*c*. 'Mapping the Europeanization of Contention,' in Imig and Tarrow (eds.) (2001*a*), 27–52.

INGLEHART, R. F. 1997. *Modernization and Postmodernization*. Princeton, NJ: Princeton University Press.

—— and BAKER, W. 2000. 'Modernization, Cultural Change, and the Persistence of Traditional Values.' *American Sociological Review* 65/1: 19–51.

—— RABIER, J. and REIF, K. 1991. 'The Evolution of Public Attitudes Toward European Integration, 1970–1986,' in K. Reif and R. Inglehart (eds.), *Eurobarometer: The Dynamics of European Public Opinion*. London: Macmillan.

JEANRENAUD, C., and KESENNE, S. 1999. *Competition Policy in Professional Sports*. Antwerp: Standaard Editions.

JENSEN, M. C., and MECKLING, W. H. 1974. 'The Theory of the Firm.' *Journal of Financial Economics* 3/4: 305–60.

JOERGES, C., and NEYER, J. 1997. 'From Intergovernmental Bargaining to Deliberative Political Processes: The Constitutionalisation of Comitology.' *European Law Journal* 3/3: 273–99.

JUDT, T. 2005. *Postwar: A History of Europe Since 1945*. New York: Penguin.

KATZENSTEIN, P. J. 2005. *A World of Regions: Asia and Europe in the American Imperium*. Ithaca, NY: Cornell University Press.

KEANE, J. 1998. *Civil Society: Old Images, New Visions*. Cambridge: Polity.

KEOHANE, R. O., and HOFFMANN, S. 1991. 'Institutional Change in Europe in the 1980s,' in R. Keohane and S. Hoffman (eds.), *The New European Community*. Boulder: Westview.

KETTNAKER, V. 2001. 'The European Conflict over Genetically Engineered Crops, 1995–1997,' in Imig and Tarrow (eds.) (2001*a*), 205–32.

KIELMANSEGG, P. 1996. 'Integration and Democracy,' in M. Jachtenfuchs and B. Kohler-Koch (eds.), *European Integration*. Opladen: Leske & Budrich, 47–71.

KINDLEBERGER, C. P. (ed.), 1970. *The International Corporations*. Cambridge, Mass.: MIT.

KING, A. 1988. *The End of the Terraces*. London: Leicester University Press.

KING, R. 2002. 'Towards a New Map of European Migration.' *International Journal of Population Geography* 8/2: 89–106.

—— and RUIZ-GELICES, E. 2003. 'International Student Migration and the European "Year Abroad".' *International Journal of Population Geography* 9/3: 229–52.

KMPG. 2003. *The European Defense Industry*. London: KMPG.

KOOPMANS, R. 2005. 'The Transformation of Political Mobilization and Communication in European Public Spheres.' Final Report to the European Commission. <www.europub.wz-berlin.de>, accessed 15 October 2007.

—— and ERBE, J. 2003. *Towards a European Public Sphere? Vertical and Horizontal Dimensions of Europeanised Political Communication*. Berlin: Wissenschaftszentrum Berlin für Sozialforschung (WZB).

—— NEIDHARDT, F., and PFETSCH, B. 2004. 'Conditions for the Constitution of a European Public Sphere.' Berlin: Wissenschaftszentrum Berlin für Sozialforschung (WZB).

KRASNER, S. D. 1988. 'Sovereignty: An Institutionalist Perspective.' *Comparative Political Studies* 21: 66–94.

KUYPERS, T., and SZYMANSKI, S., 1999. *Winners and Losers: The Business Strategies of Football*. Harmondsworth: Viking.

LAFFAN, B., O'DONNELL, R., and SMITH, M. 2000. *Europe's Experimental Union*. London: Routledge.

LAITIN, D. D. 2002. 'Culture and National Identity: "The East" and European Integration.' *West European Politics* 25/2: 55–80.

LAUMANN, E., and KNOKE, E. O. 1987. *The Organizational State*. Madison: University of Wisconsin Press.

LAWLOR, E. 1992. 'Affective Attachments to Nested Groups.' *American Sociological Review* 57/3: 327–39.

LEIBFRIED, S., and PIERSON, P. 1995. *European Social Policy: Between Fragmentation and Integration*. Washington, DC: Brookings Institution.

LINDBERG, L. N., and SCHEINGOLD, S. A. 1970. *Europe's Would-Be Polity*. New York: Prentice-Hall.

LODGE, J. 1993. *The European Community and the Challenge of the Future*. 2nd edn. London: Pinter.

—— 1996. 'Federalism and the European Parliament.' *Publicus* 26/4: 63–79.

LUTZ, W., KRITZINGER, S., and SKIRBEKK, V. 2006. 'The Demography of Growing European Identity.' *Science* 314: 425.

McChesney, R. 2004. *The Problem of the Media*. New York: Monthly Review Press.

McCormick, J. 2002. *Understanding the European Union*. New York: Palgrave.

Majone, D. (ed.) 1996. *Regulating Europe*. London: Routledge.

—— 1998. 'Europe's Democratic Deficit.' *European Law Journal* 4/1: 5–28.

Marks, G., Hooghe, L., and Blank, K. 1996. 'European Integration from the 1980s: State-Centric v. Multilevel Governance.' *Journal of Common Market Studies* 34/3: 341–78.

Mattli, W. 1999. *The Logic of Regional Integration*. Cambridge: Cambridge University Press.

Mazey, S., and Richardson, J. 1993. *Lobbying in the European Community*. Oxford: Oxford University Press.

—— —— 2001. 'Institutionalizing Promiscuity: Commission—Interest Group Relations in the EU,' in Stone Sweet, Sandholtz, and Fligstein (eds.) (2001).

Merand, F. 2003. 'Soldiers and Diplomats: The Institutionalization of European Security and Defense Policy, 1989–2003.' Dissertation, Department of Sociology, University of California.

Meyer, J., and Scott, W. R. 1983. 'The Organization of Societal Sectors,' in Meyer and Scott (eds.), *Organizational Environments: Ritual and Rationality*. Los Angeles: Sage.

Miller, V. 2007. 'EU Legislation.' United Kingdom House of Commons Standard Note SN/1A/2888.

Milward, A. 1997. 'The Springs of Integration,' in P. Gowan and P. Anderson (eds.) *The Question of Europe*. London: Verso.

Missiroli, A. 2002. 'European Football Cultures and their Integration.' *Culture, Sports, and Society* 5/1: 1–20.

Moore, B. 1966. *Social Origins of Dictatorship and Democracy*. New York: Beacon.

Moravcsik, A. 1991. Negotiating the Single European Act. *International Organization* 45/1: 19–56.

—— 1995. 'Liberal Intergovernmentalism and Integration: A Rejoinder.' *Journal of Common Market Studies* 33/4: 611–23.

—— 1998. *The Choice for Europe: Social Purpose and State Power from Massina to Maastricht*. Ithaca, NY: Cornell University Press.

—— 2002. 'In Defence of the "Democratic Deficit": Reassessing Legitimacy in the European Union.' *Journal of Common Market Studies* 40: 603–44.

Mörth, U. 2003. *Organizing European Cooperation—The Case of Armaments*. Lanham, Md.: Rowman & Littlefield.

—— and Britz, M. 2004. 'European Integration as Organizing: The Case of Armaments.' *Journal of Common Market Studies* 42/5: 57–73.

Murroni, C., and Irvine, N. 1998. *Access Matters*. London: IPPR.

Musso D. 1998. 'Le Modèle européen du sport professionnel en sursis.' *Revue Juridique et Économique du Sport* 48: 28–43.

Noel, E. 1994. *Working Together: The Institutions of the European Community*. Luxembourg: Office for Official Publications of the European Community.

OCCAR. 2007. *The Multinational Defense Acquisition Organization*. Brochure. <http://www.occar-ea.org/media/raw/occar_brochure_2006.pdf>, accessed 27 October 2007.

OECD. 2002. *International Direct Investment Statistics Yearbook*. Paris: OECD.

—— 2006. *Trends in International Migration (SOPEMI Report)*. Paris: OECD.

Offe, Claus. 1996 *Modernity and the State: East, West*. Cambridge: Polity.

Parsons, C. 2003. *A Certain Idea of Europe*. Ithaca, NY: Cornell University Press.

Pauly, L., and Reich, S. 1997. 'National Structures and Multinational Corporate Behavior.' *International Organization* 51: 1–31.

PETERS, B. G. 1992. 'Bureaucratic Politics and the Institutions of the European Community'. in A. M. Sbragia (ed.), *Europolitics*. Washington, DC: Brookings, Institution.

PETERSON, J. 2004. 'Policy Networks,' in A. Wiener and T. Diez (eds.), *European Integration Theory*. Oxford: Oxford University Press, 117–35.

PFETSCH, B. 2004. 'The Transformation of Political Mobilization and Communication in European Public Spheres.' Report WP2 EUROPUB.com. Wissenschaftzentrum, Berlin, FRG.

PHILIP, A. B., and GRAY, O. (eds.) 1997. *Directory of Pressure Groups in the EU*. London: Catermill.

PIERSON, P. 1996. 'The Path to European Integration: A Historical Institutionalist Analysis.' *Comparative Political Studies* 29: 123–63.

POIARES, M. M. 1998. *We, the Court: The European Court of Justice and the European Economic Constitution*. Oxford: Hart.

POLLACK, M. A. 1997. 'Delegation, Agency, and Agenda Setting in the European Community.' *International Organization* 51/3: 99–134.

—— 1998. 'The Engines of Integration? Supranational Autonomy and Influence in the European Union.' in Sandholtz and Stone Sweet (eds.) (1998), 217–49.

PRIMAULT, D., and ROUGER, A. 1997. 'Contribution économique à la réforme du statut juridique de clubs.' *Revue Juridique et Économique du Sport* 45: 283–305.

PURKIS, R. H. A., and STAFFORD, D. C. 1999. *The World Directory of Multinational Enterprises*. 4th edn. London: Palgrave.

RAVINET, P. 2005. 'The Sorbonne Meeting and Declaration: Actors, Shared Vision, Europeanization.' Paper presented at the Third Conference on Knowledge and Politics, University of Bergen, Norway, 18–20 May 2005.

RECCHI, E., TAMBINI, D., BALDONI, E., WILLIAMS, D. and SURAK, K. and FAVELL, A., 2003. 'Intra-EU Migration: A Socio-Demographic Overview'. Working Paper WP3. PIONEUR project, <http://www.obets.ua.es/pioneur/>, accessed 15 October 2007.

REICHERT, S., and C. TAUCH. 2005. *Trends IV: European Universities Implementing the Bologna Process*. Brussels: EUA.

RENDEIRO, M. 2003. 'Communicating the Future of Europe: A French—Portuguese Press Comparison.' Paper presented at the Communicating European Integration Conference, Lisbon, Portugal, 30–1 March 2003.

RICHARDSON, J. (ed.) 2001. *European Union: Power and Policymaking*. London: Routledge.

RISSE, T. 2002. 'How Do We Know a European Public Sphere When We See One? Theoretical Clarifications and empirical Indicators,' Paper prepared for the IDNET Workshop 'Europeanization and the Public Sphere,' European University Institute, Florence, 20–1 February 2002.

—— 2003. 'Toward a European Public Sphere? Theoretical Considerations.' Paper presented at the European Union Studies Association Meeting in Nashville, Tenn., 20 March 2003.

—— 2005. 'European Institutions and Identity Change: What Have We Learned?', in R. Hermann, M. Brewer, and T. Risse (eds.) *Identities in Europe and the Institutions of the European Union*. Lanham, Md.: Rowman & Littlefield.

—— Engelmann-Martin, D., Knopf, H., and Rosher, K. 1999. 'To Euro or not to Euro?' *European Journal of International Relations* 5: 147–87.

ROBINSON, W. 2004. *A Theory of Global Capitalism: Production, Class, and State in a Transnational World*. Baltimore: Johns Hopkins University Press.

RODRÍGUEZ-POSE, A. 2002. *The European Union: Economy, Society, and Polity*. Oxford: Oxford University Press.

RODRIK, D. 1996. 'Why Do More Open Economies Have Bigger Governments?' NBER Working Paper 5537. Cambridge, Mass.: NBER.

RODRIK, D. 1997. *Has Globalization Gone Too Far?* Washington, DC: Institute for International Economics.

ROE, M. 2003. *Political Determinants of Corporate Governance.* Oxford: Oxford University Press.

ROKKAN, S. 1973. 'Cities, States, Nations,' in S. N. Eisenstadt and S. Rokkan (eds.) *Building States and Nations.* Beverly Hills: Sage.

—— and URWIN, D. W. 1983. *Economy, Territory, Identity.* London: Sage.

ROSS, G. 1995. *Jacques Delors and European Integration.* Cambridge: Polity.

RUCHT, D. 2000. 'Zur Europäisierung Politischer Mobilisierung.' *Berliner Journal für Soziologie* 10/2: 185–202.

RUSSELL, D. 1997. *Football and the English.* Preston: Carnegie.

SANDHOLTZ, W. 1993. 'Institutions and Collective Action: The New Telecommunications in Western Europe.' *World Politics* 45/2: 242–70.

—— 1998. 'The Emergence of a Supranational Telecommunications Regime.' in Sandholtz and Stone Sweet (eds.) (1998), 134–63.

—— and A. STONE SWEET (eds.) 1998. *European Integration and Supranational Governance.* Oxford: Oxford University Press.

—— and J. ZYSMAN. 1989. '1992: Recasting the European Bargain.' *World Politics* 42/1: 95–128.

SBRAGIA, A. 1992. 'Europe as a Federal Structure,' in A Sbragia (ed.), *Europolitics.* Washington, DC: Brookings Institution.

SCHAKE, K. 2002. 'Constructive Duplication: Reducing EU Reliance on US Military Assets.' Centre for European Reform Working Paper.

SCHARPF, F. W. 1988. 'The Joint Decision Trap: Lessons from German Federalism and European Integration.' *Public Administration* 66/3: 239–72.

—— 1996. 'Negative and Positive Integration in the Political Economy of European Welfare States,' in G. Marx, F. Scharpf, P. Schmitter, and W. Streeck (eds.), *Governance in the European Union.* London: Sage.

—— 1999. *Governing in Europe: Effective and Democratic?* Oxford: Oxford University Press.

SCHISSLER, H., and SOYSAL, Y. N. 2005. *The Nation, Europe, and the World: Textbooks and Curricula in Transition.* New York: Berghahn.

SCHLESINGER, P. 1999. 'Changing Spaces of Political Communication: The Case of the European Union.' *Political Communication* 16/3: 263–79.

—— and KEVIN, D. 2000. 'Can the European Union Become a Sphere of Publics?' in E. Eriksen and J. E. Fossum (eds.) *Democracy in the European Union: Integration Through Deliberation?* London: Routledge.

SCHMITT, B. 2003. 'The European Union and Armaments, Getting a Bigger Bang for the Euro.' Cahier de Chaillot 63. Institute for Security Studies. Paris: European Union.

SCHMITTER, P. 1996. 'Examining the Present Euro-Polity with the Help of Past Theories,' in G. Marks, F. W. Scharpf, P. C. Schmitter, and W. Streeck (eds.), *Governance in the European Union.* London: Sage, 1–14.

SHORE, C. 2000. *Building Europe: The Cultural Politics of European Integration.* London: Routledge.

SIMMONS, R. 1997. 'Implications of the Bosman Ruling for Football Transfer Markets', in the Institute of Economic Affairs (ed.), *Economic Affairs.* Oxford: Blackwell, 18.

SLAUGHTER, A. M., STONE SWEET, A., and WEILER, J. H. H. 1997. *The European Court and the National Courts—Doctrine and Jurisprudence: Legal Change in its Social Context.* Oxford: Hart.

SNOW, D. A., and BENFORD, R. D. 1992. 'Master Frames and Cycles of Protest,' in A. D. Morris and C. McClurg Mueller (eds.), *Frontiers in Social Movement Theory*. New Haven: Yale University Press, 133–55.

SOYSAL, Y. N. 2002. 'Locating Europe.' *European Societies* 4/3: 265–84.

—— BERTILOTTI, T., and MANNITZ, S. 2005. 'Projections of Identity in French and German History and Civics Textbooks,' in H. Schissler and Y. Soysal (eds.), *The Nation, Europe, and the World: Textbooks and Curricula in Transition*. Oxford: Berghahn.

SPERLING, J. E., and KIRCHNER, E. 1997. *Recasting the European Order: Security Architecture and Economic Cooperation*. Manchester: Manchester University Press.

STAFFORD, R., and PURKIS, C. 1989. 3rd edn. *The World Directory of Multinationals*. London: Palgrave.

—— —— 1999. 4th edn. *The World Directory of Multinationals*. London: Palgrave.

STANDARD AND POOR'S. 2003. *Company Reports*. New York: Standard & Poor's.

STONE SWEET, A. 2000. *Governing with Judges: Constitutional Politics in Europe*. Oxford: Oxford University Press.

—— and BRUNELL, T. L. 1998. 'Constructing a Supranational Constitution: Dispute Resolution and Governance in the European Community.' *American Political Science Review* 92/1: 63–81.

—— and SANDHOLTZ, W. 1998. 'Integration, Supranational Governance, and the Institutionalisation of the European Policy,' in Sandholtz and Stone Sweet (eds.) (1998).

—— SANDHOLTZ, W. and FLIGSTEIN, N. 2001. *The Institutionalization of Europe*. Oxford: Oxford University Press.

STRANGE, S. 1996. *The Retreat of the State*. Cambridge: Cambridge University Press.

STREECK, W., and SCHMITTER, P. C. 1991. 'From National Corporatism to Transnational Pluralism: Organized Interests in the Single European Market.' *Politics and Society* 19: 133–64.

SWEDBERG, R. 1994. 'The Idea of Europe.' *Zeitschrift für Soziologie* 23/5: 378–87.

TAJFEL, H. 1981. *Human Groups and Social Categories*. Cambridge: Cambridge University Press.

TARROW, S. 2001. 'Contentious Politics in a Composite Polity,' in Imig and Tarrow (eds.) (2001a), 233–52.

TAYLOR, P. 1983. *The Limits of European Integration*. New York: Columbia University Press.

TAYLOR, R. 1992. *Football and its Fans*. Leicester: Leicester University Press.

TEICHLER, U. 2004. 'Temporary Study Abroad: The Life of ERASMUS Students.' *European Journal of Education* 39/4: 395–408.

—— and JAHR, V. 2001. 'Mobility During the Course of Study and After Graduation. *European Journal of Education* 36/4: 443–58.

THERBORN, G. 1995. *European Modernity and Beyond*. London: Sage.

TILLY, C. 1975. 'Reflections on the History of European State Making,' in C. Tilly and G. Ardant (eds.), *The Formation of Nation States in Western Europe*. Princeton, NJ: Princeton University Press.

TOMLINSON, A. 1991. 'North and South: The Rivalry of the Football League and the Football Association,' in J. Williams and S. Wagg (eds.) *British Football & Social Change*. Leicester: Leicester University Press.

TRENZ, H-J. 2004. 'Media Coverage on European Governance.' *European Journal of Communication* 19/3: 291–319.

TSEBELIS, G. 1994. 'The Power of the European Parliament as a Conditional Agenda Setter.' *American Political Science Review* 88/1: 128–42.

TURNER, J. C. 1975. 'Social Comparisons and Social Identity.' *European Journal of Social Psychology* 5: 5–34.

UNESCO. 1998. *Higher Education in Europe.* New York: United Nations.

UNION OF INTERNATIONAL ORGANIZATIONS. 2000. *Yearbook of International Organizations.* Munich: K. G. Sauer.

UNITED NATIONS. 2000. *World Investment Report.* New York: United Nations.

——2006. *World Investment Report.* New York: United Nations.

VAN APELDOORN, B. 2002. *Transnational Capitalism and the Struggle over European Integration.* London: Routledge.

VAN DE STEEG, M. 2002. 'Rethinking the Conditions for a Public Sphere in the European Union.' *European Journal of Social Theory* 5: 499–519.

——RAUER, V., RIVET, S., and RISSE, T. 2003. 'The EU as a Political Community.' Paper presented at the Annual Meeting of the European Union Studies Association, Nashville, Tenn., 27–30 March 2003.

VERNON, R. 1971. *Sovereignty at Bay.* New York: Basic Books.

VOICH, B. 2003. *Progress Toward a European Higher Education Area: Results of a Survey.* Brussels: EUA.

WADE, R. 1996. 'Globalization and its Limits: Reports of the Death of the National Economy are Greatly Exaggerated,' in S. Berger and R. Dore (eds.), *National Diversity and Global Capitalism,* Ithaca, NY: Cornell University Press.

WALLACE, H. S., and YOUNG, A. R. 1997. *Participation and Policymaking in the European Union.* Oxford: Oxford University Press.

——2000. 'The Institutional Setting,' in H. Wallace and W. Wallace (eds.), *Policy-Making in the European Union,* Oxford: Oxford University Press, 3–37.

WALTZ, K. 1979. *The Theory of International Politics.* New York: McGraw-Hill.

WATERS, M. C. 1990. *Ethnic Options.* Los Angeles: University of California Press.

WEBER, E. 1976. *Peasants into Frenchmen.* Stanford, Calif.: Stanford University Press.

WEILER, J. H. H. 1991. 'The Transformation of Europe.' *Yale Law Review* 100/8: 2403–83.

——1994. 'A Quiet Revolution: The European Court and its Interlocutors.' *Comparative Political Studies* 26/4: 510–34.

——1999. *The Constitution of Europe. 'Do the New Clothes Have an Emperor?' and Other Essays on European Integration.* Cambridge: Cambridge University Press.

WESSELS, W. 1997. 'An Ever Closer Fusion? A Dynamic Macropolitical View on Integration Processes.' *Journal of Common Market Studies* 35/2: 267–99.

WINCOTT, D. 1995. 'Institutional Interaction and European Integration.' *Journal of Common Market Studies* 33/4: 597–610.

WINDHOFF-HÉRETIER, A. 1999. *Policymaking and Diversity in Europe.* Cambridge: Cambridge University Press.

WORLD TRADE ORGANIZATION. Various years. *Annual Report on World Trade.* Geneva: World Trade Organization.

European Union Documents

COMMISSION OF THE EUROPEAN COMMUNITIES. 1983. 'Communication from the Commission to the Council on Telecommunications: Lines of Action.' COM, 573.

——1987. 'Green Paper on the Development of the Common Market for Telecommunications Services and Equipment.' COM, 290.

——1995. White Paper on Education and Training.

—— 2002. *Report by the Economic and Financial Committee on EU Financial Integration* 171, May 2002.

—— 2003. 'European Defence: Industrial and Market Issues.' COM, 113 Final. Brussels.

—— 2004. *Report on Regulatory Framework for Electronic Communication in the EU.*

EUROBAROMETER. 1997. No. 48. Fall 1997.

—— 2000. No. 54LAN. December 2000.

—— 2004. No. 91. April 2004.

EUROPEAN COURT OF JUSTICE. 1963. Van Gend en Loos, Case 26/62. *European Court Reports*, 1.

—— 1964. Costa, Case 6/64. *European Court Reports*, 585.

—— 1974. Van Duyn, Case 41/74. *European Court Reports*, 1337.

—— 1996. Belgian FA *v.* Bosman, Case 97. *European Court Report*, 1603.

EUROPEAN ECONOMY. 2004. *Annex.* Luxembourg: Office for Official Publications of the European Communities.

EUROPEAN UNION. 1957. *Treaty Establishing the European Economic Community.* Luxembourg: Office for Official Publications of the European Communities.

—— 1981. *The European Community's Legal System.* Luxembourg: Office for Official Publications of the European Communities.

—— 1987. *Single European Act.* Luxembourg: Office for Official Publications of the European Communities.

—— 1993. *Treaty of European Union.* Luxembourg: Office for Official Publications of the European Communities.

—— 1995. *Directory of Community Legislation in Force.* Luxembourg: Office for Official Publications of the European Communities.

—— 1997. *Treaty of Amsterdam.* Luxembourg: Office for Official Publications of the European Communities.

—— 2001. *Treaty of Nice.* Luxembourg: Office for Official Publications of the European Communities.

—— 2003. *Draft Treaty for Establishing a Constitution for Europe.* Luxembourg: Office for Official Publications of the European Communities.

—— 2005. *Key Data on Teaching Languages at Schools in Europe.* Luxembourg: Office for Official Publications of the European Communities.

—— 2005 Erasmus Statistics. <http://europa.eu.int/comm/education/programmes/socrates/ erasmus/stat_en.html>, accessed 15 October 2007.

Websites and Databases

Eurobarometer <http://europa.eu.int/comm/public_opinion/index_en.htm>.

European Audiovisual Database <http://www.obs.coe.int>.

European Union (EU) <http://www.europa.eu>.

European University Association <http://www.eua.be>.

Federation International Football Associations (FIFA) <http://www.fifa.com>.

Union of European Football Associations (UEFA) <http://www.uefa.com>.

G-14 European Football Clubs Grouping <http://www.g14.com>.

Letter of Intent between 6 defence ministers to facilitate the restructuring of the European Defence Industry: <http://www.grip.org/bdg/g1015.html>.

Lumière Database <http://www.lumiere.obs.coe.int>.

OCCAR <http://www.occar-ea.org>.

Official Charts and Box Office <http://www.allcharts.org>.

PIONEUR <www.obets.ua.es/pioneur>.
All sites were accessed 15 October 2007.

Newspapers and Magazines Cited in Text

Business Week
The Economist
Financial Times
The Guardian
Glasgow Sunday Times
International Herald Tribune
The London Times
Wall Street Journal

Index